# CliffsNotes®

# HiSET®

# CRAM PLAN™

*by Tim Collins, Ph.D.*

Houghton Mifflin Harcourt
Boston • New York

### About the Author

**Tim Collins, Ph.D.,** Associate Professor at National-Louis University (Chicago), specializes in test preparation and teacher education. He is the author of more than 26 books in the fields of adult education, English as a Second Language, and test preparation.

### Dedication

This book is dedicated to the success of all candidates for the HiSET credential.

### Editorial

**Executive Editor:** Greg Tubach
**Senior Editor:** Christina Stambaugh
**Copy Editor:** Donna Wright
**Technical Editors:** Andrew Beams, Jane Burstein, Jeff Johnson, Tom Page, Scott Ryan, and Mary Jane Sterling
**Proofreader:** Mary Bednarek

**CliffsNotes® HiSET® Cram Plan™**

Library of Congress Control Number: 2014956585
ISBN: 978-0-544-37330-3 (pbk)

Printed in the United States of America
DOC 10 9 8 7 6 5 4 3 2 1

For information about permission to reproduce selections from this book, write to Permissions, Houghton Mifflin Harcourt Publishing Company, 215 Park Avenue South, New York, New York 10003.

www.hmhco.com

# Table of Contents

Congratulations on your decision to obtain a high school diploma through the HiSET program! The HiSET program is an outstanding opportunity for individuals who have not completed high school to obtain a high school credential from their state or local education agency. Private and public employers, as well as educational institutions, accept the HiSET certificate as they would a high school diploma.

A HiSET certificate can help you in many ways:

- Improved employment prospects—makes getting a promotion or finding a new job much easier
- Enhanced educational opportunities at trade and vocational schools, colleges, and universities
- Enhanced personal satisfaction

## About the HiSET

The HiSET assessment tests the knowledge and skills measured in these five test sections: Language Arts: Reading; Language Arts: Writing; Mathematics; Science; and Social Studies. No specialized knowledge is required to answer the items. Instead, you will need to read and interpret passages and other information, and use your reading, critical thinking, and problem solving skills to answer the items. Complete information on each test section is presented in Chapters III through VIII of this book.

| Test Section | Number of Items | Time Available |
|---|---|---|
| Language Arts: Reading | 40 | 65 minutes |
| Language Arts: Writing | | |
|    Part 1 | 50 | 75 minutes |
|    Part 2 | 1 | 45 minutes |
| Mathematics | 50 | 90 minutes |
| Science | 50 | 80 minutes |
| Social Studies | 50 | 70 minutes |

HiSET is given in paper-and-pencil and online versions in English and in Spanish. You can take any or all of the test sections in a single sitting, or you can take the test sections one at a time. Note that Language Arts: Writing, Parts 1 and 2 are given together.

## Where to Take the HiSET

The HiSET is given at test centers in 12 U.S. states where HiSET is currently offered, with other states expected to join in the future. Test centers are generally located at adult education program centers, local community colleges, regional offices of education, and other locations. Each state's and/or local agency's requirements for HiSET testing are different. To view your state's requirements, go to http://hiset.ets.org/requirements.

Some states require you to register for the test at the local test center, while in other states, you can register through a HiSET online account. If you require special accommodations, you must register through the HiSET online account or by calling 1-855-MyHiSET (1-855-694-4738) and completing a simple form. To find out how to schedule an exam, go to https://ereg.ets.org/ereg-web/public/testcenter/search/HSE.

Your HiSET online account will let you register for test sections, find out your results, and keep track of your progress on each section of the test. Your account will also give information on testing fees, accommodations, and procedures for test day. To open an account, go to http://hiset.ets.org/test_takers.

When you sign up for the HiSET, you have a year to complete all the sections of the test. Your fee to take the HiSET includes all five sections, including two retakes for each section. If you cannot pass all of the tests in the 12-month period, you will need to pay additional fees.

# When to Take the HiSET

HiSET is given periodically throughout the year. This book can help you determine when you will be ready to pass the test. The Diagnostic Test in Chapter I will help you determine your strengths and areas for improvement on each section of the test. Then you can use the Cram Plans in Chapter II to figure out how much study time you should dedicate to each section of the test—two months, one month, or two weeks. The Cram Plans will help you work through the detailed information about each section of the test in Chapters III through VIII and take the Full-Length Practice Tests for each section of the HiSET in Chapters IX through XIII. Then you can schedule your tests based on when you will be ready to pass each one.

Check with your testing center to find out what you can bring with you into the testing center on test day. For the Mathematics test, a calculator will be supplied for you. You will also be given three pieces of scratch paper for all sections of the test you take in a session. You will also need photo identification and an admission ticket the day of the test. Generally, you will not be able to bring your phone, keys, computer, or food into the testing room with you. You can leave these things in a locker and access them during breaks or after the test.

# Accommodations for Special Needs

HiSET offers special accommodations for test-takers with special needs. Special needs include hearing and visual impairments, learning and other cognitive disabilities, attention deficit/hyperactivity disorder, and psychological or psychiatric disorders. Test-takers with these conditions can obtain accommodations, such as large-print test booklets, extended time, a separate testing room, a talking calculator, or a scribe or keyboard entry aide. To find out more about these accommodations and how to receive them when you take the test, go to http://hiset.ets.org/take/disabilities/.

# HiSET Scoring

Multiple-choice sections of the HiSET are scored by computer. Essays are scored by trained readers using the HiSET Essay Rubric. Complete information on the HiSET Essay Rubric is in Chapter V (pages 149–150).

All HiSET test multiple-choice sections are reported as scaled scores from 1 to 20. On the Writing test, scores from the multiple-choice and essay sections are combined into a composite scaled score from 1 to 20. Both the scaled score and the score on the essay are included in your score report. To pass the HiSET, you need to

- Score at least 8 out of 20 on the Reading, Mathematics, Science, and Social Studies sections
- Score a composite at least 8 on Writing, with a minimum score of 2 out of 6 on the Essay
- Achieve a total combined score on all five subtests of at least 45 out of 100

Some states set higher score requirements. Check with your local test center or go to http://hiset.ets.org/requirements to see your state's score requirements.

You will receive your test results via your HiSET online account. Generally, on computer-based administrations, you will receive an unofficial score on multiple-choice test sections as soon as you complete the section. For both online and paper-based tests, official scores are delivered to your online account in 3 to 5 business days for multiple-choice sections and in 6 to 10 business days for the essay section.

# HiSET Hotline

For any questions about registration, scores, requirements, accommodations, or any other matter, contact the HiSET Hotline at 1-855-MyHiSET (1-855-694-4738).

# How to Use This Book

To use this book, follow these instructions:

1. Take the Diagnostic Test in Chapter I.
2. Review the answer explanations at the end of the Diagnostic Test to find out your areas of strength and areas for improvement.
3. Use the "Your HiSET Cram Plan" chart on page 65 to record your scores on each section of the Diagnostic Test.
4. For each section of the HiSET, determine whether the Two-Month, One-Month, or One-Week Cram Plan is best for you.
5. Work through your Cram Plans. Each Cram Plan will tell you when to take the end-of-book Full-Length Practice Test for that section of the HiSET and how to use results from the Full-Length Practice Test to prepare for test day.
6. You are ready to take the HiSET after you finish the Cram Plan for each section of the test.

This Diagnostic Test will help you find your strengths and areas for further study for the HiSET test. This Diagnostic Test consists of half-length test sections for Language Arts: Reading; Language Arts: Writing, Part 1; Mathematics; Science; and Social Studies and a full-length Language Arts: Writing, Part 2 (essay).

As on the actual HiSET test, you can take the five sections of this test together at the same time or one at a time. The total amount of time to take all five sections is approximately 7 hours. This table shows the number of items and the time available for each section of this Diagnostic Test. The total time for this Diagnostic Test is approximately 3.5 hours.

| Test Section | Number of Items | Time Available |
|---|---|---|
| Language Arts: Reading | 20 | 33 minutes |
| Language Arts: Writing | | |
| Part 1 | 25 | 37 minutes |
| Part 2 | 1 | 45 minutes |
| Mathematics | 25 | 45 minutes |
| Science | 25 | 40 minutes |
| Social Studies | 25 | 35 minutes |

For all the multiple-choice sections, you have to choose the best answer to each item from the answer options given and fill in the corresponding circle on the answer sheet. HiSET is given in online and paper-and-pencil formats. Paper-and-pencil tests are scored by a machine, so you need to mark your answers carefully. Fill in each circle completely.

On the actual paper-and-pencil test, you will mark all of your answers on the answer sheet. If you change an answer, be sure to erase your first answer completely. Mark only one answer per item and make every mark heavy and dark:

Correct     Incorrect

TIP: On paper-and-pencil administrations of the HiSET, it's easy to mark your answer on the wrong row. To avoid making an error, write the letters of your answers on your scratch paper and copy them to your answer sheet in groups of five items at a time.

Answer all the items. HiSET does not have a penalty for guessing, so do not leave any items blank. Work as quickly as you can without becoming careless. Don't spend a lot of time on any single item. Instead, leave it and return to it later if you have time remaining. Try to answer every item, even if you have to guess.

When taking this Diagnostic Test, use the clock or timer on your mobile phone to keep track of the time. If you run out of time on any section, mark the place where you stopped working. Then complete the rest of the items as quickly as possible, so you can use the results to figure out which skill areas to study later in this book. When you finish all the items, use the Answer Key to determine your score on the Diagnostic Test. (For Language Arts: Writing, Part 2, use the instructions and sample essays to evaluate your essay.) Use the Answer Explanations (pages 47–64) to review your performance. Then follow the instructions in Chapter II, "Cram Plans," to prepare for the actual test.

# Language Arts: Reading

**20 Items**

**33 Minutes**

**Directions:** This is a test of your skills in understanding various kinds of reading material. The reading texts come from a variety of published works. Some are literary and some are informational. A number of items follow each passage.

Each passage begins with an introduction that presents information that may help you while you read. After you read each passage, continue on to the items that follow it. For each item, choose the best answer. You may refer back to the passage as often as you wish.

*Items 1 through 4 refer to the poem below.*

**English poet William Blake wrote this poem about the effect of anger on his relationships with other people.**

### A Poison Tree

I was angry with my friend:
I told my wrath, my wrath did end.
I was angry with my foe:
I told it not, my wrath did grow.

(5)     And I watered it in fears
Night and morning with my tears,
And I sunned it with smiles
And with soft deceitful wiles.

    And it grew both day and night,
(10)     Till it bore an apple bright,
And my foe beheld it shine,
And he knew that it was mine,

    And into my garden stole
When the night had veiled the pole;
(15)     In the morning, glad, I see
My foe outstretched beneath the tree.

"A Poison Tree," by William Blake.

1. How did the speaker deal with his anger toward his friend and toward his foe?

    A. He repressed his anger toward his friend and expressed his anger toward his foe.

    B. He expressed his anger toward both his friend and his foe.

    C. He expressed his anger toward his friend and repressed his anger toward his foe.

    D. He repressed his anger toward both his friend and his foe.

2. What caused the death of the speaker's foe?

    A. Suicide
    B. Murder
    C. Accidental poisoning
    D. Police gunshots

3. What is being described in lines 5–8?

    A. The speaker is making his anger worse and worse.

    B. The speaker is trying to stop thinking about his anger.

    C. The speaker has forgotten about his anger.

    D. The speaker is trying to ignore his anger.

4. What message does the author most likely want the reader to take away from this poem?

    A. When you are angry, you should ignore the anger and try to get along.

    B. When you are angry, you should deal with the anger so it won't worsen.

    C. When you are angry, you should get revenge against the person who caused the anger.

    D. When you are angry, you should try to ignore the anger by having fun.

*Items 5 through 8 refer to the passage below.*

**This excerpt is from a novel that takes place in fictional East and West Egg, where wealthy New Yorkers live in beautiful mansions. But to get to and from New York, they have to pass through the location described in this excerpt, a kind of landfill for ash from coal burned as fuel in New York. The excerpt is told from the point of view of a narrator.**

About half way between West Egg and New York the motor-road hastily joins the railroad and runs beside it for a quarter of a mile, so as to shrink away from a certain desolate area of land. This is a valley of ashes—a fantastic farm where ashes grow like wheat into ridges and hills and grotesque gardens where ashes take the forms of houses and chimneys and rising smoke and finally, with a transcendent

(5)     effort, of men who move dimly and already crumbling through the powdery air. Occasionally a line of grey cars crawls along an invisible track, gives out a ghastly creak and comes to rest, and immediately the ash-grey men swarm up with leaden spades and stir up an impenetrable cloud which screens their obscure operations from your sight.

But above the grey land and the spasms of bleak dust which drift endlessly over it, you perceive, after

(10)    a moment, the eyes of Doctor T. J. Eckleburg. The eyes of Doctor T. J. Eckleburg are blue and gigantic—their retinas are one yard high. They look out of no face but, instead, from a pair of enormous yellow spectacles which pass over a nonexistent nose. Evidently some wild wag of an oculist set them there to fatten his practice in the borough of Queens, and then sank down himself into eternal blindness or forgot them and moved away. But his eyes, dimmed a little by many paintless days under

(15)    sun and rain, brood on over the solemn dumping ground.

The valley of ashes is bounded on one side by a small foul river, and when the drawbridge is up to let barges through, the passengers on waiting trains can stare at the dismal scene for as long as half an hour.

Excerpt from *The Great Gatsby,* by F. Scott Fitzgerald.

5. The location described in the passage can best be summarized as

 A.   a bleak and depressing area that many people have to travel through unwillingly.

 B.   an open and inviting spot where people can relax and enjoy themselves.

 C.   a safe place that it is kept under watchful vigilance at all times.

 D.   a typical place one would find in New York City.

6. What are the men in lines 5–8 doing?

 A.   Unloading trash from garbage trucks

 B.   Dumping hazardous waste illegally

 C.   Sorting refuse for recycling

 D.   Unloading ashes from train cars

7. Why does the narrator mention that to get to their homes, the wealthy residents must pass through this location?

 A.   To show he believes that rich and poor people are the same in some ways

 B.   To indicate that the location was once a much nicer place

 C.   To show that he is disdainful of the wealthy residents of East and West Egg

 D.   To make West Egg seem attractive to visit

8. What is the significance of the advertising sign?

 A.   To show that people are always under observation

 B.   To indicate that some of the characters need glasses

 C.   To show that the narrator does not fit into wealthy society

 D.   To indicate that a tragedy is soon going to take place

*Items 9 through 12 refer to the passage below.*

**This excerpt from a play about the Nazi occupation of Greece during World War II focuses on a Jewish family trying to escape deportation to a Concentration Camp. The play is narrated by one of the characters as an adult.**

NARRATOR/ADULT ANDY: By the Fall of 1943, the Nazis occupying Greece had deported most of the 56,000 Jewish people who had lived in and around the port city of Salonika. The Algava family—my family—had found a hiding place, thanks to brave Greeks, like Marika. My mother, Allegra, pretended to be a cousin to Marika. She was supposed to be a widow named Angyela. My father remained
(5)     out of sight. But I was only a child. I would forget her name. So Allegra and Marika would drill me.
*(NARRATOR hands comb to ALLEGRA, returns to his place. But NARRATOR is more emotionally and sometimes physically drawn into the activities of YOUNG ANDY.)*
ALLEGRA: *(combing Andy's hair)* Now Andy, remember. My name is not Allegra. It is...?
ANDY: Angyela.
(10)    *(ALLEGRA hugs him.)*
ALLEGRA: Just for that, you shall have some baklava when Marika's guest arrives. Remember, he is Marika's friend, even though he wears a uniform.
MARIKA: *(straightening the tablecloth)* Friedrich comes at eight.
ALLEGRA: Henry, hurry, please, under the bed.
(15)    HENRY: *(getting under the bed reluctantly)* Alright, alright.
*ANDY bends way down to speak to him.*
HENRY: Don't look over here, Andy. Pretend I'm not in the room, no matter what anyone says.
ANDY: I'm going to have baklava, Papa.
HENRY: *(out of sight under the bed)* Yes, good, enjoy it.
(20)    *ALLEGRA pulls down the bedspread, then helps MARIKA set out the coffee.*
MARIKA: I speak Turkish to Friedrich. This is why he comes, to speak Turkish with me. I'm not a collaborator, don't worry.
*ALLEGRA folds the napkins in a special way, her hands shaking a bit.*
MARIKA: *(continuing)* He is a kind man, Friedrich. You are my cousin from Albania. Andy is your
(25)    little boy. Your husband died in the Italian campaign.
ALLEGRA: Yes, yes I know...I'll be silent.
MARIKA: *(looking at Allegra with a trace of jealousy)* You've got a pretty smile. How long did you know my Leonidas?
ALLEGRA: Only when he comes to get us in his truck. We climb in and hide under the fruit.
(30)    MARIKA: Good, otherwise I am very jealous.
*KNOCK AT THE DOOR, ALLEGRA freezes.*
MARIKA: I'll get the door.
*TURKISH MUSIC ON A SCRATCHY RECORD.*
*FRIEDRICH ENTERS. The jacket of his German uniform is open. A revolver shows at his belt, but his*
(35)    *manner is affable.*
MARIKA: Friedrich, come in. I have baklava, Turkish coffee. This is my cousin from Albania and her son.
*FRIEDRICH BOWS TO HER*
MARIKA: She doesn't understand the language.
(40)    FRIEDRICH: *(to the boy)* Come, sit near me. I have a boy of my own, you know.
*FRIEDRICH motions to ANDY, who is playing on the floor with a tin soldier.*
*FRIEDRICH sits on the bed, the same one under which HENRY is hiding.*

ANDY: Is that a real gun?

FRIEDRICH: Forget that. Here's a piece of baklava for you. I know what boys like.

(45)    *ANDY looks to his mother. She nods permission as she glances down to where HENRY is hiding. ANDY goes to FRIEDRICH who scoops him up on his lap.*

FRIEDRICH: But you mustn't get it on the bed or Marika will have me demoted to a foot soldier and sent to the Russian front.

*ANDY eats the baklava carefully, taking it apart leaf by leaf. At one point a layer drops on the floor,*
(50)    *dangerously near Henry's hiding place. ALLEGRA tears over to clean it up before Friedrich can see it.*

Excerpt from *Safe Harbor* based on the true story of rescue during the Nazi occupation of Greece by Joanne Koch.
Copyright © 1999. All rights reserved. Used by permission of the author.

9.  Why is it important that Andy remember Allegra's new name?

    **A.**  Because he keeps forgetting it

    **B.**  Because Allegra is a jealous person

    **C.**  To avoid revealing the family's secret to Marika

    **D.**  To prevent the Nazis from discovering them

10. What is the <u>most likely</u> reason Marika is spending time with Friedrich?

    **A.**  She is a Nazi collaborator.

    **B.**  She wants him to learn Turkish.

    **C.**  She wants to gain the assistance of a Nazi occupier.

    **D.**  She believes in the Nazi ideology.

11. Why does Allegra rush to clean up the piece of baklava that Andy dropped?

    **A.**  She doesn't want Friedrich to get sent to the Russian front.

    **B.**  She is afraid that Friedrich will pick it up and spot Henry.

    **C.**  She is a careful housekeeper and doesn't want Andy to make a mess.

    **D.**  She wants to keep the house clean while a guest is in the house.

12. Based on details in the passage, which of the following statements best characterizes the relationship between Marika and Allegra?

    **A.**  Allegra and Marika do not get along well.

    **B.**  Marika and Allegra have a guarded trust between them.

    **C.**  Allegra resents having to depend on Marika so deeply.

    **D.**  Allegra is jealous of Marika.

*Items 13 through 20 refer to the passage below.*

**This article addresses rumors of a huge volcanic eruption in the area of Yellowstone Park.**

Yellowstone Park was in the news because of fears that the caldera under it, a huge pool of magma (underground molten rock), was on the verge of a major eruption. Stories predicting an eruption in the near future flooded the Internet, and were even reported on some news sources. Some people believed that a massive eruption was about to take place, in which a massive explosion would allow huge amounts
(5)    of lava (above-ground molten rock) to cover the land, accompanied by the release of large amounts of poisonous gases and ash. Some people predicted millions of deaths from the lava flow, poisonous gases, and an ash cloud that would block sunlight. A few sources even predicted that the eruption would come within a few weeks or months, and some even predicted the exact date.

Yet, there has not been a major eruption in Yellowstone for more than 1.6 million years, and the last
(10)   series of minor eruptions was more than 70,000 years ago. So why did people become convinced that a new eruption was imminent?

Some background on Yellowstone can help explain.

Yellowstone Park, considered by many as the world's first national park, is best known for its intense geothermal activity. Yellowstone has over 10,000 different geothermal features, including about 465
(15)   active geysers. Experts believe that about half of the world's geothermal features and two-thirds of the world's geysers are located within Yellowstone Park. Geysers, which shoot large amounts of hot liquid water high in the air, are probably Yellowstone's most well-known geothermal feature. The most famous geyser in the world is Yellowstone's Old Faithful, which erupts approximately every 91 minutes. Yellowstone also has the world's largest active geyser, Steamboat Geyser, which has major eruptions up
(20)   to 300 feet high. Unlike Old Faithful, Steamboat Geyser does not erupt on a predictable schedule. During or after an eruption, a geyser can release liquid water, steam, or gases. Other important geother-mal features are steam vents, hot springs, and mudpots. Steam vents are openings in the ground that release small amounts of water vapor (steam) and other gases. Hot springs are flows of hot water from within the earth. Mudpots look like small pools of bubbling mud. They form when water rising from a
(25)   hot spring contains hydrogen sulfide. Microorganisms in the water use the hydrogen sulfide as fuel and release sulfuric acid as waste. The acid breaks down the surrounding rock into particles that mix with the water and make it look like mud.

Some other examples of Yellowstone's intense geothermal activity are hotspots and caldera. A hotspot is a place of high volcanic activity because of magma rising from the earth's core toward the
(30)   surface. A caldera is a large deposit of magma deep within the earth's surface. The Yellowstone caldera is a chamber 37 miles long, 18 miles wide, and 3 to 7 miles deep. Above the caldera, in solid rock, is a deposit of brine, or salty water. The porous rock above the brine allows the water to be replenished from runoff that sinks into the earth, while the caldera heats the water from below. The superheated water rises to the surface through the porous rock above, resulting in the large number of geysers and other
(35)   geothermic activity we observe today. Yellowstone also experiences a large number of small earthquakes each year—as many as 3,000. Most of these earthquakes cannot be detected by humans or animals, and are unrelated to Yellowstone's geothermal system.

The caldera under Yellowstone has not erupted for millions of years. So why did people think it was going to erupt? First, a seismograph malfunctioned and began reporting stronger and more frequent
(40)   earthquakes. Since this seismograph is connected to the Internet, many people noticed it and became alarmed. Apparently, rumors then swirled out of control. Scientists believe that there is no risk or indi-cation that an eruption will happen soon.

13. What is the author's main purpose in writing this article?

   **A.** To ensure that people are ready for a natural disaster

   **B.** To describe the natural features in Yellowstone Park

   **C.** To explain why rumors of a coming eruption were a false alarm

   **D.** To show pride in the world's first national park

14. What is the difference between magma and lava?

   **A.** There is no difference; both are molten rock.

   **B.** Magma is molten rock that has risen to the earth's surface, and lava is molten rock that is below the earth's surface.

   **C.** Magma is molten rock below the earth's surface, and lava is molten rock that has risen to the earth's surface.

   **D.** Lava is magma that has hardened and solidified, while magma is liquid rock.

15. What is the purpose of Paragraph 3 (line 12)?

   **A.** To provide an answer to the question asked at the end of the previous paragraph

   **B.** To show that people's fears of an eruption are groundless

   **C.** To show that most people do not know much about Yellowstone Park

   **D.** To provide a transition to the next section of the article

16. What is the meaning of the word "imminent" (line 11)?

   **A.** Very important

   **B.** Possible in the future

   **C.** Coming very soon

   **D.** Impossible to predict

17. Which of the following is <u>NOT</u> one of the causes of Yellowstone's intense geothermic activity?

   **A.** The hotspot under it

   **B.** The presence of a huge caldera

   **C.** A large underground deposit of brine

   **D.** Frequent minor earthquakes

18. What is the main difference between a geyser and a steam vent?

   **A.** A steam vent releases more water than a geyser.

   **B.** A geyser releases liquid water, and a steam vent releases water vapor.

   **C.** Only steam vents release gases.

   **D.** Geysers erupt on a predictable schedule, and steam vents do not.

19. Which of the following phrases best describe the tone of the article?

   **A.** Rational and scientific

   **B.** Alarmist and emotional

   **C.** Lyrical and poetic

   **D.** Loving and caring

20. Based on the information in the article, what should people planning a trip to Yellowstone Park do?

   **A.** Cancel their plans immediately

   **B.** Go anyway, because there is no special risk of a volcanic eruption

   **C.** Go as soon as they can, before Yellowstone is destroyed forever

   **D.** Postpone their plans until there is more evidence that travel to Yellowstone is safe

IF YOU FINISH BEFORE TIME IS CALLED, CHECK YOUR WORK ON THIS SECTION ONLY. DO NOT WORK ON ANY OTHER SECTION IN THE TEST.

# Language Arts: Writing

## Part 1

**25 Items**
**Time: 37 Minutes**

**Directions:** This is a test of the skills involved in writing and revising written materials. There are two text selections similar to the kinds of documents high school students typically write. Each selection is presented twice: first in a box in a normal format, and then in a spread-out format with certain parts of the text underlined and numbered.

Skim the boxed text quickly to get an idea of the text's purpose, organization, and style. Then continue to the spread-out version.

Each numbered section of the text corresponds to an item in the right-hand column. Select the answer option that

- Makes the sentence grammatically correct
- Expresses the idea in the clearest or most appropriate way
- Is worded consistently with the style and purpose of the writing
- Organizes the ideas most effectively

If you believe that the underlined original version is best, choose Option A, "No change." For organization items, you may find it helpful to refer to the boxed text. For spelling items, indicate which of the three words is misspelled in the context of the passage, or choose Option A, "None."

*Items 1 through 15 are based on the following text selection.*

**The draft article below is about interviewing for a job. Quickly skim the draft article in the box below. Then go to the spread-out version and review the suggested revisions, choosing the best option for each item.**

A vital step to getting a job is a successful interview. While your resume and job application are important, they only get your foot in the door. To get the job you need to interview for success. Before your interview, make sure you know something about your future workplace.

Research the company online. Make sure you know what type of business the company is in, the kinds of customers' it has, and the company's size and locations. If the workplace is a restaurant, for example, visit the restaurant's Website and read reviews of the restaurant online. Look over the menu, too.

Prepare for the day of the interview. Plan your outfit and get a good night's sleep the evening before your interview. Go to the barber or beauty salon if necessary. Prepare clean, pressed clothes. For many jobs, you may not need to wear a suit or dress to the interview, but you should wear clothes that are neat and clean. According to experts, it's best to go for a conservative look.

The night before, find the location of the interview on a map if you are not familiar with it. Figure out how you will get to the interview, the amount of travel time needed, and find out where you can park. Organize any information or materials you will need, such as: your driver's license or ID card, your Social Security number, and a pen. If you have any special licenses or certifications for the job, consider bringing along proof that you hold them. Prepare answers to some of the questions that are typically asked at an interview. You might think of questions you have been asked in previous job interviews and write down answers to those questions. For example, one commonly question asked at a job interview is, "Can you tell me a little about yourself"? This question is frequently asked first in an interview and is used to figure out if you can think quickly and answer succinctly. A short, informative answer ready to give to the interviewer. Give a bit of background about yourself and tell why you are interested in the job. Prepare a few questions to ask about the job, in case you are asked if you have any questions. Moreover, don't ask about the pay. Wait for the interviewer to do that.

The day of the interview, arrive a few minutes early. If you find yourself getting nervous as you wait, use a simple relaxation technique, such as taking a deep breath, closing your eyes, and counting to ten. Smile warmly and shake hands firmly where you meet the interviewer. Try to look the interviewer in her eyes as you talk to them. Answer all the questions completely and truthfully. At the end of the interview, thank the interviewer for her time and interest. Politely ask when the company expects to make a decision, and make sure the interviewer has your correct contact information. Get follow-up information, such as the interviewer's phone number and email address. As soon as you get home, write a thank-you note or email. Include your contact information (email and phone number) in the email.

## [1]

[1] A vital step to getting a job is a successful interview. [2] While your resume and job application are important, they only get your foot in the door. [3] To get the <u>job you</u> need to interview for success.
<sub>1</sub>
[4] <u>Before your interview, make sure you know</u>
<sub>2</sub>
<u>something about your future workplace.</u>
<sub>2</sub>

## [2]

Research the company online. Make sure you know what type of business the company is in, the kinds of <u>customers'</u> it has, and the <u>company's</u> size
<sub>3</sub>               <sub>3</sub>
and <u>locations</u>. If the workplace is a restaurant, for
<sub>3</sub>
example, visit the restaurant's <u>Website</u> and read
<sub>4</sub>
reviews of the restaurant online. Look over the menu, too. |5|

1. **A.** (No change)
   **B.** job, you
   **C.** job; you
   **D.** job,

2. Which of the following would be the best placement for Sentence 4?
   **A.** Before Sentence 1
   **B.** Before Sentence 2
   **C.** Before the first sentence in Paragraph 2
   **D.** Remove the sentence completely.

3. Which of the following words, if any, is misspelled?
   **A.** (None)
   **B.** customers'
   **C.** company's
   **D.** locations

4. **A.** (No change)
   **B.** websight
   **C.** website
   **D.** websites'

5. The writer is considering whether or not to use the following sentence.

   Companies may check your Facebook page or other locations on the Internet, so make sure that your online presence is appropriate before you begin your job search.

   What would be the best placement for this sentence?
   **A.** Make it the last sentence of Paragraph 2
   **B.** Make it the first sentence of Paragraph 3
   **C.** Make it the second sentence of Paragraph 3
   **D.** (Do not use this sentence; the article is best as written.)

**[3]**

Prepare for the day of the interview. Plan your outfit and get a good night's sleep the evening before your interview. Go to the barber or beauty salon if necessary. Prepare clean, pressed clothes. For many jobs, you may not need to wear a suit or dress to the interview, but you should wear clothes that are neat and clean. According to experts, <u>it's</u> best to go for a
6
conservative look.

**[4]**

The night before, find the location of the interview on a map if you are not familiar with it. <u>Figure out</u>
7
<u>how you will get to the interview, the amount of</u>
7
<u>travel time needed, and find out where you can park.</u>
7
Organize any information or materials you will <u>need,</u>
8
<u>such as:</u> your driver's license or ID card, your Social
8
Security number, and a pen. If you have any special licenses or certifications for the job, consider bringing along proof that you hold them. Prepare answers to some of the questions that are typically asked at an interview. You might think of questions you have been asked in previous job interviews and write down answers to those questions. For example, one <u>com-</u>
9
<u>monly question asked</u> at a job interview <u>is, "Can you</u>
9                                                        10
<u>tell me a little about yourself"?</u> This question is
10

6. **A.** (No change)
   **B.** its
   **C.** its'
   **D.** it

7. **A.** (No change)
   **B.** Figure out how you will get to the interview, the amount of travel time needed, and where you can park.
   **C.** Figure out how you will get to the interview, how much travel time you need, and find out where you can park.
   **D.** Figure out how you will get to the interview, how much travel time you need, and where you can park.

8. **A.** (No change)
   **B.** need, such as
   **C.** need such as
   **D.** need; such as

9. **A.** (No change)
   **B.** commonly asked question
   **C.** question common asked
   **D.** question asked common

10. **A.** (No change)
    **B.** is "Can you tell me a little about yourself?"
    **C.** is, Can you tell me a little about yourself?
    **D.** is, "Can you tell me a little about yourself?"

frequently asked first in an interview and is used to figure out if you can think quickly and answer succinctly. <u>A short, informative answer ready to give to the interviewer.</u> Give a bit of background about yourself and tell why you are interested in the job. Prepare a few questions to ask about the job, in case you are asked if you have any questions. <u>Moreover,</u> don't ask about the pay. Wait for the interviewer to do that.
<sub>11</sub>
<sub>11</sub>
<sub>12</sub>

## [5]

[1] The day of the interview, arrive a few minutes early. [2] If you find yourself getting nervous as you wait, use a simple relaxation technique, such as taking a deep breath, closing your eyes, and counting to ten. [3] Smile warmly and shake hands <u>firmly where</u> you
<sub>13</sub>
meet the interviewer. [4] Try to look the interviewer in her eyes as you talk to <u>them</u>. [5] Answer all the ques-
<sub>14</sub>
tions completely and truthfully. [6] At the end of the interview, thank the interviewer for her time and interest. [7] Politely ask when the company expects to make a decision, and make sure the interviewer has your correct contact information. [8] Get follow-up information, such as the interviewer's phone number and email address. [9] As soon as you get home, write a thank-you note or email. [10] Include your contact information (email and phone number) in the email. 15

11. **A.** (No change)
    **B.** A short, informative answer is ready to give to the interviewer.
    **C.** Have a short, informative answer ready to give to the interviewer.
    **D.** Should have a short, informative answer ready to give to the interviewer.

12. **A.** (No change)
    **B.** However,
    **C.** Nor
    **D.** In addition,

13. **A.** (No change)
    **B.** firmly who
    **C.** firmly when
    **D.** firmly which

14. **A.** (No change)
    **B.** him
    **C.** her
    **D.** it

15. The writer is considering splitting Paragraph 5 into two paragraphs. The best place to begin a new paragraph would be with

    **A.** Sentence 5
    **B.** Sentence 6
    **C.** Sentence 7
    **D.** Sentence 8

*Items 16 through 25 are based on the following text selection.*

**A magazine writer wrote the following article about the history of mobile phones. Quickly skim the draft in the box below. Then go to the spread-out version and review the suggested revisions, choosing the best option for each item.**

Because many people believe that the mobile phone is a relatively recent invention, people have been thinking about the possibility of mobile telephones for more than 100 years. Within 30 years of the invention of the telephone in 1876 by Alexander Graham Bell, people were already speculating about mobile phones. In 1906, a German company declared that it had developed a wireless phone that claim was quickly dismissed as a fraud. But German Railroad Companies began to experiment with mobile phones on its trains as early as 1918. By 1926, first-class passengers could use special mobile phones on certain roots on the railway network. However, these earlier mobile phones, like the radio telephones used a few years later by both sides in World War II, operated on radio frequencies and had many limitations.

The first viable mobile phones in the United States date to the 1940s. The dominant American telephone company, then a monopoly, developed its first commercial mobile phone service in the 1940s. Like their predecessors, these phones operated on radio frequencies. On the first phones, customers could not dial numbers. The operator had to dial for them. In addition, only three conversations could take place in each city where the service was offered. These phones were large and bulky. In fact, callers could only use them from their cars because of their large size and they needed so much electricity. By 1948, mobile telephone services had about 5,000 customers who made about 30,000 calls per week.

People continued to dream about mobile phones. In 1959, science fiction author Arthur C. Clarke wrote about "a personal transceiver, so small and compact that everyone carries one." He said, "The time will come when we will be able to call a person anywhere on Earth merely by dialing a number." Such a device would also, in Clarke's vision, include means for global positioning. Clarke hoped, "No one need ever again be lossed." Clarke's predictions have been remarkably accurate.

The possibility of achieving Clarke's vision became closer to reality in 1978 when the first portable mobile phones were introduced. These first portable phones were bulky, heavy, and expensive. The first true portable mobile phone had a talk time of 30 minutes and took 10 hours to recharge. Since then, phones have continued to become smaller, lighter, and cheaper. Users can now text, access the Internet, view multimedia, and accomplish many tasks. As the functionality of phones have increased, so has the size, primarily to allow for larger screens. However, these phones also have limitations. The screens of these phones are breakable silicone, and there is still limits on battery size and life. Innovators are continuing to address these issues, and new and improved phone models are introduced on a regular basis. Mobile phones are barely 100 years old. Who knows what the next 100 years will bring?

## [1]

<u>Because</u> many people believe that the mobile
<sub>16</sub> phone is a relatively recent invention, people have
been thinking about the possibility of mobile telephones for more than 100 years. Within 30 years of
the invention of the telephone in 1876 by Alexander
Graham Bell, people were already speculating about
mobile phones. In 1906, a German company
declared that it had developed a wireless <u>phone that</u>
claim was quickly dismissed as a fraud. But <u>German
Railroad Companies</u> began to experiment with
mobile phones on <u>its</u> trains as early as 1918. By
1926, first-class <u>passengers</u> could use special mobile
phones on certain <u>roots</u> on the <u>railway</u> network.
However, these earlier mobile phones, like the radio
telephones used a few years later by both sides in
World War II, operated on radio frequencies and
had many limitations.

## [2]

The first viable mobile phones in the United
States date to the 1940s. The dominant American
telephone company, then a monopoly, developed its
first commercial mobile phone service in the 1940s.

16. **A.** (No change)
    **B.** Although
    **C.** When
    **D.** Since

17. **A.** (No change)
    **B.** phone, that
    **C.** phone; however, that
    **D.** phone; although that

18. **A.** (No change)
    **B.** German railroad companies
    **C.** German Railroad companies
    **D.** german railroad companies

19. **A.** (No change)
    **B.** theirs
    **C.** their
    **D.** his

20. Which of the following words, if any, is misspelled?
    **A.** (None)
    **B.** passengers
    **C.** roots
    **D.** railway

Like their predecessors, these phones operated on radio frequencies. On the first phones, customers could not dial numbers. The operator had to dial for them. In addition, only three conversations could take place in each city where the service was offered. These phones were large and bulky. In fact, callers could only use them from their cars <u>because of their large size and they needed so much electricity</u>. By
21
1948, mobile telephone services had about 5,000 <u>customers who</u> made about 30,000 calls per week.
22

### [3]

People continued to dream about mobile phones. In 1959, science fiction author Arthur C. Clarke wrote about "a personal transceiver, so small and compact that everyone carries one." He said, "The time will come when we will be able to call a person anywhere on Earth merely by dialing a number." Such a device would also, in Clarke's vision, include means for global positioning. Clarke <u>hoped</u>, "No
23
one need ever again be <u>lossed</u>." Clarke's predictions
23
have <u>been</u> remarkably accurate.
23

21. **A.** (No change)
   **B.** because of their large size and high electricity consumption
   **C.** because of their large size and so much electricity needed
   **D.** because they were large and high electricity consumption

22. **A.** (No change)
   **B.** customers, when
   **C.** customers which
   **D.** customers, which

23. Which of the following words, if any, is misspelled?
   **A.** (None)
   **B.** hoped
   **C.** lossed
   **D.** been

## [4]

The possibility of achieving Clarke's vision became closer to reality in 1978 when the first portable mobile phones were introduced. These first portable phones were bulky, heavy, and expensive. The first true portable mobile phone had a talk time of 30 minutes and took 10 hours to recharge. Since then, phones have continued to become smaller, lighter, and cheaper. Users can now text, access the Internet, view multimedia, and accomplish many tasks. As the functionality of phones <u>have</u> increased,
24
so has the size, primarily to allow for larger screens. However, these phones also have limitations. The screens of these phones are breakable silicone, and there <u>is</u> still limits on battery size and life. Innovators
25
are continuing to address these issues, and new and improved phone models are introduced on a regular basis. Mobile phones are barely 100 years old. Who knows what the next 100 years will bring?

24. **A.** (No change)
    **B.** has
    **C.** had
    **D.** having

25. **A.** (No change)
    **B.** was
    **C.** were
    **D.** are

IF YOU FINISH BEFORE TIME IS CALLED, CHECK YOUR WORK ON THIS SECTION ONLY. DO NOT WORK ON ANY OTHER SECTION IN THE TEST.

# Part 2

**1 Essay Item**

**Time: 45 Minutes**

**Directions:** This is a test of your writing skills. You have 45 minutes to prepare and write your response. Your essay will be scored based on the following criteria:

- Development and support of a main idea with examples and details
- Clear and effective organization of ideas, including an introduction, body, and conclusion; logical paragraphs; and effective transitions between and within paragraphs
- Appropriate language use, including varied vocabulary, varied sentence patterns, and appropriate voice
- Clarity and use of Standard Written English

---

A group of teachers recently was interviewed on TV about excessive Internet surfing. They believe that people, especially children, spend too much time online. They believe that excessive Internet surfing is a reason children do not do well in school. They also believe that it is harmful to adults. Do you agree that excessive Internet surfing is a problem?

Write a letter to the editor of the TV station's website that explains whether or not you believe excessive Internet surfing is a problem. Think carefully about reasons that will help others understand your position as well as examples and details that you can use to support your position. Write in the form of an essay. Do not use greetings or closings.

IF YOU FINISH BEFORE TIME IS CALLED, CHECK YOUR WORK ON THIS SECTION ONLY. DO NOT WORK ON ANY OTHER SECTION IN THE TEST.

# Mathematics

**25 Items**

**Time: 45 Minutes**

**Directions:** This is a test of your skills in applying mathematical concepts and solving mathematical problems. Read each item carefully and decide which of the five alternatives best answers the item.

There are relatively easy problems scattered throughout the test. Thus, do not waste time on problems that are too difficult; go on, and return to them if you have time.

1. Chris and Diane need to purchase a new cell phone to go with their 2-year contract. They can purchase a phone for $425 or rent the phone for $20 per month. How much will they save over the term of the contract if they purchase the phone?

   A. $25
   B. $55
   C. $385
   D. $405
   E. $480

2. A recipe for fried chicken that serves 8 people uses 1.5 cups of buttermilk. How much buttermilk is needed when using this same recipe to serve 20 people?

   A. 2.5
   B. 3.25
   C. 3.5
   D. 3.75
   E. 4

3. The sales tax in Wigginham County is 6.5%. The negotiated price on the car that Alice just purchased is $17,800. Assuming there are no other fees associated with the purchase, what is the total Alice will pay for the car?

   A. $1,157
   B. $11,570
   C. $16,643
   D. $18,957
   E. $29,370

4. The following graph shows the population of the United States since 1950. Which of the following is the best estimate of the population of the United States in 1980?

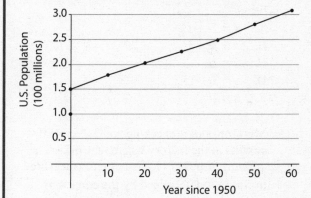

   A. 201,000,000
   B. 229,000,000
   C. 249,000,000
   D. 278,000,000
   E. 301,000,000

5. A coat that normally sells for $190 is on sale at a discount of 20%. Patty has a store coupon that entitles her to an additional 5% discount off the sale price. Which expression represents the price of the coat after all the discounts have been taken?

   A. $190 \times 0.25$
   B. $190 \times 0.75$
   C. $190 \times 0.20 \times 0.05$
   D. $190 \times 0.80$
   E. $190 \times 0.80 \times 0.95$

**19**

6. What is the value of $5(2p + 3r) - 4(3p - 2r)$ when $p = 5$ and $r = -4$?

   A. 18
   B. 38
   C. -102
   D. -82
   E. 82

7. The number of seats in a row at a theater increases by two from one row to the next so as to make for a clearer view of the stage. If there are 15 seats in the first row, which equation expresses the relationship between the number of rows from the front of the auditorium, $r$, and the number of seats in that row, $s$?

   A. $s = 2r + 13$
   B. $s = 2r + 15$
   C. $s = 2r - 13$
   D. $s = 2r - 15$
   E. $s = 2r$

8. Mr. Gonzales is checking some electrical circuits at the factory where he works. The amount of power ($P$) in a circuit (measured in watts) is determined by the equation $P = \dfrac{V^2}{R}$, where $V$ represents the number of volts and $R$ represents the amount of resistance (the resistance of the flow of electricity through the wires) measured in ohms. How many volts are in a circuit if it is producing 19.6 watts with a resistance of 10 ohms?

   A. 1.4
   B. 3.1
   C. 4.4
   D. 5.4
   E. 14.0

9. One cup of fat-free milk contains 300 grams of calcium, while each cup of calcium-enriched orange juice contains 350 grams of calcium. If the minimum daily requirement for the number of grams of calcium for an adult aged 19 to 50 is 1,000 grams, which statement best expresses this nutritional need? (*Note:* $m$ = the number of glasses of fat-free milk; $j$ = the number of glasses of calcium-enriched orange juice.)

   A. $300m + 350j \geq 1,000$
   B. $300m + 350j \leq 1,000$
   C. $300m + 350j = 1,000$
   D. $m + j > 1,000$
   E. $m + j < 1,000$

10. Which of the following curves best represents the graph of $x = 4$?

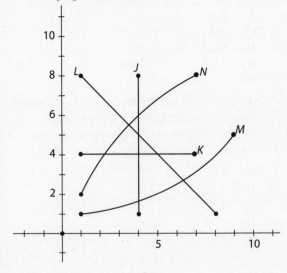

   A. $J$
   B. $K$
   C. $L$
   D. $M$
   E. $N$

*Use this information to answer items 11 through 14.*

The town council has determined that the community pool is in need of some repair. The water needs to be drained, the repairs made, and then the pool needs to be refilled. In addition, new synthetic turf will be laid on the deck around the outside of the pool. The depth of the pool is 8 feet.

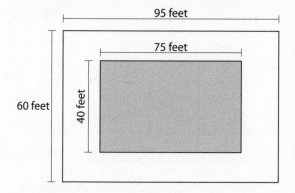

11. After the repairs to the pool have been made, the interior walls and bottom of the pool need to be painted. One gallon of the paint covers 350 square feet. Which expression represents the number of gallons of paint needed to paint the walls and bottom of the pool?

A. $\dfrac{40 \times 75 \times 8}{350}$

B. $\dfrac{2(40 \times 8) + 2(75 \times 8)}{350}$

C. $\dfrac{2(40 \times 8) + 2(75 \times 8) + (40 \times 75)}{350}$

D. $\dfrac{2(40 \times 8) + 2(75 \times 8) + 2(40 \times 75)}{350}$

E. $40 \times 75 \times 8 \times 350$

12. Which expression represents the number of gallons of water needed to refill the pool? (*Note:* 1 gallon = 0.134 cubic feet.)

A. $40 \times 75 \times 0.134$

B. $40 \times 75 \times 8 \times 0.134$

C. $\dfrac{40 \times 75}{0.134}$

D. $\dfrac{40 \times 75 \times 8}{0.134}$

E. $60 \times 95 \times 8 \times 0.134$

13. The cost of the synthetic turf is $12 per square yard. How much money will it cost to put the turf around the pool?

A. $3,600
B. $5,700
C. $22,800
D. $32,400
E. $68,400

14. Maintaining the pH of the pool water requires that 2.5 kilograms of a certain chemical be used for every 1 million liters of water in the pool. How many kilograms of chemicals must be used for the 680,000 liters of water in this pool?

A. 0.7
B. 1.7
C. 2.7
D. 3.7
E. 4.7

15. The graph of the line $y = -4x + 10$ intersects the $x$-axis at what point?

A. (2.5, 0)
B. (–2.5, 0)
C. (0, 2.5)
D. (0, –2.5)
E. (6, 0)

16. The Personal Identification Number (PIN) for an ATM card consists of a 4-digit code of numbers from 0 to 9. If the digits in the code may be repeated, how many possible PINs can there be?

A. 40
B. $10^4$
C. $4^{10}$
D. $10 \times 9 \times 8 \times 7$
E. $10 + 9 + 8 + 7$

17. An outline of a house, symmetric about the centerline, is shown. Determine the number of feet in the roofline, $m$, shown in the diagram.

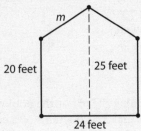

20 feet    25 feet

24 feet

    A.   5
    B.   12
    C.   13
    D.   17
    E.   20

*Data collected from a survey of small businesses in a town are summarized below. Use this information to answer items 18 and 19.*

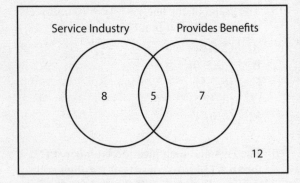

Service Industry    Provides Benefits

8   5   7

12

18. How many businesses were surveyed in total?

    A.   8
    B.   12
    C.   13
    D.   20
    E.   32

19. If one of the survey responders that provides benefits is selected at random, what is the probability that the responder is a service industry?

    A.   $\dfrac{5}{32}$
    B.   $\dfrac{5}{12}$
    C.   $\dfrac{5}{13}$
    D.   $\dfrac{13}{32}$
    E.   $\dfrac{12}{32}$

20. Max spends $\dfrac{1}{4}$ of his monthly income on housing, $\dfrac{1}{5}$ on utilities, and $\dfrac{3}{8}$ on entertainment. He spends $\dfrac{1}{2}$ of his remaining monthly income on food for eating at home. What part of his monthly income goes into buying food for eating at home?

    A.   $\dfrac{7}{80}$
    B.   $\dfrac{33}{80}$
    C.   $\dfrac{7}{40}$
    D.   $\dfrac{7}{20}$
    E.   $\dfrac{33}{40}$

21. Mrs. Quinn is analyzing the cost of manufacturing products at the factory where she is a manager. She has determined that the cost $(C)$ of producing $n$ units of one of the company's products is $C = 9{,}000n - 50n^2$. What is the cost of producing 25 units of the product?

    A.   256,250
    B.   227,500
    C.   223,750
    D.   222,500
    E.   193,750

22. The workers at Acme manufacturing produced 120 units by 9 a.m. and 480 units by 2 p.m. on a given day. What was the average rate of change of production during the time period?

    A.  60 units per hour
    B.  72 units per hour
    C.  90 units per hour
    D.  300 units per hour
    E.  360 units per hour

*The chart below summarizes the percent change in the population for each of the 50 states in the U.S. from 2010 to 2013. Use this data to answer item 23.*

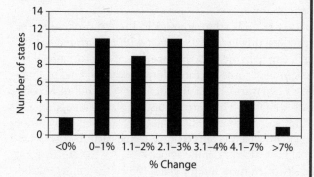

23. What percent of the states had an increase of more than 3% in the population during this time?

    A.  12
    B.  17
    C.  18
    D.  24
    E.  34

24. Molly has a total of 80 coins in her purse, quarters and dimes only, which have a total value of $16.70. If $q$ represents the number of quarters in her purse, which equation can be used to determine the number of coins of each type that are in her purse?

    A.  $q + 10 = 80$
    B.  $25q + 10 = 80$
    C.  $25q + 10q = 80$
    D.  $0.25q + 0.10(80 - q) = 16.70$
    E.  $0.25q + 0.10(q - 80) = 16.70$

25. A summary of the 2010 population of each U.S. state in 2010 (rounded to the nearest million) is shown in the table below. What was the median population for the states in 2010?

| Population (in Millions) | Frequency |
|---|---|
| 1 | 11 |
| 2 | 4 |
| 3 | 6 |
| 4 | 4 |
| 5 | 5 |
| 6 | 5 |
| 7 | 3 |
| 8 | 1 |
| 9 | 1 |
| 10 | 4 |
| 14 | 2 |
| 20 | 2 |
| 26 | 1 |
| 38 | 1 |

    A.  4,000,000
    B.  4,500,000
    C.  5,000,000
    D.  6,000,000
    E.  6,460,000

**IF YOU FINISH BEFORE TIME IS CALLED, CHECK YOUR WORK ON THIS SECTION ONLY. DO NOT WORK ON ANY OTHER SECTION IN THE TEST.**

# Science

**25 Items**

**Time: 40 Minutes**

**Directions:** This is a test of your skills in analyzing information in the area of science. Read each item and decide which of the four answer options is the best answer.

Sometimes, several items are based on the same information or graphic. You should read this material carefully and use it to answer the items.

*Items 1 through 5 refer to the following information.*

Tornados and hurricanes are two forms of dangerous weather. Both are extremely powerful and can cause great damage. Each of them is formed in a different way.

A tornado is a violently rotating funnel of air that extends from a cloud in the atmosphere to the ground. A funnel cloud is not considered a tornado until it is in actual contact with the ground. At the ground, a cloud of dust and debris may form, which can help identify the location of the tornado.

Tornados form during strong thunderstorms. The strongest tornados form during a certain kind of thunderstorm called a supercell. These thunderstorms occur when warm, moist air, often from the Gulf of Mexico, meets cool, dry air. The two air masses form an area of instability. The warm, moist air rises in an updraft. At higher altitude, this air cools, which leads to a downdraft with heavy rainfall, winds, hail, and lightning. If the updraft is strong enough, it creates a rotating funnel cloud, which is pulled down to the earth by the downdraft. In the northern hemisphere, the rotation is almost always counter-clockwise. As the storm gains strength, the funnel rotates faster and faster, and the sky often turns a dark green. When the funnel touches down, the storm is officially called a tornado. The resulting damage can be heavy, especially if the tornado touches down in a populated area. Most tornados form in the spring and fall when weather conditions are appropriate, but they have been recorded in every month on the year in the continental United States.

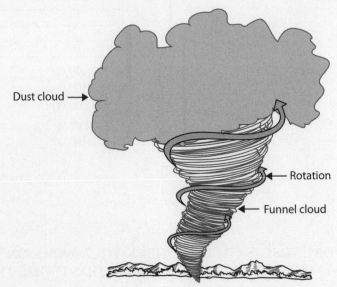

Dust cloud →

← Rotation

← Funnel cloud

Hurricanes also form from rotation in the atmosphere, but hurricanes form over the open ocean, while tornados form over land. Hurricanes get their energy from warm ocean water. For a hurricane to form, warm moist air begins to rise from sea level. If enough warm air rises fast enough, an area of low pressure forms. This area of low pressure is called a tropical depression. As the moist air rises, more air rushes into to the area of depression, absorbs moisture, and also rises, and begins to rotate. If this pattern continues, the tropical depression will become a tropical storm with strong winds and heavy rain. A tropical storm is characterized by winds from about 60 to 120 kilometers per hour. If the storm continues to draw warm, moist air, the rotation will increase and the storm will gain strength. The storm is considered a hurricane when winds exceed about 120 kilometers per hour. As the storm grows and gains strength, the central area of rotation, called the eye of the storm, is formed. A hurricane is dangerous when it hits land, where it can produce high winds, extremely heavy rainfall, and a storm surge (a rising in the sea). The storm surge is probably the most destructive aspect of a hurricane. Once the hurricane makes landfall, it will begin to weaken since it no longer can draw in warm ocean air. There are cases when a hurricane has struck land and weakened, but then passed back over the ocean again, where it regained strength. This is the case of hurricane Irene, which made landfall nine times. This destructive hurricane occurred in late August 2011. At different times, this storm was classified as a Category 1, 2, and 3 hurricane, as well as a tropical storm. It first struck the island of St. Croix and then struck Puerto Rico, the Bahamas, the Outer Banks of North Carolina, New Jersey, and Brooklyn, New York, before finally hitting New England.

1. What weather conditions are necessary for a supercell thunderstorm to form?

   A. Warm, moist air and cool, dry air come together and an area of instability forms.

   B. Heavy rainfall, winds, hail, and lightning cause a strong updraft that begins to rotate.

   C. Warm, moist air rises from the ocean surface, forming an area of low pressure.

   D. A downdraft pulls the funnel cloud to the earth's surface.

2. Which of the following causes a funnel cloud to touch down?

   A. Strong winds from the funnel cloud create rotation.

   B. Condensation causes rain, which creates a downdraft that pulls the funnel cloud to the earth.

   C. Cool, dry air high in the atmosphere moves toward the earth in a downdraft.

   D. A supercell thunderstorm created by the tornado causes heavy rainfall, high winds, and lightning.

3. Which of the following is a characteristic of both hurricanes and tornados?

   A. They both form over land.

   B. They both have rotation.

   C. They both touch the ground.

   D. They both produce storm surges.

4. After a hurricane strikes and moves inland, which of the following will most likely happen?

   A. The hurricane will go back out to sea again and become stronger.

   B. The hurricane will stop moving because it needs warm, moist air to stay in motion.

   C. The wind and rain caused by the hurricane will continue to increase.

   D. The hurricane will lose strength because it no longer gets warm, moist ocean air.

5. Storm chasers study tornados by getting as close to them as they can in order to photograph the storms and take measurements of their wind speeds, rotation, and other characteristics. Which of the following is true of storm chasers, based on the information in the passage?

   A. Storm chasers cannot provide valuable information about tornados because tornados form high in the atmosphere.

   B. May will most likely be a busy month for storm chasers.

   C. Storm chasers are not really scientists because they do not use the scientific method.

   D. Storm chasers cannot do their research because tornados cannot be predicted.

*Use the following table to answer items 6 and 7.*

Tropical storms are categorized according to the Saffir-Simpson Hurricane Wind Scale:

| Saffir-Simpson Hurricane Wind Scale | |
|---|---|
| Category | Wind Speed |
| 5 | 157 mph<br>252 km/h |
| 4 | 130–156 mph<br>209–251 km/h |
| 3 | 111–129 mph<br>178–208 km/h |
| 2 | 96–110 mph<br>154–177 km/h |
| 1 | 74–95 mph<br>119–153 km/h |
| Additional Classifications | |
| Tropical Storm | 39–73 mph<br>63–118 km/h |
| Tropical Depression | < 38 mph<br>< 62 km/h |

6. Scientists are tracking a hurricane that is forming off the coast of Cuba. A weather station in Cuba just reported that storm winds have just reached 125 km/h. What category is the storm?

   A. Category 3
   B. Category 2
   C. Category 1
   D. Tropical storm

7. Which of the following is the strongest wind that can be expected from a tropical storm?

   A. 34 mph
   B. 60 km/h
   C. 118 km/h
   D. 125 km/h

*Items 8 through 12 refer to the following information.*

Vitamin C is a necessary nutrient used by our bodies in many ways. It has long been known that vitamin C is important to the health of our blood vessels, bones, and muscles. Some studies have suggested that vitamin C is also important for maintaining skin health, but these studies are less conclusive. People whose diet does not contain adequate quantities of vitamin C, which is obtained from natural sources such as fruit and vegetables, are at risk of developing scurvy. This disease initially causes tiredness, spots on the skin, and spongy gums. As it advances, it causes more severe symptoms such as sores on the skin. The relationship between vitamin C and scurvy was not identified until vitamin C was isolated in 1932, though it had been known for some time that eating citrus fruits such as oranges, lemons, and limes would ward off scurvy.

It was not until the 1970s that people began to claim that vitamin C had a role in preventing the common cold. At that time, many healthcare professionals began recommending vitamin C supplements to prevent colds or make them shorter and less severe. Since then, numerous studies have examined the relationship between taking vitamin C supplements and the common cold. The research methods employed in the studies, as well as the results, have been inconsistent. Recently, a group of scientists conducted a meta-analysis of all studies on this topic. A meta-analysis looks at all the research and findings in order to find the most certain conclusions. The meta-analysis examined two research questions:

1. Does taking vitamin C supplements regularly reduce the number of colds people catch?
2. Does taking vitamin C regularly or at the onset of a cold reduce the severity or length of the cold?

To answer the first question, 29 studies on vitamin C were examined. Results of these studies showed that for most people, taking regular doses of vitamin C supplements did not have any effect on preventing colds when compared to control groups who did not take vitamin C supplements. However, for people who are exposed to periods of high physical stress, such as marathon runners in one study or soldiers involved in subarctic exercises in another, studies showed reduced risk for getting a cold when compared to control groups.

To answer the second question, 31 studies were examined. Overall, the results showed that the duration or severity of colds was reduced by 11% in adults and 14% in children who took vitamin C supplements. However, when seven more rigorous, therapeutic trials were examined, vitamin C supplementation was shown to have no significant effect on the duration or severity of colds.

In interpreting the results, researchers indicate that taking regular doses of vitamin C to prevent colds is not warranted, except for people who are under unusual short-term physical stress. The results about taking vitamin C to reduce the severity or duration of colds are mixed. Researchers recommend that people interested in taking vitamin C supplements monitor their own success taking vitamin C and make decisions accordingly. Results also suggest older adults and individuals with chronic health concerns take vitamin C supplements, especially if the people believe they have been helpful in the past. Of course, vitamin C is still an essential nutrient for bone, blood vessel, and muscle health, though most people get enough of this nutrient from the food they eat. Researchers recommend talking to your doctor or health care provider before making any changes to diet or nutrition.

8. Why did the group of scientists conduct the meta-analysis?

    **A.** Scurvy is a serious medical condition, and the scientists wanted to find out how to prevent it.

    **B.** Results from the many studies conducted over the years presented confusing information, and the scientists wanted to find solid conclusions.

    **C.** The scientists believed that the previous studies were not valid, so they conducted a new study.

    **D.** The scientists are certain that vitamin C supplements prevent colds, so they wanted to find results that support their belief.

9. Why do the scientists recommend that people evaluate the effectiveness of vitamin C themselves?

    **A.** The scientists do not trust the results of the meta-analysis.

    **B.** The scientists are convinced that vitamin C will prevent colds despite their findings.

    **C.** The results of the meta-analysis of the benefits of the supplements in reducing the duration or severity of colds are contradictory.

    **D.** The results of the meta-analysis show that additional research is needed.

10. Which of the following is a benefit of conducting a meta-analysis of previous studies?

    **A.** Scientists can better understand the health risks of short-term physical stress.

    **B.** Scientists can use the results to evaluate the effectiveness of vitamin C supplements on other diseases.

    **C.** The public will take more vitamin C supplements, which will reduce the incidence of the common cold.

    **D.** Scientists will have a better understanding of the effectiveness of different ways to investigate a research question.

11. The meta-analysis gave results on the effects of vitamin C supplements on people under short-term physical stress. A researcher is interested in studying the effects of this vitamin on people experiencing short-term psychological stress. The researcher developed a short quiz that estimates the amount of short-term psychological stress people are under. How can the investigator use the quiz to find out the relationship between short-term psychological stress and the effects of vitamin C supplements on colds?

    **A.** Use the quiz to find groups of people who are or are not experiencing psychological stress, give each group vitamin C supplements during summer months, and ask the people to track the number, length, and severity of their colds.

    **B.** Use the quiz to find people under psychological stress, give vitamin C supplements to half the people during winter months, and ask all the people to track the number, length, and severity of their colds.

    **C.** Use the quiz to find people who are experiencing psychological stress, have half the people take vitamin C supplements in winter and the other half take the supplements in summer, and ask the people to track the number, length, and severity of their colds.

    **D.** Use the quiz to find people who are under psychological stress and use another test to find people under physical stress, have all the people take the supplements in winter, and ask the people to track the number, length, and severity of their colds.

12. Jessica is exposed to a lot of colds at her child-care facility job. Last winter, she got three bad colds and missed a few days of work. She read the meta-analysis and wants to begin taking vitamin C supplements if they improve her health. Which of the following is the best way for Jessica to answer her question?

    **A.**  Take vitamin C supplements this winter and compare the number, length, and severity of her colds this winter to those from last winter.

    **B.**  Eat more citrus fruit this winter and compare the number, length, and severity of her colds this winter to those from last winter.

    **C.**  Improve simple hygiene, such as washing her hands more frequently and using hand sanitizer while in her classroom, and compare the number, length, and severity of her colds this winter to those from last winter.

    **D.**  Take a multivitamin with high vitamin C content daily this winter and compare the number, length, and severity of her colds this winter to those from last winter.

*Items 13 and 14 refer to the following information.*

Sir Isaac Newton, an English scientist who lived from 1642 to 1727, formulated the following laws, which explain the movement of objects.

1.  An object at rest tends to stay at rest, and an object in motion tends to stay in motion, unless another force acts on it to make it stop. For this reason, if you throw an object, such as a ball, the ball will eventually slow down, fall to the ground, and roll to a stop. A number of forces act on the ball to make it stop: Gravity pulls it down, friction from the air slows it down, and friction from the ground causes it to roll to a stop.

2.  Acceleration happens when a force acts on an object. The greater the force, the greater the acceleration. The greater the mass of the object, the more force required to move it. For example, it takes more force to pick up a 5 kilogram box than a 1 kilogram box.

3.  For every action, there is an equal and opposite reaction. Forces always occur in pairs: an action force and a reaction force. So when a firework is lit, for example, there is an action force—thrust pushing down against the ground. There is also a reaction force—the firework flying into the air.

13. Which part of Newton's laws explains what happened to the child?

    A.  The piñata was swinging toward the child when the child hit it. The action force from the piñata was transferred to the stick, which, combined with the reaction force of hitting the piñata, caused the child to fall down.

    B.  After the child hit the piñata, it swayed back and forth violently and struck the child. The force of the piñata striking the child caused the child to fall down.

    C.  The child fell down because the force affected the child more than it affected the piñata because of their difference in mass.

    D.  Striking the piñata with the stick caused an equal and opposite reaction that caused the child to fall down.

14. The piñata continued to sway after the child hit it, but then the swaying stopped as the child got up. No one touched the piñata. Which part of Newton's laws explains why the swaying stopped?

    A.  Two forces—gravity pulling the piñata down and friction of air on the piñata— caused it to stop moving.

    B.  The piñata stopped moving because the reaction force caused all the energy to transfer back to the child.

    C.  The piñata used up all the energy so it stopped moving.

    D.  The piñata stopped moving because such a small child is not strong enough to make the piñata move for a long time.

*Items 15 through 19 refer to the following information.*

The composition of water is $H_2O$. That is, a water molecule is composed of two atoms of hydrogen and one atom of oxygen. Hydrogen and oxygen usually occur as diatomic molecules, $O_2$ and $H_2$. It takes two $H_2$ molecules and one $O_2$ molecule to produce two $H_2O$ molecules. Creating water from hydrogen and oxygen is called an exothermic reaction, a reaction that produces energy. In the case of water, a very large amount of energy is produced. This type of reaction is also considered a combustion reaction—a reaction in which a substance is combined with oxygen. Combustion reactions are particularly violent kinds of reactions and can produce tremendous heat and flames.

Water can also be broken down into its component parts through a process called electrolysis. In electrolysis, an electric current is passed through a liquid. Electrolysis of water is therefore an endothermic reaction. To electrolyze water, only a few materials are needed: a beaker, two glass test tubes, electrodes, two pieces of insulated copper wire, a battery, and water. First, place water in the beaker. Then fill the test tubes with water, too. Place an electrode inside each test tube, attach a wire to each one, and mount the test tubes to the side of the beaker using clips. Next, connect the wires to the battery leads one at a time. Watch carefully as the test tubes fill with hydrogen and oxygen.

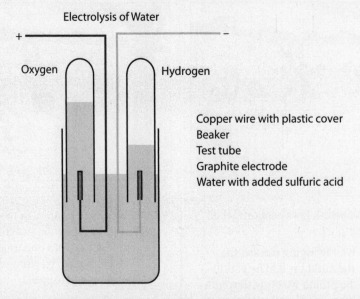

This process is slow and expensive because a lot of electricity is required. One way to speed the reaction is to add a catalyst to the water. A catalyst is a substance that speeds the reaction without affecting the result. In this case, adding sodium bicarbonate ($NaHCO_3$) to the water will speed the reaction.

15. How many $O_2$ molecules are needed to produce 20 water molecules?

    A.  5
    B.  10
    C.  20
    D.  30

16. Why is electrolysis of water an endothermic reaction?

    A.  It is slow and expensive.
    B.  A catalyst such as baking soda is needed to speed it up.
    C.  It uses a source of energy.
    D.  It gives off heat and light.

17. Which of the following is a potential risk associated with conducting this experiment?

    A.  The hydrogen gas produced could explode if not handled properly.
    B.  Heat and light from the electrolysis could start a fire.
    C.  The bicarbonate of soda will break down and produce a dangerous acid.
    D.  The battery can give off a dangerous electric shock.

18. Scientists want to use electrolysis of water to produce hydrogen for use as fuel. Which of the following is the biggest obstacle to using hydrogen derived from water as fuel?

    A.  Electrolysis produces hazardous chlorine gas as a by-product.
    B.  Hydrogen fuel is more expensive than fossil fuels.
    C.  Water is inexpensive and abundant.
    D.  Hydrogen is not easy to ignite.

19. Which of the following is an example of a combustion reaction?

    A.  A cast iron skillet gradually rusts and forms iron oxide when it is in contact with oxygen and water.
    B.  Methane gas produced in a swamp bursts into flames when it comes into contact with oxygen.
    C.  Carbon dioxide is produced when baking soda is combined with a mild acid.
    D.  Dry ice left on a plate in a kitchen gives off a cloud and gradually disappears.

*Items 20 through 22 refer to the following information.*

Plants are the only organisms that can make their own food. This happens in a process called photosynthesis. Photosynthesis is a process that uses energy from the sun, plus water and carbon dioxide, to synthesize various kinds of simple sugar molecules. These simple sugars are stored in the plants for use as food.

Photosynthesis is a complicated process involving many different parts of a plant and several chemical reactions. However, components of photosynthesis can be easily expressed as follows:

$$\text{Sunlight} + \text{Water} + \text{Carbon Dioxide} \xrightarrow{\text{Chlorophyll}} \text{Simple Sugars} + \text{Oxygen (waste)} + \text{Water (waste)}$$

Various parts of a plant participate in photosynthesis. Special proteins in the leaves of plants take in energy from the sun. Roots take in water, and special openings in the underside of leaves take in carbon dioxide from the air and release oxygen and water (in the form of vapor) as waste. The plant's stems move water and simple sugars through the plant so they can be used or stored. Chlorophyll has two roles in photosynthesis, and two kinds of chlorophyll have been isolated within plants. One type of chlorophyll is key in absorbing energy from sunlight and transferring it to the part of the leaves where it is used in photosynthesis. The second role of chlorophyll is to act as a catalyst in some of the chemical reactions used to convert energy, water, and carbon dioxide to energy. While sunlight is vital to photosynthesis, not all the chemical reactions involved in photosynthesis take place during the day. The chemical reactions in photosynthesis can be divided into two groups: light reactions (which take place during the day) and dark reactions (which take place at night).

20. Which of the following is both a component of photosynthesis and a waste product?

    A. Carbon dioxide
    B. Oxygen
    C. Simple sugars
    D. Water

21. Which of the following would <u>most likely</u> happen if plants in a greenhouse are lit with artificial light 24 hours a day?

    A. Photosynthesis will increase because of the increased light.
    B. There will be no change to the amount of photosynthesis.
    C. Photosynthesis will slow down or stop because dark reactions cannot take place.
    D. Photosynthesis will slow down or stop because the amount of light will affect the amount of water the plant's roots will absorb.

22. Which of the following plant parts do NOT have a role in photosynthesis?

    A. Leaves
    B. Flowers
    C. Stems
    D. Roots

*The following information applies to items 23 and 24.*

A group of researchers developed special LED lamps for greenhouses. The scientists believed that the lamps give off light in the exact wavelength that plants need to grow quickly. The lamps also use less electricity and produce less light pollution when used at night. The researchers tested their new LED lamps by growing spinach under regular greenhouse lights and under the new LED lamps for 28 days. The plants were grown in two separate greenhouses that were lit 16 hours a day and dark for 8 hours a day. The scientists measured the amount of biomass produced. The results are summarized in the following table.

| Plant Growth with Regular Greenhouse Lights and with New LED Lamps | |
|---|---|
| Type of Lighting | Biomass Produced per Unit of Land ($kg/m^2$) |
| Regular greenhouse lights | 7.6 |
| New LED lamps | 8.8 |

23. Which of the following can be concluded from the data?

   A. The new LED lamps resulted in greater spinach production.

   B. The new LED lamps are more effective than natural sunlight for growing vegetables.

   C. Food produced with the new LED lamps may taste or look different than food grown with regular greenhouse lights or sunlight.

   D. The cost of the new LED lamps is too great to make them competitive with the regular greenhouse lights.

24. Which of the following is NOT a limitation of this study?

   A. The effectiveness of the new LED lamps when combined with regular sunlight has not been tested.

   B. The type of light produced by the new LED lamps may benefit some plants more than others.

   C. The LED lamps were not tested with plants that need light for an exact amount of time each day in order to bloom or grow fruit.

   D. The amount of carbon dioxide available to the plants in different places may affect the results.

25. Weathering is the gradual breakdown of rock because of the effects of rain, wind, and plants on them. Which of the following is NOT an example of weathering?

   A. In the middle of the desert, blowing sands cause the side of a rocky cliff to become smooth.

   B. Over millions of years, a river carves a canyon out of rock.

   C. An unusually high tide during a storm surge from a hurricane washes away all the rocks and pebbles on a beach.

   D. Ice and snow get in small cracks in around the entrance of a cave causing the entrance to collapse.

**IF YOU FINISH BEFORE TIME IS CALLED, CHECK YOUR WORK ON THIS SECTION ONLY. DO NOT WORK ON ANY OTHER SECTION IN THE TEST.**

# Social Studies

**25 Items**

**Time: 35 Minutes**

**Directions:** This is a test of your skills in analyzing information in the area of social studies. Read each item and decide which of the four answer options is the best answer.

Sometimes, several items are based on the same information. You should read this material carefully and use it to answer the items.

*Items 1 through 5 refer to the following information and timeline.*

Queen Cleopatra, along with King Tutankhamen (or Tut), is among the best known rulers of ancient Egypt. Born in 69 B.C., the daughter of Pharaoh Ptolemy XII, she ascended the throne at age 18. At that time, Egypt was a protectorate of Rome, which was the leading power in the region. After being briefly removed from power, Cleopatra regained control. During her reign, Egypt had tremendous natural resources and was one of the richest countries in the Mediterranean. Cleopatra was considered a strong and powerful ruler, and Egypt continued to prosper under her rule. Despite her success as a ruler, she is probably best remembered for her love affairs with two Roman Emperors, Julius Caesar and Mark Antony, and for her death by suicide following Egypt's defeat by Rome in 30 B.C.

| Key Events in Queen Cleopatra's Life | |
|---|---|
| 69 B.C. | Cleopatra is born. |
| 51 B.C. | On the death of their father, Cleopatra ascends the throne along with her brother, Ptolemy XIII, at age 18. |
| 48 B.C. | Cleopatra is removed from power and held by supporters of her brother. Cleopatra meets Julius Caesar in Alexandria. |
| 47 B.C. | Caesar defeats Ptolemy XIII, and Cleopatra returns to the throne. |
| 46–44 B.C. | Cleopatra goes to Rome with Julius Caesar. |
| 44 B.C. | Julius Caesar is assassinated; Cleopatra flees to Egypt with the son she had with Caesar. |
| 41 B.C. | Mark Antony, now a ruler of Rome, meets Cleopatra while fighting in Egypt. |
| 40 B.C. | Antony returns to Rome. |
| 35 B.C. | Antony returns to Alexandria. |
| 31 B.C. | Antony's co-ruler, Octavian, defeats Antony and Cleopatra, and captures Cleopatra. |
| 30 B.C. | Cleopatra fakes her death. Thinking Cleopatra is dead, Mark Antony commits suicide. Cleopatra then commits suicide. Octavian annexes Egypt and returns to Rome where he displays the captured gold and slaves in a huge parade. |

1. Cleopatra first met Julius Caesar by having herself smuggled into his rooms in the palace inside a rolled-up rug. Why did she do this?

   A. She was out of power and a captive of the Egyptian government.

   B. She wanted to give Julius Caesar a nice surprise.

   C. She thought that Julius Caesar would refuse to see her unless she snuck in.

   D. She was secretly plotting to kill Caesar.

2. Why did Cleopatra become involved with Julius Caesar?

   A. She wanted his support in order to regain power.

   B. She was no longer interested in being Queen of Egypt and wanted to move to Rome.

   C. She wanted to use her relationship with Caesar to gain independence for Egypt.

   D. She needed his vast wealth to shore up Egypt's finances.

3. Which of the following is the most logical reason for Cleopatra to leave Rome?

   A. She was overcome with grief at the loss of her lover.

   B. She feared that she or her son with Caesar would be killed by Caesar's enemies.

   C. She thought that people would blame her for Caesar's death.

   D. After Caesar died, she needed the backing of another powerful Roman leader.

4. Historians believe that love is not the main reason Cleopatra took her own life. What is the most logical reason Cleopatra committed suicide?

   A. She thought that her son with Julius Caesar should be the Roman Emperor, not Octavian.

   B. She could not live without Mark Antony.

   C. She feared that Octavian would humiliate her by taking her to Rome as a slave.

   D. She wanted to use her death to rally Egypt to defeat Octavian.

5. If Cleopatra's life were a television show, which of the following kinds of shows would it most likely be?

   A. A game show, such as *The Price is Right*

   B. A soap opera, such as *The Young and the Restless*

   C. A late night talk show, such as *The Tonight Show*

   D. A courtroom reality show, such as *The People's Court*

*Items 6 through 10 refer to the following graph.*

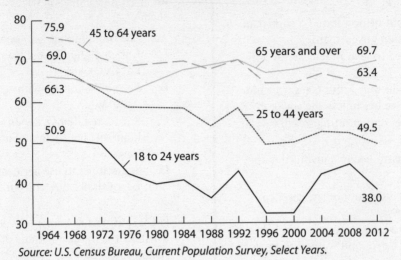

**Voting Rates Over Time for the Voting-age Population: 1964–2012** (In percent)

Source: U.S. Census Bureau, Current Population Survey, Select Years.

6. Which of the following individuals would most likely have voted in the 1988 elections?

   A. a 19-year-old community college student

   B. a 26-year-old woman

   C. a 44-year-old father

   D. a 69-year-old grandmother

7. Which of the following statements best sums up voting trends in the period covered by the graph?

   A. Voter turnout increased regularly.

   B. Participation in elections remained constant.

   C. Voter turnout cannot be predicted.

   D. Overall, the percentage of people voting declined.

8. Which of the following statements can most logically be concluded from voter participation rates in 1992?

   A. American voting trends do not follow a predictable pattern.

   B. The progressive decline in voter participation ended that year.

   C. People vote in higher numbers if they feel an election is important.

   D. Voters were especially concerned about international relations that year.

9. Which of the following statements best explains the increase in voting among 18 to 24 year olds in 2008?

   A. Barak Obama's promises of change captured young voters' attention in 2008.

   B. Many of these voters had lost their homes during the mortgage crisis and wanted change.

   C. Young voters were not excited by Barak Obama's candidacy.

   D. The turnout of young voters is erratic and cannot be explained.

10. Which of the following issues would most likely motivate voters age 65 and up to vote in record numbers?

   A. A proposal to cut federal assistance for adult education programs

   B. A proposal to increase taxes on Social Security and Medicare benefits

   C. A proposal to cut higher education financial aid and scholarship programs

   D. A proposal to require utility companies to use more renewable energy sources

*Items 11 through 15 refer to the following map and information.*

By the 1860 election, Sectionalism had brought the United States to the point of crisis. The Democratic Party had split over sectional lines and fielded two candidates, one in the North and one in the South. Several other smaller parties fielded candidates as well. Lincoln won the election, but without any support from the South, even though he had pledged in the election not to end slavery.

Before Lincoln reached the White House, seven Southern states seceded from the Union. War did not break out right away. Lincoln refused to start hostilities because he felt that the U.S. government should not attack its own citizens without provocation.

The immediate cause of the Civil War was the Confederate decision to fire upon Fort Sumter, South Carolina, on April 12, 1861. After the battle, more Southern states seceded from the Union. In all, the following states had seceded: Virginia, North Carolina, South Carolina, Georgia, Florida, Tennessee, Alabama, Mississippi, Louisiana, Arkansas, and Texas. Four slaveholding states—Missouri, Kentucky, Delaware, and Maryland—remained in the union, but did not give up slavery.

The map shows Union and Confederate states at the start of the Civil War. (West Virginia broke away from Virginia in 1863 to join the Union.)

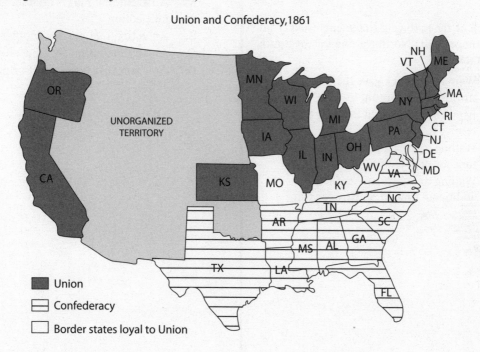

Union and Confederacy, 1861

11. What was the immediate cause of the secession crisis, according to the information?

   A. Lincoln's election as President
   B. Increasing sectionalism in the 1850s
   C. Lincoln's inauguration as President
   D. The Confederate decision to fire on Fort Sumter

12. How many states seceded from the Union in total?

   A. nine
   B. ten
   C. eleven
   D. twelve

13. Which of the following statements is NOT an advantage of the North waiting for the South to attack first?

   A. Waiting to attack gave the benefit of surprise to the South.
   B. Attacking first might increase Southern resolve to win the war.
   C. Waiting to attack permitted additional time for negotiation.
   D. Waiting to attack gave the Union additional time to prepare for war.

14. Why did more Southern states secede from the Union after the Battle of Fort Sumter?

   A. Lincoln said he would end slavery in their states.
   B. They thought that the Union would attack them next.
   C. The Confederate victory made them think the war would be quickly won.
   D. They believed that they had to support the Confederacy.

15. What is the meaning of the word "provocation" as it appears at the end of the second paragraph in the information?

   A. An event that makes another person take action
   B. An action that pleases another person
   C. An action that makes someone angry
   D. An event that is the result of previous action

*Items 16 and 17 refer to the following information.*

For many years, Americans have been concerned about the growing amount of inexpensive goods imported from China. Many Americans feel that these imports jeopardize American jobs and cause a ballooning balance of payments deficit. However, imports from China and other low-labor-cost nations are beneficial to consumers, too. First, Americans have access to inexpensive goods, which boosts their spending power. In addition, many manufacturing jobs pay low wages and do not offer much potential for personal growth or advancement. By buying imported goods, then, the American economy can focus on other, better-paying jobs.

Lately, another trend has emerged. Many Chinese companies are using their new wealth to buy American companies. This is a major change that was not anticipated even a few years ago. Recently, Joel Backaler, a noted management consultant on doing business with China, wrote, "China is going West. Its firms will irrevocably shape the global business landscape and their investments herald both tangible benefits as well as potential concerns. Adopting an appropriate response by all parties is critical to ensure that the maximum political and economic benefits are achieved."

16. What has changed about Chinese companies?

   A. They are only interested in low-wage manufacturing.
   B. They are buying up U.S. companies.
   C. They no longer want to export goods to the United States.
   D. They think that the U.S. should focus on better-paying jobs.

17. What is Backaler's opinion about China going West?

   A. He believes that it is a threat to U.S. jobs and companies.
   B. He believes it cannot be stopped, so it should be managed appropriately.
   C. He is certain that it will be beneficial to both sides.
   D. He doubts that China will succeed in taking over many companies.

*Items 18 and 19 refer to the following table.*

Parks are an important part of urban geography, especially in densely populated urban areas. The Trust for Public Land recently prepared an annual report on parks in the United States. This table presents the 15 U.S. cities with the highest percentage of land dedicated to parks.

| Parkland as a Percentage of Total Area in High-Density Cities | | | |
|---|---|---|---|
| City | Adjusted City Area (Acres) | Parkland (Acres) | Percent Parkland |
| Washington, D.C. | 38,955 | 8,513 | 21.9% |
| New York | 187,946 | 38,606 | 20.5% |
| San Francisco | 29,980 | 5,685 | 19.0% |
| Oakland | 33,181 | 6,063 | 18.3% |
| Jersey City | 9,261 | 1,660 | 17.9% |
| Boston | 29,175 | 4,916 | 16.9% |
| Minneapolis | 33,958 | 5,055 | 14.9% |
| Philadelphia | 82,913 | 11,211 | 13.5% |
| Los Angeles | 295,015 | 36,112 | 12.2% |
| Arlington, Virginia | 15,878 | 1,795 | 11.3% |
| Seattle | 52,765 | 5,546 | 10.5% |
| Long Beach | 31,066 | 3,121 | 10.0% |
| Baltimore | 51,318 | 4,905 | 9.6% |
| Chicago | 136,796 | 12,485 | 9.1% |
| Newark | 14,054 | 847 | 6.0% |
| Miami | 22,949 | 1,180 | 5.1% |
| Santa Ana | 17,453 | 515 | 3.0% |
| Hialeah | 13,666 | 175 | 1.3% |

Source: The Trust for Public Land

18. Which of these cities could most logically be called, "The City in a Garden" in a tourism campaign?

   A. Chicago
   B. Philadelphia
   C. Oakland
   D. Miami

19. Consider the two statements below.

   | I. | To remind people that parks are vital resources for all Americans. |
   |---|---|
   | II. | To encourage cities to maintain their current parks and create new ones. |

   Which of the statements, if either, best summarizes The Trust for Public Land's reasons for preparing the report?

   A. I only
   B. II only
   C. I and II
   D. Neither I nor II

*Items 20 and 21 refer to the following information and table.*

As the U.S. economy changes and grows, the kinds of jobs that are available and growing are different than in the past. Not long ago, there were many good jobs in the manufacturing sector, but there are fewer and fewer of those jobs. To help people plan their education and careers, the U.S. Bureau of Labor Statistics prepared a report on the jobs that are growing the fastest.

| Five High-Growth Careers for the Next 10 Years | | | |
|---|---|---|---|
| **Job** | **Education Required** | **Average Annual Pay** | **Projected Growth** |
| Office supervisor | High school diploma or equivalent | $49,330 | 171,500 |
| Licensed practical nurse | Associate's degree | $44,450 | 182,900 |
| Bookkeeper, accounting clerk, etc. | High school diploma or equivalent | $35,170 | 204,600 |
| Elementary school teacher | Bachelor of Arts degree | $53,400 | 161,900 |
| Dental hygienist | Associate's degree | $45,810 | 64,200 |

*Source: Bureau of Labor Statistics*

20. Marge has a high school diploma. Which of the jobs listed can she get?

   **A.** Dental hygienist
   **B.** Licensed practical nurse
   **C.** Accounting clerk
   **D.** Elementary school teacher

21. Consider the two statements below.

| | |
|---|---|
| **I.** | They can find jobs that they know will be in demand in the future. |
| **II.** | They can figure out the education they need to get the job they want. |

Which of the following statements, if either, best summarizes how people can use the table?

   **A.** I only
   **B.** II only
   **C.** I and II
   **D.** Neither I nor II

*Items 22 through 24 refer to the following cartoon and information.*

This political cartoon, first published in 1754, is considered the first known political cartoon produced in North America. Benjamin Franklin, a printer and newspaper publisher, was dismayed by the disunited response of the American colonies to the threat of the French and Indian War. The cartoon shows a snake cut into eight segments, corresponding to these colonies or regions: South Carolina, North Carolina, Virginia, Maryland, Pennsylvania, New Jersey, New York, and New England (Massachusetts, Connecticut, Rhode Island, and New Hampshire). The drawing did not include either of Britain's northernmost possessions, Nova Scotia and Newfoundland, which would later become part of Canada, nor its possessions in the Caribbean. In an accompanying editorial, Franklin urged the colonies to join together with Britain to fight against the French and their Native American allies.

Later, the drawing became a symbol of the American Revolution. The words at the bottom were changed to Unite or Die. The cartoon appeared in newspapers all over the colonies. During the Revolution, some newspapers ran the cartoon in every issue for a year or more.

22. What was the main idea of the cartoon in 1754?

   A. The colonies should rebel against Britain and declare independence.

   B. The colonists were dangerous and untrustworthy and should be killed.

   C. The colonies needed to work together with Britain to defeat their enemies.

   D. Colonists should work together to eradicate poisonous snakes.

23. What does Franklin's omission of Nova Scotia and Newfoundland in 1754 indicate about the North American colonies?

   A. Nova Scotia and Newfoundland were not British colonies so they did not concern Franklin.

   B. The colonies that would form the United States were already developing a separate identity.

   C. Franklin was concerned about the 13 American colonies gaining independence from Britain.

   D. Franklin did not know that these colonies existed.

24. Which of the following quotations from Benjamin Franklin most closely resembles the meaning of the cartoon as it was used during the American Revolution?

   A. "We must, indeed, all hang together, or assuredly we shall all hang separately."

   B. "Do not anticipate trouble, or worry about what may never happen. Keep in the sunlight."

   C. "Freedom of speech is a pillar of free government."

   D. "Those who would give up essential liberty, to purchase a little temporary safety, deserve neither liberty nor safety."

*Item 25 refers to the following graph.*

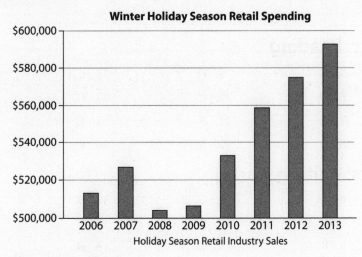

**Winter Holiday Season Retail Spending**

Holiday Season Retail Industry Sales

*Source: U.S. Census Bureau*

25. Which of the following statements can <u>most logically</u> be concluded from the graph?

    **A.**  The winter holiday period is the time of highest retail spending.

    **B.**  Beginning in 2009, retail sales increased every year.

    **C.**  2014 retail sales increased over 2013 sales.

    **D.**  The U.S. economy improved steadily every year since 2009.

IF YOU FINISH BEFORE TIME IS CALLED, CHECK YOUR WORK ON THIS SECTION ONLY. DO NOT WORK ON ANY OTHER SECTION IN THE TEST.

# Answer Key

## Language Arts: Reading

| | | | | |
|---|---|---|---|---|
| 1. C | 5. A | 9. D | 13. C | 17. D |
| 2. B | 6. D | 10. C | 14. C | 18. B |
| 3. A | 7. A | 11. B | 15. D | 19. A |
| 4. B | 8. A | 12. B | 16. C | 20. B |

## Language Arts: Writing, Part 1

| | | | | |
|---|---|---|---|---|
| 1. B | 6. A | 11. C | 16. B | 21. B |
| 2. C | 7. D | 12. B | 17. C | 22. A |
| 3. B | 8. B | 13. C | 18. B | 23. C |
| 4. C | 9. B | 14. C | 19. C | 24. B |
| 5. D | 10. D | 15. B | 20. C | 25. D |

## Mathematics

| | | | | |
|---|---|---|---|---|
| 1. B | 6. C | 11. C | 16. B | 21. E |
| 2. D | 7. A | 12. D | 17. C | 22. B |
| 3. D | 8. E | 13. A | 18. E | 23. E |
| 4. B | 9. A | 14. B | 19. B | 24. D |
| 5. E | 10. A | 15. A | 20. A | 25. B |

## Science

| | | | | |
|---|---|---|---|---|
| 1. A | 6. C | 11. B | 16. C | 21. C |
| 2. B | 7. C | 12. A | 17. A | 22. B |
| 3. B | 8. B | 13. D | 18. B | 23. A |
| 4. D | 9. C | 14. A | 19. B | 24. D |
| 5. B | 10. D | 15. B | 20. D | 25. C |

## Social Studies

| | | | | |
|---|---|---|---|---|
| 1. A | 6. D | 11. A | 16. B | 21. C |
| 2. A | 7. D | 12. C | 17. B | 22. C |
| 3. B | 8. C | 13. A | 18. C | 23. B |
| 4. C | 9. A | 14. D | 19. C | 24. A |
| 5. B | 10. B | 15. A | 20. C | 25. B |

# Answer Explanations

## Language Arts: Reading

1. **C. He expressed his anger toward his friend and repressed his anger toward his foe. (Comprehension and Synthesis/Poetry)** Option C is correct. This answer is stated directly in the first four lines of the poem: "I was angry with my friend:/I told my wrath, my wrath did end./I was angry with my foe:/I told it not, my wrath did grow." For this reason, the other options (A, B, and D) are incorrect.

2. **B. Murder (Inference/Poetry)** Option B is correct because clearly the apple is a symbol that represents the speaker's accumulated anger and its fatal effect on the speaker's foe. The speaker deliberately made his anger grow and grow until it resulted in the death of his foe. Therefore, the other options (A, C, and D) are incorrect.

3. **A. The speaker is making his anger worse and worse. (Analysis/Poetry)** Option A is correct. These four lines contain two symbols that show how the speaker made his anger stronger and stronger. The tears represent how his fears made the anger stronger, and the smiles represent how he hid his anger from his enemy as it continued to grow. For this reason, Option A is correct. Options B and C are incorrect because the speaker is obviously thinking about his anger, so he has not forgotten about it. Option D is contradicted by the lines; the speaker is dwelling on his anger, not trying to ignore it.

4. **B. When you are angry, you should deal with the anger so it won't worsen. (Synthesis/Poetry)** Option B is correct because for the speaker, dealing with his anger with his friend had a better outcome than repressing his anger toward his enemy. Options A and D are both ways of repressing anger, which resulted in murder, so they are incorrect. Getting revenge (Option C) is another kind of violence, so this is also incorrect.

5. **A. a bleak and depressing area that many people have to travel through unwillingly. (Comprehension/Prose Fiction)** Option A is correct. The mountains of coal ash, the dust-covered workers unloading the ash, and the strange advertising sign, combined with the narrator's description of how drivers and railroad passengers were forced to pass through this place, show that Option A is correct. For this reason, Option B is incorrect. Option C shows a misunderstanding of the "eyes of Dr. Eckleburg," (lines 9–15), which are not actual eyes, but a forgotten advertising sign. Option D does not make sense.

6. **D. Unloading ashes from train cars (Comprehension/Prose Fiction)** Option D is correct because the context and details make it clear that this place is a dumping ground for coal ashes which arrive in "a line of grey cars…along an invisible track" (lines 5–6). For this reason, the other options are incorrect.

7. **A. To show he believes that rich and poor people are the same in some ways (Inference/Prose Fiction)** Option A is correct because the wealthy residents, along with the train passengers and the workers and residents of the area, all have to pass through this place. This indicates that these people are all the same in some way. Option B is not supported by the details in the passage. Though Option C is later revealed to be true of the narrator, it is not supported by the details in this passage. Option D is most likely untrue—having to pass through such an area would most likely make West Egg unattractive to visit.

8. **A. To show that people are always under observation (Analysis/Prose Fiction)** Option A is correct. The constant presence of the eyes indicate that people are constantly subject to one another's scrutiny. Option B is the literal meaning of the sign, not its significance in the novel. Options C and D are not supported by information in the passage.

9. **D. To prevent the Nazis from discovering them (Comprehension/Drama)** Option D is correct because the family has changed names to hide from the Nazis. If Andy forgets Allegra's new name, the family risks discovery. Option A is not a reason why it is important for Andy to remember her new name, so is it incorrect. Option B is incorrect because Marika, not Allegra, admits to being jealous, and Marika's jealousy is not related to Allegra's new name. Option C is incorrect because Marika is already aware of the family's secret. The family is worried about their secret being revealed to the Nazis.

10. **C. She wants to gain the assistance of a Nazi occupier. (Interpretation/Drama)** Option C is correct. Life under Nazi rule was hard, and having the support of a Nazi occupier would make life easier for Marika. Marika denies being a collaborator in lines 21–22, so Option A is incorrect. Option B is the reason Friedrich gives for wanting to spend time with Marika, not Marika's reason for spending time with him, so it is incorrect. Option D is contradicted by Marika's actions. If she believed in Nazi ideology, she would not be hiding Jews in her home.

11. **B. She is afraid that Friedrich will pick it up and spot Henry. (Interpretation/Drama)** Option B is correct because Henry is hiding under the bed. If Friedrich bends down and looks under the bed he may see Henry; their whole plan would be exposed, and everyone would suffer the consequences. For this reason, Options C and D are incorrect. Option A is merely a joke of Friedrich's and is not a serious possibility, so it is incorrect.

12. **B. Marika and Allegra have a guarded trust between them. (Interpretation/Drama)** Option B is correct because although Marika has taken the refugees into her home at great personal risk, she still feels somewhat jealous and insecure about Allegra's relationship with her husband, Leonidas (lines 27–30). Option A is contradicted by the details in the passage. They seem to work together well in deceiving Friedrich. Option C is not supported by details in the passage. Option D is contradicted by details in the passage. It seems that Marika is jealous of Allegra and suspicious of Allegra's relationship with her husband Leonidas.

13. **C. To explain why rumors of a coming eruption were a false alarm (Analysis/Informational Texts)** Option C is correct because the author's attitude toward the predictions is skeptical in the first few paragraphs, and in the final paragraph he explains why the rumors started and went out of control. For this reason, Option A is incorrect. Option B is incorrect because the author discusses Yellowstone's natural features only to help explain why the rumors are a false alarm. While the author mentions the park's status as the world's first national park and the home of well-known and significant geysers, he brings those details up only as background, and they are not the main focus of the article (Option D).

14. **C. Magma is molten rock below the earth's surface, and lava is molten rock that has risen to the earth's surface. (Synthesis/Informational Texts)** Option C is correct because in line 2 the writer refers to magma as "underground molten rock" and in line 5, refers to lava as "above-ground molten rock." For this reason, the other options (A, B, and D) are incorrect.

15. **D. To provide a transition to the next section of the article (Analysis/Informational Texts)** Option D is correct because this sentence indicates that background information necessary to answer the question posed at the end of Paragraph 2. Since the following paragraphs provide background and not the answer to the question, which is given in the last paragraph of the passage, Option A is incorrect. Option B is the main idea of the passage, not of this sentence. Option C does not make sense.

16. **C. Coming very soon (Comprehension/Informational Texts)** Option C is correct because phrases such as "near future" (line 3), "about to take place" (line 4), and "within a few weeks or months" (line 8) in the preceding sentences suggest this meaning. For this reason, Option D is incorrect. Option A is the

definition of the near homonym *eminent*, so it is incorrect. Option B does not express the near certainty implied in the word, so it is incorrect.

17. **D. Frequent minor earthquakes (Comprehension/Informational Texts)** Option D is correct because the passage states directly at the end of Paragraph 5 that Yellowstone's frequent small earthquakes are unrelated to the geothermal activity. The remaining options (A, B, and C) are mentioned in Paragraph 5, so they are incorrect.

18. **B. A geyser releases liquid water, and a steam vent releases water vapor. (Synthesis/Informational Texts)** Option B is correct. This information is stated directly in the passage: Geysers "shoot large amounts of hot liquid water high in the air" (lines 16–17) and steam vents "release small amounts of water vapor, or steam" (lines 22–23). For this reason, Option A is incorrect. Option C is incorrect because the passage indicates that geysers release steam (a gas) as well as other gases during and after eruptions (line 21). Option D is incorrect because the passage states that Steamboat geyser does not erupt on a regular schedule. In addition, the name Old Faithful implies that the regularity of this geyser is unusual.

19. **A. Rational and scientific (Interpretation/Informational Text)** Option A is correct because the author's logical reasoning and detailed presentation of geological data indicate a rational and scientific tone. For this reason, the other options (B, C, and D) are incorrect. In addition, Option B is incorrect because the author's intention is to debunk the alarmist rumors that have spread about Yellowstone. Option C is incorrect because the logical presentation of fact and detail are not lyrical or poetic. Option D is incorrect because although it's clear that the author likes and respects Yellowstone Park, his intention is to present a logical and scientific refutation of the rumors.

20. **B. Go anyway, because there is no special risk of a volcanic eruption (Inference/Informational Text)** Option B is correct because if there is no special risk of an eruption, there is no reason to change one's travel plans. For this reason, the remaining options (A, C, and D) are incorrect.

# Language Arts: Writing

## Part 1

1. **B. job, you (Punctuation/Writing Conventions)** Option B is correct because a comma is needed after this introductory phrase. Therefore, Option A is incorrect. Option C is incorrect because semicolons are used to join two clauses together, not to join a phrase and a clause. Option D is incorrect because deleting the subject pronoun *you* changes the sentence to a sentence fragment.

2. **C. Before the first sentence in Paragraph 2 (Paragraph Structure/Organization)** Option C is correct because this sentence is not related to Paragraph 1, but it does provide a good topic sentence for Paragraph 2. Therefore, Options A, B, and D are incorrect.

3. **B. customers' (Writing Conventions/Possessive Nouns)** Option B is misspelled because this word is not possessive, so there is no reason to include an apostrophe. For this reason, Option A is incorrect. Option C is spelled correctly. An apostrophe is needed because this is a singular, possessive noun. Option D is a correctly spelled plural noun.

4. **C. website (Writing Conventions/Capitalization)** Option C is correct; *website* is a common noun, so it does not need to be capitalized. Therefore, Option A is incorrect. Option B is incorrect because there is no such word as *websight*. Option D is incorrect because there is no reason to make *website* plural and possessive.

5. **D. (Do not use this sentence; the article is best as written.) (Relevance/Organization)** Option D is correct. The sentence is about a step in the job search process that is not relevant to Paragraph 2 (which is about learning about the company) or Paragraph 3 (which is about what to do the night before your interview). Therefore, Options A, B, and C are incorrect.

6. **A. (No change) (Contractions/Writing Conventions)** Option A is correct because this contraction is the subject and verb of the sentence. Option B is incorrect because a possessive adjective is not needed in this location. There is no such word as *its'*, so Option C is incorrect. Option D is incorrect because deleting the word *is* makes the sentence a fragment.

7. **D. Figure out how you will get to the interview, how much travel time you need, and where you can park. (Parallel Structure/Language Facility)** This sentence has faulty parallel structure because it mixes independent clauses (beginning with *Figure out* and *find out,* which are imperatives) and a noun phrase (*the amount of travel time needed*). Therefore, Option A is incorrect. Only Option D makes the three parts of the sentence parallel by making all three items relative clauses that are the objects of the verb *figure out*. The remaining options have faulty parallel structure because they mix relative clauses and a noun clause (Option B) or two independent clauses and a relative clause (Option C).

8. **B. need, such as (Punctuation/Writing Conventions)** Option B is correct because a comma, not a colon is used to introduce a list of examples starting with *such as.* Therefore, Option A is incorrect. Option C incorrectly omits the comma after *need.* There is no reason to use a semicolon, which is used to join independent clauses, so Option D is incorrect.

9. **B. commonly asked question (Adjectives and Adverbs/Writing Conventions)** Option B is correct because *commonly,* an adverb, appropriately modifies *asked,* an adjective. Option A is incorrect because *commonly* modifies the noun *question,* and adverbs can only modify adjectives or other adverbs. Options C and D are incorrect because, in these options, *common* is a misplaced modifier, since adjectives usually go before nouns.

10. **D. is, "Can you tell me a little about yourself?" (Punctuation/Writing Conventions)** Option D is correct because it uses a comma before the quote, has open quotation marks at the beginning of the quotation, and has a question mark followed by closing quotation marks at the end of the quotation. Option A is incorrect because the question mark should go before the final quotation marks. Option B incorrectly deletes the comma after *is,* and Option C incorrectly omits the quotation marks.

11. **C. Have a short, informative answer ready to give to the interviewer. (Sentence Fragments/Language Facility)** Option C is correct. The original sentence is a fragment. Option C corrects the fragment by adding the imperative form of a verb to the sentence, which has the implied subject *you.* Therefore, Option A is incorrect. Option B does not make sense. Option D is still a fragment because it lacks a subject: *should have* is not an imperative, so it needs a subject.

12. **B. However, (Transitional Words and Phrases/Organization)** Option B is correct because this sentence introduces a contrasting idea, so *however* makes sense in this sentence. Options A and D are incorrect because *moreover* and *in addition* are used to add an additional supporting idea, not a contrast. Option C is incorrect because *nor* is usually a coordinating conjunction, not a transitional word.

13. **C. firmly when (Relative Clauses/Language Facility)** Option C is correct because this relative clause needs to be introduced by the relative pronoun *when,* since the clause gives information about the time the event happens. The other options (A, B, and D), which use different relative pronouns, are incorrect.

14. **C. her (Pronoun Reference/Writing Conventions)** Option C is correct because earlier in the sentence, the interviewer is referred to as *her*. The remaining options (A, B, and D), which use different pronouns, are incorrect.

15. **B. Sentence 6 (Paragraph Structure/Organization)** Option B is correct because the paragraph has two main ideas, the day of the interview and the end of the interview. The discussion of what to do at the end of the interview begins with Sentence 6, so that is the best place to start a new paragraph. Therefore, the other options (A, C, and D) are incorrect.

16. **B. Although (Subordination/Language Facility)** Option B is correct because *although* is the subordinating conjunction that indicates the correct relationship between the clauses: contradiction. The subordinating conjunctions in the remaining options are therefore incorrect: *because* (Option A) indicates cause; *when* (Option C) indicates time; and *since* (Option D) indicates reason.

17. **C. phone; however, that (Run-On Sentences/Language Facility)** Option C is correct. The original sentence is a run-on. Option C corrects the run-on by joining the two clauses with a semicolon and adding the transitional word *however* and a comma to indicate the relationship between the two clauses: contrast.

18. **B. German railroad companies (Capitalization/Writing Conventions)** Of the three words in the phrase, only *German* is a proper adjective, so Option B is correct. Options A and C capitalize common nouns unnecessarily. Option D incorrectly lowercases the proper adjective *German*.

19. **C. their (Pronoun Reference/Writing Conventions)** Option C is correct because the antecedent of this possessive adjective is *companies,* which is third person plural. Therefore, the correct pronoun is *their*. Option A is incorrect because *its* is singular. Option B is incorrect because *theirs* is a possessive pronoun, not a possessive adjective. Option D is incorrect because *his* is a singular pronoun used to refer to people or animals, and the antecedent is plural and not human.

20. **C. roots (Spelling/Writing Conventions)** Option C is correct because *roots* is used incorrectly in place of its homonym, *routes*. The remaining words in Options B and D are spelled correctly.

21. **B. because of their large size and high electricity consumption (Parallel Structure/Language Facility)** Option B is correct. The original sentence has faulty parallel structure. *Because of* needs to be followed by noun phrases, and only Option B has two noun phrases after *because of*. Option A is incorrect because it has a noun phrase and an independent clause. Option C is incorrect because it has a noun phrase and a participial phrase. Option D is incorrect because *because* is followed by an independent clause and a noun phrase.

22. **A. (No change) (Relative Clauses/Language Facility)** Option A is correct because the sentence introduces an essential relative clause with *who* and does not use a comma before the clause. Option B is incorrect because the relative pronoun *when* is used to refer to a time, not to people. Options C and D are incorrect because *which* is not used to refer to people. In addition, *which* is generally used in inessential relative clauses.

23. **C. lossed (Irregular Verbs/Writing Conventions)** Option C is correct. The past participle of *lose* is *lost*. The words in the other options (B and D) are spelled correctly.

24. **B. has (Subject-Verb Agreement/Writing Conventions)** Option B is correct because the subject of this verb is *functionality,* which is singular, so a singular verb, *has,* is required. Option A is incorrect because *have* is a plural verb. Option C is incorrect because there is no reason to change the verb to the past tense. Option D is incorrect because *having* is not a complete verb, which makes the sentence into a fragment.

25. **D. are (Subject-Verb Agreement/Writing Conventions)** Option D is correct because the subject of this verb is *limits,* which is plural, so a plural verb is needed. For this reason, Option A, which has a singular verb, is incorrect. Options B and C are incorrect because there is no reason to change the verb to the past tense. In addition, *was* is singular, and a plural verb form is needed in this sentence.

# Part 2

Use the Learner-Friendly HiSET Essay Scoring Rubric on pages 149–150 and these sample essays with score explanations to evaluate and score your essay. If possible, ask a teacher or a friend who is good at writing to evaluate and score your writing for you. Whether or not you can get another person to review your essay, you should always use the rubric and sample essays to evaluate and score your essay yourself. Set aside your essay for a day or two so you can view it with fresh eyes. Then compare your essay to the sample essays. Find the sample essay that most closely resembles your essay. Then read the descriptions in the rubric for that score as well as the scores above and below it. Select the description that best matches your essay. That should give you a good idea of your final score. If you were able to have another person score your essay, compare the two results. Use the information you learn to figure out ways you can improve your writing.

## Sample Response, Score = 1

I do not no much about the internet, in fact I hate it. I think that sit by your computer and type all day is boring and stupid and a waste of time. I prefer to go out and meeting my friends. We hang out, talk, watch TV, and chat. I use a computer at my job, but not the internet. I think that if I have to use the internet at my job, even for a little bit, I would quit and find another job.

**Explanation:** The information in the essay is not relevant to the topic. It does not have an introduction or a conclusion, and it does not organize ideas into paragraphs or use transitions. It has little variety in vocabulary and many errors in grammar and usage.

## Sample Response, Score = 2

Everybody nos that nowadays many people spend a long time on internet. My oldest sun likes to use internet, and uses it for a lot of different activitys, such as study, meet friends, play games, listen music and a lot more that I don't even know about. My sun is a good boy and does good in school. Therefore, I think that for him internet is not a problem. In fact, he does a lot of home works on internet, and plays games. I checked these games, and they look fun. So I think that as long as people are not having problems, their Internet usage is not a problem at all.

**Explanation:** The essay has one relevant idea, but the essay is repetitious. There is an attempt to write an introduction and conclusion, but the ideas are not organized into paragraphs. The vocabulary is limited and awkward, and there are many errors in grammar and spelling that interfere with understanding.

## Sample Response, Score = 3

As a parent of a teenager, I think that internet use can be a problem for many families. My daughter likes to spend time with her friends on internet, but recently it has become a problem. Her grades went down a lot after she began spending so much time with friends on the Internet.

Even more serious, in my daughter's school some other girls began to bullie girls. They put negative comments on some of her web pages. They even sent her mean text messages. The girl became very depressed, tried to kill herself.

My daughter and her friends are not very active. They spend a lot of time sitting in front of their computer alone. They don't want to spend time with their families, exercising, or doing active activities. For these reasons, I agree that a lot of Internet is bad for people, especially students.

**Explanation:** The essay includes relevant ideas, but they are not explained fully. The essay has an introduction and a conclusion, but they are very short. The essay has the beginning of a paragraph structure, but lacks separate introductory and concluding paragraphs, and does not provide a body paragraph for each supporting idea. The essay does not use transitions, but ideas are in a logical order. The essay has many errors in vocabulary, grammar, and sentence structure, and some of these interfere with understanding.

## Sample Response, Score = 4

On TV recently, a group of teachers complained about the Internet. They think that excessive Internet use is bad for people, especially students. I disagree with these teachers. The internet helps me with my studies, let's me find out about fun activities, and helps me with my money.

Most important, internet helps me with my studies. Right now, I am preparing for the HiSET test. I can find a lot of preparation materials to help me prepare online. I can also look up more information on subjects that are important for the test. Yesterday, I used internet to find out more about photosinthesis to help me get ready for the test.

Second, I can find out about fun activities from the internet. I like to go to music concerts. I use a website called Bands in Town to find out about concerts, my friends and I can go to. I also have my own website for my soccer team. We keep track of our games and practices on my website.

Finally, the internet helps me with my money. I use internet and mobile banking to make my life easyer. Now I don't have to go to the bank alot. I can use Internet and phone to do everything I need. I only need to go to an ATM Machine when I need money.

In conclusion, the internet helps me do many valuable things. I can study, have fun, and take care of my money with the internet. I hope that these teachers reconsider their idea about the internet.

**Explanation:** This essay has three main supporting ideas, each of which is somewhat developed, though there is still not enough information and detail. The essay has fairly well developed introductory and concluding paragraphs, and groups related ideas into three supporting paragraphs. The essay mostly uses simple transitions between paragraphs. There are some problems with sentence structure and variety, as well as some errors in spelling and grammar, but these do not interfere with understanding.

## Sample Response, Score = 5

Some teachers were on TV recently complaining about the Internet. They raised many important issues. I believe that they have a good point—all things are good in moderation. The Internet has many good features, but many people use it too much. I believe that too much Internet use makes us inactive, prevents us from doing other activities, and is bad for our health.

First, I recently read that some people spend up to 12 to 16 hours online every day. 12 to 16 hours a day is too much time! They are on Facebook, playing games, chatting with friends, listening to music, and doing a lot of other unimportant things. In some extreme cases, people have played games for a whole weekend without ever taking a break or getting some sleep. While some game playing is good, people need more variety in their lives.

Second, because people are spending so much time in front of their computers, they are not doing other important things. The teachers were concerned that students were spending time online that they could use for studying. While studying is important the teachers need to remember that the Internet is a valuable learning tool. But I still agree that people need to get away from their computers more. Excessive Internet use keeps people from sports, concerts, family, and friends. One of my friends has a teenage son. He says that he seldom sees his son because he is always in his room with his computer. Another one of my friends became a Facebook adict. She was on Facebook all the time. She checked Facebook constantly, and she even got in trouble at work because she accessed Facebook at work all the time.

Third, all of this Internet use is bad for our physical and emotional health. When people stay inside all the time, they donot get any fresh air or exercise. In addition, many people eat unhealthy food and too many snacks in front of their screens. The kinds of food people tend to eat are often junk food with too much sugar, chemicals, and, salt. In addition, people need to be in contact with one another in order to have healthy, balanced lives. We need to talk to people and spend time with them in the real world, not just the online one. We need to go places together and have fun together.

In conclusion, while the Internet has many valuable uses, the phrase, "All things are good in moderation, is true about it. Many people are online for too much time, which prevents them from doing other important activities and damages their physical and mental health. We need to be careful about using the Internet for the right amount of time so that we can have balanced, healthy lives.

**Explanation:** This essay has three main supporting ideas, and each one has well-developed supporting reasons, examples, or details. It also brings up and addresses a counterargument: students can use the Internet to help with their studies. The essay has an introduction and a conclusion and organizes ideas into supporting paragraphs. The essay uses transitions in many places. It has few errors, and some variety in sentence patterns.

## Sample Response, Score = 6

Would you rather drive across town to go to the bank or take care of your banking with just a few clicks? Would you rather take the bus to the library to check out a book or use the library's website to download a free e-book? These are just two of the ways that the Internet helps us. Recently, a group of teachers complained about the Internet, but I believe that the Internet makes our lives more convenient, brings us in contact with the world, and can help us with our careers.

First of all, my life is much easier today than 10 years ago because of the Internet. In addition to online banking, I can manage my credit cards, pay my mortgage, and do many other tasks. My apartment building recently started using a new Internet tool in our laundry room. Now I don't have to go to the laundry room as much because of this new website. I can use the website to see if the washing machines are free or in use. And after I put my laundry in, I can use the website to find out when the laundry is done. I don't have to keep going to the laundry room to check. I also can do a lot of my shopping online. Now I buy all my family's socks, underwear, pajamas, and towels online, and I don't have to go to the store, find parking, and spend time walking around.

Second, the Internet keeps me in contact with the world. My town's newspaper is too expensive and not very good. I can get all then news and information I need from the Internet. Each morning, I get a free emailed digest of top news stories, and I can click to see the stories I want. The front page of my Internet service provider also carries top news stories that are updated constantly. If I am interested in a particular story, I can request updates on particular stories. For example, when my husband was in Iraq, I set my computer to get updates whenever a new story about Iraq posted. Those notices were sent to my computer and my mobile phone. That way, I always felt informed. Of course, we also communicated all the time through email. That was a lot better than waiting for a letter to arrive in the male.

Third, the Internet can really help us with our careers. I got my last two jobs through online job postings. But the Internet can help our careers in other ways, too. Now I use a free online tool to help me build my resume. This website stores all the information about my work history, and uses it to create a beautiful resume that I can print or email to people. As my work history changes, I can add updates to the website and my resume. But many people earn their livings directly from the Internet. My neighbor really loves making beautiful, fragrant homemade candles. Her candles are much nicer than ones sold in stores, and a lot cheaper, too. She started a website and began selling her candles online. Now she has so much business that she asked me if I was interested in a part-time job helping her.

In conclusion, I think that these teachers really do not understand the Internet. I agree that sometimes the Internet can keep us from our studies, and that sometimes children use it too much. But the Internet has changed my life in so many ways. I really cannot imagine my life without the Internet, and I hope that these teachers can realize that the Internet can help us in many ways.

**Explanation:** This essay has three main supporting ideas, and each one has well-developed supporting reasons, examples, or details. It has an introduction that gets the reader's attention by asking some provocative questions. It also brings up and addresses counterarguments in key places. The essay organizes ideas into effective supporting paragraphs and uses transitions between and within paragraphs. It has few errors and variety in sentence patterns, and grammar, vocabulary, and usage are sophisticated.

# Mathematics

1. **B. $55 (Numbers and Operations on Numbers/Computation)** Chris and Diane will pay a total of $480 over the 2-year period (24 months × $20) if they rent the phone. The difference between $480 and $425 is $55.

2. **D. 3.75 (Numbers and Operations on Numbers/Computation)** As a proportion, this problem can be solved as $\frac{1.5 \text{ cups}}{8 \text{ people}} = \frac{x \text{ cups}}{20 \text{ people}}$. Cross-multiply to get $8x = 30$, and then divide both sides by 8 to get $x = 3.75$.
A second way to look at the problem is that the recipe is to be used to make 2.5 times as much chicken: $20 \div 8 = 2.5$. Therefore, multiply 1.5 by 2.5 to get 3.75.

3. **D. $18,957 (Numbers and Operations on Numbers/Computation)** The tax on the purchase is $1,157:$17,800 × 0.065 = $1,157. The total price is $17,800 + $1,157 = $18,957.

4. **B. 229,000 (Data Analysis: Probability, and Statistics/Statistics)** 1980 is 30 years after 1950. The graph of the population shows a point approximately midway between 2.0 and 2.5, or about 2.25, which is 225,000,000 people. The answer option closest to this value is B, 229,000,000.

5. **E. 190 × 0.80 × 0.95 (Numbers and Operations on Numbers/Computation)** The sale price of the coat is 80% of the original price: 190 × 0.80. Patty then pays 95% of the sale price when she uses her coupon. Therefore, the final cost of the coat is 190 × 0.80 × 0.95.

6. **C. –102 (Algebraic Concepts/Number Properties)** Substitute the values for $p$ and $r$ into the equation and follow the order of operations.

$$5(2 \times 5 + 3 \times -4) - 4(3 \times 5 - 2 \times -4) = 5(10 - 12) - 4(15 + 8) = 5(-2) - 4(23) = -10 - 92 = -102$$

7. **A. $s = 2r + 13$ (Algebraic Concepts/Slope)** The slope of the relationship is 2 as given by the statement "The number of seats in a row at a theater increases by *two* from one row to the next." Therefore, the equation must be of the form $s = 2r + b$. When $r = 1$, $s = 15$, so, $15 = 2(1) + b$. Solve this equation to determine the value of $b$, subtracting 2 from both sides: $15 = 2 + b$; $15 - 2 = b$; $b = 13$. Therefore, the equation that expresses the relationship between the number of rows, $r$, from the front of the auditorium and the number of seats, $s$, in that row is $s = 2r + 13$.

8. **E. 14.0 (Algebraic Concepts/Distributive Property)** With $P = 19.6$ and $R = 10$, the equation $P = \dfrac{V^2}{R}$ becomes $19.6 = \dfrac{V^2}{10}$. Multiply both sides of the equation by 10 to get $196 = V^2$. Take the square root of both sides of the equation to get $V = 14$.

9. **A. 300m + 350j ≥1,000 (Algebraic Concepts/Inequalities)** The minimum daily requirement is the least amount needed, so getting more than 1,000 grams of calcium in a day is acceptable. This indicates that the inequality should be greater than or equal to. Each glass of fat-free milk contains 300 grams of calcium, so $m$ glasses contain $300m$ grams of calcium. Similarly, $j$ glasses of calcium-enriched orange juice contain $350j$ grams of calcium. Therefore, the statement that best expresses this nutritional need is $300m + 350j \geq 1,000$.

10. **A. J (Algebraic Concepts/Coordinate Plane)** The line $x = 4$ consists of all the points whose $x$-coordinate is 4. For example, the points $(4, 0)$, $(4, 1)$, $(4, 2)$ would all be on this line. When plotted, they all lie on the vertical line passing through the point $(4, 0)$, $J$.

11. **C. $\dfrac{2(40 \times 8) + 2(75 \times 8) + (40 \times 75)}{350}$ (Measurement and Geometry/Area)** The smaller walls on the pool each have an area $40 \times 8$ square feet, and the longer walls have an area $75 \times 8$ square feet. The floor of the pool has an area $40 \times 75$ square feet. The total number of square feet that need to be painted is $2(40 \times 8) + 2(75 \times 8) + (40 \times 75)$. Divide this number by 350 square feet to determine the number of gallons of paint that will be needed: $\dfrac{2(40 \times 8) + 2(75 \times 8) + (40 \times 75)}{350}$.

12. **D. $\dfrac{40 \times 75 \times 8}{0.134}$ (Measurement and Geometry/Volume of a Cube or Rectangular Prism)** The number of cubic feet of water needed is $40 \times 75 \times 8$. Multiply this by the conversion factor $\dfrac{1 \text{ gallon}}{0.134 \text{ cubic feet}}$, or divide by 0.134, to calculate the number of gallons needed: $\dfrac{40 \times 75 \times 8}{0.134}$.

13. **A. $3,600 (Measurement and Geometry/Area)** The number of square feet of turf needed is $(60 \times 95) - (40 \times 75) = 5,700 - 3,000 = 2,700$. Divide this number by the conversion factor $\dfrac{1 \text{ square yard}}{9 \text{ square feet}}$ to calculate the number of square yards needed: $2,700 \div \dfrac{1 \text{ square yard}}{9 \text{ square feet}} = 300$. Multiply the number of square yards by the cost of one square yard, $12, to get the cost of laying the turf: $300 \times \$12 = \$3,600$.

14. **B. 1.7 (Numbers and Operations on Numbers/Ratio and Proportion)** Solve the proportion $\dfrac{2.5}{1,000,000} = \dfrac{c}{680,000}$ to find $c$. Use the cross-products proportion rule to find $c$: $2.5 \times 680,000 = 1,000,000c$; $1,700,000 = 1,000,000c$; $1.7 = c$.

15. **A. (2.5, 0) (Algebraic Concepts/Coordinate Plane)** All points on the $x$-axis have a $y$-coordinate that is 0. To determine the point where the line crosses the $x$-axis, set $y = 0$ in the equation and solve for $x$. That is, $0 = -4x + 10$ becomes $4x = 10$ or $x = 2.5$. Therefore, the coordinate of the point is $(2.5, 0)$.

16. **B. $10^4$ (Data Analysis: Probability and Statistics/Probability)** There are 10 choices for each digit in the code, so the number of possible PINs is $10 \times 10 \times 10 \times 10 = 10^4$.

17. **C. 13 (Measurement and Geometry/Pythagorean Theorem)** Draw a line from the bottom of $m$ to the centerline. The right triangle formed has legs with lengths 5 feet and 12 feet. Use the Pythagorean theorem to solve for $m$: $a^2 + b^2 = c^2$; $12^2 + 5^2 = c^2$; $144 + 25 = c^2$; $169 = c^2$; $\sqrt{169} = c$; $13 = c$. Therefore, $m = 13$ feet.

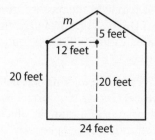

18. **E. 32 (Data Analysis: Probability and Statistics/Venn Diagram)** Add the numbers from each of the regions in the Venn diagram, $8 + 5 + 7 + 12 = 32$.

19. **B. $\dfrac{5}{12}$ (Data Analysis: Probability and Statistics/Probability)** Twelve responders indicate that they provide benefits. Of these, 5 are service industries. Therefore, the probability that the responder is a service industry is 5:12, or $\dfrac{5}{12}$.

20. **A. $\dfrac{7}{80}$ (Numbers and Operations on Numbers/Computation)** Max spends a total of $\dfrac{1}{4} + \dfrac{1}{5} + \dfrac{3}{8} =$ $\dfrac{10}{40} + \dfrac{8}{40} + \dfrac{15}{40} = \dfrac{33}{40}$ on housing, utilities, and entertainment. (Note that you must find the lowest common denominator before you can add the three fractions.) The remaining money is $\dfrac{7}{40}$ of his monthly income. Half of the remaining money, $\dfrac{1}{2} \times \dfrac{7}{40} = \dfrac{7}{80}$, is used to buy food for eating at home.

21. **E. 193,750 (Algebraic Concepts/Number Properties)** Substitute 25 for $n$ into the expression $9,000n - 50n^2$: $9,000(25) - 50(25)^2 = 225,000 - 31,250 = 193,750$. (Note that you must follow the order of operations, finding $25^2$ before multiplying by 50.)

22. **B. 72 (Algebraic Concepts/Ratio and Proportion)** The average rate of change of production is the ratio of the change in production and the number of hours: $\dfrac{480 - 120}{5} = 72$.

23. **E. 34 (Data Analysis: Probability and Statistics/Statistics)** There are a total of 17 states whose population increase was more than 3%: 12 in the 3.1–4% range, 4 in the 4.1–7% range, and 1 greater than 7%. These 17 states represent 34% of all the states: $17 \div 50 = 0.34$, or 34%.

24. **D. 0.25q + 0.10(80 – q) = 16.70 (Algebraic Concepts/Number Properties)** If Molly has $q$ quarters in her purse, then the difference between 80 and $q$ must be dimes. Therefore, $80 - q$ represents the number of dimes. The equation needed to solve this item is about the value of the coins. Each quarter is worth 25 cents, or 0.25 dollars, so the total value of the $q$ quarters is $0.25q$ and the value of the $80 - q$ dimes is $0.10(80 - q)$. Add these two terms together to get the value of all the coins in the purse, $16.70: 0.25q + 0.10(80 - q) = 16.70$.

25. **B. 4,500,000 (Data Analysis: Probability and Statistics/Central Tendency)** The median value is midway between the 25th data point (4 million) and the 26th data point (5 million): 4,500,000.

# Science

1. **A. Warm, moist air and cool, dry air come together and an area of instability forms. (Analyzing Information/Earth Science)** Option A integrates information stated directly in the passage, so it is correct. Option B misstates key information in the passage. A downdraft, not an updraft, accompanies the heavy rainfall. Option C is an explanation of how hurricanes, not tornados, form. Option D is incorrect because this is an explanation of how a funnel cloud becomes a tornado, not an explanation of how a supercell thunderstorm forms.

2. **B. Condensation causes rain, which creates a downdraft that pulls the funnel cloud to the earth. (Interpreting Information/Earth Science)** Option B is correct because according to the information, rising warm air cools, causing condensation and rainfall, which creates a downdraft that pulls the funnel cloud toward the earth. Option A is incorrect because rotation causes the funnel cloud to form. The downdraft, not the rotation, pulls the tornado to the earth. Option C is incorrect because the cool, dry air causes condensation and rainfall. The rainfall, not the cool, dry air, falls to the earth causing the downdraft.

3. **B. They both have rotation. (Analyzing Information/Earth Science)** Option B is directly stated in the article at the beginning of paragraph 4. Options A and C are contradicted by the information; only tornados form over land (Option A) or touch the ground (Option C). Only hurricanes produce storm surges (Option D).

4. **D. The hurricane will lose strength because it no longer gets warm, moist ocean air. (Analyzing Information/Earth Science)** Option D is correct because the passage indicates that hurricanes get their strength from rising ocean air. After the hurricane moves inland, it can no longer obtain warm, moist air, so it will lose strength. For this reason, Option C is incorrect. Option A happens with some hurricanes, but not all, so it is incorrect. Option B is not supported by information in the passage. Ocean air gives hurricanes their strength. The speed and direction of a hurricane are affected by the hurricane's strength and also by other factors, such as prevailing winds.

5. **B. May will most likely be a busy month for storm chasers. (Applying Information/Earth Science)** Option B is correct because the information says that most tornados occur in the spring and fall. May is in the spring, so this is statement is an accurate inference. Option A is incorrect because storm chasers can learn a lot about tornados by observing them from the ground. Option C is incorrect because many scientists use observational methods. Option D is not supported by the information in the passage. However, storm chasers need patience, luck, and hard work to find tornados they can study.

6. **C. Category 1. (Applying Information/Earth Science)** A Category 1 storm has winds from 119–153 km/h, so this storm belongs in Category 1. Option A is incorrect because Category 3 storms have winds from 178–208 km/h. Option B is incorrect because Category 2 storms have winds of 154–177 km/h. Option D is incorrect because tropical storms have winds of 63–118 km/h.

7. **C. 118 km/h (Interpreting Information/Earth Science)** Option C is correct because according to the table, tropical storms have winds of 63–118 km/h. Option A is incorrect because a storm with winds of 34 mph is a tropical depression, not a tropical storm. Option B is incorrect because a storm with winds of 60 km/h is a tropical depression, not a tropical storm. Option D is incorrect because a storm with winds of 125 km/h is a Category 1 hurricane.

8. **B. Results from the many studies conducted over the years presented confusing information, and the scientists wanted to find solid conclusions. (Interpreting Information/Life Science)** Option B is correct because the passage says, "A meta-analysis looks at all the research and findings in order to find the

most certain conclusions." Option A is incorrect because scientists have long known the connection between vitamin C and scurvy. Option C is incorrect because the scientists accepted the claims of many of the studies, and conducted a kind of review of them, not a new study. Option D is not supported by the information in the passage; in addition, this option is inconsistent with the scientific method.

9. **C. The results of the meta-analysis of the benefits of the supplements in reducing the duration or severity of colds are contradictory. (Interpreting Information/Life Science)** Option C is correct because the more rigorous therapeutic studies give different results than the other studies. Since the results are inconclusive, but give some indication that the benefits are not fully understood, some people may benefit from the supplements and should take them. Options A and B are not supported by the information. Option D may be true, but is not a reason for members of the public to continue to evaluate the effectiveness of the supplements themselves.

10. **D. Scientists will have a better understanding of the effectiveness of different ways to investigate a research question. (Generalizing/Life Science)** Option D is correct because the information says that the meta-analysis compared methods and results. One of the benefits of this comparison is a better understanding of research methods that give valuable results. Option A is incorrect because the meta-analysis studied the common cold, not short-term physical stress. Option B is not supported by the information. Option C is incorrect because the results of the meta-analysis seem to show that vitamin C supplements are less effective than many people previously thought, which would make fewer people take them.

11. **B. Use the quiz to find people under psychological stress, give vitamin C supplements to half the people during winter months, and ask all the people to track the number, length, and severity of their colds. (Applying Information/Life Science)** Option B is correct because only this research design will let the researcher compare the results of taking the supplements on people under psychological stress. Option A will be less effective than the design in Option B because people catch fewer colds in summer than in winter. In addition, this design will not show whether results are different for people under stress who are not taking the supplement. Option C is incorrect because it will show the effectiveness of the supplements in different seasons, which is not the researcher's goal. Option D is incorrect because it compares people who are under physical and psychological stress, which is not the researcher's goal.

12. **A. Take vitamin C supplements this winter and compare the number, length, and severity of her colds this winter to those from last winter. (Applying Information/Life Science)** Option A is correct because only this method will help Jessica evaluate whether the supplements helped her avoid colds or reduce their length and severity. Options B and C are incorrect because these practices will not let her evaluate the effect of vitamin C supplements. Option D is incorrect because she will not be able to determine if the results are because of vitamin C or because of another vitamin in the multivitamin supplement.

13. **D. Striking the piñata with the stick caused an equal and opposite reaction that caused the child to fall down. (Applying Information/Physical Science)** Option D is correct because Newton's Third Law says that every action has an equal and opposite reaction. The reaction force caused the child to lose his balance and fall down. Option A is incorrect because the illustration shows that the piñata was at rest before the child hit it. Option B is contradicted by the drawing. The piñata is too high in the air to hit the child. Option C is not consistent with Newton's Second Law. The action force would affect the piñata more than the reaction force would affect the child because these equal forces would affect the piñata more than the child due to the piñata's smaller mass.

14. **A. Two forces—gravity pulling the piñata down and friction of air on the piñata—caused it to stop moving. (Applying Information/Physical Science)** Option A is correct because Newton's First Law says that an object in motion stays in motion unless another force affects it. In this case, the forces of gravity and friction stopped the piñata from swaying. Option B is incorrect because each action has an equal and opposite reaction; the action force and reaction force do not cancel each other out in this case. Option C is contradicted by Newton's First Law: Motion is not "used up." The object will stay in motion until affected by another force.

15. **B. 10 (Interpreting Information/Physical Science)** Option B is correct because each water molecule has 1 oxygen atom. Since each $O_2$ molecule has 2 atoms of oxygen, 10 $O_2$ molecules are needed ($20 \div 2 = 10$). Option A will produce only 10 water molecules. Option C will produce 40 water molecules. Option D will produce 60 water molecules.

16. **C. It uses a source of energy. (Interpreting Information/Physical Science)** Option C is correct because endothermic reactions require energy. The battery is a source of energy. Options A and B are true statements, but they are not related to whether electrolysis of water is endothermic or exothermic. Option D is a characteristic of an exothermic reaction.

17. **A. The hydrogen gas produced could explode if not handled properly. (Applying Information/Physical Science)** Option A is correct because the passage discusses the explosive nature of hydrogen, which can produce a combustion reaction. While this possibility is remote, care should be exercised. Option B is not correct because this endothermic reaction consumes energy and does not produce it. Option C is incorrect because the bicarbonate of soda is a catalyst in the reaction; it is not used or changed during the reaction. Option D is not correct because a battery of the size and power depicted in the illustration does not produce enough electricity to cause a bad shock.

18. **B. Hydrogen fuel is more expensive than fossil fuels. (Applying Information/Physical Science)** Option B is correct because cost is a major factor in people's acceptance of new fuels. Option A is not supported by information in the passage. Option C is an advantage of hydrogen fuel, so it is incorrect. Option D is contradicted by the information; hydrogen readily ignites in a combustion reaction.

19. **B. Methane gas produced in a swamp bursts into flames when it comes into contact with oxygen. (Applying Information/Physical Science)** A substance combining with oxygen in an exothermic reaction is an example of a combustion reaction. Only Option B matches this definition. Option A is an example of oxidation. Option C is incorrect because oxygen is not involved. Option D is an example of a change in state, not a chemical reaction.

20. **D. Water (Interpreting Information/Life Science)** Option D is correct because the equation shows water on both sides of the arrow. Option A is incorrect because carbon dioxide is used in photosynthesis, but it is not a product of it. Option B is incorrect because oxygen is only a waste product of photosynthesis. Simple sugars are a product of photosynthesis, so are neither an ingredient nor a waste product.

21. **C. Photosynthesis will slow down or stop because dark reactions cannot take place. (Applying Information/Life Science)** Option C is correct because the information says that some of the chemical reactions involved in photosynthesis take place in the dark. Therefore, Options A and B are incorrect. Option D is incorrect because daylight does not regulate the amount of water absorbed into plants from the roots.

22. **B. Flowers (Interpreting Information/Life Science)** Option B is correct because flowers are the only plant part among the answer options that are not mentioned in the information as having a role in

photosynthesis. The remaining options are all mentioned in the information as having a role in photosynthesis.

23. **A. The new LED lamps resulted in greater spinach production. (Interpreting Information/Life Science)** Option A is correct because the new LED lamps resulted in 8.8 kg of spinach grown per $m^2$. The regular greenhouse lighting resulted in 7.6 kg of spinach per $m^2$. Option B is incorrect because the study compared the results from the new LED lamps and regular greenhouse lights, not sunlight. Options C and D cannot be concluded from the information.

24. **D. The amount of carbon dioxide available to the plants in different places may affect the results. (Interpreting Information/Life Science)** Option D is not a limitation because plants can get enough carbon dioxide from the atmosphere regardless of location. The remaining options are limitations of the study, so they are incorrect. The study examined plant growth using only the two kinds of artificial light (Option A). The study examined only one kind of plant. The information indicates that photosynthesis works differently in different plants, and some plants may benefit from different wavelengths of light (Option B). Some plants, such as poinsettias, need light for a certain amount of time in order to bloom or grow fruit. The study did not examine the light when used with these kinds of plants (Option C).

25. **C. An unusually high tide during a storm surge from a hurricane washes away all the rocks and pebbles on a beach. (Applying Information/Earth Science)** Option C is correct because this is an example of erosion, not weathering. The pebbles and stones were not broken down, but washed away. The remaining options (A, B, and D) are all examples of weathering, so they are incorrect.

# Social Studies

1. **A. She was out of power and a captive of the Egyptian government. (Analyzing Information/History)** Option A is correct because during that time, Cleopatra was a captive of the government. The only way she could see Julius Caesar was to sneak past the guards. Option B is therefore incorrect. Option C is not supported by the information. Option D is contradicted by the information. Her purpose was to seek an ally in order to regain the power she had lost. She had no reason to kill Caesar.

2. **A. She wanted his support in order to regain power. (Analyzing Information/History)** Option A is correct because the next event in the timeline is her return to power with Caesar's backing. Therefore, Option B is incorrect. Option C makes no sense, since Caesar, as a leader of Rome, would never agree to losing one of its wealthiest protectorates. Option D is not supported by the information, which makes it clear that Egypt had important natural resources and was prosperous under Cleopatra.

3. **B. She feared that she or her son with Caesar would be killed by Caesar's enemies. (Analyzing Information/History)** Option B is correct because she owed her position to Caesar, who had restored her to the throne and was the father of her son. Those are good reasons for her to fear Caesar's enemies. Options A and C do not make sense. Option D is probably a true statement, since she subsequently looked to Mark Antony as a Roman backer, but this is a reason to stay in Rome, not to return to Egypt.

4. **C. She feared that Octavian would humiliate her by taking her to Rome as a slave. (Analyzing Information/History)** Option C is correct because Cleopatra had allied herself with Octavian's enemy, and Octavian had defeated her in war and was holding her in captivity. It is logical that she would fear being displayed to the people in Rome with all of the treasure and slaves captured in Egypt.

5. **B. A soap opera, such as *The Young and the Restless* (Applying Information/History)** Option B is correct because Cleopatra's life is characterized by lovers, betrayals, and turns of fate. The kind of television program that her life most resembles is a soap opera. Therefore, the other options (A, C, and D) are incorrect.

6. **D. A 69-year-old grandmother (Interpreting Information/Civics and Government)** Option D is correct because the line representing voters of 65 years of age and older shows this age group voted at the highest rate for that year. For this reason, the other options (A, B, and C) are incorrect.

7. **D. Overall, the percentage of people voting declined. (Generalizing/ Civics and Government)** Option D is correct because the percentage of people voting in each age group declined during the period, except for adults age 65 years and older. For this reason, Options A and B are incorrect. Option C does not make sense because the item is not about predicting voter behavior but analyzing past behavior.

8. **C. People vote in higher numbers if they feel an election is important. (Analyzing Information/Civics and Government)** Option C is correct because a perception that an election is important would increase people's participation. Option A is incorrect because many patterns can be identified in this data. Option B is incorrect because in the following year, voter participation declined again. Option D is not supported by the data in the graph.

9. **A. Barak Obama's promises of change captured young voter's attention in 2008. (Analyzing Information/ Civics and Government)** Option A is correct because a promise of change would appeal to young voters. Option B is incorrect because people in this age group typically rent their homes or live with their families, so they would not be concerned about the mortgage crisis. Option C is not supported by the information and would not be a reason for voter participation to increase. Option D does not make sense. Though young voters' participation in elections shows the greatest volatility of all the groups, this does not mean that their voting behavior lacks an explanation.

10. **B. A proposal to increase taxes on Social Security and Medicare benefits (Applying Information/Civics and Government)** Of the four issues, increasing taxes on Social Security and Medicare benefits would interest voters age 65 and older the most because they use those programs; therefore, Option B is correct. For this reason, the other options (A, C, and D) are incorrect.

11. **A. Lincoln's election as President (Interpreting Information/History)** Option A is correct. This answer is stated directly in the passage. Sectionalism (Option B) was the long-term cause of the crisis, so it is incorrect. Option C is incorrect because the states seceded from the Union before Lincoln's inauguration. Option D is incorrect because the decision to fire on Fort Sumter was the immediate cause of the outbreak of the Civil War, not the secession crisis.

12. **C. eleven (Interpreting Information/History)** Option C is correct. The answer is stated directly in the information (eleven states are listed as having seceded) and can also be counted on the map (eleven states are indicated as belonging to the Confederacy). Therefore, the remaining options (A, B, and D) are incorrect.

13. **A. Waiting to attack gave the benefit of surprise to the South. (Analyzing Information/History)** Option A is correct because surprise can be an important advantage in a war. Waiting to attack gave the South this advantage, not the North. The remaining options are benefits of waiting to attack and so are incorrect. The Union attacking first (Option B) could boost Confederate commitment to the war. Lincoln wanted to avoid war if possible, so gaining additional negotiation time (Option C) would be a benefit of waiting to attack. While waiting, the Union could muster its resources (Option D).

14. **D. They believed that they had to support the Confederacy. (Analyzing Information/History)** Option D is correct because the attack on Fort Sumter made them feel that they had to support other slave states. Option A is incorrect because Lincoln had promised not to end slavery during the election campaign. Option B does not make sense because Lincoln had refrained from attacking until attacked. In addition, Lincoln would be more likely to attack the states that had seceded than those that had not. Option C is not supported by the information. In addition, thinking that the Confederacy would win quickly might be less reason for them to enter the war.

15. **A. An event that makes another person take action (Interpreting Information/History)** Option A is correct because Lincoln was waiting for the South to act first in order to take action himself. Therefore, Option B is incorrect. Option C is incorrect because Lincoln was not waiting for the South to anger him. He was waiting for it to attack first to gain public sympathy in the North and avoid provoking the South himself. Option D does not make sense.

16. **B. They are buying up U.S. companies. (Interpreting Information/History)** Option B is correct. This answer is stated directly in the information. Therefore, Option A is incorrect. China is interested in buying foreign companies as well as providing low-wage manufacturing. Option C is not supported by the information. Just because they are buying U.S. companies does not mean they are giving up on exporting to the U.S. Option D is the opinion of the writer of the passage, not the Chinese companies, so it is incorrect.

17. **B. He believes it cannot be stopped, so it should be managed appropriately. (Analyzing Information/History)** Option B is correct because he says that it is inevitable, ("China is going West.") and urges politicians and business leaders to respond in a way that provides benefits to all. The other options (A, C, and D) are incorrect.

18. **C. Oakland (Applying Information/History)** Option C is correct because of the four cities given, Oakland has the highest percentage of parkland (18.3%) according to the table. The remaining options have lower percentages of parkland: Option A, Chicago (9.1%); Option B, Philadelphia (13.5%); and Option D, Miami (5.1%).

19. **C. I and II (Analyzing Information)** The reasons given in Statements I and II are consistent with the association's name, the table, and the information about The Trust for Public Land in the passage. Therefore, the other options (A, B, and D) are incorrect.

20. **C. Accounting clerk (Analyzing Information/Economics)** Option C is correct because this is the only job in the options that is available to someone with a high school diploma. The other options require more education. Option A (dental hygienist) and Option B (licensed practical nurse) both require an associate's degree. Option D (elementary school teacher) requires a bachelor's degree.

21. **C. I and II (Analyzing Information/Economics)** Option C is correct because the information can be used to find jobs that will be in demand for the next 10 years (Statement I) and it tells people the education they need to get the job (Statement II). The other options (A, B, and D) are incorrect.

22. **C. The colonies needed to work together with Britain to defeat their enemies. (Interpreting Information/History)** Option C is correct. This answer is stated directly in the information. Option A was true in 1776, not 1754. There is no support for Option B in the information. Option D does not make sense.

23. **B. The colonies that would form the United States were already developing a separate identity. (Analyzing Information/History)** Option B is correct because the French and Indian War was a global conflict that involved all of Britain's colonies and possessions. Since Franklin focused only on the colonies that

would rebel against Britain, it shows that those colonies were already developing a separate identity. Option A is contradicted by the passage. Option C is incorrect because colonists were not concerned about independence during the French and Indian War. Option D does not make sense.

24. **A. "We must, indeed, all hang together, or assuredly we shall all hang separately." (Applying Information/History)** Option A is correct because both the quotation and the cartoon are about unit. Option B is incorrect because the colonists were not anticipating trouble in 1776. They were already at war with Britain. Option C is incorrect because the cartoon is not about free speech. Option D is incorrect because the cartoon is about unity, not safety.

25. **B. Beginning in 2009, retail sales increased every year. (Analyzing Information/Economics)** Option B is correct. Beginning with 2009, each successive bar on the chart is higher than the previous bar. This shows that retail sales increased each year starting in 2009. While Options A, C, and D and may be true, these statements cannot be concluded from the graph.

# II. Cram Plans

## A. Your HiSET Cram Plan

Follow these steps to figure out *your* HiSET Cram Plan:

1. Take the Diagnostic Test in Chapter I, if you have not taken it already.
2. Use the answer explanations to figure out your scores on each section. Write your scores in the second column of the chart below.
3. Review your answers to the items and compare them to the answer explanations. Identify your difficult areas.
4. Check the box of the Cram Plan that's right for you for each section of the test: two-month, one-month, or one-week.

| Your HiSET Cram Plan | | | | |
|---|---|---|---|---|
| Test Section | Your Score | Your Cram Plan | | |
| Language Arts: Reading | | ❑ Two-Month | ❑ One-Month | ❑ One-Week |
| Language Arts: Writing, Part 1 | | ❑ Two-Month | ❑ One-Month | ❑ One-Week |
| Language Arts: Writing, Part 2 | | ❑ Two-Month | ❑ One-Month | ❑ One-Week |
| Mathematics | | ❑ Two-Month | ❑ One-Month | ❑ One-Week |
| Science | | ❑ Two-Month | ❑ One-Month | ❑ One-Week |
| Social Studies | | ❑ Two-Month | ❑ One-Month | ❑ One-Week |

Follow the Cram Plans you choose on the following pages.

**TIP: For all of the Cram Plans listed, your tasks for the day of the test and the night before are the same. See "The Day of the Test and the Night Before" on page 82.**

# B. Language Arts: Reading

| Language Arts: Reading — Two-Month Cram Plan | |
|---|---|
| 8 weeks before the test | **Study Time:** 1.5 hours<br>❏ **Topic:** Test Format. Chapter III, Section A<br>❏ Read the section, answer the sample items, and review your answers. |
| 7 weeks before the test | **Study Time:** 0.5 hour<br>❏ **Topic:** Comprehension. Chapter III, Section B.1<br>❏ Read the section, answer the sample items, and review your answers. |
| 6 weeks before the test | **Study Time:** 0.5 hour<br>❏ **Topic:** Inference and Interpretation. Chapter III, Section B.2<br>❏ Read the section, answer the sample items, and review your answers. |
| 5 weeks before the test | **Study Time:** 0.5 hour<br>❏ **Topic:** Analysis. Chapter III, Section B.3<br>❏ Read the section, answer the sample items, and review your answers. |
| 4 weeks before the test | **Study Time:** 0.5 hour<br>❏ **Topic:** Synthesis and Generalization. Chapter III, Section B.4<br>❏ Read the section, answer the sample items, and review your answers. |
| 3 weeks before the test | **Study Time:** 1.5 hours<br>❏ **Practice:** Chapter III, Section C<br>❏ Answer the practice items and review your answers. Identify any sections you should review. |
| 2 weeks before the test | **Study Time:** 1.5 hours<br>❏ Use your results from the practice items to review any sections prior to taking the Language Arts: Reading Full-Length Practice Test next week. |
| 7 days before the test | **Study Time:** 2 hours<br>❏ Take the Language Arts: Reading Full-Length Practice Test (Chapter IX).<br>❏ Review your answers. Based on your errors on the Practice Test, identify difficult topics and their corresponding sections. Target those sections for extra review. |
| 6 days before the test | **Study Time:** 0.5 hour<br>❏ **Topic:** Comprehension. Chapter III, Section B.1<br>❏ Review any content you identified from your Practice Test results. |
| 5 days before the test | **Study Time:** 0.5 hour<br>❏ **Topic:** Inference and Interpretation. Chapter III, Section B.2<br>❏ Review any content you identified from your Practice Test results. |
| 4 days before the test | **Study Time:** 0.5 hour<br>❏ **Topic:** Analysis. Chapter III, Section B.3<br>❏ Review any content you identified from your Practice Test results. |
| 3 days before the test | **Study Time:** 0.5 hour<br>❏ **Topic:** Synthesis and Generalization. Chapter III, Section B.4<br>❏ Review any content you identified from your Practice Test results. |
| 2 days before the test | **Study Time:** 1.5 hours<br>❏ **Practice Test Review:** Review your Practice Test results one more time.<br>❏ Review any content you identified from your Practice Test results. |

## Language Arts: Reading — One-Month Cram Plan

| | |
|---|---|
| **4 weeks before the test** | **Study Time:** 2 hours<br>❏ **Topic:** Test Format. Chapter III, Section A<br>❏ **Topic:** Comprehension. Chapter III, Section B.1<br>❏ Read the sections, answer the sample items, and review your answers. |
| **3 weeks before the test** | **Study Time:** 2 hours<br>❏ **Topic:** Inference and Interpretation. Chapter III, Section B.2<br>❏ **Topic:** Analysis. Chapter III, Section B.3<br>❏ Read the sections, answer the sample items, and review your answers. |
| **2 weeks before the test** | **Study Time:** 2 hours<br>❏ **Topic:** Synthesis and Generalization. Chapter III, Section B.4<br>❏ Read the section, answer the sample items, and review your answers. |
| **1 week before the test** | **Study Time:** 1.5 hours<br>❏ **Practice:** Chapter III, Section C<br>❏ Answer the practice items and review your answers. Identify any sections you should review. |
| **6 days before the test** | **Study Time:** 2 hours<br>❏ Take the Language Arts: Reading Full-Length Practice Test (Chapter IX).<br>❏ Review your answers. Based on your errors on the Practice Test, identify difficult topics and their corresponding sections. Target those sections for extra review. |
| **5 days before the test** | **Study Time:** 1 hour<br>❏ **Topic:** Comprehension. Chapter III, Section B.1<br>❏ **Topic:** Inference and Interpretation. Chapter III, Section B.2<br>❏ Review any content you identified from your Practice Test results. |
| **4 days before the test** | **Study Time:** 0.5 hour<br>❏ **Topic:** Analysis. Chapter III, Section B.3<br>❏ Review any content you identified from your Practice Test results. |
| **3 days before the test** | **Study Time:** 0.5 hour<br>❏ **Topic:** Synthesis and Generalization. Chapter III, Section B.4<br>❏ Review any content you identified from your Practice Test results. |
| **2 days before the test** | **Study Time:** 1.5 hours<br>❏ **Practice Test Review:** Review your Practice Test results one more time.<br>❏ Review any content you identified from your Practice Test results. |

| Language Arts: Reading — One-Week Cram Plan | |
|---|---|
| **7 days before the test** | **Study Time:** 2 hours<br>❏ **Topic:** Test Format. Chapter III, Section A<br>❏ **Topic:** Comprehension. Chapter III, Section B.1<br>❏ Read the sections, answer the sample items, and review your answers. |
| **6 days before the test** | **Study Time:** 1 hour<br>❏ **Topic:** Inference and Interpretation. Chapter III, Section B.2<br>❏ **Topic:** Analysis. Chapter III, Section B.3<br>❏ Read the sections, answer the sample items, and review your answers. |
| **5 days before the test** | **Study Time:** 0.5 hour<br>❏ **Topic:** Synthesis and Generalization. Chapter 3, Section B, Part 4<br>❏ Read the section, answer the sample items, and review your answers. |
| **4 days before the test** | **Study Time:** 1.5 hours<br>❏ **Practice:** Chapter III, Section C.<br>❏ Answer the practice items and review your answers. Identify any sections you should review. |
| **3 days before the test** | **Study Time:** 2 hours<br>❏ Take the Language Arts: Reading Full-Length Practice Test (Chapter IX).<br>❏ Review your answers. Based on your errors on the Practice Test, identify difficult topics and their corresponding sections. Target those sections for extra review. |
| **2 days before the test** | **Study Time:** 1.5 hours<br>❏ **Practice Test Review:** Review your Practice Test results one more time.<br>❏ Review any content you identified from your Practice Test results. |

# C. Language Arts: Writing, Parts 1 and 2

| Language Arts: Writing, Parts 1 and 2 — Two-Month Cram Plan | |
|---|---|
| **8 weeks before the test** | **Study Time:** 2.5 hours<br>❏ **Topic:** Test Format. Chapter IV, Section A<br>❏ **Topic:** Test Content and Types of Items. Chapter IV, Section B<br>❏ Read the sections, answer the sample items, and review your answers.<br>❏ Write one essay this week (see pages 163–164 for sample essay topics).<br>❏ Evaluate your essay using the instructions and scoring rubric in Chapter V (pages 149–150). |
| **7 weeks before the test** | **Study Time:** 1.5 hours<br>❏ **Topic:** Organization. Chapter IV, Section C.1.a–c<br>❏ Read the section, answer the sample items, and review your answers.<br>❏ **Practice 1: Organization.** Chapter IV, Section C.1.d<br>❏ Answer the practice items and review your answers. Identify any sections you need to review. |
| **6 weeks before the test** | **Study Time:** 2.5 hours<br>❏ **Topic:** Language Facility. Chapter IV, Section C.2.a–h<br>❏ Read the section, answer the sample items, and review your answers.<br>❏ **Practice 2: Language Facility.** Chapter IV, Section C.2.i<br>❏ Answer the practice items and review your answers. Identify any sections you need to review.<br>❏ Write one essay this week (see pages 163–164 for sample essay topics).<br>❏ Evaluate your essay using the instructions and scoring rubric in Chapter V (pages 149–150). |
| **5 weeks before the test** | **Study Time:** 2 hours<br>❏ **Topic:** Writing Conventions. Chapter IV, Section C.3.a–f<br>❏ Read the section, answer the sample items, and review your answers.<br>❏ **Practice 3: Writing Conventions.** Chapter IV, Section C.3.g<br>❏ Answer the practice items and review your answers. Identify any sections you need to review. |
| **4 weeks before the test** | **Study Time:** 2.5 hours<br>❏ **Topic:** Test Format. Chapter V, Section A<br>❏ **Topic:** How Your Writing Is Evaluated—The Writing Rubric. Chapter V, Section B<br>❏ Read the sections.<br>❏ **Practice 1: Applying the Rubric.** Chapter V, Section B.1<br>❏ Answer the practice items and review your answers. Identify any sections you need to review.<br>❏ Write one essay this week (see pages 163–164 for sample essay topics).<br>❏ Evaluate your essay using the instructions and scoring rubric in Chapter V (pages 149–150). |
| **3 weeks before the test** | **Study Time:** 2.5 hours<br>❏ **Topic:** The Five-Paragraph Essay. Chapter V, Section C.1<br>❏ **Topic:** The Three Rs Writing Process. Chapter V, Section C.2<br>❏ Read the sections.<br>❏ **Practice 2: Essay Writing.** Chapter V, Section C.3<br>❏ Write your essay response to the topic in Practice 2.<br>❏ Compare your essay to the provided sample essays and evaluate it using the instructions and scoring rubric in Chapter V (pages 149–150). |
| **2 weeks before the test** | **Study Time:** 2.5 hours<br>❏ Take the Language Arts: Writing Full-Length Practice Test (Chapter X).<br>❏ Review your answers. Based on your errors on the Practice Test, identify difficult topics and their corresponding sections. Target those sections for extra review. |

*continued*

| 7 days before the test | **Study Time:** 1 hour<br>❏ **Topic:** Organization. Chapter IV, Section C.1a–c<br>❏ Review any content you identified from your Practice Test results. |
|---|---|
| 6 days before the test | **Study Time:** 1.5 hours<br>❏ **Topic:** Language Facility. Chapter IV, Section C.2.a–h<br>❏ Review any content you identified from your Practice Test results. |
| 5 days before the test | **Study Time:** 1.5 hours<br>❏ **Topic:** Writing Conventions. Chapter IV, Section C.3a–f<br>❏ Review any content you identified from your Practice Test results. |
| 4 days before the test | **Study Time:** 1.5 hours<br>❏ **Topic:** The Five-Paragraph Essay. Chapter V, Section C.1<br>❏ **Topic:** The Three Rs Writing Process. Chapter V, Section C.2<br>❏ Review any content you identified from your Practice Test results. |
| 3 days before the test | **Study Time:** 2 hours<br>❏ Review the essays you have written. Look for common errors you can easily correct.<br>❏ Write one more essay (see pages 163–164 for sample essay topics).<br>❏ Evaluate your essay using the instructions and scoring rubric in Chapter V (pages 149–150).<br>❏ Review any content you identified from your Practice Test results. |
| 2 days before the test | **Study Time:** 1.5 hours<br>❏ **Practice Test Review:** Review your Practice Test results one more time.<br>❏ Review any content you identified from your Practice Test results. |

## Language Arts: Writing, Parts 1 and 2 — One-Month Cram Plan

| | |
|---|---|
| **4 weeks before the test** | **Study Time:** 3 hours<br>❑ **Topic:** Test Format. Chapter IV, Section A<br>❑ **Topic:** Test Content and Types of Items. Chapter IV, Section B<br>❑ **Topic:** Organization. Chapter IV, Section C.1a–c<br>❑ Read the sections, answer the sample items, and review your answers.<br>❑ **Practice 1: Organization.** Chapter IV, Section C.1.d<br>❑ Answer the practice items and review your answers. Identify any sections you need to review.<br>❑ Write one essay this week (see pages 163–164 for sample essay topics).<br>❑ Evaluate your essay using the instructions and scoring rubric in Chapter V (pages 149–150). |
| **3 weeks before the test** | **Study Time:** 1.5 hours<br>❑ **Topic:** Language Facility. Chapter 4, Section C.2a–h<br>❑ Read the section, answer the sample items, and review your answers.<br>❑ **Practice 2: Language Facility.** Chapter IV, Section C.2.i<br>❑ Answer the practice items and review your answers. Identify any sections you need to review. |
| **2 week before the test** | **Study Time:** 2 hours<br>❑ **Topic:** Writing Conventions. Chapter IV, Section C.3.a–f<br>❑ Read the section, answer the sample items, and review your answers.<br>❑ **Practice 3: Writing Conventions.** Chapter IV, Section 3.g<br>❑ Answer the practice items and review your answers. Identify any sections you need to review. |
| **1 week before the test** | **Study Time:** 1.5 hours<br>❑ **Topic:** Test Format. Chapter V, Section A<br>❑ **Topic:** How Your Writing Is Evaluated—The Writing Rubric. Chapter V, Section B<br>❑ Read the sections.<br>❑ **Practice 1: Applying the Rubric.** Chapter V, Section B.1<br>❑ Answer the practice items and review your answers to identify any sections you need to review. |
| **6 days before the test** | **Study Time:** 2.5 hours<br>❑ **Topic:** The Five-Paragraph Essay. Chapter V, Section C.1<br>❑ **Topic:** The Three Rs Writing Process. Chapter V, Section C.2<br>❑ Read the sections.<br>❑ **Practice 2: Essay Writing.** Chapter V, Section C.3<br>❑ Write your essay response to the topic in Practice 2.<br>❑ Compare your essay to the provided sample essays and evaluate it using the instructions and scoring rubric in Chapter V (pages 149–150).<br>❑ Review all of the essays you have written thus far. Look for common errors you can easily correct. |
| **5 days before the test** | **Study Time:** 2.5 hours<br>❑ Take the Language Arts: Writing Full-Length Practice Test (Chapter X).<br>❑ Review your answers. Based on your errors on the Practice Test, identify difficult topics and their corresponding sections. Target those sections for extra review. |
| **4 days before the test** | **Study Time:** 1.5 hours<br>❑ Review any content you identified from your Practice Test results. |
| **3 days before the test** | **Study Time:** 1.5 hours<br>❑ Write one more essay.<br>❑ Evaluate your essay using the instructions and scoring rubric in Chapter V (pages 149–150). |
| **2 days before the test** | **Study Time:** 1.5 hours<br>❑ **Practice Test Review:** Review your Practice Test results one more time.<br>❑ Review any content you identified from your Practice Test results. |

| Language Arts: Writing, Parts 1 and 2 — One-Week Cram Plan | |
|---|---|
| **7 days before the test** | **Study Time:** 2 hours<br>❑ **Topic:** Test Format. Chapter IV, Section A<br>❑ **Topic:** Test Content and Types of Items. Chapter IV, Section B<br>❑ **Topic:** Organization. Chapter IV, Section C.1<br>❑ Read the sections, answer the sample items, and review your answers.<br>❑ **Practice 1: Organization.** Chapter IV, Section C.1.d<br>❑ Answer the practice items and review your answers. Identify any sections you need to review. |
| **6 days before the test** | **Study Time:** 1.5 hours<br>❑ **Topic:** Language Facility. Chapter IV, Section C.2<br>❑ Read the section, answer the sample items, and review your answers.<br>❑ **Practice 2: Language Facility.** Chapter IV, Section C.2.i<br>❑ Answer the practice items and review your answers. Identify any sections you need to review. |
| **5 days before the test** | **Study Time:** 2 hours<br>❑ **Topic:** Writing Conventions. Chapter IV, Section C.3.a–f<br>❑ Read the section, answer the sample items, and review your answers.<br>❑ **Practice 3: Writing Conventions.** Chapter IV, Section C.3.g<br>❑ Answer the practice items and review your answers. Identify any sections you need to review. |
| **4 days before the test** | **Study Time:** 1.5 hours<br>❑ **Topic:** Test Format. Chapter V, Section A<br>❑ **Topic:** How Your Writing Is Evaluated—The Writing Rubric. Chapter V, Section B<br>❑ Read the sections.<br>❑ **Practice 1: Applying the Rubric.** Chapter V, Section B.1<br>❑ Answer the practice items and review your answers. Identify any sections you need to review. |
| **3 days before the test** | **Study Time:** 2.5 hours<br>❑ **Topic:** The Five-Paragraph Essay. Chapter V, Section C.1<br>❑ **Topic:** The Three Rs Writing Process. Chapter V, Section C.2<br>❑ Read the sections.<br>❑ **Practice 2: Essay Writing.** Chapter V, Section C.3<br>❑ Write your essay response to the topic in Practice 2.<br>❑ Compare your essay to the provided sample essays and evaluate it using the instructions and scoring rubric in Chapter V (pages 149–150). |
| **2 days before the test** | **Study Time:** 2.5 hours<br>❑ Take the Language Arts: Writing Full-Length Practice Test (Chapter X).<br>❑ Review your answers. Based on your errors on the Practice Test, identify difficult topics and their corresponding sections. Target those sections for extra review. |

# D. Mathematics

| Mathematics Two-Month Cram Plan | |
|---|---|
| 8 weeks before the test | **Study Time:** 0.5 hour<br>❑ **Topic:** Test Content and Types of Items. Chapter VI, Section A<br>❑ Read the section. |
| 7 weeks before the test | **Study Time:** 1 hour<br>❑ **Topic:** Computation and Estimation. Chapter VI, Section B.1–2<br>❑ Read the section, answer the sample items, and review your answers.<br>❑ **Practice 1:** Answer the practice items and review your answers. Identify any sections you need to review. |
| 6 weeks before the test | **Study Time:** 1 hour<br>❑ **Topic:** Ratios, Proportions, and Percents. Chapter VI, Section B.3–4<br>❑ Read the section, answer the sample items, and review your answers.<br>❑ **Practice 2:** Answer the practice items and review your answers. Identify any sections you need to review. |
| 5 weeks before the test | **Study Time:** 1 hour<br>❑ **Topic:** Algebraic Concepts Part 1: Combining Terms. Chapter VI, Section C.1–3<br>❑ Read the section, answer the sample items, and review your answers.<br>❑ **Practice 3:** Answer the practice items and review your answers. Identify any sections you need to review. |
| 4 weeks before the test | **Study Time:** 1 hour<br>❑ **Topic:** Algebraic Concepts Part 2: Solving Equations and Inequalities. Chapter VI, Section D.1–3<br>❑ Read the section, answer the sample items, and review your answers.<br>❑ **Practice 4:** Answer the practice items and review your answers. Identify any sections you need to review. |
| 3 weeks before the test | **Study Time:** 1 hour<br>❑ **Topic:** Algebraic Concepts Part 3: Graphs and Functions. Chapter VI, Section E.1–2<br>❑ Read the section, answer the sample items, and review your answers.<br>❑ **Practice 5:** Answer the practice items and review your answers. Identify any sections you need to review. |
| 2 weeks before the test | **Study Time:** 1 hour<br>❑ **Topic:** Measurement and Geometry. Chapter VI, Section F.1–5<br>❑ Read the section, answer the sample items, and review your answers.<br>❑ **Practice 6:** Answer the practice items and review your answers. Identify any sections you need to review. |
| 7 days before the test | **Study Time:** 1 hour<br>❑ **Topic:** Data Analysis: Probability and Statistics. Chapter VI, Section G.1–3<br>❑ Read the section, answer the sample items, and review your answers.<br>❑ **Practice 7:** Answer the practice items and review your answers. Identify any sections you need to review. |
| 6 days before the test | **Study Time:** 2 hours<br>❑ Take the Mathematics Full-Length Practice Test (Chapter XI).<br>❑ Review your answers. Based on your errors on the Practice Test, identify difficult topics and their corresponding sections. Target those sections for extra review. |

*continued*

| 5 days before the test | **Study Time:** 1.5 hours<br>❏ Redo items that you answered incorrectly on the Practice Test.<br>❏ Review the answer explanations. |
|---|---|
| 4 days before the test | **Study Time:** 1.5 hours<br>❏ **Topic:** Computation and Estimation. Chapter VI, Section B.1<br>❏ **Topic:** Ratios, Proportions, and Percents. Chapter VI, Section B.3<br>❏ **Topic:** Algebraic Concepts Part 1: Combining Terms. Chapter VI, Section C.1–2<br>❏ **Topic:** Algebraic Concepts Part 2: Solving Equations and Inequalities. Chapter VI, Section D.1–2<br>❏ Review any content you identified from your Practice Test results. |
| 3 days before the test | **Study Time:** 1.5 hours<br>❏ **Topic:** Algebraic Concepts Part 3: Graphs and Functions. Chapter VI, Section E.1<br>❏ **Topic:** Measurement and Geometry. Chapter VI, Section F.1–4<br>❏ **Topic:** Data Analysis: Probability and Statistics. Chapter VI, Section F.1–4<br>❏ Review any content you identified from your Practice Test results. |
| 2 days before the test | **Study Time:** 1.5 hours<br>❏ **Practice Test Review:** Review your Practice Test results one more time.<br>❏ Review any content you identified from your Practice Test results. |

| \multicolumn{2}{c}{**Mathematics One-Month Cram Plan**} |
|---|---|
| **4 weeks before the test** | **Study Time:** 1.5 hours<br>❑ **Topic:** Test Content and Types of Items. Chapter VI, Section A<br>❑ **Topic:** Computation and Estimation. Chapter VI, Section B.1–2<br>❑ Read the sections, answer the sample items, and review your answers.<br>❑ **Practice 1:** Answer the practice items and review your answers. Identify any sections you need to review. |
| **3 weeks before the test** | **Study Time:** 1.5 hours<br>❑ **Topic:** Ratios, Proportions, and Percents. Chapter VI, Section B.3–4<br>❑ Read the section, answer the sample items, and review your answers.<br>❑ **Practice 2:** Answer the practice items and review your answers. Identify any sections you need to review. |
| **2 weeks before the test** | **Study Time:** 2 hours<br>❑ **Topic:** Algebraic Concepts Part 1: Combining Terms. Chapter VI, Section C.1–3<br>❑ **Topic:** Algebraic Concepts Part 2: Solving Equations and Inequalities. Chapter VI, Section D.1–3<br>❑ Read the sections, answer the sample items, and review your answers.<br>❑ **Practice 3 and 4:** Answer the practice items and review your answers. Identify any sections you need to review. |
| **7 days before the test** | **Study Time:** 3 hours<br>❑ **Topic:** Algebraic Concepts Part 3: Graphs and Functions. Chapter VI, Section E.1–2<br>❑ **Topic:** Measurement and Geometry. Chapter VI, Section F.1–5<br>❑ **Topic:** Data Analysis: Probability and Statistics. Chapter VI, Section G.1–3<br>❑ **Practice 5, 6 and 7:** Answer the practice items and review your answers. Identify any sections you need to review. |
| **6 days before the test** | **Study Time:** 2 hours<br>❑ Take the Mathematics Full-Length Practice Test (Chapter XI).<br>❑ Review your answers. Based on your errors on the Practice Test, identify difficult topics and their corresponding sections. Target those sections for extra review. |
| **5 days before the test** | **Study Time:** 1.5 hours<br>❑ Redo items that you answered incorrectly on the Practice Test.<br>❑ Review the answer explanations. |
| **4 days before the test** | **Study Time:** 1.5 hours<br>❑ **Topic:** Computation and Estimation. Chapter VI, Section B.1<br>❑ **Topic:** Ratios, Proportions, and Percents. Chapter VI, Section B.3<br>❑ **Topic:** Algebraic Concepts Part 1: Combining Terms. Chapter VI, Section C.1–2<br>❑ **Topic:** Algebraic Concepts Part 2: Solving Equations and Inequalities. Chapter VI, Section D.1–2<br>❑ Review any content you identified from your Practice Test results. |
| **3 days before the test** | **Study Time:** 1.5 hours<br>❑ **Topic:** Algebraic Concepts Part 3: Graphs and Functions. Chapter VI, Section E.1<br>❑ **Topic:** Measurement and Geometry. Chapter VI, Section F.1–4<br>❑ **Topic:** Data Analysis: Probability and Statistics. Chapter VI, Section F.1–4<br>❑ Review any content you identified from your Practice Test results. |
| **2 days before the test** | **Study Time:** 1.5 hours<br>❑ **Practice Test Review:** Review your Practice Test results one more time.<br>❑ Review any content you identified from your Practice Test results. |

## Mathematics One-Week Cram Plan

| | |
|---|---|
| **7 days before the test** | **Study Time:** 1.5 hours<br>❑ **Topic:** Test Content and Types of Items. Chapter VI, Section A<br>❑ **Topic:** Computation and Estimation. Chapter VI, Section B.1–2<br>❑ Read the sections, try to answer the sample items, and review your answers.<br>❑ **Practice 1:** Answer the practice items and review your answers. Identify any sections you need to review. |
| **6 days before the test** | **Study Time:** 1.5 hours<br>❑ **Topic:** Ratios, Proportions, and Percents. Chapter VI, Section B.3–4<br>❑ Read the section, answer the sample items, and review your answers.<br>❑ **Practice 2:** Answer the practice items and review your answers. Identify any sections you need to review. |
| **5 days before the test** | **Study Time:** 2 hours<br>❑ **Topic:** Algebraic Concepts Part 1: Combining Terms. Chapter VI, Section C.1–3<br>❑ **Topic:** Algebraic Concepts Part 2: Solving Equations and Inequalities. Chapter VI, Section D.1–3<br>❑ Read the sections, answer the sample items, and review your answers.<br>❑ **Practice 3 and 4:** Answer the practice items and review your answers. Identify any sections you need to review. |
| **4 days before the test** | **Study Time:** 3 hours<br>❑ **Topic:** Algebraic Concepts Part 3: Graphs and Functions. Chapter VI, Section E.1–2<br>❑ **Topic:** Measurement and Geometry. Chapter VI, Section F.1–5<br>❑ **Topic:** Data Analysis: Probability and Statistics. Chapter VI, Section G.1–3<br>❑ **Practice 5, 6 and 7:** Answer the practice items and review your answers. Identify any sections you need to review. |
| **3 days before the test** | **Study Time:** 2 hours<br>❑ Take the Mathematics Full-Length Practice Test (Chapter XI).<br>❑ Review your answers. Based on your errors on the Practice Test, identify difficult topics and their corresponding sections. Target those sections for extra review. |
| **2 days before the test** | **Study Time:** 1.5 hours<br>❑ Redo items that you answered incorrectly on the Practice Test.<br>❑ Review the answer explanations. |

# E. Science

| Science Two-Month Cram Plan | |
|---|---|
| **8 weeks before the test** | **Study Time:** 0.5 hour<br>❑ **Topic:** Test Format. Chapter VII, Section A<br>❑ Read the section, answer the sample items, and review your answers. |
| **7 weeks before the test** | **Study Time:** 0.5 hour<br>❑ **Topic:** Interpret and Apply. Chapter VII, Section B.1<br>❑ Read the section, answer the sample items, and review your answers. |
| **6 weeks before the test** | **Study Time:** 0.5 hour<br>❑ **Topic:** Analyze. Chapter VII, Section B.2<br>❑ Read the section, answer the sample items, and review your answers. |
| **5 weeks before the test** | **Study Time:** 0.5 hour<br>❑ **Topic:** Evaluate and Generalize. Chapter VII, Section B.3<br>❑ Read the section, answer the sample items, and review your answers. |
| **4 weeks before the test** | **Study Time:** 1 hour<br>❑ **Topic:** Physical Science. Chapter VII, Section C.1<br>❑ Read the section, answer the sample items, and review your answers. |
| **3 weeks before the test** | **Study Time:** 1 hour<br>❑ **Topic:** Earth Science. Chapter VII, Section C.2<br>❑ Read the section, answer the sample items, and review your answers. |
| **2 weeks before the test** | **Study Time:** 1 hour<br>❑ **Topic:** Life Science. Chapter VII, Section C.3<br>❑ Read the section, answer the sample items, and review your answers. |
| **7 days before the test** | **Study Time:** 1 hour<br>❑ **Practice:** Chapter VII, Section D<br>❑ Answer the practice items and review your answers. Identify any sections you need to review. |
| **6 days before the test** | **Study Time:** 2 hours<br>❑ Take the Science Full-Length Practice Test (Chapter XII).<br>❑ Review your answers. Based on your errors on the Practice Test, identify difficult topics and their corresponding sections. Target those sections for extra review. |
| **5 days before the test** | **Study Time:** 1.5 hours<br>❑ Redo items that you answered incorrectly on the Practice Test.<br>❑ Review the answer explanations. |
| **4 days before the test** | **Study Time:** 1.5 hours<br>❑ **Topic:** Interpret and Apply. Chapter VII, Section B.1<br>❑ **Topic:** Analyze. Chapter VII, Section B.2<br>❑ **Topic:** Evaluate and Generalize. Chapter VII, Section B.3<br>❑ Review any content you identified from your Practice Test results. |
| **3 days before the test** | **Study Time:** 1 hour<br>❑ **Topic:** Physical Science. Chapter VII, Section C.1<br>❑ **Topic:** Earth Science. Chapter VII, Section C.2<br>❑ **Topic:** Life Science. Chapter VII, Section C.3<br>❑ Review any content you identified from your Practice Test results. |
| **2 days before the test** | **Study Time:** 1.5 hours<br>❑ **Practice Test Review:** Review your Practice Test results one more time.<br>❑ Review any content you identified from your Practice Test results. |

| Science One-Month Cram Plan | |
|---|---|
| **4 weeks before the test** | **Study Time:** 1 hour<br>❏ **Topic:** Test Format. Chapter VII, Section A<br>❏ **Topic:** Interpret and Apply. Chapter VII, Section B.1<br>❏ Read the section, answer the sample items, and review your answers. |
| **3 weeks before the test** | **Study Time:** 1 hour<br>❏ **Topic:** Analyze. Chapter VII, Section B.2<br>❏ **Topic:** Evaluate and Generalize. Chapter VII, Section B.3<br>❏ Read the sections, answer the sample items, and review your answers. |
| **2 weeks before the test** | **Study Time:** 2.5 hours<br>❏ **Topic:** Physical Science. Chapter VII, Section C.1<br>❏ **Topic:** Earth Science. Chapter VII, Section C.2<br>❏ **Topic:** Life Science. Chapter VII, Section C.3<br>❏ Read the sections, answer the sample items, and review your answers. |
| **7 days before the test** | **Study Time:** 1 hour<br>❏ **Practice:** Chapter VII, Section D<br>❏ Answer the practice items and review your answers. Identify any sections you need to review. |
| **6 days before the test** | **Study Time:** 2 hours<br>❏ Take the Science Full-Length Practice Test (Chapter XII).<br>❏ Review your answers. Based on your errors on the Practice Test, identify difficult topics and their corresponding sections. Target those sections for extra review. |
| **5 days before the test** | **Study Time:** 1.5 hours<br>❏ Redo items that you answered incorrectly on the Practice Test.<br>❏ Review the answer explanations. |
| **4 days before the test** | **Study Time:** 1.5 hours<br>❏ **Topic:** Interpret and Apply. Chapter VII, Section B.1<br>❏ **Topic:** Analyze. Chapter VII, Section B.2<br>❏ **Topic:** Evaluate and Generalize. Chapter VII, Section B.3<br>❏ Review any content you identified from your Practice Test results. |
| **3 days before the test** | **Study Time:** 1 hour<br>❏ **Topic:** Physical Science. Chapter VII, Section C.1<br>❏ **Topic:** Earth Science. Chapter VII, Section C.2<br>❏ **Topic:** Life Science. Chapter VII, Section C.3<br>❏ Review any content you identified from your Practice Test results. |
| **2 days before the test** | **Study Time:** 1.5 hours<br>❏ **Practice Test Review:** Review your Practice Test results one more time.<br>❏ Review any content you identified from your Practice Test results. |

| Science One-Week Cram Plan | |
|---|---|
| **7 days before the test** | **Study Time:** 1 hour<br>❑ **Topic:** Test Format. Chapter VII, Section A<br>❑ **Topic:** Interpret and Apply. Chapter VII, Section B.1<br>❑ Read the sections, answer the sample items, and review your answers. |
| **6 days before the test** | **Study Time:** 1 hour<br>❑ **Topic:** Analyze. Chapter VII, Section B, Part 2<br>❑ **Topic:** Evaluate and Generalize. Chapter VII, Section B, Part 3<br>❑ Read the sections, answer the sample items, and review your answers. |
| **5 days before the test** | **Study Time:** 2.5 hours<br>❑ **Topic:** Physical Science. Chapter VII, Section C.1<br>❑ **Topic:** Earth Science. Chapter VII, Section C.2<br>❑ **Topic:** Life Science. Chapter VII, Section C.3<br>❑ Read the sections, answer the sample items, and review your answers. |
| **4 days before the test** | **Study Time:** 1 hour<br>❑ **Practice:** Chapter VII, Section D<br>❑ Answer the practice items and review your answers. Identify any sections you need to review. |
| **3 days before the test** | **Study Time:** 2 hours<br>❑ Take the Science Full-Length Practice Test (Chapter XII).<br>❑ Review your answers. Based on your errors on the Practice Test, identify difficult topics and their corresponding sections. Target those sections for extra review. |
| **2 days before the test** | **Study Time:** 1.5 hours<br>❑ Redo items that you answered incorrectly on the Practice Test.<br>❑ Review the answer explanations. |

# F. Social Studies

| Social Studies Two-Month Cram Plan | |
| --- | --- |
| **8 weeks before the test** | **Study Time:** 2 hours<br>❑ **Topic:** Test Format. Chapter VIII, Section A<br>❑ Read the section, answer the sample items, and review your answers. |
| **7 weeks before the test** | **Study Time:** 0.5 hour<br>❑ **Topic:** Interpret and Apply. Chapter VIII, Section B.1<br>❑ Read the section, answer the sample items, and review your answers. |
| **6 weeks before the test** | **Study Time:** 0.5 hour<br>❑ **Topic:** Analyze. Chapter VIII, Section B.2<br>❑ Read the section, answer the sample items, and review your answers. |
| **5 weeks before the test** | **Study Time:** 0.5 hour<br>❑ **Topic:** Evaluate and Generalize. Chapter VIII, Section B.3<br>❑ Read the section, answer the sample items, and review your answers. |
| **4 weeks before the test** | **Study Time:** 0.5 hour<br>❑ **Topic:** History. Chapter VIII, Section C.1<br>❑ Read the section, answer the sample items, and review your answers. |
| **3 weeks before the test** | **Study Time:** 0.5 hour<br>❑ **Topic:** Civics/Government. Chapter VIII, Section C.2<br>❑ Read the section, answer the sample items, and review your answers. |
| **2 weeks before the test** | **Study Time:** 0.5 hour<br>❑ **Topic:** Economics. Chapter VIII, Section C.3<br>❑ **Topic:** Geography. Chapter VIII, Section C.4<br>❑ Read the sections, answer the sample items, and review your answers. |
| **7 days before the test** | **Study Time:** 1 hour<br>❑ **Practice:** Chapter VIII, Section D<br>❑ Answer the practice items and review your answers. Identify any sections you need to review. |
| **6 days before the test** | **Study Time:** 2 hours<br>❑ Take the Social Studies Full-Length Practice Test (Chapter XIII).<br>❑ Review your answers. Based on your errors on the Practice Test, identify difficult topics and their corresponding sections. Target those sections for extra review. |
| **5 days before the test** | **Study Time:** 1.5 hours<br>❑ Redo items that you answered incorrectly on the Practice Test.<br>❑ Check the answer explanations. |
| **4 days before the test** | **Study Time:** 1.5 hours<br>❑ **Topic:** Interpret and Apply. Chapter VIII, Section B.1<br>❑ **Topic:** Analyze. Chapter VIII, Section B.2<br>❑ **Topic:** Evaluate and Generalize. Chapter VIII, Section B.3<br>❑ Review any content you identified from your Practice Test results. |
| **3 days before the test** | **Study Time:** 1 hour<br>❑ **Topic:** History. Chapter VIII, Section C.1<br>❑ **Topic:** Civics/Government. Chapter VIII, Section C.2<br>❑ **Topic:** Economics. Chapter VIII, Section C.3<br>❑ **Topic:** Geography. Chapter VIII, Section C.4<br>❑ Review any content you identified from your Practice Test results. |
| **2 days before the test** | **Study Time:** 1.5 hours<br>❑ **Practice Test Review:** Review your Practice Test results one more time.<br>❑ Review any content you identified from your Practice Test results. |

## Social Studies One-Month Cram Plan

| 4 weeks before the test | **Study Time:** 2 hours<br>❏ **Topic:** Test Format. Chapter VIII, Section A<br>❏ **Topic:** Interpret and Apply. Chapter VIII, Section B.1<br>❏ Read the sections, answer the sample items, and review your answers. |
|---|---|
| 3 weeks before the test | **Study Time:** 1 hour<br>❏ **Topic:** Analyze. Chapter VIII, Section B.2<br>❏ **Topic:** Evaluate and Generalize. Chapter VIII, Section B.3<br>❏ Read the sections, answer the sample items, and review your answers. |
| 2 weeks before the test | **Study Time:** 1.5 hours<br>❏ **Topic:** History. Chapter VIII, Section C.1<br>❏ **Topic:** Civics/Government. Chapter VIII, Section C.2<br>❏ **Topic:** Economics. Chapter VIII, Section C.3<br>❏ **Topic:** Geography. Chapter VIII, Section C.4<br>❏ Read the sections, answer the sample items, and review your answers. |
| 7 days before the test | **Study Time:** 1 hour<br>❏ **Practice:** Chapter VIII, Section D<br>❏ Answer the practice items and review your answers. Identify any sections you need to review. |
| 6 days before the test | **Study Time:** 2 hours<br>❏ Take the Social Studies Full-Length Practice Test (Chapter XIII).<br>❏ Review your answers. Based on your errors on the Practice Test, identify difficult topics and their corresponding sections. Target those sections for extra review. |
| 5 days before the test | **Study Time:** 1.5 hours<br>❏ Redo items that you answered incorrectly on the Practice Test.<br>❏ Check the answer explanations. |
| 4 days before the test | **Study Time:** 1.5 hours<br>❏ **Topic:** Interpret and Apply. Chapter VIII, Section B.1<br>❏ **Topic:** Analyze. Chapter VIII, Section B.2<br>❏ **Topic:** Evaluate and Generalize. Chapter VIII, Section B.3<br>❏ Review any content you identified from your Practice Test results. |
| 3 days before the test | **Study Time:** 1 hour<br>❏ **Topic:** History. Chapter VIII, Section C.1<br>❏ **Topic:** Civics/Government. Chapter VIII, Section C.2<br>❏ **Topic:** Economics. Chapter VIII, Section C.3<br>❏ **Topic:** Geography. Chapter VIII, Section C.4<br>❏ Review any content you identified from your Practice Test results. |
| 2 days before the test | **Study Time:** 1.5 hours<br>❏ **Practice Test Review:** Review your Practice Test results one more time.<br>❏ Review any content you identified from your Practice Test results. |

| Social Studies One-Week Cram Plan | |
|---|---|
| **7 days before the test** | **Study Time:** 2 hours<br>❑ **Topic:** Test Format. Chapter VIII, Section A<br>❑ **Topic:** Interpret and Apply. Chapter VIII, Section B.1<br>❑ Read the sections, answer the sample items, and review your answers. |
| **6 days before the test** | **Study Time:** 1 hour<br>❑ **Topic:** Analyze. Chapter VIII, Section B.2<br>❑ **Topic:** Evaluate and Generalize. Chapter VIII, Section B.3<br>❑ Read the sections, answer the sample items, and review your answers. |
| **5 days before the test** | **Study Time:** 1.5 hours<br>❑ **Topic:** History. Chapter VIII, Section C.1<br>❑ **Topic:** Civics/Government. Chapter VIII, Section C.2<br>❑ **Topic:** Economics. Chapter VIII, Section C.3<br>❑ **Topic:** Geography. Chapter VIII, Section C.4<br>❑ Read the sections, answer the sample items, and review your answers. |
| **4 days before the test** | **Study Time:** 1 hour<br>❑ **Practice:** Chapter VIII, Section D<br>❑ Answer the practice items and review your answers. Identify any sections you need to review. |
| **3 days before the test** | **Study Time:** 2 hours<br>❑ Take the Social Studies Full-Length Practice Test (Chapter XIII).<br>❑ Review your answers. Based on your errors on the Practice Test, identify difficult topics and their corresponding sections. Target those sections for extra review. |
| **2 days before the test** | **Study Time:** 1.5 hours<br>❑ Redo items that you answered incorrectly on the Practice Test.<br>❑ Check the answer explanations. |

# G. The Day of the Test and the Night Before

| The Day of the Test and the Night Before | |
|---|---|
| **The night before the test** | **Reminders:**<br>❑ Relax and have positive thoughts.<br>❑ Eat a good dinner.<br>❑ Get a good night's sleep.<br>❑ Set an alarm if you need to get up early. |
| **The day of the test** | **Reminders:**<br>❑ Have a good breakfast.<br>❑ Take these things with you:<br>　❑ Your admission ticket and photo ID<br>　❑ A watch<br>❑ Food, such as a snack or a sandwich, if you will be at the test center for a long time. |

# III. Language Arts: Reading

The HiSET Language Arts: Reading section tests your ability to understand, comprehend, interpret, and analyze different kinds of reading material. It has 40 multiple-choice items, and you will have 65 minutes to complete the section. Items test your understanding of two main kinds of reading passages:

- Literary Texts—fiction, poetry, drama (60%)
- Informational Texts—memoirs, essays, short biographies, editorials, and so on (40%)

You do not need any specialized knowledge in these areas to answer the items. Rather, the test asks you to read and interpret reading passages. Generally, reading passages range from 400 to 600 words (though poetry selections may be shorter) and are followed by six to nine items. The HiSET Language Arts: Reading section will ask you to show your ability to answer items in these four areas:

- **Comprehension**—Understand restatements of details or information in the passage, determine the meaning of words in the passage, and analyze the impact of the writer's word choices on the passage's meaning and tone.
- **Inference and Interpretation**—Make inferences about character's' feelings, motives, or personalities; apply information or details in the passage to new settings; and interpret figurative language.
- **Analysis**—Analyze multiple interpretations of a passage; determine the main idea or theme of a passage; identify the writer's or speaker's purpose, intent, or point of view; distinguish among fact and opinion, assumptions, observations, and conclusions; and recognize literary and argumentative techniques.
- **Synthesis and Generalization**—Draw conclusions, make generalizations, make predictions based on information or details in the passage, compare and contrast, and synthesize information or details across multiple sources or points of view.

## A. Test Format

This section gives an overview of the kinds of literary texts and informational texts that you will read and interpret on the HiSET Language Arts: Reading section. Each reading text will be followed by six to nine items.

## 1. Literary Texts

**Literary texts** include prose fiction, poetry, and drama. These texts will be drawn from both popular literature (recently published works) and classical literature (older works that are considered by experts as masterpieces that have stood the test of time). Most literary passages are from 400 to 600 words (except for poetry selections, which may be shorter).

# a. Prose Fiction

**Fiction** is writing that is about imaginary ideas and events. Fiction is the invention of the author and is not real. Prose fiction includes both novels and short stories. Look at the following example:

**This excerpt is from a novel that explores the relationships among the European colonizers of an African country, as well as their relationships with the colonized people.**

The Nellie, a cruising yawl, swung to her anchor without a flutter of the sails, and was at rest. The flood had made, the wind was nearly calm, and being bound down the river, the only thing for it was to come to and wait for the turn of the tide.

(5) The sea-reach of the Thames stretched before us like the beginning of an interminable waterway. In the offing the sea and the sky were welded together without a joint, and in the luminous space the tanned sails of the barges drifting up with the tide seemed to stand still in red clusters of canvas sharply peaked, with gleams of varnished sprits. A haze rested on the low shores that ran out to sea in vanishing flatness. The air was dark above Gravesend, and farther back still seemed condensed into a mournful gloom, brooding motionless over the biggest, and the greatest, town on earth.

(10) The Director of Companies was our captain and our host. We four affectionately watched his back as he stood in the bows looking to seaward. On the whole river there was nothing that looked half so nautical. He resembled a pilot, which to a seaman is trustworthiness personified. It was difficult to realize his work was not out there in the luminous estuary, but behind him, within the brooding gloom.

Between us there was, as I have already said somewhere, the bond of the sea. Besides holding our
(15) hearts together through long periods of separation, it had the effect of making us tolerant of each other's yarns—and even convictions. The Lawyer—the best of old fellows—had, because of his many years and many virtues, the only cushion on deck, and was lying on the only rug. The Accountant had brought out already a box of dominoes, and was toying architecturally with the bones. Marlow sat cross-legged right aft, leaning against the mizzen-mast. He had sunken cheeks, a yellow complexion, a straight back,
(20) an ascetic aspect, and, with his arms dropped, the palms of hands outwards, resembled an idol. The Director, satisfied the anchor had good hold, made his way aft and sat down amongst us. We exchanged a few words lazily. Afterwards there was silence on board the yacht. For some reason or other we did not begin that game of dominoes. We felt meditative, and fit for nothing but placid staring. The day was ending in a serenity of still and exquisite brilliance. The water shone pacifically; the sky, without a
(25) speck, was a benign immensity of unstained light; the very mist on the Essex marshes was like a gauzy and radiant fabric, hung from the wooded rises inland, and draping the low shores in diaphanous folds. Only the gloom to the west, brooding over the upper reaches, became more somber every minute, as if angered by the approach of the sun.

Excerpt from *Heart of Darkness,* by Joseph Conrad.

All reading passages (both literary and informational) follow the same format. First, a boldfaced headnote gives important background about the text.

> TIP: Always read the boldfaced headnote first. It gives important background about the text. Use the information to help you read and answer the items.

After the headnote, the passage will follow. Unlike reading passages on HiSET Science and Social Studies sections, passages on the HiSET Reading section will have line numbers. The line numbers are used in the items that follow to identify the location of key words, phrases, and information referenced in the text.

TIP: If you find you are running out of time but have a few minutes remaining to answer items, look for items that have line numbers. You can quickly and easily try to answer a few of those items by reading only the passage headnote and the lines of the text referenced in the line numbers.

After the reading passage, the items begin.

TIP: After you read the headnote, read the items and then read the passage. Use the items and line numbers to focus your reading. Then try to answer the items. If necessary, go back and read the passage more carefully as you answer the items.

Look at the following example items for prose fiction:

What is the mood of the characters as they await the changing of the tide?

A. Anxious and afraid
B. Bored and unimpressed
C. Peaceful and friendly
D. Happy and excited

Option C is correct. Words and phrases such as, "affectionately" (line 10), "holding our hearts together" (lines 14–15), "tolerant" (line 15), "the best of old fellows" (line 16), and "placid" (line 23) show that the characters feel peaceful and friendly. For this reason, Options A and B are incorrect. Option D is incorrect because they seem to be quiet and meditative, not happy and excited.

Why does the author mention, "Only the gloom to the west, brooding over the upper reaches, became more somber every minute, as if angered by the approach of the sun" (lines 27–28)?

A. To show that bad weather has delayed their departure
B. To show the writer's dislike of London
C. To show that the writer considers Africa a better place than London
D. To show that some bad events are forthcoming later in the story

Option D is correct. The foreboding darkness and gloom are used to show that characters will face some bad events later in the story. For this reason, Options B and C are incorrect. Option A is incorrect because their departure is delayed until the tide goes out, not because of the bad weather behind them to the west.

What is the meaning of "yawl" (line 1)?

A. A kind of sailing ship
B. A way of saying, "you-all"
C. A kind of ice pick
D. A change in direction of an airplane or ship

Option A is correct. The context (the words and sentences that come before and after the word) makes it clear that the characters are passengers on a boat with sails. Option B is incorrect because the usual way to write *you-all* is *ya'll,* and it is clear from the context that *yawl* is not a pronoun-adjective combination. Another word for ice pick is *awl,* so Option C is incorrect. A change in direction of a plane or ship is *yaw,* so Option D is incorrect.

# b. Poetry

**Poetry** is a kind of writing that uses the sound of language (rhythm, rhyme, beat, and the sounds of the words), imagery, and other literary techniques to communicate a figurative meaning in addition to the literal meaning of the words. Poetry is not generally written in sentences and paragraphs, but rather in lines and stanzas. Poems, limericks, song lyrics, and rap music are all examples of poetry. Look at the following example:

**Alfred, Lord Tennyson, a British poet, wrote this poem about a tragic battle in the Crimean war that occurred on October 25, 1854, in which a British regiment charged into a valley on horseback only to be ambushed and killed.**

> Half a league, half a league,
> Half a league onward,
> All in the valley of Death
> Rode the six hundred.
> (5)   "Forward, the Light Brigade!
> "Charge for the guns!" he said:
> Into the valley of Death
> Rode the six hundred.

The first stanza from "The Charge of the Light Brigade," by Alfred, Lord Tennyson.

---

What is the purpose of the strong rhythmic beat of the poem?

**A.** To reproduce the sound of a sad funeral song
**B.** To emphasize heroism of the soldiers
**C.** To imitate the sound of horse hooves galloping into battle
**D.** To criticize the enemy for its sneak ambush

---

Option C is correct. The strong beat and rhythm of the poem sounds like hooves of many horses galloping. For this reason, Option A is incorrect. Options B and D are not supported by the excerpt.

**TIP:** When an item asks you to interpret the sound or rhythm of a poem, say a few lines of the poem quietly to yourself. Pay attention to the rhythm, beat, and sounds of the words.

---

Why does the speaker repeat the phrases "All in the valley of Death/Rode the six hundred" (lines 3–4) and "Into the valley of Death/Rode the six hundred" (lines 7–8)?

**A.** To show the size and importance of the British army
**B.** To strengthen his case for opposing the war
**C.** To indicate the cowardice of the soldiers
**D.** To emphasize the impending doom of the soldiers

---

Option D is correct. The repetition of these lines emphasizes that the soldiers are all about to die. Option A is not supported by the passage. Though Britain was proud of its military might, this is not the reason the speaker mentions the size of the regiment in this case. Option B is incorrect because the speaker seems to think that the soldiers were heroic. For this reason, Option C is also incorrect.

---

Which of the following sentences best states the author's attitude toward the soldiers?

  **A.** They were foolish to charge before finding out they would be surrounded.
  **B.** They were brave soldiers who experienced tragic deaths.
  **C.** They were loyal soldiers who lacked proper leadership.
  **D.** They were poor soldiers who were unprepared for battle.

---

Option B is correct. The poem's mood of impending doom contrasted with the bravery of the charge indicate that Option B is correct. For this reason, Option D is incorrect. Option A may be true, but is not Tennyson's attitude toward the soldiers in the poem. While today, many historians would agree that the soldiers would not have charged into the battle if they had had proper leadership, this is not Tennyson's attitude, so Option C is incorrect.

## c. Drama

**Drama** is a kind of fiction that is intended to be performed by actors for an audience. Drama can include short and long plays, movies, and television dramas or comedies. Look at the following example:

**In this excerpt from a play, Dunyasha, a female servant, is waiting for the return of her employer Madame Lubov Andreyevna, a wealthy aristocrat, with her friend Lopakhin, a wealthy merchant.**

> LOPAKHIN. The train's arrived, thank God. What's the time?
> DUNYASHA. It will soon be two. *(Blows out candle)* It is light already.
> LOPAKHIN. How much was the train late? Two hours at least. *(Yawns and stretches)* I have made a terrible mess of it! I came here on purpose to meet them at the station, and then overslept myself... in my
(5) chair. It's a pity. I wish you'd wakened me.
> DUNYASHA. I thought you'd gone away. *(Listening)* I think I hear them coming.
> LOPAKHIN. *(Listens)* No.... They've got to collect their luggage and so on.... *(Pause)* Lubov Andreyevna has been living abroad for five years; I don't know what she'll be like now.... She's a good sort—an easy, simple person. I remember when I was a boy of fifteen, my father, who is dead—he used
(10) to keep a shop in the village here—hit me on the face with his fist, and my nose bled.... We had gone into the yard together for something or other, and he was a little drunk. Lubov Andreyevna, as I remember her now, was still young, and very thin, and she took me to the washstand here in this very room, the nursery. She said, "Don't cry, little man, it'll be all right in time for your wedding." *(Pause)* "Little man".... My father was a peasant, it's true, but here I am in a white waistcoat and yellow shoes... a pearl
(15) out of an oyster. I'm rich now, with lots of money, but just think about it and examine me, and you'll find I'm still a peasant down to the marrow of my bones. *(Turns over the pages of his book)* Here I've been reading this book, but I understood nothing. I read and fell asleep. *(Pause.)*
> DUNYASHA. The dogs didn't sleep all night; they know that they're coming.
> LOPAKHIN. What's up with you, Dunyasha...?
(20) DUNYASHA. My hands are shaking. I shall faint.

LOPAKHIN. You're too sensitive, Dunyasha. You dress just like a lady, and you do your hair like one too. You oughtn't. You should know your place.

Excerpt from *The Cherry Orchard,* by Anton Chekov.

---

Based on Lopakhin's words, Madame Lubov Andreyevna can best be described as

**A.** a wealthy aristocrat who is obsessed with money and power.
**B.** a miserly landlord who exploits people under her power.
**C.** a spendthrift who cannot manage her money well.
**D.** a simple, kind-hearted person who cares for others.

---

Option D is correct. Lopakhin's words and his description of Madame Lubov Andreyevna's kindness to him when he was hurt as a child show that this option is correct. The other options are not supported by details in the passage and are incorrect.

---

What does Lopakhin mean when he says he is "a pearl out of an oyster" (lines 14–15)?

**A.** He is much poorer than his ancestors.
**B.** He thinks he is better than the aristocratic Madame Lubov Andreyevna.
**C.** He thinks that wealth is not that important.
**D.** He believes his life is a rags-to-riches story.

---

Option D is correct. In his speech (lines 14–17), Lopakhin says that his family has risen from humble peasant origins, and he is now a wealthy merchant who can stand in an aristocrat's home dressed in fine clothes. For this reason, Option A is incorrect. Option B is not supported by details in the passage. Option C is contradicted by the passage. Lopakhin's words show that he gives great attention to wealth.

---

Which of the following is a theme developed in the text?

**A.** The meaning of true love
**B.** Understanding and dealing with death
**C.** The relationship between social class and wealth
**D.** The meaning of life

---

Option C is correct. In two places, Lopakhin mentions wealth or its trappings, and their relationship to social class. In lines 14–16, he says that even though he is wealthy now and dresses well, he is "still a peasant down to the marrow of my bones." Later, he reproaches Dunyasha, a servant for dressing inappropriately: "You dress just like a lady, and you do your hair like one too. You oughtn't. You should know your place" (lines 21–22). Option A is incorrect because the people are not talking about love. Option B is incorrect because the people are not talking about death. Option D is too general to be correct.

# 2. Informational Texts

**Informational texts** are **non-fiction.** They are about real or factual actions, events, descriptions, and interpretations. Look at the following example:

**The essay excerpted below looks at myths and realities about bats.**

      Bats are among the most feared and misunderstood animals. When most people think of bats, they think of blood-sucking vampires, flying rodents, or old tales of flying bats getting tangled in people's hair. In truth, bats are a fascinating group of mammals that serve vital functions.

      In actuality, bats are not rodents at all, but are members of a mammal order of their own. In addition,
(5)  bats are the only mammals that can fly. Bats also carry out vital functions. Most bats are insectivores. Without bats, insect populations would go out of control. In fact, some cities, such as Austin, Texas, have built special bridges or caves to attract bats in order to control mosquitos and other pests. Other bats are fruit-eating. Many plant species depend on bats to pollinate their flowers or spread their seeds. Only one kind of bat, the vampire bat, drinks blood. These bats' habitat ranges from Mexico to Peru and
(10) Argentina. While vampire bats have been known to drink the blood of people, they more commonly drink the blood of birds or other mammals.

---

What is the meaning of the word "insectivores" (line 5)?

A.   Bat-eating
B.   Blood-drinking
C.   Fruit-eating
D.   Insect-eating

---

Option D is correct. The context makes it clear that these bats eat insects, so Option D is correct. For this reason, Options B and C are incorrect. Option A is incorrect; bats do not eat other bats.

---

Which of the following states the main idea of the passage?

A.   Bats serve vital functions.
B.   Bats are very dangerous.
C.   Bats are very misunderstood creatures.
D.   Bats have a key role in plant reproduction.

---

Option C is correct. The main idea is stated directly in the first sentence of the passage. For this reason, Option B is incorrect; bats are not described as dangerous. Option A is incorrect because identifying bats' functions is one way the writer supports the main idea. Option D is incorrect because bats' role in plant reproduction is just one of the details in the text.

---

Why does the author mention vampire bats in lines 9–11?

A.   To prove that bats are dangerous
B.   To show that only a few bats drink blood
C.   To demonstrate that bats serve useful functions
D.   To prove that bats are misunderstood

Option B is correct. Of the many kinds of bats, only the vampire bat drinks blood. For this reason, Option A is incorrect. The insect-eating and fruit-eating bats mentioned earlier in the passage, unlike vampire bats, serve useful functions so Option C is incorrect. The many other useful kinds of bats, not vampire bats, show that bats are misunderstood, so Option D is incorrect.

**TIP:** On the HiSET test, you can skip items and return to them later. So if prose fiction, poetry, drama, or informational text is hard for you, choose one of them to skip, and focus on the genres that are easier for you. Then go back to the more difficult genres and take your best guess.

# B. Types of Items: A Detailed Look

Items on the HiSET Language Arts: Reading section are divided into four types:

- Comprehension
- Inference and interpretation
- Analysis
- Synthesis and generalization

This section gives detailed information on how to answer each type of item.

# 1. Comprehension

Comprehension items ask you to identify reworded statements of information from the text. In other words, you are asked to figure out the meaning of new or unfamiliar words as they are used in the text, and analyze the impact of the writer's word choices on the text's meaning and tone.

Restating information in new words assesses whether you have understood the meaning of the text. Figuring out the meaning of new or unfamiliar words shows whether you can use the overall meaning of the passage to deepen your understanding of it. And analyzing word choice shows that you understand how writers use word choice to express their ideas clearly and vividly. Look at the following example items:

*Items 1 through 15 refer to the passage below.*

**Pip, a poor orphan who lives with his older sister and her husband, Joe, encountered and helped a mysterious stranger as a child. In this excerpt from a novel, Pip finds out from a lawyer that an unknown benefactor is interested in helping him become a gentleman.**

"Now, I return to this young fellow. And the communication I have got to make is, that he has Great Expectations."

Joe and I gasped, and looked at one another.

"I am instructed to communicate to him," said Mr. Jaggers, throwing his finger at me sideways, "that

(5) he will come into a handsome property. Further, that it is the desire of the present possessor of that property, that he be immediately removed from his present sphere of life and from this place, and be brought up as a gentleman—in a word, as a young fellow of great expectations."

My dream was out; my wild fancy was surpassed by sober reality; Miss Havisham was going to make my fortune on a grand scale.

(10)     "Now, Mr. Pip," pursued the lawyer, "I address the rest of what I have to say, to you. You are to understand, first, that it is the request of the person from whom I take my instructions that you always bear the name of Pip. You will have no objection, I dare say, to your great expectations being encumbered with that easy condition. But if you have any objection, this is the time to mention it."

     My heart was beating so fast, and there was such a singing in my ears, that I could scarcely stammer
(15)    I had no objection.

     "I should think not! Now you are to understand, secondly, Mr. Pip, that the name of the person who is your liberal benefactor remains a profound secret, until the person chooses to reveal it. I am empowered to mention that it is the intention of the person to reveal it at first hand by word of mouth to yourself. When or where that intention may be carried out, I cannot say; no one can say. It may be years
(20)    hence. Now, you are distinctly to understand that you are most positively prohibited from making any inquiry on this head, or any allusion or reference, however distant, to any individual whomsoever as the individual, in all the communications you may have with me.

Excerpt from *Great Expectations,* by Charles Dickens.

---

1.  Why are Pip and his family talking to a lawyer?

    **A.**  Pip needs advice about a valuable inheritance he received.

    **B.**  The lawyer is communicating to Pip some exceptionally good news from one of his clients.

    **C.**  Pip was involved in a crime when he met the mysterious stranger, so he needs the help of a lawyer.

    **D.**  The lawyer is informing Pip about how he became an orphan.

---

Option B is correct. The passage makes clear that Pip is going to receive a valuable gift from a person for whom the lawyer works. For this reason, the other options (A, C, and D) are incorrect.

---

2.  Which of the following is NOT one of the conditions imposed on Pip by his benefactor?

    **A.**  The identity of the individual helping Pip is to remain unknown to him.

    **B.**  Pip is not allowed to investigate the identity of the benefactor.

    **C.**  Pip is not allowed to make hints about the identity of the benefactor to Mr. Jaggers.

    **D.**  Pip is not allowed to spend any of the money without the benefactor's direct authorization.

---

Option D is correct. In this item, you are presented with three paraphrases of Mr. Jagger's instructions to Pip, and one which is not mentioned by Jaggers. All the options but Option D are mentioned by Mr. Jaggers, so Option D is correct and the remaining options (A, B, and C) are incorrect.

TIP: Be careful when answering items with negative words like *not* or *except*. It is very easy to forget that you are looking for an option that is not in the passage or is contradicted by it and choose the first answer that is supported by the passage. Whenever you see one of these items, read each option carefully and eliminate the options that are supported by the passage. The option that remains is the correct answer.

3. What is the meaning of the word "handsome" (line 5)?

   A.  Valuable
   B.  Good-looking
   C.  Skillful
   D.  Unexpected

Option A is correct. You can figure out this meaning because the lawyer's words, and even his involvement, indicate that a large amount of money or possessions are involved. For this reason, Option B, which is a more usual meaning of the word, is incorrect. Option C is not supported by the details in the text. While receiving this money obviously was unexpected, this is not a possible meaning of the word "handsome," so Option D is incorrect.

TIP: Vocabulary items often use words with more than one meaning. For example, the word *handsome* in item 3 can mean "attractive or good-looking" or "extremely valuable." Therefore, do not choose the first option that you recognize as having the same meaning as the word, since the word may be used with another of its meanings in the passage. Read all the options, and then insert the one you believe is correct into the original sentence in the passage to check your answer.

To answer a vocabulary item, do the following:

■ If you already know the meaning of the word, find it in the list, and then plug it in to the original sentence in the passage to make sure that the meaning makes sense. If it has the same meaning, choose that option and go on to the next item.

■ If you cannot find the correct answer, use clues in the sentence and surrounding sentences. For example, the phrases "Great Expectations" (lines 1–2), "gentleman" (line 7), and "make my fortune on a grand scale" (lines 8–9) all indicate that a large or important sum of money is involved.

■ If you still cannot find the right answer, eliminate options you know to be incorrect and then choose one of the remaining options at random. For example, in item 3, you can eliminate Option C as incorrect, since *skillful* does not make sense because the passage seems to suggest that Pip's luck, more than skill, is involved.

4. What is the main effect of stating that Mr. Jaggers was "throwing" his finger sideways at Pip (line 4)?

   A.  To indicate that the information he is about to give can be disregarded
   B.  To indicate the importance of the information he is about to give
   C.  To indicate that the information he is about to give is confidential
   D.  To indicate that he does not believe that Pip is deserving of this good fortune

Option B is correct. You can figure out this meaning because the information that follows indicates the news is important and life-changing. Therefore, Option A is incorrect. Mr. Jaggers gives the warnings about confidentiality and secrecy later in the text, so Option C is not a reason he would make this gesture. Option D is not supported by details in the passage.

# 2. Inference and Interpretation

## a. Inferences

Inference items ask you to use information from the passage to figure out new information. For example, you have been waiting for an important phone call about a new job. Suddenly, the phone rings. You can infer that someone is calling you about the new job. Items may ask you to draw conclusions from information in the passage or to use information from the passage to make inferences about the personalities, feelings, or motivation of characters or individuals. Try these example inference items:

5. Which of the following statements can be inferred about Mr. Jaggers?

   A. He is Pip's benefactor.
   B. He does not believe that Pip should accept the benefactor's offer.
   C. His actions are dictated by the benefactor.
   D. He does not agree with the benefactor's decision to help Pip.

Option C is correct. Phrases such as, "it is the request of the person from whom I take my instructions" (line 11) indicate that the benefactor is dictating the lawyer's actions. Option A is not supported by information in the passage. Option B is contradicted by the passage when Mr. Jaggers says, "I should think not!" (line 16) after Pip expresses no disagreement with conditions the benefactor wants to imposed on him. Option D is not supported by information in the passage.

6. Which of the following is <u>most likely</u> true of Pip at the time of Mr. Jaggers' visit?

   A. He has a bad relationship with his brother-in-law, Joe.
   B. He is not from an upper-class background.
   C. He loved Miss Havisham.
   D. He wanted to leave his small town and move to London.

This item asks you to use information in the text to make an inference about Pip. Option B is correct. In lines 6–7, the text makes it clear that he is to be "removed from his present sphere of life and from this place, and be brought up as a gentleman." This statement strongly implies that Pip is not from an upper-class background. Option A is not supported by information in the passage. Options C and D are not supported by information in the passage. There is no information that shows that Pip loved Miss Havisham (Option C) or that he wanted to leave his town (Option D).

## b. Interpretation

Interpretation items ask you to apply information from the text to a new context or situation and to figure out the meaning of non-literal, or figurative, language.

Interpretation items may ask you, for example, to speculate about what a character would most likely do in a different time or location, or in a hypothetical situation. Look at the following example item:

---

7.  Imagine that Pip asked Mr. Jaggers whether Miss Havisham was his benefactor. Which of the following would <u>most likely</u> happen?

    **A.**  Mr. Jaggers would reveal the true identity of the benefactor.
    **B.**  Mr. Jaggers would remind Pip that he is forbidden to ask about this topic.
    **C.**  Mr. Jaggers would lie to cover up that Miss Havisham was the benefactor.
    **D.**  Pip would finally get to meet Miss Havisham.

---

Option B is correct. Mr. Jaggers explained the rule carefully and seems to be a person who sets and follows rules, so he would most likely remind Pip that he is not supposed to ask about the identity of the benefactor. For this reason, Options A and D are incorrect; Option D is also incorrect because it seems that Pip already knows Miss Havisham. Option C is incorrect because it is not clear from the passage whether Miss Havisham is the benefactor or not, and Mr. Jaggers would most likely refuse to answer the question, rather than cover up the truth.

## i. Figurative Language

**Figurative language** refers to words that are used in creative and non-literal ways. An example of figurative language is, "I'm so hungry I could eat a horse." Figurative language does not use the literal meanings of the words. Instead figurative language uses the words in fresh, more expressive ways.

Many kinds of figurative language involve similes and metaphors. A **simile** is a comparison between two things—two things are said to be like one another. For example, the famous English poet Robert Burns once wrote, "My love is like a red, red rose." A **metaphor** is when one thing is said to be another. For example, one might say of an uncomfortable bus, "That bus is a tin can on wheels."

**Understatement** and **overstatement** are two other kinds of figurative language. The first example about being hungry (*I'm so hungry I could eat a horse*) is an example of exaggeration. An example of understatement is a very hungry person saying, "I wouldn't mind nibbling on something." Clearly, the speaker is hungry but expresses this meaning indirectly using understatement. The purpose of all figurative language is to make writing more vivid and expressive.

---

8.  What does Pip mean when he says that there was "such a singing in my ears" that he could not respond to Mr. Jagger's question?

    **A.**  Pip's sister and her husband Joe were singing out of happiness so loudly Pip could not hear Mr. Jaggers.
    **B.**  Pip was so happy that he was singing.
    **C.**  Pip was sick and experiencing ringing in his ears.
    **D.**  Pip was experiencing an outpouring of happiness.

---

This item asks you to determine the meaning of figurative language. Option D is correct. Pip felt so happy and excited that he could not concentrate on Mr. Jaggers' words. Options A, B, and C are based on the literal meaning of the word *singing* and are therefore incorrect.

# 3. Analysis

Analysis items may ask you to analyze multiple interpretations of a passage; determine the main idea or theme of a passage; identify the writer's or speaker's purpose, intent, or point of view; distinguish among fact and opinion, assumptions, observations, and conclusions; and recognize literary and argumentative techniques.

In general, one characteristic of good writing is that it can have multiple interpretations. That is, different people can read a passage and interpret it in different ways. Good fiction writing has a **theme**—an underlying thought or idea about people or society. Good non-fiction writing has a **main idea**—the main point that the author is trying to get across. Writers usually have an intent or purpose in writing such as providing entertainment; commenting on an important social issue; proposing their idea about how to improve the world; or revealing their belief about love, truth, or beauty. Writers may include opinions, assumptions, observations, and conclusions in their writing, and in order to understand and evaluate the writer's ideas, it is important to distinguish those ideas from facts. Finally, fiction writers can employ literary techniques, and non-fiction writers can employ argumentative techniques. For example, fiction writers can employ theme, imagery, foreshadowing, symbols, tone, and point of view. Non-fiction writers can use organizational patterns such as compare/contrast and order of importance to make their cases. Look at these example analysis items:

---

9. One of the text's main themes is

   A. the problems caused by the Industrial Revolution in England.
   B. the social class system in England.
   C. the problem of trying to find true love.
   D. the abuses of the legal system in England.

---

Option B is correct. Pip's benefactor wants Pip to become a gentleman—that is, change social classes, which brings up topics such as the differences between social classes and social mobility (the ability of people to move upward socially). The other options (A, C, and D) are themes found in Charles Dickens' work, but not in this passage, so they are incorrect.

---

10. The best way to describe Mr. Jaggers' tone is

   A. relaxed and happy.
   B. serious and matter-of-fact.
   C. angry and jealous.
   D. bored and indifferent.

---

Option B is correct. Mr. Jaggers' words and gestures show that he takes this matter seriously, and his enumeration of the conditions of Pip's great expectations are expressed in a direct, matter-of-fact way. Therefore, the other options (A, C, and D) are incorrect.

11. What is the effect on the reader of these words of Pip's: "My dream was out; my wild fancy was surpassed by sober reality; Miss Havisham was going to make my fortune on a grand scale" (lines 8–9)?

    **A.** Humor—because Pip really does not understand what is happening to him, while the reader does

    **B.** Irony—because Pip is calling a moment of great happiness "sober reality"

    **C.** Disbelief—because the reader knows that Miss Havisham is really not the benefactor

    **D.** Mistrust—because Mr. Jaggers' offer seems too good to be true

Option B is correct. While this is a moment of great happiness for Pip, he considers it sober reality. Option A is incorrect because Pip fully understands Mr. Jaggers' offer, even though it is not yet clear whether Miss Havisham or some other person is the benefactor. Option C is incorrect because nothing in the passage indicates whether Pip's supposition is correct or not. Option D may be true—the benefactor's offer to Pip is hidden by so much secrecy that it may not be as good as it seems, but this is not signaled by the quotation.

# 4. Synthesis and Generalization

## a. Synthesis

**Synthesis** involves bringing together different pieces of information and analyzing it in some way. Synthesis items may ask you to compare and contrast or synthesize information from multiple sources or points of view.

12. What difference between Pip and Mr. Jaggers is <u>most strongly</u> implied in the passage?

    **A.** Pip is a member of a lower social class than Mr. Jaggers.

    **B.** Pip has great expectations for the future, and Mr. Jaggers does not.

    **C.** Pip is wealthier than Mr. Jaggers because of his great expectations.

    **D.** Pip needs to follow the benefactor's instructions, but Mr. Jaggers does not.

This is an example of an item that asks you to compare and contrast. Option A is correct. The text indicates that Pip is a poor orphan, while Mr. Jaggers is an attorney. Option B is incorrect because the passage gives no information about Mr. Jaggers' expectations for the future. Option C is incorrect because the text gives no information about Mr. Jaggers' or Pip's relative wealth. Option D is incorrect because both Mr. Jaggers and Pip need to follow the benefactor's instructions: Pip in order to get his new wealth, and Mr. Jaggers in order to follow the instructions of his client.

13. Which statement best expresses the role of Mr. Jaggers with regard to Pip and the unknown benefactor?

    **A.** Mr. Jaggers urged the benefactor to help Pip.

    **B.** Mr. Jaggers is opposed to the benefactor helping Pip.

    **C.** Mr. Jaggers believes that Pip should not accept the benefactor's help or instructions.

    **D.** Mr. Jaggers is the intermediary between Pip and the benefactor.

This item asks you to synthesize information from multiple points of view. Option D is correct. Mr. Jagger's role seems to be a bridge between the unknown benefactor and Pip. Options A and B are not supported by information in the passage. Option C is contradicted by the passage. Mr. Jaggers believes that Pip should accept the benefactor's condition that he continue to be called Pip, for example.

## b. Generalization

Generalizing involves using specific facts or details to make broader conclusions, or **generalizations.** Items may ask you to decide whether a generalization is justified, to identify supporting details for a generalization, or to use specific facts or details from the passage to make a generalization. Other generalization items may ask you to use specific facts in the passage to make predictions about what will happen later in the passage.

14. Which of the following is the <u>most logical</u> reason Mr. Jaggers refers to the main character as Mr. Pip throughout the passage?

    A.    He wants to show his dislike of Pip because he is from a poor family.
    B.    He wants to convince Pip to accept the benefactor's offer of assistance.
    C.    He believes that Pip is unworthy of the benefactor's assistance.
    D.    He wants to emphasize that Pip is to become a gentleman.

Option D is correct because using a title such as *Mr.* indicates that Mr. Jaggers, a lawyer, wants Pip to begin to consider himself a gentleman and his social equal. Option A is incorrect because using a title such as *Mr.* shows respect, not disdain. Option B is incorrect because calling Pip by this title is not a way to convince him to accept the benefactor's offer. Option C is not supported by the details in the passage.

15. Which of the following is the primary reason for Mr. Jaggers' meeting with Pip?

    A.    To teach Pip become a gentleman
    B.    To tell Pip that he is not to change his name
    C.    To inform Pip about sudden and unexpected news
    D.    To warn Pip not to violate the rules set by his benefactor

Option C is correct. Mr. Jaggers is meeting with Pip because his client, the secret benefactor, engaged him to tell Pip of the news. Option A is incorrect, because the benefactor wants Pip to become a gentleman, but Mr. Jaggers is the intermediary between the benefactor and Pip, not Pip's teacher. Options B and D are incorrect because they are merely details of the conversation, not the primary purpose of the meeting.

# C. Practice

## 1. Items

*Items 1 through 5 refer to the passage below.*

**This excerpt from a traditional Chinese story tells how a young woman, Li-niang, finds the love of her life.**

A long time ago in Old China, a beautiful girl named Li-niang lived with her father in a beautiful city full of old temples, ancient shrines, well-tended gardens, and inviting tea pavilions, all around a beautiful lake.

(5) Li-niang means "beautiful woman" in Chinese. Her family name, Hua, means "flower," and Li-niang was as beautiful as a flower. She was thin and graceful, and she had long, silky black hair that she wore in braids wrapped tightly atop her head like a crown. Her cheeks and lips were as pink and fresh as a peony blossom on a dewy summer morning. Like all Chinese girls, she wore brightly colored silk gowns. Her favorite gowns were red, which made her pink cheeks and lips look even brighter and more beautiful.

(10) Li-niang always dreamed about meeting the man she would marry one day, but her father didn't want her to get married. Li-niang's father was an important official in the imperial government, and he was very old-fashioned.

Whenever Li-niang talked about getting married, her father would say, "Li-niang, remember, your mother died many years ago. A daughter's first duty is to her family. Without you, I will be all alone in (15) this big house." That made Li-niang very sad. She loved her father very much and wanted to please him, but she also wanted to find a love of her own.

At this time, girls from important Chinese families did not go out of the house much, even to go to school. Tutors came to their homes to teach them. So Li-niang's only friend was her maid, Lin. Lin was just a year younger than Li-niang. One day in early summer, Li-niang and Lin were in her room. (20) Suddenly, Li-niang saw a boy out the window. He was the most handsome boy she'd ever seen! He was tall and thin. His eyes were clear and dark, and he had a friendly smile. He was riding a proud white horse and wearing the clothes of a student. As he rode by, he held a willow branch in his hand.

"Look at the boy on the horse!" said Li-niang, blushing. "He's so handsome. And he looks so kind. That's what I want my future husband to look like! And look at his clothes! He's a student! Maybe he'll (25) be an imperial official some day! He's just the kind of boy that Father might like. What if I never see him again?"

"Quick!" said Lin. "Let's go outside. Maybe we can talk to him. Hurry!"

Li-niang and Lin flew downstairs as fast as they could. When they got to the front door, they hurriedly slid their feet into their shoes, threw open the door, and rushed outside. But the boy was nowhere (30) to be seen. Lin ran down the street to look for the boy, but soon came back saying that the boy was nowhere to be found. His only trace was the willow branch, which he had dropped near the front door. A single tear slipped down Li-niang's face.

"Oh, no," said Li-niang, now breaking into tears. "He's gone forever. I'll never meet a nice boy and get married."

Excerpt from *The Peony Pavilion,* by Tang Xianzu, as retold by Tim Collins. Copyright © 2014 by Multimodal Learning, LLC. Used with permission.

1. What is the meaning of the braids wrapped tightly around Li-niang's head (line 6)?

   A. She is very beautiful.
   B. Her hair is not attractive when worn long.
   C. She lacks freedom.
   D. She is regal, like a princess.

2. How did Li-niang feel when she saw the boy out her bedroom window?

   A. Curious
   B. Fearful
   C. Shy
   D. Excited

3. What is the significance of the willow branch dropped at Li-niang's door (line 31)?

   A. The boy is probably going to return to the town and meet Li-niang.
   B. The boy is not very interested in getting married.
   C. Li-niang's dream of marrying a nice boy will be crushed.
   D. Li-niang will soon meet another nice boy.

4. What will the father most likely do when he finds out that Li-niang has seen the boy?

   A. Help her find the boy
   B. Encourage her to find another boy from her town
   C. Tell her that soon she will meet another boy
   D. Forbid her to think or talk about the boy

5. What is the meaning of the word "flew" (line 28), as used in the text?

   A. Jumped out the window
   B. Slid down the bannister
   C. Climbed down a rope
   D. Ran down the stairs as quickly as possible

*Items 6 through 10 refer to the poem below.*

**Written by a young African American poet from Ohio, this poem explores how our dreams can fade as time goes by.**

### Dreams

What dreams we have and how they fly
Like rosy clouds across the sky;
Of wealth, of fame, of sure success,
Of love that comes to cheer and bless;
(5)    And how they wither, how they fade,
The waning wealth, the jilting jade—
The fame that for a moment gleams,
Then flies forever,—dreams, ah—dreams!

O burning doubt and long regret,
(10)   O tears with which our eyes are wet,
Heart-throbs, heart-aches, the glut of pain,
The somber cloud, the bitter rain,
You were not of those dreams—ah! well,
Your full fruition who can tell?
(15)   Wealth, fame, and love, ah! love that beams
Upon our souls, all dreams—ah! dreams.

"Dreams," by Paul Laurance Dunbar

6. What is being described in lines 1–4?

   A. The speaker's original optimistic dreams
   B. The speaker's inability to have dreams
   C. The disillusionments that caused his dream to fade away
   D. The speaker's fearful dreams that have floated away, like clouds in the sky

7. What does the speaker mean at the end of the poem when he says, "Wealth, fame, and love, ah! love that beams/Upon our souls, all dreams—ah! dreams" (lines 15–16)?

   A. We should hope for many things in life.
   B. All the things we hope for are fruitless dreams.
   C. We should try to find dreams we can achieve.
   D. We should stop dreaming completely.

8. Which of the following is the closest synonym for "waning" (line 6)?

   A. Growing
   B. Replacing
   C. Declining
   D. Resplendent

9. One of the poem's main themes is

   A. death will overtake all of us eventually.
   B. there is no point in having dreams.
   C. our dreams drift away and escape us over time.
   D. life can be unfair.

10. Overall, the poem's tone can be described as

   A. melancholic and somewhat cynical.
   B. optimistic and hopeful.
   C. disinterested and unengaged.
   D. angry and resentful.

*Items 11 through 15 refer to the passage below.*

**The passage below explores the benefits of walking for our brains.**

## Tired of Thinking? Go for a Walk!

Scientists have recently documented the benefits of walking on mental processes. People have long thought that walking can help us clear our minds, focus our thinking, and increase our creativity. Now scientists at two major universities report that their studies show that walking has important mental benefits.

(5)    First, a series of studies conducted at Stanford University show that walking can improve memory and creativity. The researchers themselves had observed that going for walks helped them, as well as their students, clear their minds and focus their thinking, so they decided to put their observations to the test. The researchers gave a series of memory and creativity tasks to volunteer subjects. Some of the volunteers had gone for walks, but others had not. According to the researchers, the subjects who had

(10)   gone for walks performed better on both memory tasks and creativity tasks than the subjects who had not gone on walks.

Another set of experiments, conducted at the University of South Carolina, focused on the benefits of where we walk. They measured memory of people who had gone for walks on city streets or in a park. They found that people who had walked in a park performed better on a memory test than people

(15)   who had walked on city streets. These studies back up other studies that show that contact with nature has important benefits for our mental and physical health.

Scientists say that the study results can be explained from physiological data. Walking raises our heart rates, which increases blood flow to the brain. The increased flow of blood and oxygen to the brain can stimulate memory and fresh thinking. They also say that regular walking helps the brain cre-

(20)   ate new connections between brain cells, which benefits memory and staves off some the changes to the brain that occur with age. Scientists caution that while these changes cannot be avoided altogether, they are delayed or reduced in people who walk regularly.

So if you're tired of studying or need a break, look no further than a walk in your nearest local park!

11. The Stanford scientists tested the insights about the benefits of walking by

   A. observing that their own memory and creativity increased after going for walks.

   B. going on walks with their students and seeing the benefits on memory and creativity.

   C. creating a scientific test to assess the effects of walking on memory and creativity.

   D. taking some tests after going on walks with their students.

12. The results of the studies conducted by Stanford and University of South Carolina scientists are presented primarily in which two paragraphs?

   A. Paragraphs 1 and 2

   B. Paragraphs 2 and 3

   C. Paragraphs 3 and 4

   D. Paragraphs 4 and 5

13. Which of the following best summarizes the general point the writer makes in Paragraph 4 (lines 17–22)?

   A. The researchers' studies were not necessary because the benefits of walking were already well understood.

   B. Walking might prevent serious conditions such as Alzheimer's disease.

   C. Walking benefits the brain by increasing its supply of oxygen.

   D. Other kinds of scientific data provide support and explanation for the findings of the researchers.

14. What is the meaning of "staves off" (line 20), as used in the passage?

   A. Slows down

   B. Stops

   C. Accelerates

   D. Steadies

15. Why does the last paragraph (line 23) consist of a single sentence?

   A. The writer made a mistake because a paragraph should always have several sentences.

   B. The sentence does not really belong to the essay, so it is in a separate paragraph.

   C. The sentence offers another important supporting idea so should be in a separate paragraph.

   D. The writer wanted to increase the dramatic effect of this final idea.

*Items 16 through 20 refer to the excerpt from a play below.*

**In Nazi-occupied Greece, most Jews have been rounded up and sent to concentration camps. Henry and his family are attempting to use false identity papers to deceive the occupiers.**

     *In a police station, German and Greek police are questioning Henry about his identity papers as the rest of the family watches.*

     HENRY: My union card.

     GREEK POLICEMAN *(handing it to CLERK):* His union card.

(5)     GERMAN OFFICER: This is not an identity card.

     HENRY: My identity card was stolen.

     GERMAN OFFICER: So you say. Union card...union men were Communist dogs.

     HENRY: Yes, but we were forced to join the union.

     GERMAN OFFICER: Let me see your hands.

(10)     *(HENRY extends his hands, trying to keep them from trembling.)*

     GERMAN OFFICER: Awfully clean, aren't they?

     HENRY: I haven't had work for some time.

     GERMAN OFFICER: So you say... *(looking at ANDY huddling beside ALLEGRA)* Is that your son?

     HENRY: Yes, but he...

(15)     GERMAN OFFICER: I will speak with him.

     HENRY: There's no need to—

     GERMAN OFFICER: I will determine what is necessary. Sit.

     *HENRY reluctantly sits.*

     GERMAN OFFICER: *(beckoning ANDY with a smile)* Come here...Come...You only need tell me

(20) the truth. You are an honest boy, are you not?

     *ANDY nods his head, comes forward, terrified.*

16. What will <u>most likely</u> happen to Henry and his family if the police discover the truth about them?

    A.  They will get new identity papers.
    B.  They will suffer a terrible fate.
    C.  They will be released by the police.
    D.  They will be allowed to move to another country.

17. Which of the following is <u>most likely</u> the reason Henry does not have an identity card?

    A.  He destroyed his identity card because it would reveal that he is Jewish.
    B.  His identity card was stolen.
    C.  He never had an identity card in the first place.
    D.  He is secretly a member of the Communist Party.

18. Why does the German officer ask, in reference to Henry's hands, "Awfully clean, aren't they?"

    A.  He thinks that Henry takes very good care of himself.
    B.  He thinks that Henry is lying about the union card.
    C.  He thinks that Henry is a member of the Communist Party.
    D.  He is changing the subject to distract Henry and catch him in a lie.

19. Why does the German officer want to speak to Henry's son?

    A.  He hopes that the child's words will reveal the truth.
    B.  He enjoys talking to children.
    C.  He thinks that children are more reliable than adults.
    D.  He thinks that children are better liars than adults.

20. Which of the following phrases best describes the mood of the passage?

    A.  Gloomy and pessimistic
    B.  Dark and fearful
    C.  Sad and mournful
    D.  Quiet and peaceful

# 2. Answer Explanations

1. **D. She is regal, like a princess. (Analysis/Prose Fiction)** Option D is correct because the passage says that the braids are "like a crown" (line 6). The closest answer to this is Option D. Option A is incorrect because braids do not have anything to do with beauty. Option B is contradicted by the passage, which says that her hair was long and silky (line 5). Option C is not supported by details in the passage. Though she lacks freedom, this has nothing to do with her hair.

2. **D. Excited (Comprehension/Prose Fiction)** Option D is correct because after she sees him, she runs out the door and tries to meet him. She was more than simply curious, so Option A is incorrect. Running out the door is not the reaction of a person who is fearful or shy about meeting another person, so Options B and C are incorrect.

3. **A. The boy is probably going to return to the town and meet Li-niang. (Analysis/Prose Fiction)** Option A is correct because the boy was holding the branch as he rode by Li-niang's house. Since he dropped it near her door, it most likely foreshadows that he will return one day. For this reason, the other options (B, C, and D) are incorrect.

4. **D. Forbid her to think or talk about the boy (Synthesis and Generalization/Prose Fiction)** Option D is correct because the father has already made it very clear that he does not want his daughter to marry. Therefore, the other options (A, B, and C) are incorrect.

5. **D. Ran down the stairs as quickly as possible (Inference and Interpretation/Prose Fiction)** This is an example of figurative language, and it means that they hurried as fast as they could. Therefore, Option D is correct. Option A is too close to the literal meaning of the word and does not make sense, so it is incorrect. Option B is not supported by the passage. Option C does not make sense.

6. **A. The speaker's original optimistic dreams (Comprehension/Poetry)** Option A is correct because the phrase "rosy clouds," (line 2) indicates that these are the optimistic dreams the speaker started with. Option D is incorrect because these dreams were optimistic, not fearful. Option B is contradicted by the lines; the speaker seems to have many dreams. Option C summarizes the speaker's attitude toward dreams later in the poem.

7. **B. All the things we hope for are fruitless dreams. (Comprehension/Poetry)** Option B is correct, because the preceding lines are all about the speaker's dreams being dashed. Therefore, all of his dreams were fruitless. For this reason, Option A is incorrect. Options C and D are not supported by the poem. While the speaker believes that dreams are fruitless, he never indicates that we should change our dreams or stop dreaming.

8. **C. Declining (Comprehension/Poetry)** Option C is correct because the poem is about how our dreams are destroyed over time. Of the four options, only Option C expresses this meaning. For this reason, Options A and D are incorrect. Wealth would not be growing (Option A) or resplendent (Option D), since resplendent means "with glowing splendor." Option B does not make sense.

9. **C. our dreams drift away and escape us over time. (Analysis/Poetry)** The speaker says in line 14 that our dreams are all fruitless. This option is closest in meaning to that belief. The poem is not about death, so Option A is incorrect. The speaker only says that dreams are fruitless, so Option B is incorrect. While Option D may be true, the speaker seems to believe that everyone's dreams are fruitless.

10. **A. melancholic and somewhat cynical. (Analysis/Poetry)** Option A is correct because the speaker seems sad about his dashed dreams and somewhat cynical, since he has come to the conclusion that all dreams are fruitless. For this reason, Option B is incorrect. Options C and D cannot be concluded from the details in the poem.

11. **C. creating a scientific test to assess the effects of walking on memory and creativity. (Comprehension/ Informational Texts)** Option C is correct because the scientists created a carefully constructed study to test their hypothesis about the mental benefits of walking. Options A and B are how the scientists developed the hypothesis they tested in their study. Option D is incorrect because the scientists tested their hypothesis on volunteer subjects, not on themselves.

12. **B. Paragraphs 2 and 3 (Comprehension/Informational Texts)** The results of the Stanford study are presented in Paragraph 2, and the results of the University of South Carolina studies are presented in Paragraph 3, so Option B is correct. The other options (A, C, and D) are incorrect.

13. **D. Other kinds of scientific data provide support and explanation for the findings of the researchers. (Analysis/Informational Texts)** This main idea is stated in the first sentence of the paragraph (line 17), so Option D is correct. Therefore, Option A is incorrect. Option B is an inference that can be drawn from the information in the paragraph, but it is not the main idea of the paragraph so it is incorrect. Option C is a detail in the paragraph that supports the main idea, so it is incorrect.

14. **A. Slows down (Comprehension/Informational Texts)** Option A is correct because the following sentence makes clear that "while these changes cannot be avoided altogether, they are delayed or reduced." The answer option closest to this meaning is Option A. For this reason, Option B is incorrect. Options C and D are contradicted by the information in the paragraph, so they are incorrect.

15. **D. The writer wanted to increase the dramatic effect of this final idea. (Analysis/Informational Texts)** Option D is correct because putting this final thought in a paragraph of its own draws readers' attention. For this reason, Option A is incorrect. Option B is incorrect because the final sentence relates back directly to the title of the passage, "Tired of Thinking? Go for a Walk!" so it belongs in the passage. The final paragraph is a kind of conclusion, not an additional supporting idea, so Option C is incorrect.

16. **B. They will suffer a terrible fate. (Inference and Interpretation/Drama)** Option B is correct because under Nazi rule, Jews were killed or sent to concentration camps. Since most Jews in occupied Greece had already been deported, the family might simply be killed for lying or sent to one of the camps. For this reason, the other options (A, C, and D) are incorrect.

17. **A. He destroyed his identity card because it would reveal that he is Jewish. (Inference and Interpretation/ Drama)** Option A is correct. The family does not want to reveal their true identities, so they have hidden or destroyed their old papers so that they cannot be used against them. Option B is incorrect because it is the lie Henry tells in order to cover up not wanting to show his real identity card. Option C does not make sense. If this were the case, he would simply say so. In addition, the officer's demeanor implies that everyone is supposed to have an identity card. Option D is contradicted by the details in the passage. He does not want to identify himself because he is Jewish, not because he is a Communist.

18. **B. He thinks that Henry is lying about the union card. (Inference and Interpretation/Drama)** Option B is correct. The police officer believes that a union worker would have rough or dirty hands from manual work, and Henry's clean hands are a sign that the union card is not really his. For this reason, Option A is incorrect. Henry already answered the officer's question about being a member of the Communist Party, so Option C is incorrect. Option D is not supported by the details in the passage.

19. **A. He hopes that the child's words will reveal the truth. (Inference and Interpretation/Drama)** Option A is correct because he hopes that the child may not be able to lie as well as Henry or will reveal a clue to the truth by mistake. For this reason, Option B is incorrect. Option C is not supported by the details in the passage. Though the child may lie, he may reveal the truth by mistake. Option D does not make sense. If the officer thinks that children are better liars than adults, he would not bother talking to the child.

20. **B. Dark and fearful (Analysis/Drama)** Option B is correct because the badgering questions of the police officer, Henry's trembling hands, and the child's terror at having to answer the police officer's questions all make the mood of the passage dark and fearful. For this reason, Option D is incorrect. Option A is not strong enough to capture the mood of the passage. The people are afraid, not sad, so Option C is incorrect.

HiSET Language Arts: Writing tests your ability to use clear and effective **Standard Written English,** or SWE. SWE is the kind of English that is used in many business, professional, and community settings. News articles, business emails, community newsletters, and letters from government offices are most likely written in SWE. You probably receive writings in SWE from your workplace, businesses, community organizations, your child's teachers, religious institutions, and the government. SWE is different from the way we talk or write in everyday situations.

The Language Arts: Writing section contains two parts:

- Part 1 has 50 multiple-choice items that assess your ability to recognize Standard Written English. In this part of the test, you have 75 minutes to show your knowledge of SWE by editing and revising written texts. Part 1 is covered in this chapter.
- Part 2 has one essay item that assesses your ability to write a short essay in SWE on a topic of general interest. Part 2 is covered in Chapter V.

## A. Test Format

Part 1 of the HiSET Language Arts: Writing test asks you to revise text to improve it or to fix errors. The kinds of texts include letters, essays, news articles, personal accounts, and reports. The test items are embedded into the texts. Underlining shows the parts of the text that may need revision. Items suggest possible ways to correct or improve the writing.

First, you will see the entire text. On the actual exam, the initial text will have paragraph numbers above each paragraph. Some paragraphs of the text will have sentence numbers. You will refer to these numbers later when you answer the items about the passage.

TIP: Try to read the passage text as quickly as you can so you can go on to the items.

Residents of the Buena Park neighborhood will be glad to know that three new businesses will make our neighborhood even more convenient. The three new businesses, Sam's 24/7 Deli, The Haircuttery, and The Mobile Phone Source, are open and ready for customers.

Sam's 24/7 Deli is located on the corner of Green Street and Broadway Avenue, near the subway station and two bus stops. Owned by Sam Gouletas, the location offers all the usual convenience store items. For customers on the go, Sam's has a Grab-and-Go Breakfast Buffet with a variety of hot and cold breakfast items, such as yogurt, muffins, breakfast sandwiches, breakfast tacos, and wraps. As well as several kinds of gourmet coffee and tea. Sam's 24/7 Deli is true to its name. "We never close," says Sam. "You're welcome any time of the day or knight for a beverage, a snack, groceries, or any of the hundreds of other items we carry."

Just down the block, The Haircuttery opened a little over a month ago. The four stylists in the shop can give you a quick trim or the latest hairstyle. Men and boys' haircuts are always just $6. Women's haircuts start at $7. Prices for other services are just as low. Soon women will be able to get their nails done right next door when their new nail salon opens. Owner Madge Miner, who is a very nice person, says that all services will be half-price during the salon's grand opening the first week of July.

Finally, The Mobile Phone Source just opened just across the street from Martino's Supermarket. At this handy location, you can pay your phone bill or get a new or replacement phone for most major carriers. You can also check out the latest accessories for your phone, such as covers, screen protectors, and cases.

These new businesses and services are three more reasons our neighborhood is a great place to live. Be sure to patronize these and other local shops and services.

After you read the entire text, you will move to a spread-out version with the text on the left and the items on the right. Items can refer to a specific sentence, a number of sentences, or an entire paragraph. The HiSET uses this numbering system to identify items and parts of the passage:

- The numbers above the paragraphs are paragraph numbers.
- The numbers below underlined sections of the text refer to the corresponding item numbers. A word, a phrase, a whole sentence, or parts of sentences can be underlined. In some items, several individual words, phrases, or sentences can be underlined.
- Numbers in front of sentences are sentence numbers. Some items will refer to sentence numbers.
- Numbers inside of boxes show that the item with that number refers to the whole paragraph. Boxed numbers can appear at the beginning or end of a paragraph.

Study the following example and items:

## [1]

Residents of the Buena Park neighborhood will be glad to know that three new businesses will make our neighborhood even more convenient. The three new businesses, Sam's 24/7 Deli, The Haircuttery, and The Mobile Phone Source, <u>are</u> open and ready
1
for customers.

## [2]

[1] Sam's 24/7 Deli is located on the corner of Green Street and Broadway Avenue, near the subway station and two bus stops. [2] Owned by Sam Gouletas, the location offers all the usual

1. **A.** (No change)
   **B.** is
   **C.** was
   **D.** were

convenience store items. [3] For customers on the go, Sam's has a Grab-and-Go Breakfast Buffet with a variety of hot and cold breakfast items, such as yogurt, muffins, breakfast sandwiches, breakfast tacos, and <u>wraps. [4] As well as several kinds of</u>
<sub>2</sub>
<u>gourmet coffee and tea</u>. [5] Sam's 24/7 Deli is true to
<sub>2</sub>
its name. [6] "We never close," says Sam. [7] "<u>You're</u>
<sub>3</sub>
welcome any time of the day or <u>knight</u> for a <u>beverage</u>,
<sub>3</sub>       <sub>3</sub>
a snack, groceries, or any of the hundreds of other items we carry." [4]

2. **A.** (No change)
  **B.** wraps, as well as several kinds of gourmet coffee and tea
  **C.** wraps; several kinds of gourmet coffee and tea
  **D.** wraps, several kinds of gourmet coffee, tea

3. Which of these words, if any, is misspelled?

  **A.** (None)
  **B.** You're
  **C.** knight
  **D.** beverage

4. Which of these sentences, if any, should begin a new paragraph?

  **A.** (There should be no new paragraph.)
  **B.** Sentence 5
  **C.** Sentence 6
  **D.** Sentence 7

TIP: A boxed number in the passage indicates that the item with that number refers to the whole paragraph. For example, [4] in this passage shows that Item [4] refers to paragraph 2. A boxed number can come at the beginning of a paragraph or at the end.

In this book, all items, whether in examples, exercises, or practice tests, are accompanied by complete answer explanations.

1. **A. No change (Subject-Verb Agreement)** Option A is correct because the plural subject *businesses* requires a plural verb, *are.* For this reason, Option B, which agrees with *Source,* the last word of a phrase following the subject, is incorrect. Options C and D are incorrect because there is no reason to change the verb to the past tense. In addition. Option C is not possible because it is the singular form of the verb, and a plural verb form is required.

2. **B. wraps, as well as several kinds of gourmet coffee and tea (Commas)** Option B is correct because a comma is needed to join the fragment to the preceding sentence. For this reason, Options A and C are incorrect. Option D is incorrect because there is no reason to remove *as well as* and to remove *and* after *coffee* and insert a comma.

3. **C. knight (Spelling)** Option C is correct because the word *night* ("evening") is needed here, not its homonym *knight* ("soldier from the middle ages"). For this reason, the other options, A, B, and D, are all incorrect.

4. **A. (There should be no new paragraph.) (Paragraph Structure)** Option A is correct because this paragraph is all about one topic, Sam's 24/7 Deli, so a new paragraph is not necessary. For this reason, the other options (B, C, and D) are incorrect.

# B. Test Content and Types of Items

Test items may ask you to revise the text to improve the organization, use appropriate style, use logical transitions, improve word choice, or fix sentence structure, usage, and mechanics. **Organization** refers to the overall ordering of information in the text, or the ordering of information in one part of the text, such as a paragraph. Organization also includes relevance—whether the information relates to the main idea of the text. **Appropriate style** refers to the way the text is written—formal or casual, businesslike or friendly, serious or funny. Each of these styles may be appropriate in some situations and inappropriate in others. **Logical transitions** refer to words that show relationships among ideas in the text, such as *first, second, third* (order); *therefore, so, because* (cause-effect); *in addition, also* (adding an idea); *but, however* (contrast); and *for instance, for example* (giving examples). **Word choice** refers to using the best, most descriptive vocabulary to express your ideas. **Sentence structure** refers to whether your sentences follow the grammar rules of SWE. **Usage** refers to whether words and phrases are used correctly in sentences. **Mechanics** refers to rules in SWE about details such as capital letters and punctuation (for example, periods and commas).

# C. Types of Items: A Detailed Look

Language Arts: Writing, Part 1 test items fall into three groups:

- **Organization—20 percent or about 10 items** These items ask you to identify logical or effective opening, transitional, and final sentences; decide whether information is relevant to the text; decide whether the paragraph structure is logical; and evaluate or choose logical transitions. These items may ask you to correct sentences, add sentences, delete sentences, combine paragraphs, or divide paragraphs.

- **Language Facility—25 percent or about 13 items** These items ask you to identify correct sentence structure. Items may ask you to correct sentences or join two sentences into a single sentence.
- **Writing Conventions—55 percent or about 28 items** These items ask you to use correct mechanics (punctuation, spelling, capitalization), use the correct forms of verbs and other words, and use other details of SWE.

In this section, we will review the conventions of Standard Written English used to answer all the types of items typically assessed on Part 1 of the Language Arts: Writing test.

# 1. Organization

When writing, it's important to have plenty of good ideas and detail. It's also important to present these ideas and details in an order that is logical and easy to understand. Organization items assess all of these areas. Some organization items ask you to evaluate whether information in the text is relevant. Some items ask whether, and where, a sentence with an additional detail can be added to the text. Other organization items ask you to evaluate the overall organization of a text or specific parts of a text, such as the order of sentences in a paragraph. These items can also ask you to decide if a paragraph needs a topic sentence or if a text needs a more effective introduction or conclusion. Other items ask whether combining paragraphs or dividing paragraphs will improve the organization of the text.

## a. Relevance Items

In an effective text, all of the information is related to the main idea. Information in the text may be in the wrong paragraph or may not belong in the essay at all. Try these example items:

[3]

Just down the block, The Haircuttery opened a little over a month ago. The four stylists in the shop can give you a quick trim or the latest hairstyle. Men and boys' haircuts are always just $6. Women's haircuts start at $7. Prices for other services are just as low. <u>Soon women will be able to get their nails done right next door</u>
<u>5</u>
<u>when a new nail salon opens.</u> Owner Madge Miner, <u>who is a very nice person</u>, says that all services will be
<u>5</u>                                                                        <u>6</u>
half-price during the salon's grand opening the first week of July.

---

5. Which of the following would be the best choice for this sentence?
   - **A.** (No change)
   - **B.** Move the sentence so that it comes before the preceding sentence.
   - **C.** Move the sentence to become the first sentence of the paragraph.
   - **D.** Omit the sentence

---

Option D is correct. This sentence is not related to the main idea of the paragraph, which is a description of services available at The Haircuttery. In addition, the text is about businesses that opened recently, not businesses that may open in the future. For these reasons, the new nail salon is not a relevant detail, so it should be omitted. Since this irrelevant detail should not be in the text at all, Options A, B, and C are all incorrect.

6. Which of the following facts would be the <u>most</u> relevant to include here?

   **A.** (No change)
   **B.** who retired from her old job last year
   **C.** who studied hair care in Paris and Rome
   **D.** who is an expert in make-up

Option C is correct because this detail, which is about Madge's training in hair care, is relevant to a passage about a hair salon. Options A, B, and D may be true, but are not relevant to the main idea of the paragraph.

# b. Paragraph Structure Items

Paragraph structure items ask you to evaluate whether the essay follows a logical paragraph structure. In general, each paragraph should be about a single main idea. In the example text, each paragraph is about one of the new businesses in the neighborhood.

Good texts often have an introductory paragraph, body paragraphs, and a concluding paragraph. An **introductory paragraph** is organized from general to specific. It introduces the topic of the text and gives an overview of the paragraphs to follow. In the example text, the first paragraph gives a general overview of the topic in the first sentence. The second sentence, called the **thesis statement,** gives an indication of the main idea of each body paragraph that follows: "The three new businesses, Sam's 24/7 Deli, The Haircuttery, and The Mobile Phone Source, are open and ready for customers."

Each of the paragraphs that follow the introduction is called a body paragraph. **Body paragraphs** give specific detail. Each body paragraph is organized from general to specific. First, a **topic sentence** gives the main idea of the paragraph. Then each sentence that follows gives specific detail about the topic sentence. For example, in Paragraph 2, the first sentence gives a general introduction to the first business: "Sam's 24/7 Deli is located on the corner of Green Street and Broadway Avenue, near the subway station and two bus stops." The sentences that follow give detail on the kinds of things customers can buy at the store.

Good texts usually have a **concluding paragraph** that sums up the ideas in the text. Concluding paragraphs are organized from specific to general. In the sample text, Paragraph 5 is the concluding paragraph. The first sentence sums up information on the three new businesses. The second, and final, sentence is more general, and encourages residents to use these new businesses.

Texts that follow this pattern of introduction-body-conclusion will frequently have a total of three or five paragraphs.

**Three-Paragraph Text**
1. Introductory paragraph
2. Body paragraph
3. Concluding paragraph

**Five-Paragraph Text**
1. Introductory paragraph
2. Body paragraph A
3. Body paragraph B
4. Body paragraph C
5. Concluding paragraph

> TIP: Use your knowledge of three- and five-paragraph texts to answer items about paragraph structure. Items may ask you to evaluate and make corrections so that texts have appropriate introductions, thesis statements, body paragraphs, topic sentences, and conclusions.

Part 1 items may ask you to evaluate and improve the paragraph structure of a text by moving sentences, combining paragraphs, dividing paragraphs, or adding thesis statements or topic sentences. Look at the following example:

## NOTICE TO POOL USERS

### [1]

Hill Park Pool will close on June 1 for approximately 4 weeks to allow the installation of a new filtration system. During this time, park patrons can use a number of other nearby park district pools and beaches.

### [2]

1 [1] Wells Park, Germain Park, and Freedson Park are all located within 2 miles of Hill Park and offer similar daytime and evening hours and services to Hill Park. [2] The pool at Unity High School offers adult and lap swimming after work. [3] Finally, park district beaches all open on June 15. [4] Beaches at Green Street and Brown Avenue offer special areas for adult swimmers. [5] These beaches have lifeguards on duty from sunrise to sundown 7 days a week. [6] We hope that all swimmers will be able to find a pool or beach that meets their needs. [7] We will place notices at all of these locations when Hill Park pool reopens. 2

1. The writer is considering adding a sentence to the beginning of Paragraph 2 to improve the transition from Paragraph 1. Which of the following would be the best choice?
   A. (No change; the paragraph is best as written.)
   B. Several excellent pools are available for the use of people who usually swim at Hill Park.
   C. Four nearby pools and several beaches are available for Hill Park patrons.
   D. Our city has excellent recreation facilities.

Option C is correct. This item asks you to decide whether adding a new sentence will improve Paragraph 2. In fact, the paragraph lacks a topic sentence. The main idea of Paragraph 2 is that there are several places where park patrons can swim. The new sentence in Option C works as an effective topic sentence since it is a general introduction to the main idea of the paragraph. Therefore, Option A is incorrect. Option B is incorrect because it does not include beaches. Option D is too general to be the topic sentence of this paragraph. The paragraph is about beaches and pools Hill Park swimmers can use, not about recreation facilities in general.

2. Which of these sentences, if any, should begin a new paragraph?

   **A.** (There should be no new paragraph.)
   **B.** Sentence 5
   **C.** Sentence 6
   **D.** Sentence 7

Option C is correct. This item asks you to decide whether the text needs a separate concluding paragraph. In fact, the writer improperly joined the body and concluding paragraphs. Therefore, Option A is incorrect. You need to decide which sentence should begin the concluding paragraph. Option C is correct because Sentence 6 is where a summary of the main idea of the essay begins. Option B is incorrect because Sentence 5 is a detail that belongs to the body paragraph. Option D is incorrect because both Sentences 6 and 7 are the kinds of general summarizing sentences that belong in a concluding paragraph, so they should not be separated.

## c. Transitional Word and Phrase Items

Transitional words and phrases such as *first, therefore, so, however, in addition*, and *in contrast* show the relationship among the ideas in a text. Look at these examples:

He was hungry. *However*, he waited for his wife to get home before eating dinner.

There are many good places to find bargains on clothing. *For example*, thrift stores are a good choice.

Transitional words and phrases can show that an idea is a contrast, an example, a step in a process, or several other kinds of relationships. Look at the following chart:

| Transitional Words and Phrases | |
|---|---|
| **Transitional Words and Phrases** | **Function** |
| For instance,….; For example,…. | To give an example |
| First,….; Second,….; Third,….; Next,….; Then,….; Last,…. | To show order of past events or steps in a process. |
| In order to….; In order that….; Because….; Since…. | To show reason or purpose |
| More importantly,…. | To show importance |
| In addition,….; Moreover,….; Also,…. | To add a supporting idea |
| However,….; In contrast,…. | To indicate a contrast |

Part 1 Writing items may ask you to insert or change transitional words or phrases to make the relationships among the ideas clear. Try these examples:

Making the perfect cup of tea requires following a few simple steps. <u>First,</u> start with freshly drawn tap
<sub>1</sub>
water. Put the water in a tea kettle or pan and bring the water to a boil. While you are waiting for the water to boil, get out a teabag and put it in your cup or teapot. When the water is just beginning to boil, carefully pour the water over the teabag. <u>For example,</u> dip the teabag up and down a few times in the water and remove it
<sub>2</sub>
when the tea is ready. Then add milk or cream and sugar, if desired, and stir. Now you can sit back and enjoy a relaxing cup of tea.

---

1. **A.** (No change)
   **B.** For example,
   **C.** So
   **D.** However,

---

Option A is correct because the passage is about steps in a process. This is the first step, so the word *First* is an appropriate transitional word. Option B is incorrect because the sentence is the first step in a process, not an example. Option C is incorrect because *so* indicates that the idea is a consequence of another event. Option D is incorrect because *however* signals a contrasting idea, not the first step in a process, so it does not make sense here.

---

2. **A.** (No change)
   **B.** Next,
   **C.** Last
   **D.** Before that,

---

Option B is correct. This is the next step in the process, so *Next,* makes sense. Option A is incorrect because the sentence is a step in a process, not an example. Option C is incorrect because more steps follow this step. Option D is incorrect because it does not make sense to move the teabag up and down until after there is water is in the cup or teapot.

## d. Practice 1: Organization

### i. Items

**FOUNDERS' DAY PARADE
PARTICIPANT INSTRUCTIONS**

**[1]**

Founders' Day is our community's most important annual celebration. The parade and picnic are only a week away. We are glad that your club or group is participating in this year's parade. <u>We want to have an orderly parade. We</u> ask that groups follow a few simple instructions to prepare for the parade, the parade line up, and the parade itself.
<sub>1</sub>

**[2]**

[1] <u>First</u>, prepare for the weather. [2] Saturday we are
<sub>2</sub>
expected to set another record for heat, so wear light clothes appropriate to the weather. [3] Individuals sensitive to the sun should put on sunblock. [4] Groups and individuals should ensure that they have plenty of water on hand. [5] Line-up for the parade is on Industrial Avenue from 6 to 8:30 a.m. on Saturday morning. [6] A representative from each group should check in at the marshal's table by 7 a.m. [7] <u>In contrast,</u> all large floats,
<sub>3</sub>
cars, and other vehicles should be at your group's assigned position in the line-up by 7:00 a.m. [8] By 8:30 a.m., all parade participants should be in position in the line-up. [4]

1. **A.** (No change)
   **B.** In order to have an orderly parade, we
   **C.** In addition, we want to have an orderly parade, we
   **D.** However, we want to have an orderly parade, so

2. **A.** (No change)
   **B.** Moreover,
   **C.** However,
   **D.** In contrast,

3. **A.** (No change)
   **B.** In addition,
   **C.** Next,
   **D.** Last,

4. The writer is considering splitting Paragraph 2 into two paragraphs. The best place to begin a new paragraph would be with

   **A.** Sentence 3
   **B.** Sentence 4
   **C.** Sentence 5
   **D.** Sentence 6

**[3]**

|5| Be ready to start on time. The parade steps off at 9 a.m. sharp. We set this early start time in order to avoid marching in the midday sun. Parade marshals will signal when each group should start marching. The parade officially begins when your group reaches the intersection of Green Street and Industrial Avenue. The parade will continue south on Green Street to Founders' Park. At the entrance to the park, all floats, cars, and other vehicles should turn left onto Brown Avenue. Parade participants should continue marching into the park, where the Founders' Day Community Picnic will begin at 11 a.m. <u>If you drive to the park, you should use Parking Lot A.</u>
6

**[4]**

The Founders' Day Parade Committee hopes that by following these simple instructions participants and spectators can all enjoy this year's Founders' Day Parade and Picnic.

5. The writer is considering adding a sentence to the beginning of Paragraph 3 to improve the transition from Paragraph 2. Which of the following would be the best choice?

   A. (No change; the paragraph is best as written.)
   B. Following a few simple rules will make the parade run more smoothly.
   C. The parade begins at 9:00 and ends at 11:00.
   D. Pay attention to parade marshals during the parade.

6. Which of the following would be the best choice for this sentence?

   A. (No change; the paragraph is best as written.)
   B. Move the sentence so it comes before the preceding sentence.
   C. Move the sentence so it becomes the first sentence of the next paragraph (Paragraph 4).
   D. Omit the sentence.

## ii. Answer Explanations

1. **B. In order to have an orderly parade, we (Transitional Words and Phrases)** Option B is correct because *In order to* indicates purpose or reason. The purpose of the instructions is to have an orderly parade, so *In order to* shows the correct relationship among the ideas. Therefore, Option A is incorrect. Options C and D are incorrect because the transitional words *In addition* and *However* do not show the correct relationship among the ideas. The sentence does not introduce a new idea or a contrast.

2. **A. (No change) (Transitional Words and Phrases)** Option A is correct because preparing for the parade is the first thing people should do. Therefore, the sentence is correct as written. Option B is incorrect because this paragraph does not add an idea. Options C and D are incorrect because this paragraph does not introduce a contrast.

3. **B. In addition, (Transitional Words and Phrases)** Option B is correct because the sentence adds an additional idea. Option A is incorrect because the sentence adds an additional idea, not a contrast. Option C does not make sense because this sentence is not the next step in a process. The actions in this sentence and the sentence before both take place at the same time. This is not the last thing people do to line up, so Option D does not make sense.

4. **C. Sentence 5 (Paragraph structure)** Option C is correct because the writer incorrectly joined two paragraphs about different topics: preparing for the parade and lining up for the parade. The writer begins discussing the parade line-up in Sentence 5, so a new paragraph should start there. Options A and B do not make sense because these sentences are about preparing for the parade, not lining up. Option D does not make sense because Sentence 6 is a detail about lining up, and beginning a new paragraph with this sentence leaves Sentence 5 (also about lining up) in the paragraph about preparing for the parade.

5. **B. Following a few simple rules will make the parade run more smoothly. (Paragraph Structure)** Option B is correct. Paragraph 3 lacks a topic sentence. Since this paragraph is about rules for marching in the parade, Option B is the best choice. Option A is incorrect because Paragraph 3 lacks a topic sentence. Options C and D are too specific to be topic sentences for Paragraph 3.

6. **D. Omit the sentence. (Relevance)** Option D is correct because the paragraph and the article are about the parade, which ends at the park. This sentence is about parking, so it does not belong in the article. Therefore, Options A, B, and C are incorrect.

# 2. Language Facility

Language facility items test your ability to use sentence structure correctly. Items may ask you to evaluate and correct sentence structure. Other items may ask you to combine sentences correctly.

## a. Correcting Sentence Fragment Items

These items will ask you to evaluate whether sentences are complete or fragments. A **complete sentence** has a subject and a verb. In the following examples, the subjects are underlined <u>once</u> and the verbs <u>twice</u>:

> <u>Stephan</u> <u>is sleeping</u> on the sofa.
>
> Last Saturday, <u>Pat and Mary Jane</u> <u>bought</u> eggs, butter, and cheese at the farmers' market.

> TIP: A complete sentence has a subject and a verb. A dependent clause has a subject and a verb but cannot stand alone as a sentence.

Some items will ask you to decide whether a sentence is complete or a **fragment**—lacking a subject or a verb or expressing an incomplete thought. Look at the following fragment examples:

> Stephan off work today. (*Lacks a verb.*)
>
> Luckily, were on sale for half price. (*Lacks a subject.*)

TIP: Imperatives, or commands, do not have a subject but are still considered complete sentences. The subject "you" is implied.

Other items will ask you to distinguish between a complete sentence and a dependent clause. A **dependent clause** begins with a word such as *after, although, because, if, since, though, when*, and *until* and has a subject and a verb. However, a dependent clause cannot stand alone as a sentence because it doesn't express a complete thought. Look at the following example:

Although <u>apples</u> <u>were</u> very cheap. (*A dependent clause starting with* Although.)

Fragments can be corrected by adding missing words or combining the fragment with another sentence.

Stephan **is** off work today. (*Added a verb.*)

Luckily, **eggs** were on sale for half price. (*Added a subject.*)

Although apples were very cheap, **Mary Jane and Pat, bought berries, not apples.** (*Combined with another sentence.*)

Now try these examples:

[1] The Flagship Hotel offers several breakfast options to guests. [2] Our free breakfast buffet opens at 6:30. <u>[3] Offers a variety of breakfast items</u>: juice, cereal, yogurt, muffins, bagels, pastries, and more. [4] <u>Over</u>
1                                                                                                                                                              2

<u>50 selections to choose from, as well as freshly brewed hot coffee and a selection of gourmet teas</u>. [5] Guests
2

can also order their favorite breakfast from our regular <u>menu eggs, omelets, pancakes, waffles, French</u>
3

<u>toast are all available for a small additional charge</u>. [6] Finally, guests in a hurry can request our free
3

Grab-and-Go Breakfast <u>Bag, it</u> includes fresh fruit, yogurt, a breakfast muffin, and a choice of hot or iced
4

coffee or tea.

1. **A.** (No change)
   **B.** 6:30 it offers a variety of breakfast items
   **C.** 6:30. Offering a variety of breakfast items
   **D.** 6:30. It offers a variety of breakfast items

Option D is correct. The underlined sentence is a fragment. Option D begins a new sentence that has a complete subject and a complete verb. For this reason, Option A is incorrect. Option B is incorrect because it creates a run-on sentence by adding a complete subject and a verb but joining the sentence to the previous sentence without the correct punctuation. Option C creates a new fragment that lacks a complete subject and a complete verb.

2. The writer is considering revising Sentence 4. Which version should she use?

    **A.** (No change)

    **B.** There are over 50 selections to choose from, as well as freshly brewed hot coffee and a selection of gourmet teas.

    **C.** Over 50 selections that you can choose from, as well as freshly brewed hot coffee and a selection of gourmet teas.

    **D.** Over 50 selections choose from for breakfast, as well as freshly brewed hot coffee and a selection of gourmet teas.

Option B is correct. The original sentence is a fragment, and Option B corrects the fragment by adding *There are*. For this reason, Option A is incorrect. Option C is incorrect because it only adds a relative clause (*that you can choose from*), but does not fix the fragment in the main clause. Option D does not make sense; *selections* cannot make choices.

## b. Correcting Improperly Joined Sentences Items

Sometimes writers join two complete sentences improperly. When two independent clauses are joined with a comma, this creates a **comma splice.**

> My mother is in the hospital, I visited her there yesterday.

Sometimes writers do not use any punctuation or linking words to join sentences. (**Linking words** are words such as *and, but, so, then,* and *because.*) This is called a **run-on sentence.**

> My mother is in the hospital I visited her yesterday.

Both comma splices and run-on sentences can be corrected by adding the necessary punctuation and linking words.

> My mother is in the hospital, **so** I visited her yesterday.

TIP: A comma splice or run-on sentence can also occur when a phrase or sentence fragment is joined to an independent clause with or without a comma:

My mother is in the hospital, getting out tomorrow. *(comma splice)*
My mother is in the hospital getting out tomorrow. *(run-on)*

Items will ask you to correct comma splices and run-ons by choosing a response that corrects the error. Try this example:

[1] The Flagship Hotel offers several breakfast options to guests. [2] Our free breakfast buffet opens at 6:30. [3] <u>Offers a variety of breakfast items</u>: juice, cereal, yogurt, muffins, bagels, pastries, and more. [4] <u>Over 50</u>
<sub> </sub>        1        2

<u>selections to choose from, as well as freshly brewed hot coffee and a selection of gourmet teas</u>. [5] Guests can also
       2

order their favorite breakfast from our regular <u>menu eggs, omelets, pancakes, waffles, and French toast are all</u>
       3

<u>available for a small additional charge</u>. [6] Finally, guests in a hurry can request our free Grab-and-Go
       3

Breakfast <u>Bag, it</u> includes fresh fruit, yogurt, a breakfast muffin, and a choice of hot or iced coffee or tea.
     4

---

3. **A.** (No change)
   **B.** menu. Eggs, omelets, pancakes, waffles, and French toast are all available for a small additional charge
   **C.** menu, eggs, omelets, pancakes, waffles, and French toast are all available for a small additional charge
   **D.** menu. Eggs, omelets, pancakes, waffles, and French toast all available for a small additional charge

---

Option B is correct because it corrects the run-on sentence by separating the two sentences with a period and a capital letter. For this reason, Option A is incorrect. Option C is incorrect because adding a comma after *menu* creates a comma splice. Option D is incorrect. While it separates the two sentences with a period and a capital letter, removing the verb *are* creates a sentence fragment.

---

4. **A.** (No change)
   **B.** Bag it includes
   **C.** Bag, which includes
   **D.** Bag. Includes

---

Option C is correct because it changes the second clause of this comma splice to a relative clause. Option A is incorrect because it is a comma splice. Option B is incorrect because it changes the comma splice to a run-on by removing the comma. Option D is incorrect because it creates a sentence fragment by removing the subject (*it*) and starting a new sentence.

# c. Correcting Faulty Coordination Items

**Coordination** involves joining together sentences or sentence parts with linking words, such as *and, but, or, for, nor, yet*, and *so.* These words are called coordinating conjunctions. **Coordinating conjunctions** join together two or more sentences into a single sentence. (When a sentence is made of two or more sentences combined together, each of the sentences is called an **independent clause.** An independent clause can stand alone as a sentence.) Look at the following example:

> Diego works for a large company, **and** Maria runs a family business. (*Joins together two complete sentences, or independent clauses.*)

Coordinating conjunctions can also join together two or more similar sentence parts, such as subjects, verbs, or objects of verbs. Look at these examples:

> Diego **and** Maria always speak Spanish at home. (*Joins together two subjects.*)
>
> Diego can speak English **and** Spanish. (*Joins together two objects.*)
>
> Maria works during the day **and** studies for the HiSET exam at night. (*Joins together two verb phrases:* works during the day *and* studies for the HiSET exam at night.)

> **TIP:** When two independent clauses are joined together with a coordinating conjunction *(and, or, nor, for, yet, but, or so)*, a comma is required before the coordinating conjunction, unless the clauses are very short.

Coordination items often ask you to determine the following:

- Whether the correct coordinating conjunction is used
- Whether the elements joined together are equivalent (two subjects, two verbs, two objects, etc.)
- Whether a comma is used correctly to join the elements

Try these examples, which are based on the following email:

To: Mike Tahiri
From: Jacqui Jones
Subject: Payroll Errors

    As you know, several employees complained about mistakes in their paychecks. I checked into the problem, and found several errors that needed to be corrected immediately. First, Mike and Ali were
     1
paid the wrong rate of pay. Mike should be paid $10.25 per hour and Ali should be paid $11.10 per
                                                      2
hour. Second, we paid Henka and Josie for the wrong number of hours. Both of them worked a 40-hour week last week, so they were paid for only 30 hours. We have corrected the errors and issued new pay-
     3
checks to the employees.

1. **A.** (No change)
   **B.** problem so found
   **C.** problem and found
   **D.** problem, yet found

Option C is correct. *And* is the correct coordinating conjunction, but a comma is not needed before it, since it does not join independent clauses. For this reason, Option A is incorrect. Option B is incorrect because the coordinating conjunction *so* does not make sense in this sentence. Option D is incorrect because the coordinating conjunction *yet* does not make sense in this sentence, and a comma is not needed to join two verbs.

2. **A.** (No change)
   **B.** hour, yet Ali
   **C.** hour so Ali
   **D.** hour, and Ali

Option D is correct because *and* joins two independent clauses, so a comma is needed. For this reason, Option A is incorrect. Option B is incorrect because *yet* does not make sense in this sentence. Option C is incorrect because *so* does not make sense in this sentence, and a comma is also needed to join the two independent clauses.

3. **A.** (No change)
   **B.** week, but
   **C.** week, and
   **D.** week, nor

Option B is correct because the coordinating conjunction *but* (which shows contrast) makes sense in this sentence. *So* shows cause/effect and does not make sense in this sentence. For this reason, Option A is incorrect. Options C and D are incorrect because *and* and *nor* do not make sense in this sentence.

## d. Correcting Relative Clause Items

A **relative clause** is a kind of subordinate clause that gives more information about one of the nouns in a sentence. For this reason, a relative clause is sometimes called an adjective clause. A relative clause is always introduced by a **relative pronoun,** such as *that, who, which, whom, whose,* and *what.*

In general, a relative pronoun that adds essential information to the sentence is not set off by commas. Relative clauses that add nonessential information are set off by commas. The relative pronouns *who* and *whom* are used to refer to people (and sometimes animals, such as pets). The relative pronouns *which* and *that* are used to refer to things, not people. *Which* is generally used in nonessential relative clauses, while *that* is used in essential relative clauses. Look at these examples:

The team *that* wins this game will go on to the Super Bowl. (*Adds essential information*)

The team won the chance to play in the Super Bowl, *which* will take place in Miami. (*Adds nonessential information.*)

The player *who* scores the most points will probably win the most valuable player award. (*Adds essential information.*)

Items will test whether the correct relative pronoun was used to join the sentences. Items may also require you to figure out how to join two sentences correctly using a relative pronoun or whether a comma (or commas) are needed. Try these examples:

Dear Global Airlines:

I am writing about the bad experience <u>when</u> I had on flight 101 from Chicago to Dallas on Sunday,
1
April 27. I was traveling to visit my best <u>friend. She</u> was celebrating her 50th birthday that night. <u>Because</u>
3
2
I arrived at the airport three hours before my flight, I was told that there was not a seat for me. The

agent told me to go to the gate and wait for a seat assignment. At the gate, I was told that there was not

a seat for <u>me. The</u> flight was overbooked. The agent told me that I <u>have</u> to take a later flight. However,
4 5

the later flight was cancelled, and I <u>will be</u> unable to reach my destination. I would like to get a complete
6

refund of my ticket price plus a free flight on Global Airlines in the U.S.

| 1. A. | (No change) |
|---|---|
| B. | that |
| C. | who |
| D. | where |

Option B is correct because *that* is the only relative pronoun that makes sense in this sentence. The relative pronouns in Options A, C, and D do not make sense in this sentence, so they are incorrect.

| 2. A. | friend, who |
|---|---|
| B. | friend which |
| C. | friend where |
| D. | friend when |

Option A is correct because only the relative pronoun *who* joins the sentences in a way that makes sense. For this reason, Options B, C, and D are all incorrect.

# e. Correcting Faulty Subordination Items

**Subordination** involves joining an independent clause and a dependent clause in a single sentence. Remember, an **independent clause** has a complete subject and verb and can stand alone; a **dependent clause** has a complete subject and a verb, too, but cannot stand alone. Look at these examples:

Although it was very cold out. (*Dependent clause*)

The workers were not wearing heavy coats. (*Independent clause*)

**TIP: When a dependent clause stands alone, it is considered a sentence fragment because it does not express a complete thought.**

Independent and dependent clauses are joined together by special linking words called **subordinating conjunctions.** Some common subordinating conjunctions are *when, if, although, after, before,* and *because.* In addition, a comma is needed to join the two clauses when the dependent clause is first in the sentence. Look at these examples:

Although it was very cold out, the workers were not wearing heavy coats. (*A comma is needed.*)

The workers were not wearing heavy coats although it was very cold out. (*No comma is needed.*)

**Subordinate clauses** give more information about the main, or independent, clause. Subordinating conjunctions show different relationships between the clauses. Look at the following chart:

| Subordinating Conjunctions | |
| --- | --- |
| Subordinating Conjunctions | Function |
| after, before, since, until, when, while | To show order |
| because, since | To give a reason |
| although, even though, though | To show a contradiction or concession |
| in order that, so that | To state a result |
| if, unless | To state a condition |

Items may ask you to correct faulty subordination. You may need to decide whether the correct subordinating conjunction was used or whether two sentences should be combined with correct subordination. Try the following examples:

Dear Global Airlines:

I am writing about the bad experience <u>when</u> I had on flight 101 from Chicago to Dallas on Sunday,
<sub>1</sub> — [1]

April 27. I was traveling to visit my best <u>friend. She</u> was celebrating her 50th birthday that night. <u>Because</u>
[2]   [3]

I arrived at the airport three hours before my flight, I was told that there was not a seat for me. The

agent told me to go to the gate and wait for a seat assignment. At the gate, I was told that there was not

a seat for <u>me. The</u> flight was overbooked. The agent told me that I <u>have</u> to take a later flight. However,
[4]   [5]

the later flight was cancelled, and I <u>will be</u> unable to reach my destination. I would like to get a complete
[6]

refund of my ticket price plus a free flight on Global Airlines in the U.S.

3. **A.** (No change)
   **B.** While
   **C.** If
   **D.** Although

Option D is correct because the subordinating conjunction *although* makes sense in this sentence. *Because, while,* and *if* do not make sense, so Options A, B, and C are incorrect.

4. **A.** me after the
   **B.** me because the
   **C.** me, so the
   **D.** me when the

Option B is correct. This item requires you to choose the option that combines the two sentences most effectively. Option B is correct because the two sentences are in a cause-effect relationship. The cause is that the flight is overbooked. The effect is that the passenger does not have a seat on the plane. The only option that makes sense is Option B, which uses the subordinating conjunction *because* correctly to join the two clauses. Option A is incorrect because the subordinating conjunction *after* does not make sense in this sentence. Option C is incorrect because *so* is a subordinating conjunction that introduces an effect; in this option, it is used incorrectly to introduce a cause. Option D is incorrect because the subordinating conjunction *when* does not make sense in this situation.

## f. Correcting Inconsistent Verb Tense Items

When a sentence contains two or more verbs in a series, the verbs generally should be in the same tense.

> We ate dinner and then watched a movie.

In a sentence with a subordinate clause, the verbs in both clauses should be in the same tense unless one of the actions took place at a different time.

> Paul George, who scored the most points in the game, will probably be named most valuable player. (*George already scored the most points, but he has not been selected as MVP yet.*)

> Paul George, who scored the most points in the game, was just named most valuable player. (*George was just selected as MVP.*)

Items will ask you to determine whether verb tenses are consistent. Try these examples:

Dear Global Airlines:

I am writing about the bad experience <u>when</u> I had on flight 101 from Chicago to Dallas on Sunday,
<sub>1</sub>
April 27. I was traveling to visit my best <u>friend. She</u> was celebrating her 50th birthday that night. <u>Because</u>
<sub>2</sub> <sub>3</sub>
I arrived at the airport three hours before my flight, I was told that there was not a seat for me. The

agent told me to go to the gate and wait for a seat assignment. At the gate, I was told that there was not

a seat for <u>me. The</u> flight was overbooked. The agent told me that I <u>have</u> to take a later flight. However,
<sub>4</sub> <sub>5</sub>
the later flight was cancelled, and I <u>will be</u> unable to reach my destination. I would like to get a complete
<sub>6</sub>
refund of my ticket price plus a free flight on Global Airlines in the U.S.

5. **A.** (No change)
   **B.** has
   **C.** have had
   **D.** had

Option D is correct. The sentence has two actions that took place in the past. Only Option D contains a
verb in the past tense, so it is correct. Therefore, Option A is incorrect. Options B and C contain verbs in the
simple present and present perfect tense, so therefore they are incorrect. In addition, Option B does not
agree with the subject of the sentence, *I*.

6. **A.** (No change)
   **B.** would be
   **C.** was going to be
   **D.** was

Option D is correct because this action happened in the past, so the simple past tense is required. Option A
is incorrect because the action is in the past, not the future. Options B and C are incorrect because the action
is a completed action in the past, so *would be* (Option B) and *was going to be* (Option C), which are about
actions that did not actually happen or were going to happen, are incorrect.

## g. Correcting Faulty Parallel Structure

When a sentence contains two or more items in a series, each of the items needs to be in the same
grammatical form. Study the following examples:

**Running** and **to swim** are my favorite sports. (*Not parallel*)
**Running** and **swimming** are my favorite sports. (*Parallel*)

**Parallel structure** makes our ideas clear and easy to understand. When we write, we should make sure that nouns, verbs, adjectives, adverbs, phrases, and clauses are all parallel. Items will ask you to determine whether sentences use correct parallel structure. Try these examples:

Summer is often the time for family reunions. Families <u>will remember and cherish</u> their reunion memories
1

for years. But <u>planning and organize</u> a family reunion are important. First, it's important to choose a conve-
2

nient time, date, and a location to meet. Make sure that relatives from out of town will have a place to stay—

<u>with relatives or a hotel</u>. Plan appropriate activities, such as a dinner, a tour of your city or town, or a picnic.
3

<u>Wearing custom T-shirts, your family pride will show</u>. <u>Your family will have a fun and memorable reunion</u>
45

<u>with luck.</u>
5

---

1. **A.** (No change)
   **B.** remembered and will cherish
   **C.** will remember and would cherish
   **D.** will remember and cherishing

---

Option A is correct. The sentence has correct parallel structure. In this sentence, *will* refers to both *remember* and *cherish*. Options B, C, and D are incorrect because the verbs are not parallel.

---

2. **A.** (No change)
   **B.** planned and organizing
   **C.** plan and organize
   **D.** planning and organizing

---

Option D is correct. Both *planning* and *organizing* are gerunds. A gerund is a verb that ends in *-ing* and acts as a noun (in this case, the two gerunds act as the subject of the sentence). Therefore, Option A is incorrect. Option B is incorrect because only *organizing* is a gerund. While the verbs in Option C are parallel, gerunds are required in this sentence, so Option C is incorrect.

---

3. **A.** (No change)
   **B.** at relatives or a hotel
   **C.** relatives or hotel
   **D.** with relatives or in a hotel

---

Option D is correct. Two prepositional phrases are required to have correct parallel structure. Therefore, Option A is incorrect, since only *with relatives* is a prepositional phrase. Option B is incorrect because *at relatives* does not make sense, and the items are not parallel. Option C is incorrect because even though the items are parallel, prepositional phrases are required in this sentence.

# h. Correcting Misplaced and Dangling Modifiers

A **modifier** is a word, phrase, or sentence that modifies, or describes, another part of the sentence it is in.

A **misplaced modifier** is a modifier that seems to describe the wrong word or phrase. Look at these examples:

> We bought a new flat screen TV <u>with excitement</u> for our living room. (With excitement *can refer to we* or *TV.*)

> We watched our new TV while we ate dinner <u>happily</u>. (Happily *can modify either clause: we watched our new TV* or *we ate dinner.*)

You can correct misplaced modifiers by moving them to the proper place in the sentence, usually as close as possible to the word or words being modified.

> <u>With excitement</u>, we bought a new flat screen TV for our living room.

> <u>Happily</u>, we watched TV while we ate dinner.

A **dangling modifier** occurs when the sentence does not have an appropriate word or phrase for the modifier to describe.

> Watching the new TV, the picture was much better than on our old TV. (Watching the new TV *cannot modify* the picture *because the picture cannot watch itself.*)

Correct a dangling modifier by rewriting the sentence so the modifier describes a word that makes sense.

> Watching the new TV, we realized that the picture was much better than that of our old TV.

Now try these examples:

Summer is often the time for family reunions. Families <u>will remember and cherish</u> their reunion memories
                                                     1

for years. But <u>planning and organize</u> a family reunion are important. First, it's important to choose a conve-
                      2

nient time, date, and a location to meet. Make sure that relatives from out of town will have a place to stay—

<u>with relatives or a hotel</u>. Plan appropriate activities, such as a dinner, a tour of your city or town, or a picnic.
      3

<u>Wearing custom T-shirts, your family pride will show</u>. <u>Your family will have a fun and memorable reunion</u>
               4                                          5

<u>with luck.</u>
 5

---

4. **A.** (No change)
   **B.** By wearing custom T-shirts, your family pride will show.
   **C.** If your family wears custom T-shirts, your family pride will show.
   **D.** Wearing custom T-shirts, you can help your family pride show.

---

Option C is correct. The original sentence has a dangling modifier—the phrase *Wearing custom T-shirts* cannot refer to family pride because family pride cannot wear T-shirts. Therefore, Option A is incorrect. Option C is correct because it changes the dangling modifier to a subordinate clause. Option B is incorrect because the sentence still has a dangling modifier. Option D is incorrect because it changes the meaning of the sentence. The sentence is about family members wearing custom T-shirts. In Option D, only the reunion organizer is wearing the T-shirt.

TIP: Changing an introductory phrase to a subordinate clause is often an effective way to fix a dangling modifier.

5.  **A.**  (No change)
    **B.**  Luckily, your family will have a fun and memorable reunion.
    **C.**  Your family will have a fun, memorable, and lucky reunion.
    **D.**  With luck, your family will have a fun and memorable reunion.

Option D is correct. The original sentence contains a misplaced modifier. It's not clear whether *with luck* refers to *reunion* or to the whole sentence. Therefore, Option A is incorrect. Option D corrects the problem by moving the phrase to the beginning of the sentence, so that it clearly modifies the whole sentence. Options B and C are incorrect because they change the meaning of the sentence. In addition, Option B does not make sense.

# i. Practice 2: Language Facility

## i. Items

Listening to music with headphones, loud music
<u>                      </u>
1

can damage your hearing. According to medical

researchers, headphones can produce sound up to
2

120 decibels. Louder than most rock concerts! This
                        3

level can produce hearing loss after less than 90 min-

utes of listening. According to statistics, one in five

young adults has some form of hearing loss. A rate
                              4

that is 30 percent higher than that in the 1980s and

1990s. According to experts, the only way to avoid

hearing loss is to turn down the volume or to limit

listening to about 60 minutes per day. How can you

know if your music is too loud? Doctors say that if

you cannot hear anything going on around you, you

should have lowered the volume.
         5

1.  **A.**  (No change)
    **B.**  Listening to loud music with headphones, you
    **C.**  Listening with headphones to loud music,
    **D.**  Listening with headphones to loud music, you

2.  **A.**  (No change)
    **B.**  researchers headphones
    **C.**  researchers. Headphones
    **D.**  researchers: headphones

3.  **A.**  (No change)
    **B.**  decibels; louder
    **C.**  decibels louder
    **D.**  decibels. That is louder

4.  **A.**  (No change)
    **B.**  loss a rate
    **C.**  loss, which is a rate
    **D.**  loss that is a rate

5.  **A.**  (No change)
    **B.**  should lower
    **C.**  lowered
    **D.**  lowering

## ii. Answer Explanations

1. **D. Listening with headphones to loud music, you (Misplaced and Dangling Modifiers)** The introductory phrase is a dangling modifier because it lacks a clear subject to refer to. Option D fixes the problem by making the phrase refer to the subject of the sentence, *you.* For this reason, Option A is incorrect. Option B fixes the dangling modifier by giving it a clear subject to refer to, *you,* but introduces a misplaced modifier, *with headphones.* Option C is incorrect because the verb *can* lacks a subject.

2. **A. (No change) (Language facility)** The sentence is correct as written; therefore, the other options are incorrect. Option B removes a comma that is required after an introductory phrase. Option C changes the introductory phrase to a fragment. Option D replaces the comma with a colon, which does not make sense.

3. **D. decibels. That is louder (Sentence Fragment)** The sentence that begins with *louder* is a fragment, and Option D fixes the fragment by adding a complete subject and verb. Option B does not fix the fragment; a semicolon is used to join two complete independent clauses. Option C creates a kind of run-on sentence by joining the fragment to the previous sentence without punctuation.

4. **C. loss, which is a rate (Sentence Fragment)** Option C is correct because the sentence that begins with *a rate* is a fragment. Option C fixes the fragment by changing it to a nonessential relative clause and joining it to the preceding sentence. Therefore, Option A is incorrect. Option B is incorrect because it creates a kind of run-on sentence by joining the fragment to the preceding sentence. Option D is incorrect because a nonessential relative clause is required here.

5. **B. should lower (Inconsistent Verb Tense)** Option B is correct because a present tense verb is required in this sentence. Therefore, Options A and C are incorrect. Option D is not a complete verb, so it is incorrect.

# 3. Writing Conventions

After you organize your ideas and express them in sentences, you can turn to fixing errors in writing conventions. **Writing conventions** include details such as capitalization, punctuation, spelling, subject-verb agreement, pronoun-antecedent agreement, and correct word forms (such as using adjectives and adverbs correctly).

## a. Correcting Capitalization Items

HiSET assesses capitalization of proper nouns and proper adjectives. Proper nouns and adjectives refer to specific, unique entities, such as persons or places. In general, HiSET assesses the capitalization of the following words and phrases.

The names of specific people, places, and organizations:

> Tupac Shakur was a very talented musician.
>
> Hill Park is my favorite place to swim.
>
> I am a member of the Buena Park Neighborhood Association.

**TIP:** Do not capitalize very short words (*as, a, the, in, at,* etc.) in a title or name of an organization unless the word is the first word of the name.

He is the president of The Friends of the Library.

The titles of specific people, when used with their names:

> I admire <u>President</u> Obama.
>
> I need to speak to <u>Dr.</u> Kirk.

In general, we do not capitalize titles when they are used alone, except when used in speaking directly to the person (direct address):

> I am going to complain to the <u>mayor</u> about all the potholes in the streets.
>
> When, at long last, <u>Mayor</u>, will the potholes on Main Street be repaired? (*Direct address*)
>
> What time will you be home, <u>Daddy</u>? (*Direct address*)

Days, months, and holidays:

> This year, the <u>Independence Day</u> parade is on <u>Saturday</u>, <u>July</u> 3.

Brand names:

> Give me a large <u>Coke</u>, please.

The first word of a quotation:

> The guard shouted, "<u>Halt</u>!"
>
> Benjamin Franklin said, "<u>Early</u> to bed and early to rise make a man healthy, wealthy, and wise."

Of course, we always capitalize the first word of a sentence and the pronoun *I*. These two capitalization rules are generally not tested on Language Arts: Writing, Part 1, but you should always follow these conventions in Part 2 and in your own writing. Capitalization of words used in direct address generally is not tested on Part 1 either, because it is so uncommon.

Try these examples:

> Lucky <u>Noodles</u> is a <u>brand</u> new <u>Restaurant</u> in Los Angeles. This new eatery offers <u>noodle</u> dishes from
> <sub>1</sub>      <sub>1</sub>      <sub>1</sub>      <sub>2</sub>
>
> around the <u>World</u>, including China, Japan, <u>Thailand</u>, and Italy. Some of the dishes served at the restaurant
> <sub>2</sub>      <sub>2</sub>
>
> include Chinese beef noodle soup, Italian spaghetti, and spicy Thai noodles.

---

1. Which of these words, if any, has a capitalization error?

   A. (None)

   B. Noodles

   C. brand

   D. Restaurant

---

Option D is correct. *Restaurant* should not be capitalized in this case because it is not used as part of the name of a specific restaurant (such as Andy's Family Restaurant). For this reason, Option A is incorrect. Option B is correct because in this case, *Noodles* is part of the restaurant's name. Option C is incorrect because there is no reason to capitalize *brand*.

---

2. Which of these words, if any, has a capitalization error?

    **A.**  (None)
    **B.**  noodle
    **C.**  World
    **D.**  Thailand

---

Option C is correct because *world* is not a proper noun so should not be capitalized. For this reason, Option A is incorrect. Option B is incorrect because *noodle* is not a proper noun in this sentence. Option D is incorrect because *Thailand* is the name of a country, making it a proper noun that is capitalized correctly.

## b. Correcting Punctuation Errors

The most commonly tested punctuation errors include commas, colons and semicolons, and quotation marks.

### i. Commas

Commas are used to show how parts of a sentence are related. Comma errors are probably the most common errors in writing. In general, the HiSET tests the following areas of comma use.

Use a comma to separate three or more items in a list.

> Please buy <u>lettuce, tomatoes, and green onions</u> for the salad.
> <u>Peggy, Mario, and Tim</u> ate lunch together yesterday.

**TIP:** The last comma before *and* is optional. For this reason, commas before *and* are seldom tested on the HiSET exam.

Commas are not needed if all the items in the list are joined by coordinating conjunctions.

> Tim would like to go on vacation in June <u>or</u> July <u>or</u> August.
> We went to Disneyland on Wednesday <u>and</u> Thursday <u>and</u> Friday!

Use a comma to separate two or more adjectives that describe a noun when *and* can be used between the adjectives.

> She is one of the <u>funniest, smartest</u> comedians working today.

Use commas to set off a phrase that interrupts a sentence.

> Dujuan is on time for work every day. Larry, on the other hand, is frequently late.

Use a comma to set off a word or phrase that restates or clarifies another noun or noun phrase. These words and phrases are called **appositives.**

Jeff Gordon, <u>my favorite NASCAR driver</u>, just won a big race.

Frank's third-grade teacher, Mrs. Tafel, was also his professor many years later when he went to college. (Mrs. Tafel *restates* third-grade teacher.)

Use a comma after an introductory word.

<u>No</u>, we are out of bananas today.

<u>Fortunately</u>, our train arrived on time.

Use a comma after an introductory phrase, unless the phrase is very short.

<u>As a matter of fact</u>, I am president of the club.

<u>At exactly 12:00 noon</u>, the ceremony will begin.

<u>In 1981</u> MTV went on the air for the first time. (*No comma is needed.*)

Use commas before direct quotations or when the quotation is interrupted with a phrase such as *she said*.

Benjamin Franklin said, "Early to bed and early to rise make a man healthy, wealthy, and wise."

"Early to bed and early to rise," Benjamin Franklin said, "makes a man healthy, wealthy, and wise."

Use commas to separate items in a date.

The concert will take place on <u>Friday, August 1, 2015</u>, at 8 p.m.

Use a comma between cities and states.

Now I live in Tacoma, <u>Washington</u>.

Use a comma to join two independent clauses with *and, or, nor, for, yet,* or *so*.

I live in Annapolis<u>, and</u> my sister lives nearby in Baltimore.

Use a comma to join a dependent clause and an independent clause.

If I have time<u>,</u> I visit my sister every weekend.

A comma is *not* needed when the independent clause comes before the dependent clause.

I visit my sister every weekend if I have time.

## ii. Colons and Semicolons

In general, the HiSET tests the following areas of colon and semicolon use.

Use a colon after an independent clause to introduce a list or an idea.

We have several options for lunch: pizza, burgers, pasta, or salad.

Chris and I have finally made a decision: We are going to get married in May of next year.

Do *not* use a colon to separate a verb from its objects or a preposition from its objects.

Please buy formula, diapers, and shampoo for the baby.

I have lived in Spain, Morocco, and China.

Use a semicolon to join independent clauses.

My mother is in the hospital; I visited her there yesterday.

We looked at several apartments; however, all of them were too expensive.

**TIP: One way to fix a comma splice is to change the comma to a semicolon:**

**Comma Splice: My mother is in the hospital, I visited her there yesterday.**

**Correct: My mother is in the hospital; I visited her there yesterday.**

When a list is long and complicated (such as a list containing commas within the list items), use semicolons to separate larger parts of the list.

We have several kinds of sandwiches: peanut butter and jelly; fresh mozzarella cheese and tomato; bacon, lettuce, and tomato; and single, double, and triple hamburgers and cheeseburgers.

Now try these examples:

Memo
TO: All Employees
FROM: Marty Mickey, Manager

**[1]**

As you know, we will soon be closing the second floor of the main office building for renovations.
                1

The second floor will be completely gutted and rebuilt with new walls, and flooring.
                                                                    2

**[2]**

We have a lot of old unwanted furniture and supplies. To dispose of these things, we will hold a rummage sale on Wednesday June 18 from 10:00 to 2:00. You can buy: desks, chairs, tables, and file cabinets
                                3                                                    4
at reasonable prices. We will accept only cash or personal checks, all sales are final, and proceeds will

benefit this year's company charity, Habitat for Humanity of Washington, D.C.

---

1. **A.** (No change)
   **B.** As you know we will
   **C.** As you know, we will,
   **D.** As you know, we, will

---

Option A is correct because a comma is needed after the introductory phrase. For this reason, Option B is incorrect. Option C is incorrect because a comma is not needed after *will*. Option D is incorrect because there is no reason to use a comma after *we*.

2. **A.** (No change)
   **B.** new, walls and flooring
   **C.** new walls and flooring
   **D.** new, walls, and flooring

Option C is correct. A comma is not needed between *walls* and *flooring* because a comma is not needed when a list contains two items. Therefore, Option A is incorrect. Option B is incorrect because there is no reason to use a comma after *new*. Option D is incorrect because there is no reason to include commas after *new* and *walls*.

3. **A.** (No change)
   **B.** Wednesday, June 18, from
   **C.** Wednesday, June 18 from
   **D.** Wednesday June 18, from

Option B is correct. Dates are set off with commas after the day of the week, the date, and the year. Therefore, Options A, C, and D are all incorrect.

4. **A.** (No change)
   **B.** buy, desks, chairs, tables, and file, cabinets
   **C.** buy; desks, chairs, tables, and file cabinets
   **D.** buy desks, chairs, tables, and file cabinets

Option D is correct because a colon is not used to separate a verb from its objects. Therefore, Option A is incorrect. Option B is incorrect because a comma is not used to separate a verb from its objects, and a comma is not needed between *file* and *cabinets*. Option C is incorrect because semicolons are used to join independent clauses without a word like *and*.

## iii. Quotation Marks

We use **quotation marks** to indicate that we are repeating another person's exact words. A quotation begins with quotation marks and a capital letter. A quotation ends with appropriate punctuation and quotation marks. The quotation marks generally come after the punctuation. Look at these examples:

"I'll take it," said the customer. (*A comma ends the quotation if the sentence continues after the quotation.*)

The customer said, "I'll take it." (*A period inside the quotation marks ends the quotation and sentence.*)

The clerk asked, "Cash or charge?" (*A question mark inside the quotation marks ends the quotation and sentence.*)

When a question mark is not part of the quotation, but instead part of the whole sentence, the question mark goes outside the quotation marks.

Did the customer say, "Cash"? (*The speaker is questioning what the customer said.*)

Now try these example items:

"James" Doctor Martin advised, "you need to cut down on sweets and cholesterol. Unless you make some
<br>1

changes to your diet, you are at risk of suffering a heart attack."
<br>2

**137**

1. **A.** (No change)
   **B.** "James," Doctor Martin advised, "you
   **C.** "James," Doctor Martin advised, you
   **D.** "James, Doctor Martin advised, you

Option B is correct. A comma and quotation marks are required after *James,* and quotation marks are required before *you.* For this reason, options A, C, and D are correct.

2. **A.** (No change)
   **B.** attack".
   **C.** attack.
   **D.** attack!

Option A is correct because a quotation should end with final punctuation (a period, question mark, or exclamation point) and quotation marks. For this reason, options B, C, and D are incorrect.

## c. Correcting Subject-Verb Agreement Errors

**Subject-verb agreement** means that the subject of the sentence and the verb match—both are singular or both are plural. Look at these examples:

> Lenny and Carl always arrive at work on time. (*Plural subject and plural verb.*)

> Homer always arrives at work late. (*Singular subject and singular verb.*)

In the simple present tense, singular verbs end in -*s: arrives, lives, eats,* etc. Some verbs have irregular forms. The singular form of *have* is *has.* The verb *be* has several irregular forms. Study the following chart:

| Forms of the Verb *Be* | | |
|---|---|---|
| | Present | Past |
| **Singular** | I **am** <br> He, she, it **is** <br> You **are** | I, he, she, it **was** <br> You **were** |
| **Plural** | We, you, they **are** | We, you, they **were** |

When a sentence has a compound subject joined by *and,* the verb is plural.

> Doing laundry and washing dishes are my least favorite household tasks.

When a sentence has a compound subject joined by *or,* the verb agrees with the noun closest to it.

> Sam or the twins are watching TV in the living room.
> The twins or Sam is watching TV in the living room.

TIP: The verb agrees with the subject of the sentence, not the words that follow the subject:

Ironing clothes is boring. (The subject is *ironing*, not *clothes; is* (singular), not *are* (plural) is correct.)

The Chicago Cubs <u>is</u> Donna's favorite baseball team. In summer, Donna <u>go</u> to every game with her
<sub>1</sub> <sub>2</sub>

friends.

1. **A.** (No change)
   **B.** are
   **C.** am
   **D.** be

Option B is correct because *Cubs* is plural, so it needs a plural verb. For this reason, options A, C, and D are incorrect.

2. **A.** (No change)
   **B.** gone
   **C.** going
   **D.** goes

Option D is correct because *Donna* is singular, so it needs a singular verb. For this reason, Option A is incorrect. Options B and C are incorrect because a past participle (*gone*) and a present participle (*going*) cannot stand alone as the verb of a sentence. They need helping verbs, such as *have* or *is*.

# d. Correcting Adjective and Adverb Errors

Items may ask you to decide whether adjectives and adverbs are used correctly.

Use adjectives to modify nouns.

A **tasty** cheeseburger sounds good for lunch. (Tasty *modifies* cheeseburger.)

That cheeseburger looks **delicious.** (Delicious *modifies* cheeseburger.)

Use adverbs to modify verbs, adjectives, other adverbs, or a whole sentence.

She **quickly** threw together a few sandwiches for the children's lunch. (Quickly *modifies* threw.)

I just saw an **incredibly** good movie. (Incredibly *describes the adjective* good. *The adjective* good *describes* movie.)

TIP: Most, but not all, adverbs end in *-ly. Good* is an adjective. *Well* is usually an adverb that describes how an action was performed. Sometimes *well* is an adjective used to describe someone's health.

A few adjectives end in *-ly.* Examples include: *chilly, costly, deadly, deathly, friendly, likely, orderly,* and *silly.*

Try these examples:

In winter, certain produce, such as peas, are <u>ridiculous expensive</u>, while others, such as oranges, are much
1

cheaper. Besides being cheap in winter, oranges are <u>well</u> to eat because they are high in vitamin C.
2

> 1. **A.**   (No change)
>    **B.**   slightly expensive
>    **C.**   ridiculously
>    **D.**   ridiculously expensive

Option D is correct. *Ridiculous* modifies *expensive,* so it should be an adverb: *ridiculously.* Therefore, Option
A is incorrect. Option B is incorrect because it changes the meaning of the sentence. Option C is incorrect
because there is no reason to delete *expensive.*

> 2. **A.**   (No change)
>    **B.**   goodly
>    **C.**   good
>    **D.**   welly

Option C is correct. An adjective, *good,* is needed to modify *oranges.* For this reason, Option A is incorrect.
Options B and D are not used in Standard Written English, so they are incorrect.

## e. Correcting Pronoun Reference Errors

A **pronoun** is a word that is used to refer to a noun. *He, she, it, him, her, theirs,* and *themselves* are all
examples of pronouns. The noun that a pronoun refers to is called the **antecedent.** A pronoun and its
antecedent should agree.

Pronouns and antecedents should agree in number—singular or plural.

> **Mr. Smith** is my neighbor. **He**'s a really nice guy.
>
> Those **women** are excellent students. **They** will probably pass the HiSET exam with flying colors.

> TIP: Be careful with phrases that come after a noun. The pronoun should agree with the noun, and not with words in
> the phrase that comes after the noun:
> The students in that class are very intelligent. (Are *agrees with the subject* students, *not* in that class, *the phrase that
> follows).*

When the antecedent is a person or, sometimes, an animal, pronouns and antecedents should agree in
gender—masculine or feminine.

> **Elena** bought several lottery tickets, but **she** didn't win.
>
> My dog **Charlie** loves **his** chew toy.

Pronouns should agree with the grammatical function of the antecedent: subject, object, possessive, or reflexive. Study the following chart:

| Grammatical Function of Pronouns | |
| --- | --- |
| **Grammatical Function** | **Pronouns** |
| Subject | I, you, he, she, it, we, they |
| Object | me, you, him, her, it, us, them |
| Possessive | my, your, his, her, its, our, them, mine, yours, hers, its, ours, theirs |
| Reflexive | myself, yourself, himself, herself, itself, ourselves, yourselves, themselves |

Pronouns and antecedents should agree in person—first person, second person, or third person—as noted in the following chart:

| The Person of Pronouns | |
| --- | --- |
| **Person** | **Pronouns** |
| First Person | I, we, me, us, mine, our, ours, ourselves |
| Second Person | you, your, yours, yourselves |
| Third Person | he, she, it, they, him, her, them, his, hers, its, their, theirs, himself, herself, themselves |

Try these example items, which refer to the following email:

John, I am afraid that Stephanie and <u>me</u> will not be able to make it to your party tomorrow night.
<br>1<br>
I just found out that <u>mine</u> uncle and aunt are visiting from Canada. Of course, we are sorry to miss your
<br>2<br>
party, but I am sure you will understand.

| | | |
| --- | --- | --- |
| 1. | **A.** | (No change) |
| | **B.** | mine |
| | **C.** | I |
| | **D.** | my |

Option C is correct. The subject pronoun *I* is required in this position. Therefore, options A, B, and D are incorrect.

| | | |
| --- | --- | --- |
| 2. | **A.** | (No change) |
| | **B.** | my |
| | **C.** | ours |
| | **D.** | their |

Option B is correct because *my* is needed when the possessive word comes before a noun. For this reason, Option A is incorrect. Option C is incorrect because *ours* cannot come before a noun. Option D is incorrect because it changes the meaning of the sentence in a way that does not make sense.

# f. Correcting Spelling Errors

The most commonly tested spelling errors on the HiSET are homonyms, contractions, possessives, and irregular verbs.

TIP: Spelling error items refer to misspellings within the context of the passage.

## i. Homonyms

**Homonyms** are two, or sometimes three, words that are spelled differently but sound the same. Here are a few common homonyms:

board, bored

break, brake

hear, here

it's (*contraction*), its (*possessive*)

knew, new

know, no

maid, made

plain, plane

right, rite, write

sea, see

sight, site, cite

they're (*contraction*), their (*possessive*), there (*adverb*)

to, two, too

weak, week

wood, would

you're (*contraction*), your (*possessive*)

## ii. Contractions and Possessive Nouns

Apostrophes are used in contractions and possessive forms of nouns. An **apostrophe** is used to show the letters deleted from a contraction.

he is = he's

they are = they're

do not = don't

are not = aren't

I would = I'd

Some contractions do not follow this pattern and have to be memorized.

will not = won't

**Apostrophes** are also used to show possession. For a singular noun, add *'s* to the noun.

I loaded the baseball **team's** bats and balls in my **car's** trunk.

For a plural noun that ends in *-s,* add an apostrophe to the noun. For a plural noun that does not end in *-s,* add *'s* to the noun.

The two **girls'** model airplanes crashed into each other.

The **children's** toys were spread all over the living room floor in a big mess.

## iii. Irregular Verbs

Most verbs add *-d* or *-ed* to form the past tense or past participle. However, some verbs are irregular. Their spelling changes in the past tense and past participle.

John **cooked** dinner for all of us, but he **ate** nothing. (Cook *is a regular verb.* Eat *is an irregular verb.*)

They have **finished** all their work for the day, but they haven't **left** for home yet. (Finish *is a regular verb*; leave *is an irregular verb.*)

**TIP: A past participle always has an auxiliary verb such as *have, has, had, is, are, was,* or *were.***

Here are some common irregular verbs:

| Common Irregular Verbs | | |
|---|---|---|
| **Present Tense** | **Past Tense** | **Past Participle** |
| begin | began | begun |
| break | broke | broken |
| choose | chose | chosen |
| come | came | come |
| drink | drank | drunk |
| drive | drove | driven |
| eat | ate | eaten |
| give | gave | given |
| grow | grew | grown |
| go | went | gone |
| know | knew | known |
| make | made | made |
| see | saw | seen |
| speak | spoke | spoken |
| wear | wore | worn |

Try these example items:

When <u>you're</u> planning a long car trip, <u>its</u> important to plan and prepare for <u>your</u> trip. You, or a reliable
    1                              1                         1

mechanic, should check your car thoroughly. Check the <u>car's</u> tires, headlights, <u>taillights</u>, <u>break</u> lights, turn
                                           2                   2    2

signals, oil, radiator fluid, and windshield washer fluid. If your tires are <u>wore</u>, you should get <u>new</u> ones <u>right</u>
                                                            3            3       3

away. By following these simple tips, you can have a safe and relaxing auto trip.

1. Which of the following words, if any, is misspelled?

    **A.** (None)

    **B.** you're

    **C.** its

    **D.** your

Option C is correct because *it's,* the contraction of *it is,* is required. Therefore, Option A is incorrect. Options B and D are spelled correctly.

---

2. Which of the following words, if any, is misspelled?

    **A.** (None)
    **B.** car's
    **C.** taillights
    **D.** break

---

Option D is correct because the word *brake* is needed to refer to the system that stops a car. *Break* and *brake* are homonyms. Therefore, Option A is incorrect. Options B and C are spelled correctly.

---

3. Which of the following words, if any, is misspelled?

    **A.** (None)
    **B.** wore
    **C.** new
    **D.** right

---

Option B is correct. The past participle *worn* is required after the verb *are.* Therefore, Option A is incorrect. Options C and D are spelled correctly.

# g. Practice 3: Writing Conventions

## i. Items

**[1]**

Travel websites can help you save money on hotel rooms. A travel website that <u>compare</u> hotel rates
$\overset{\phantom{.}}{1}$
from many different websites <u>are</u> helpful for finding
$\overset{\phantom{.}}{2}$
the best deal. These websites are helpful because you can find hotel deals from many travel websites in a single location. You can compare rates and deals for the same room. For example, one recent search showed that you could find the same room at the same <u>downtown</u> <u>new</u> York <u>luxury</u> hotel at prices
$\overset{\phantom{.}}{3}\qquad\overset{\phantom{.}}{3}\qquad\quad\overset{\phantom{.}}{3}$
from $129 to $389 on 10 different websites. To get the lowest rate, you need to prepay part or all of your stay, or book and pay a week or more in advance. These websites are good for people who want to find a good deal and can afford to pay in advance. When using these sites, <u>it's</u> important to
$\overset{\phantom{.}}{4}$
read the terms <u>extremely carefully</u>, since your
$\overset{\phantom{.}}{5}$
deposit or prepayment may not be refundable.

1. **A.** (No change)
   **B.** compares
   **C.** compared
   **D.** comparing

2. **A.** (No change)
   **B.** is
   **C.** be
   **D.** was

3. Which of the following words, if any, should be capitalized?
   **A.** (None)
   **B.** downtown
   **C.** new
   **D.** luxury

4. **A.** (No change)
   **B.** its
   **C.** its'
   **D.** it

5. **A.** (No change)
   **B.** extreme carefully
   **C.** extremely careful
   **D.** extreme careful

**[2]**

With other websites, you do not find out the name or exact address of your hotel until after you book and pay. When you book, you only have infor-
6
mation on the neighborhood the hotel is located in. Generally, these websites offer the lowest prices, but you are taking some risks. These sites work best for people who are flexible and have a sense of adventure, according to many travel experts.

6. **A.** (No change)
   **B.** book you
   **C.** book; you
   **D.** book. You

## ii. Answer Explanations

1. **B. compares (Subject-Verb Agreement)** Option B is correct because the subject of this relative clause is *that,* whose antecedent, *website,* is singular, so a singular verb is required. For this reason, Option A is incorrect. Option C is incorrect because there is no reason to use the past tense in this sentence. Option D is incorrect because *comparing* is not a complete verb.

2. **B. is (Subject-Verb Agreement)** Option B is correct because the subject of this verb is *website* (not *websites*), so a singular verb is required. For this reason, Option A is incorrect. Option C is incorrect because *be* is not a complete verb. Option D is incorrect because there is no reason to use the past tense in this sentence.

3. **C. new (Capitalization)** Option C is correct because this word is part of a proper noun, *New York,* so it should be capitalized. Therefore, Option A is incorrect. Options B and D are incorrect because *downtown* and *luxury* are not proper nouns or parts of proper nouns, so there is no reason to capitalize them.

4. **A. (No change) (Spelling)** Option A is correct because *it's* is the subject and verb of the sentence, so the correct contraction is *it's.* Therefore, Option B, which is a possessive word, is incorrect. There is no such word as *its'* (Option C). Option D is incorrect because it removes the verb, *is,* making the sentence a fragment.

5. **A. (No change) (Adjectives and Adverbs)** Option A is correct because in this sentence, *carefully* is an adverb that modifies the verb *reads,* and *extremely* is an adverb that modifies *carefully.* For this reason, options B, C, and D are incorrect.

6. **A. (No change) (Punctuation)** A comma is needed when a dependent clause comes before an independent clause, so Option A is correct. For this reason, Option B is incorrect. There is no reason to use a semicolon (Option C). Option D creates a fragment, since a dependent clause cannot stand alone.

# V. Language Arts: Writing, Part 2

HiSET Language Arts: Writing, Part 2 tests your ability to write an essay on a topic of general interest using clear and effective Standard Written English, or SWE. (As you learned in Chapter IV, SWE is the kind of English that is used in many business, professional, and community settings.) For more information about SWE and how to use it to answer HiSET Language Arts: Writing, Part 1 items, see Chapter IV. This chapter will give you all the information, skills, and tips you need to write a high-scoring HiSET essay.

## A. Test Format

HiSET Language Arts: Writing, Part 2 asks you to write an essay on a topic of general interest in 45 minutes. You will need no special knowledge or information to write your response. Usually, you will be asked to write a persuasive essay that tries to convince others to support a position on an issue or topic of interest to the community. For example, you may have to persuade others to support spending more money on your community's library. Or you might have to write an essay persuading people to believe or disbelieve the point of view of a speaker at a meeting.

Each essay item has three parts:

- **Directions:** General instructions for writing your response
- **Topic:** A brief explanation of the problem, issue, topic, or situation that you will write about. For example, the topic might present background about the library and its needs. The topic will appear in a box.
- **Prompt:** The actual topic your essay needs to address.

Here is an example:

**Directions:** This is a test of your writing skills. You have 45 minutes to prepare and write your response. Your essay will be scored based on the following criteria:

- Development and support of a main idea with examples and details
- Clear and effective organization of ideas, including an introduction, body, and conclusion; logical paragraphs; and effective transitions between and within paragraphs
- Appropriate language use, including varied vocabulary, varied sentence patterns, and appropriate voice
- Clarity and use of Standard Written English

> At a community meeting, several people spoke about a need for better public transportation in the city. There was a lot of discussion during and after the meeting. Community residents offered many ideas for and against improved public transportation. Do you think that your community needs improved public transportation?

Write an essay for your community's news website that explains whether or not you think your community needs improved public transportation. Think carefully about reasons that will help others understand your position as well as examples and details that you can use to support your position.

> **TIP:** The directions for the essay section (the part before the box) are always the same. Become familiar with these directions before taking the test so you don't have to spend a lot of time reading them during the test. Instead, focus on reading the boxed topic and the prompt that follows.

# B. How Your Writing Is Evaluated—The Writing Rubric

Essays are scored by specially trained readers using a scoring guide called a rubric. Your scores on Language Arts: Writing Parts 1 and 2 are combined into a composite scaled score from 1 to 20. Both your composite scaled score and the score on the essay are reported on your official score report. To pass the Writing section, you have to achieve **both** a composite scaled score of at least 8 <u>as well as</u> a minimum score of 2 on the essay section.

Look at the sample response to the above prompt on public transportation. This essay would most likely score a 6.

Did you ever get to the bus stop only to see the bus pulling away? Or have you ever been stuck in a traffic jam for hours? Then you should be interested in enhanced public transportation for our town. All of us need to go to different places, such as work, school, doctor's appointments, and shopping. However, our town does not have enough public transportation. Improved public transportation would help our town in three ways: It would improve life for many people, reduce traffic, and reduce pollution.

First, many people depend on public transportation, but we do not have enough public transportation to meet people's needs. Right now, buses run only every 30 or 60 minutes. That means that there is not a bus at convenient times. There are also late night buses on only 3 routes. This makes it very difficult for people who work late shifts to use public transportation. Finally, buses do not go to many important places. For example, no buses run from the south end of town to River Mall. And buses do not serve Ridge Industrial Park. Many people cannot accept jobs at the Industrial Park because they do not have reliable transportation to get to work. While many people with cars may not support public transportation because of higher taxes, people who do not own cars still need public transportation in order to live happy lives in our community. In addition, the higher taxes may not be necessary because the cost will be offset by income from jobs created by public transportation.

Second, pollution in our town is a big problem. I live near route 11, and neighbors along that street always complain about the pollution from cars and trucks. Pollution is especially bad on days when the wind is from the west, because the pollution is trapped by the mountains outside of town. The only time we have fresh air is when there is a breeze from the south that brings some fresh air. Fewer cars would mean less pollution, which is dangerous for people with asthma. Reduced pollution would help everyone in town, whether or not they drive.

Finally, traffic in our town gets worse every year. There are to many cars on the road. During morning and evening rush hour, it can take more than 40 minutes to drive downtown from any part of the city. With improved public transportation, there would be less cars on the road, and people could get to their destinations more quicker.

In conclusion, while many people prefer to drive their cars, many people depend on public transportation. Improved public transportation would help people get to work, shopping, doctor's visits, and much more. It would also reduce traffic and congestion. I hope everyone supports the proposal to improve public transportation in our town.

Look at the Learner-Friendly HiSET Essay Scoring Rubric that follows. This rubric was adopted from the official rubric used by score readers. It is simplified for use by test-takers and teachers to help you prepare for the test. To see the official rubric, go to http://hiset.ets.org/s/pdf/writing_response_scoring_guide.pdf. Use the Learner-Friendly HiSET Essay Scoring Rubric to figure out why this essay scored a 6.

| Learner-Friendly HiSET Essay Scoring Rubric | |
| --- | --- |
| **Score** | **Description** |
| 1 | Essays with a score of 1 show **little or no** skill.<br>❏ **The essay lacks development of ideas.** The essay may provide a few ideas but lacks explanation of ideas, repeats ideas, or the ideas lack relevance.<br>❏ **The essay has minimal organization.** The essay does not have an introduction and conclusion. The essay does not organize ideas into logical paragraphs. The essay does not use transitions or transitions are used incorrectly.<br>❏ **The essay has minimal control of language.** Vocabulary and sentence structure are simple. The essay has errors in sentence construction, pronoun use, verb forms, and/or spelling. The errors frequently make the essay hard to understand. |
| 2 | Essays with a score of 2 show **weak** skill.<br>❏ **The essay has weak development of ideas.** The essay gives a few ideas, but the amount of explanation is very limited. The details, support, and explanation may be repetitive or lack relevance.<br>❏ **The essay has weak organization.** There is little evidence of an introduction and/or conclusion. Some related ideas are grouped together, but related ideas may not be grouped into paragraphs. The essay may use transitions, but their use is awkward or incorrect.<br>❏ **The essay has beginning skills in language use.** Vocabulary choice is awkward or repetitive. The essay has repetitive sentence structure and/or long, uncontrolled sentences. The essay has serious errors in sentence construction, pronoun use, verb forms, and/or spelling that disrupt the flow of the essay, and some errors may make parts of the essay hard to understand. |
| 3 | Essays with a score of 3 show **limited** skill.<br>❏ **The essay has limited development of ideas.** The essay focuses on a central idea through some of the response. The essay gives several supporting ideas but with limited or uneven explanation and few or only general examples and/or details.<br>❏ **The essay shows developing skill in organization.** The essay has an introduction and conclusion, but they may be too long or too short. The essay groups related ideas in paragraphs, but the relationships among ideas may be unclear at times. The essay uses a few transitions between and/or within paragraphs.<br>❏ **The essay shows developing skills in language use.** Vocabulary is general, and the essay has a little variety in sentence structure, but may have a few long, uncontrolled sentences. Errors in sentence construction, pronoun use, verb forms, and/or spelling are present and may occasionally cause problems with understanding. |
| 4 | Essays with a score of 4 show **adequate** skill.<br>❏ **The essay has adequate development of ideas.** The essay stays focused on a main idea most of the time. The essay gives several ideas with adequate explanation and offers some specific and relevant examples and/or supporting details.<br>❏ **The essay shows adequate skills in organization.** The essay has a clear introduction and conclusion that are somewhat developed. The essay groups related ideas into paragraphs and sometimes presents ideas in a logical order. The essay consistently uses simple transitions between and/or within paragraphs.<br>❏ **The essay shows adequate skills in language use.** The vocabulary is usually specific and somewhat varied. The essay shows control of sentence patterns with some variety in length and structure. The tone is usually appropriate for the audience and purpose of the essay. The essay has some errors in sentence construction, pronoun use, verb forms, and/or spelling, but the errors do not interfere with understanding. |

*continued*

| Score | Description |
|-------|-------------|
| 5 | Essays with a score of 5 show **competent** skill. <br> ❑ **The essay has competent development of ideas.** The essay stays focused on a clear main idea. The essay gives several supporting ideas with complete explanation; and the essay gives specific, relevant, and somewhat elaborated reasons, examples, and/or details to back up the supporting ideas. The essay shows some critical thinking in that it brings up complications of the issue and/or counterarguments. <br> ❑ **The essay shows competent organization skills.** The essay has clear, well-developed introductory and concluding paragraphs, and the introduction clearly states the main idea of the response. The essay has a clear and appropriate paragraph structure, and ideas are in a logical order throughout most of the response. The essay uses varied transitions between and within paragraphs. <br> ❑ **The essay shows competent skills in language use.** Vocabulary is usually precise and varied. The essay uses well-controlled sentence patterns, and sentences are varied in length and complexity. Tone is appropriate for the audience and purpose of the essay. There are few grammar, usage, or mechanics errors and most are not important and do not interfere with understanding. |
| 6 | Essays with a score of 6 show **proficient** skill. <br> ❑ **The essay shows proficient development of ideas.** The essay stays focused on a clear main idea. The essay gives several supporting ideas with complete and thorough explanation. It has relevant and fully explained reasons, examples, and/or details to back up the supporting ideas. The essay shows strong critical thinking skills and insight. It discusses complications of the issue and/or addresses counterarguments. <br> ❑ **The essay shows proficient organization skills.** The essay has effective, well-developed introductory and conclusion paragraphs, and has an interesting introduction that clearly states the organization of the response. The essay has a clear and appropriate paragraph structure. The ideas are in a logical order. The essay has effective transitions. <br> ❑ **The essay shows proficient skills in language use.** Vocabulary is precise, varied, and interesting. The essay uses sentences of varied length and complexity. The tone is appropriate for the essay's audience and purpose and makes the response more effective. The essay has no or only a few minor errors that do not affect communication and has sophisticated grammar, usage, and mechanics. |

The sample essay on page 148 shows all the features of an essay with a score of 6. This table sums up the criteria in the Learner-Friendly HiSET Essay Scoring Rubric for an essay with a score of 6 and shows how the sample fulfills the criteria.

| What Makes the Essay a 6? | |
|---|---|
| **Scoring Rubric Criteria** | **How the Sample Meets the Criteria** |
| **The essay shows proficient development of ideas.** The essay stays focused on a clear main idea. The essay gives several supporting ideas with complete and thorough explanation. It has relevant and fully explained reasons, examples, and/or details to back up the supporting ideas. The essay shows strong critical thinking skills and insight. It discusses complications of the issue and/or addresses counterarguments. | The essay is focused on the main idea, which is supporting enhanced public transportation in the writer's town. The essay has three supporting ideas: Making life easier for people, reduced pollution, and reduced traffic. Each supporting paragraph has reasons, examples, and/or details that back up the supporting ideas. The essay addresses objections of car drivers in key places, and shows ways that improved public transportation will improve life for everyone. For example, the writer admits that improving public transportation will result in increased taxes, but also says that the higher taxes will be offset by all the new jobs created because of public transportation. |

| Scoring Rubric Criteria | How the Sample Meets the Criteria |
| --- | --- |
| **The essay shows proficient organization skills.** The essay has effective, well-developed introductory and conclusion paragraphs, and has an interesting introduction that clearly states the organization of the response. The essay has a clear and appropriate paragraph structure. The ideas are in a logical order. The essay has effective transitions. | The essay has a well-developed introduction that gets readers' attention through some questions that everyone can relate to: missing a bus or being stuck in traffic. The final sentence of the introduction (the thesis statement) clearly indicates the contents and order of the body paragraphs that follow. The essay has a good paragraph structure: each of the supporting ideas has its own paragraph. The order of the ideas makes sense, and the essay has transitional words such as *first, second, finally,* and *for example.* |
| **The essay shows proficient skills in language use.** Vocabulary is precise, varied, and interesting. The essay uses sentences of varied length and complexity. The tone is appropriate for the essay's audience and purpose, and makes the response more effective. The essay has no or only a few minor errors that do not affect communication and has sophisticated grammar, usage, and mechanics. | The essay uses precise and varied vocabulary, and has sentences of various lengths and complexity. For example, the second body paragraph contains vocabulary such as *pollution, trapped, breeze,* and *asthma.* The tone of the essay is respectful and persuasive and designed to convince everyone in town to support the proposal. There are only a few errors in grammar, usage, and mechanics, which are sophisticated and appropriate. For example, *route 11* should be *Route 11, less* should be *fewer, more quicker* should be *more quickly.* |

# 1. Practice 1: Applying the Rubric

**Directions:** Read the sample essays that respond to the public transportation prompt on page 147. Use the rubric to write a score for each one.

## a. Sample Essays for Review

1. **Score:** _____

   The speaker at the meeting said that more public transportation is needed, but I disagree. I have a car, I worked very hard to get the money to buy it. My car is not expensive but it's reliable and nice. I don't think it is fair for me to pay high tacsses in order for other people to ride the bus inexpensively. I think that all people should pay their own way and not make me pay for their transportation. So I am against this idea and think that everyone should work hard and pay their own way and not make me pay a tacks for their public transportation.

2. **Score:** _____

   Do you pay too much in taxes? I do. That's why I oppose spending more money on public transportation. I do not want to pay more for more public transportation because it's too expensive already, people do not use the public transportation we have now, and bus transportation will not work for many people.

   According to the city budget, we already spend a lot of money on public transportation. I heard at a meeting that we spend nearly $30 million a year on public transportation. That is a lot of money. Our taxes are already very high. We do not need to spend more money on public transportation when there are other pressing needs. The elementary school near my house, for example needs new classrooms and computers. That's where we should spend the money.

   On top of the cost, not enough people take public transportation right now. Most of the busses I see are completely empty, or have only 1 or 2 passengers. The only routes that are busy are the ones that serve schools. So I think that maybe the solution is to have less public transportation and focus on the places where it is needed the most, such as schools.

Finally, I believe that for many people, more public transportation will not get them to use public transportation. For example, I am a salesperson for a beverage company. I have to visit many different stores and supermarkets every day on all parts of town. Often I have to carry samples of new drinks. I have to have a car to do my work. I am sure that there are many people like me who cannot use public transportation.

In conclusion, I believe that it is foolish to spend money on public transportation when we spend so much on it already and people do not use it or cannot use it. Instead, we should focus on lowering taxes and spending money where it is needed, such as improved public schools.

3. **Score:** _____

I take public transportation every day, and have many problems with good service. I think we need more busses, more bus lines, and nicer busses.

Right now, most of the bus lines in our town run every 30 or 60 minutes. That is not enough. First of all, if you are a minute late, you will miss your bus and then have to wait an hour. We need more frequent busses especially at busy times. We also need to have more busses on routes to schools. At 7:30 my bus is packed with teenagers headed to Central High School. Right now, there is only 1 bus per hour to Central High School. On rainy days, that bus is so full I cannot get on sometimes. So we need more frequent busses.

Second, we also need more bus lines. For example, there is not a convenient bus to Rosemont Beach, River Mall, or several other places in town. People who want to work or shop in the mall cannot get there by bus. Rosemont Beach is nice in summer, but people who do not have cars cannot go there. In addition, there is not even a convenient bus to get to City Hall and Downtown from my neighborhood. We have to go far out of our way to Central Terminal and change busses. We need more direct bus lines to places where people want to go.

Finally, the busses in our town are more than 20 years old. They are the same busses I took to high school when I was a student. They are old, make a lot of pollution, and do not have air conditioning, or the air conditioning does not work well. Last year, I went to Shelbyville to visit my aunt. Shelbyville just got new busses that do not pollute and are cheaper to operate. I read in the newspaper that these busses cost half as much to operate than the old busses, so Shelbyville doubled the bus service at the same cost.

I see many reasons to have improved public transportation. I hope that everyone understands that we need more frequent busses, more bus lines, and better busses. We need to be better than Shelbyville.

4. **Score:** _____

I take bus to work every day. Don't like to take bus, but don't have a car. Today some guy was smoking on the bus, driver called the police. Police took a long time comming, I was late for work. Now in trouble at work because of this bus. I want to buy car as soon as I can.

5. **Score:** _____

I take the bus every day, and I think better bus service is important.

For example, yesterday, it was raining, I mist my bus home from work. I had to wait for 30 minutes in the rain together with a lot of other people. Then the next bus was late, so we had to wait more longer. So we need more frequent bus service. Also, sometimes I need to go to my foot doctor's office. But there is not a bus that goes to this area. So I have to walk or take a cab, very expensive for me, and walking is not good for my foots. Last, these busses are old and dirty and brake down a lot. Who wants to ride these busses? We need comfortable busses that are clean and nice.

So let's all support this proposal.

## b. Answer Explanations

1. **This essay would most likely score a 2.** The essay has one relevant idea, but is repetitious and includes some irrelevant detail about the writer's car. There is an attempt to write an introduction and conclusion, but the conclusion is part of a long, run-on sentence that repeats ideas discussed earlier. Ideas are not organized into paragraphs. The vocabulary is limited and awkward, and there are many errors in sentence patterns.

2. **This essay would most likely score a 5.** It has three main supporting ideas, and each one has supporting reasons, examples, or details. It also brings up counterarguments, such as using money to improve schools. It has an introduction and conclusion and organizes ideas into supporting paragraphs. It uses transitions in many places. It has few errors, and some variety in sentence patterns, though a few sentences are too long and complicated.

3. **This essay would most likely score a 4.** It has three main supporting ideas, each of which is somewhat developed, though there is still some unnecessary information and detail. The essay has a fairly well-developed introduction and concluding paragraph and groups related ideas into three supporting paragraphs. The essay uses mostly simple transitions between paragraphs. The essay has some problems with sentence structure and variety, as well as some errors in spelling and grammar, but these do not interfere with understanding.

4. **This response would most likely score a 1.** The information in the essay is not relevant to the topic. The essay does not have an introduction or conclusion and does not organize ideas into paragraphs or use transitions. It has little variety in vocabulary and contains errors in grammar, sentence structure, and spelling, many of which interfere with understanding.

5. **This essay would most likely score a 3.** The essay includes three relevant ideas, but they are not explained fully. The essay has an introduction and a conclusion, but they are very short. The essay has the beginning of a paragraph structure but groups all the ideas into a single body paragraph that does not develop ideas fully. The essay does not use transitions, but ideas are in a logical order. The essay has many errors in vocabulary, grammar, and sentence structure, and some of these interfere with understanding. For example, the writer uses *mist* instead of *missed,* which is especially confusing in a sentence that also talks about rainy weather.

# C. Writing an Effective Essay: A Detailed Look

This section examines a good structure to use to write a high-scoring essay: the five-paragraph essay. Then we will look at a simple three-step process you can follow to write a high-scoring five-paragraph essay in 45 minutes.

# 1. The Five-Paragraph Essay

When you write, it's important that you have plenty of good ideas and detail. It's also important that to present your ideas and detail in an order that is logical and easy to understand. The scoring rubric makes clear that a high-scoring essay should have effective introductory and concluding paragraphs, as well as well-developed supporting paragraphs. A good number of supporting paragraphs is three. Therefore, one way to write an effective essay is to follow the five-paragraph format:

**Five-Paragraph Essay**

1. Introductory paragraph
2. Supporting paragraph 1
3. Supporting paragraph 2
4. Supporting paragraph 3
5. Concluding paragraph

The sample essay on page 148 successfully uses the five-paragraph format. Here's a breakdown of the essay.

# a. Introductory Paragraph

As you learned in Chapter IV, an effective **introductory paragraph** is organized from general to specific. The essay begins with some opening sentences that get the reader's attention: "Did you ever get to the bus stop only to see the bus pulling away? Or have you ever been stuck in a traffic jam for hours? Then you should be interested in enhanced public transportation for our town."

The introductory paragraph goes on to introduce the topic of the essay and gives an overview of the supporting paragraphs that follow and makes the writer's point of view clear. These sentences give a general overview of the topic: "All of us need to go to different places, such as work, school, doctor's appointments, and shopping. However, our town does not have enough public transportation." The last sentence of the introductory paragraph, called the **thesis statement,** gives an indication of the main idea of each supporting paragraph that follows: "Improved public transportation would help our town in three ways: It would improve life for many people, reduce traffic, and reduce pollution."

> **TIP:** The prompt may ask you to write a letter, such as a letter to the editor. In this case, you should still write in the form of an essay. You do not need to include greetings (such as *Dear Editor*) or closings (such as *Sincerely*).

# b. Supporting Paragraphs

The three paragraphs that follow the introduction are called **supporting paragraphs,** and each of them is about one supporting idea. Supporting paragraphs give specific reasons, explanations, and details to back up the supporting idea. Each supporting paragraph is organized from general to specific. First, a **topic sentence** gives the main idea of the paragraph. Then each sentence that follows gives specific reasons, examples, and details that back up the topic sentence. For example, in Paragraph 2, the topic sentence is, "First, many people depend on public transportation, but we do not have enough public transportation to meet people's needs." The following sentences give reasons, examples, and details that show that there is not enough public transportation to meet people's needs.

# c. Concluding Paragraph

The **concluding paragraph** sums up the ideas in the essay. Concluding paragraphs are organized from specific to general. In the sample essay, Paragraph 5 is the concluding paragraph. The first three sentences sum up information in the essay: "In conclusion, while many people prefer to drive their cars, many people depend on public transportation. Improved public transportation would help people get to work, shopping, doctor's visits, and much more. It would also reduce traffic and congestion." The final sentence is a strong, general restatement of the main idea of the entire essay: "I hope everyone supports the proposal to improve public transportation in our town."

TIP: You studied paragraph structure in the "Organization" section in Chapter IV, pages 112–119. Use what you learned about effective paragraph writing in Chapter IV to help you write your essay. If necessary, review "Writing Conventions" (pages 132–146) in Chapter IV as well.

# 2. The Three Rs Writing Process

You will have only 45 minutes to write your essay. In general, the scoring rubric gives more attention to organization and support than to grammar and other details of writing. Therefore, you should spend more of your time on gathering and organizing ideas and writing in complete, effective sentences and paragraphs, than on details of writing such as capitalization, spelling, and so on. A few errors in these areas will not lower your score excessively.

Because 45 minutes is very little time, we recommend a specific three-part writing strategy to help you plan, write, and revise your essay in 45 minutes. We call this plan the Three Rs Writing Process:

1. Get **Ready** (10 minutes)
2. **Write** (30 minutes)
3. **Revise** (5 minutes)

Following this plan will help you write a high-scoring essay in a short amount of time.

TIP: When you begin your essay, write the three Rs on your scratch paper so you can be sure to follow them as you write.

## a. Get Ready

To get ready to write, you should do the following:

1. Skim the directions very quickly.
2. Read the topic and prompt carefully and make sure you understand them.
3. Gather and organize your ideas.

Look again at the topic the writer of the sample essay responded to:

> At a community meeting, several people spoke about a need for better public transportation in the city. There was a lot of discussion during and after the meeting. Community residents offered many ideas for and against improved public transportation. Do you think that your community needs improved public transportation?

The topic gives important background information and frequently ends with a question. Usually, it will state an issue or controversy of general interest, and tell when and where the controversy took place. In this case, people at a meeting talked about a need for better public transportation. The question that follows asks your opinion about the issue.

> TIP: Not all topics end with a question to answer in your essay. Some may state a scenario and then the prompt directs you to write an essay to persuade your audience to take action or to detail the pros and cons of an issue.

Even if you do not really care that much about the issue, you should choose an opinion you can back up with examples, reasons, and details in your essay.

> TIP: When you decide how you will respond, choose the side of the issue that is easiest for you to support with examples, reasons, and details, even if you do not agree with that point of view.

Next, read the writing prompt that follows. Usually, it will specify a purpose and audience for your writing. In this example, you need to write an article for the community's news website. Other prompts might ask you to write a letter to the editor, a blog post, an email or letter to a public official, or some other type of persuasive writing. As you get ready to write, make sure your essay matches the type of writing specified in the prompt. Here is the prompt from the sample essay:

> Write an essay for your community's news website that explains whether or not you think your community needs improved public transportation. Think carefully about reasons that will help others understand your position as well as examples and details that you can use to support your position.

Try to spend only a few minutes understanding the prompt. As soon as you understand the prompt, begin to gather ideas. The writing prompt states that you should, "Think carefully about reasons that will help others understand your position as well as examples and details that you can use to support your position." A good way to do this is by structured brainstorming. When you use structured brainstorming, find your three main supporting ideas and write them on your scratch paper. Look at this example:

People need more public transportation

Reduce traffic

Reduce pollution

Next, write as many reasons, examples, and details as you can about each supporting idea on your scratch paper. Use abbreviations to save time writing. In this case, the writer used the letter *b* to save time writing the word *buses* many times. Do not worry about whether all of the ideas are good. And do not worry about grammar, vocabulary, and spelling. You can take care of those things later in the process.

People need more public transportation
b run every 30/60 min
no b to impt places—River Mall & Indust. Pk—people can't get job
only 3 night b
many people have cars, but people who don't can't live good lives

Reduce traffic
more b = less traffic
traffic worse every year
40 min drive downtown rush hour

Reduce pollution
air only fresh when breeze frm south
lots of pollution rt 11

pollution bad with west wind
pollution dangerous for asthma
reduced pollution will help all people
hybrid and electric cars will help, too

A high-scoring essay addresses counterarguments and contradictory information. For example, in the sample essay, the writer included key details about people who oppose improved public transportation. If you think of a counterargument, jot it down as you brainstorm.

After you brainstorm, number your ideas quickly. First, number your supporting paragraphs in order.

TIP: When you organize your essay, order your ideas from most important to least important. This way, if you are running out of time, you can leave off your third paragraph, add a concluding paragraph, and finish before time is up. This method will ensure that you include your strongest reasons in your essay.

In this case, the writer decided to number the paragraphs as follows:

1. People need more public transportation
b run every 30/60 min
no b to impt places—River Mall & Indust. Pk—people can't get job
only 3 night b
many people have cars, but people who don't can't live good lives

3. Reduce traffic
more b = less traffic
traffic worse every year
40 min drive downtown rush hour

2. Reduce pollution
air only fresh when breeze frm south
lots of pollution rt 11
pollution bad with west wind
pollution dangerous for asthma
reduced pollution will help all people
hybrid and electric cars will help, too

Then number the ideas in each paragraph in the most effective order. If any ideas are not related to the topic, cross them off. Look at how the writer numbered the ideas and crossed of irrelevant ones.

1. People need more public transportation
1. b run every 30/60 min
3. no b to impt places—River Mall & Indust. Pk—people can't get jobs
2. only 3 night b
4. many people have cars, but people who don't can't live good lives

3. Reduce traffic
2. more b = less traffic
1. traffic worse every year
3. 40 min drive downtown rush hour

2. Reduce pollution
3. air only fresh when breeze frm south
1. lots of pollution rt 11
2 pollution bad with west wind
4. pollution dangerous for asthma
5. reduced pollution will help all people
~~hybrid and electric cars will help, too~~

Once you have gathered and organized your ideas, you are ready to write.

## b. Write

When you are ready to write, you should use your brainstorming ideas to write strong introductory and supporting paragraphs. An effective introductory paragraph is very important to a high-scoring essay, so try to think of an interesting way to get the reader's attention.

> **TIP: A provocative first sentence or some engaging questions are good ways to get the reader's attention.**

In the sample essay (page 148), the questions the writer posed at the beginning of the essay were effective in getting the reader's attention. After you write an attention-getting beginning, write a few more general sentences about the topic. Make sure that your opinion about the topic—for or against—is clear. End your introductory paragraph with a strong topic sentence that clearly indicates the organization of the essay. Look again at the sample essay's topic sentence: "Improved public transportation would help our town in three ways: It would improve life for many people, reduce traffic, and reduce pollution." This sentence clearly states the writer's opinion and indicates the three main supporting ideas that will be discussed in the rest of the essay.

Next, write three supporting paragraphs. Begin each supporting paragraph with a strong topic sentence. A **topic sentence** is a general sentence that states the main idea of the paragraph. The topic sentence of the first supporting paragraph of the sample essay is, "First, many people depend on public transportation, but we do not have enough public transportation to meet people's needs."

An important criterion of the scoring rubric is variety in sentence patterns and vocabulary. To score well, you should avoid short, choppy sentences; instead, try to combine ideas into longer, more sophisticated sentences. For example, you can join shorter sentences with coordinating conjunctions such as *and, but, or, for, nor, yet,* and *so.* You can also create longer and more sophisticated sentences by joining shorter sentences with subordinating conjunctions. Look at the table of Subordinating Conjunctions on page 126.

Also try to use varied vocabulary. For example, in the sample essay, the writer uses both *buses* and *public transportation* in the essay.

Another important criterion of the scoring rubric is using effective transitions. **Transitions** help readers see the relationship of paragraphs and ideas in paragraphs. The chart on page 115 shows some examples of common transitional words and phrases.

As you write, be sure to include transitions at the beginning of each supporting paragraph and within each one as well. Because you are writing a persuasive essay with the supporting paragraphs in order from most important to least important, you could begin each body paragraph with *first, second,* and *finally,* as in the sample essay. You could also begin the first supporting paragraph with *Most importantly* instead of *first*. This would clearly signal to readers that you are using order of importance to organize your ideas.

Finally, write a strong concluding paragraph organized from specific to general.

**TIP: A good way to begin your concluding paragraph is with the transitional phrase *In conclusion*. This is an easy-to-remember way to include a transitional phrase that clearly shows the reader that the conclusion is beginning.**

To write a good concluding paragraph, first restate the thesis statement in new words. Then add a few more general sentences. End with a general sentence restating the main idea of the whole essay.

**TIP: If you run out of time during the essay section, leave off your third supporting paragraph and write a good conclusion as quickly as possible. Then change your thesis statement to match the supporting paragraphs in your essay.**

## c. Revise

When you revise, you should check the order and organization of your essay, grammar, sentence structure, and vocabulary, as well as writing details such as capitalization, punctuation, and spelling. Make sure you use complete sentences. If you see ways to combine short sentences into longer, more sophisticated ones, do so.

If you follow these steps in the practice essays that follow, you are well on your way to writing a high-scoring HiSET essay.

# 3. Practice 2: Essay Writing
## a. Directions, Topic, and Writing Prompt

**Directions:** This is a test of your writing skills. You have 45 minutes to prepare and write your response. Your essay will be scored based on the following criteria:

- Development and support of a main idea with examples and details
- Clear and effective organization of ideas, including an introduction, body, and conclusion; logical paragraphs; and effective transitions between and within paragraphs
- Appropriate language use, including varied vocabulary, varied sentence patterns, and appropriate voice
- Clarity and use of Standard Written English

---

A speaker at the public library recently gave a talk about ways to improve community health. One of her recommendations was to require all restaurants to print the calorie and fat content of each dish on the menu. Many people supported the idea, but the owner of a popular local restaurant strongly opposed it. Your local library is preparing a special newsletter about whether restaurants should print the calorie and fat content of each dish on their menus.

---

Write an essay for the library's newsletter that explains whether or not you think your community should require all restaurants to print the fat and calorie content of all menu items. Think carefully about reasons that will help others understand your position as well as examples and details that you can use to support your position.

# b. Sample Essays with Scores and Explanations

Use the Learner-Friendly HiSET Essay Scoring Rubric on pages 149–150 and these sample essays to evaluate and score your essay. If possible, ask a teacher or a friend who is good at writing to evaluate and score your writing for you. Whether or not you can get another person to review your essay, you should always use the rubric and sample essays to evaluate and score your essay yourself. Set aside your essay for a day or two so you can view it with fresh eyes. Then compare your essay to the sample essays. Find the sample essay that most closely resembles your essay. Then read the descriptions in the rubric for that score as well as the scores above and below it. Select the description that best matches your essay. That should give you a good idea of your final score. If you were able to have another person score your essay, compare the two results. Use the information you learn to figure out ways you can improve your writing.

## i. Sample Essay, Score = 1

I am not so fat so I do not pay attention to calories and fat. I like to eat all my favorite foods like fried chicken, ribs, burgers, and pizza. I do not like vegetables, soup and I hate salad most of all. All of these foods are high in fat but, my special favorite is hot Italian sawssage. Calorie and fat not important to me because I am not fat.

**Explanation:** The information in the essay is not relevant to the topic. It does not have an introduction or a conclusion, and it does not organize ideas into paragraphs or use transitions. It has little variety in vocabulary and many errors in grammar and usage.

## ii. Sample Essay, Score = 2

I like to eat in restrants, I always eat lunch at a different restrant every day. Sometimes I eat at a fast food restrant that rights the calories and fat on the menu, but other times I order the same food a restrant that does not right the information. Since I always order the same food, it does not make a difference whether I have the information or not. So this information is not necessary. Usually, I order what I want like a cheeseborger and fries. I will not change my order because of having this information or not, so I don't think the information makes any difference.

**Explanation:** The essay has one relevant idea, but the essay is repetitious and includes some irrelevant detail about the writer's food preferences. There is an attempt to write an introduction and conclusion, but ideas are not organized into paragraphs. The vocabulary is limited and awkward, and there are many errors in grammar and spelling that interfere with understanding.

## iii. Sample Essay, Score = 3

Like many people, I am on a diet to lose wait. So I worry a lot about food I eat, and I want to find out ways to improve my diet.

Having information on fat and calories in food will help me a lot. For example, I recently found out that 2 tacos has a lot less fat than a taco salad. That surprised me a lot and helped me because I like tacos and want to avoid a lot of fat. I also found out that many appetizers have a lot of fat and salt. Before, I liked to order 2 appetizers instead of a mane dish. Now I kno that ordering these appetizers is not a good idea. I can order a mane dish and not worry about all that salt and fat. So for me having more information about my food is a good idea and will help me have healthy food in my life.

**Explanation:** The essay includes relevant ideas, but they are not explained fully. The essay has an introduction and a conclusion, but they are very short. The essay has the beginning of a paragraph structure, but groups all the ideas into a single body paragraph that does not develop ideas fully, and the essay lacks a separate concluding paragraph. The essay does not use transitions, but ideas are in a logical order. The essay has many errors in vocabulary, grammar, and sentence structure, and some of these interfere with understanding.

## iv. Sample Essay, Score = 4

At a recent meeting, a speaker shared some ideas about nutrition when eating out. As a restaurant owner, I was concerned because she suggested that the city require all restaurants to post the fat and calories in all menu items. This seems like a good idea, but it will harm local businesses, reduce choices of restaurants for customers, and not provide better food choices for customers.

First, this idea will harm local businesses. Calculating the fat and calories in a restaurant dish requires an expensive test. Restaurants send food samples to a lab, plus the recipes. These lab tests costs thousands of dollars. Big chains can afford this cost but small family owned businesses cann't. My restaurant would have to close if faced with this cost. This will hurt families and businesses in town.

Second, because many small, local restaurants will close, consumers will be hurt too. Some of the best restaurants in town are locally owned, and these restaurants produce some of the best food in town.

Third, knowing the fat and calories in food is not enough. People need to make educated choices. And restaurants need to provide healthy options. A better way idea is for restaurants to include healthy options on their menus. I have 7 healthy items on our regular menu. One daily special is healthy, too. These healthy options, not knowing the calories and fat, will help customers make good choices.

For these reasons, I oppose the idea of making restaurants put fat and calorie counts on their menus. I hope that everyone can see the big problems this idea will cause.

**Explanation:** This essay has three main supporting ideas, each of which is somewhat developed, though there is still not enough information and detail. The essay has fairly well-developed introductory and concluding paragraphs, and groups related ideas into three supporting paragraphs. The essay mostly uses simple transitions between paragraphs. The essay has some problems with sentence structure and variety, as well as some errors in spelling and grammar, but these do not interfere with understanding.

## v. Sample Essay, Score = 5

Everyone knows that we need to eat better. Too many people in our country are overweight. At a recent meeting at the library, a guest speaker made a good suggestion: require restaurants to put the fat and calorie counts of all foods directly on the menu. This idea is good for several reasons: people can make good choices, restaurants will try to reduce excess calories and fat, and children will learn good eating habits.

Right now, most restaurant customers do not know much about the content of the food they eat. They just know it tastes good. But did you know that a single restaurant meal can contain up to a stick of butter? Restaurants use that much fat to make their food taste better, but people need to know how much fat and calories they are getting. Sometimes, just by ordering one kind of cheeseburger instead of another, customers can greatly reduce the amount of fat and calories they eat.

Second, at present, there is no incentive for restaurants to watch whether their food has excessive calories or fat. They just want the food to taste good so customers keep coming back. Putting the amount of calories and fat will encourage restaurants to reduce excessive calories and fat because the information will be out in the open for everyone to see. Restaurants may not like this, but encouraging restaurants to reduce excess fat is definitely in the public good.

Finally, children will learn good eating habits from the start. Most people today were not raised paying attention to calories and fat. This is one of the reason there are so many obese children in our country. If children see their parents checking calorie and fat counts, and if parents make sure that their children order items low in fat and calories, then they will learn better eating habits, and childhood obesity will go down.

In conclusion, this proposal will help everyone. Restaurant customers will be able to make better choices, restaurants will begin to police the amount of calories and fat in their food, and children will learn better eating habits from the start. This is a great proposal, and I hope that the city council takes up this issue very soon.

**Explanation:** This essay has three main supporting ideas, and each one has well-developed supporting reasons, examples, or details. It also brings up and addresses a counterargument from restaurant owners. The essay has an introduction and a conclusion and organizes ideas into supporting paragraphs. The essay uses transitions in many places. It has few errors, and some variety in sentence patterns, though a few sentences are too long and complicated.

## vi. Sample Essay, Score = 6

Do you feel that there is too much government regulation of our lives? Do you think that we should be free to live our lives as we wish? Then I hope you will join me in opposing a recent suggestion from a guest speaker at the library. She suggested that restaurants be required to provide fat and calorie counts for every food they serve. This sort of excessive regulation is bad for business, is too much government control of our lives, and will not solve the health problems caused by overeating or eating too much fat and calories.

First, regulations such as these are bad for business. Businesses in our country are all regulated too much. Restaurants are already required to meet very stringent requirement for such things as cleanliness and food storage. Requiring restaurants to figure out the calorie and fat content of their food will be very costly, and this cost will be passed on to consumers. This will cause business to go down, since customers will have to eat out less. This will cost our community tax revenue and jobs. While many people believe that this proposal will make us healthier, a healthy economy is important, too. If restaurants close and people lose their jobs, our community will be harmed.

A second reason that this is a bad proposal is that the government already controls our lives too much. There is too much government regulation of our lives. In my opinion, the government needs to stay out of people's business and let them make their own decisions. Right now, very few restaurants provide fat and calorie counts, which shows that people really do not want them. If customers really wanted this information, they would demand it, and government regulation would not be necessary.

Third, this proposal will not solve health problems caused by overeating and eating too much fat. People will continue to order food they like. I believe that personal responsibility, and not government regulation, will cause people to eat better. Right now, there are plenty of healthy options on most restaurants menus, but people do not order them. Putting the calorie and fat counts will not change people's behavior. People need to make their own decisions themselves.

In conclusion, this proposal is bad for our community's economy, is too much regulation, and will not solve the problems posed by overeating. Instead, we need to teach people to take responsibility for solving their problems themselves. Government regulation is not the way to solve this problem. People need to solve it themselves by making better decisions about what they eat.

**Explanation:** This essay has three main supporting ideas, and each one has well-developed supporting reasons, examples, or details. The introduction gets the reader's attention by asking some provocative questions. The essay brings up and addresses counterarguments in key places. Ideas are organized into effective supporting paragraphs, and transitions are used between and within paragraphs. This essay has few errors and shows variety in sentence patterns; grammar, vocabulary, and usage are sophisticated.

# D. Additional Writing Topics and Prompts

Use these writing topics and prompts to gain additional practice writing HiSET essays. Use the Learner-Friendly HiSET Essay Scoring Rubric on pages 149–150 and the sample essays in this chapter to evaluate and score your practice essays. If possible, ask a teacher or a friend who is good at writing to evaluate and score your writing for you. Whether or not you can get another person to review your essay, you should always use the rubric and sample essays to evaluate and score your essay yourself.

1. At a recent town hall meeting, a speaker from City Cyclers, a group dedicated to improving bicycle transportation in the city, proposed that the city eliminate a lane of traffic in each direction and replace the traffic lane with a bicycle lane. The idea generated a lot of controversy. Do you think that the community should replace a traffic lane in each direction on main streets with a bicycle lane?

Write an essay for your community's news website that explains whether or not you think your community should replace a traffic lane in each direction with a bicycle lane on main streets. Think carefully about reasons that will help others understand your position as well as examples and details that you can use to support your position.

2. At a recent Parent-Teacher Association meeting, a speaker discussed testing in school. He thinks that children have to take too many standardized tests, and that all the testing has reduced the time children spend learning. The Parent-Teacher Association has asked community members to write their ideas about this topic, so they can share people's ideas with school leaders.

Write an essay for the Parent-Teacher Association that persuades people to accept your point of view about whether the number of standardized tests schoolchildren take is excessive and should be reduced. Think carefully about reasons that will help others understand your position as well as examples and details that you can use to support your position.

3. Many communities have installed speeding cameras and red light cameras in their neighborhoods. The cameras are designed to stop people from speeding and running red lights. These cameras are highly controversial, and your city is considering whether or not to install them. Do you think your community should install speeding cameras and red light cameras?

Write an essay to your local city council member that explains whether or not you think the city should install speeding cameras and red light cameras. Think carefully about reasons that will help others understand your position as well as examples and details that you can use to support your position.

4. A local park was recently badly damaged by a major flood. The swimming pool, basketball courts, and baseball fields were ruined and cannot be used. The city is holding an election to decide whether to raise taxes to pay for the repairs. Do you think that taxes should be raised to pay for the repairs?

Write an essay for a local news blog that explains whether or not people should vote for the tax increase. Think carefully about reasons that will help others understand your position as well as examples and details that you can use to support your position.

5. Physical fitness is very important to maintaining good health. Your employer is worried about employees' physical fitness. The company built an on-site gym and offers free exercise classes, but employees are not using the facility. Your boss asked you to write an essay to convince more employees to use the facility.

Write an essay that persuades your coworkers to use the on-site gym and free exercise classes. Think carefully about reasons that will help others understand your position as well as examples and details that you can use to support your position.

6. People in your community are worried about an increase in accidents involving young drivers. Local leaders have proposed raising the driving age from 16 to 18 to reduce the number of accidents. Do you believe that the driving age should be raised to 18?

Write an essay to your newspaper that explains whether or not you think the age for getting a driver's license should be raised to 18. Think carefully about reasons that will help others understand your position as well as examples and details that you can use to support your position.

7. A new apartment complex recently decided that tenants cannot own dogs, cats, or other animals as pets. While many people agree that the complex can ban pets, other people think that people should be able to own pets.

Write an essay for your neighborhood news blog that explains whether or not you think the apartment complex should be able to ban dogs, cats, and other pets. Think carefully about reasons that will help others understand your position as well as examples and details that you can use to support your position.

8. The government has proposed building a new highway near your neighborhood. The highway will make it much easier for people to get to work and school, but it will bring a lot of traffic and pollution to the neighborhood. Do you think that the government should build the highway?

Write an essay to your local city council that explains whether or not you think the government should build the new highway. Think carefully about reasons that will help others understand your position as well as examples and details that you can use to support your position.

# VI. Mathematics

The Mathematics section of HiSET tests your ability to solve quantitative problems using math concepts and math reasoning skills. You will be tested on your knowledge of numbers and number operations (such as addition, subtraction, etc.), measurement and geometry, data analysis, and algebra.

The Mathematics section of HiSET consists of 50 multiple-choice items for which you will be given 90 minutes. There is no penalty for an incorrect answer. If you feel that you do not know how to answer a particular item, you should take a guess at the correct answer. You can use a simple, four-function calculator on the exam. You will be provided with one at the test site. You may not bring your own. We strongly recommended that you get a calculator, such as the Texas Instruments TI-108, to use while you prepare for the test; doing so will get you comfortable with using the calculator when you need it.

## A. Test Content and Types of Items

The purpose of the HiSET Mathematics test is to measure not only your ability to accurately perform computations but also your ability to use mathematics to solve problems.

## 1. Item Types

The items you will see on the exam will come from four types:

- Numbers and Operations on Numbers
- Algebraic Concepts
- Measurement and Geometry
- Data Analysis: Probability and Statistics

### a. Numbers and Operations on Numbers (25 percent; 12–13 items)

These items ask you to work with the order of operations, absolute value, exponents, radicals, ratios, proportions, and percents. Look at the following example:

> A coat that normally sells for $250 is offered at a 30% discount. What is the sale price of the coat?
>
> A. $75
> B. $175
> C. $225
> D. $325
> E. $425

### b. Algebraic Concepts (25 percent; 12–13 items)

These items ask you to analyze mathematical situations and structures using algebra. You should understand patterns, relations, and functions. Topics may include linear functions and inequalities, as well as nonlinear functional relations. You may have to analyze and interpret numeric data or graphs, figure out how to solve problems, simplify algebraic expressions, and understand ways to use math symbols to represent problems and solutions. Look at the following example:

A coat that normally sells for $190 is on sale at a discount of 20%. Patty has a store coupon that entitles her to an additional 5% discount off the sale price. Which expression represents the price of the coat after all the discounts have been taken?

**A.** $190 \times 0.25$
**B.** $190 \times 0.75$
**C.** $190 \times 0.20 \times 0.05$
**D.** $190 \times 0.80$
**E.** $190 \times 0.80 \times 0.95$

## c. Measurement and Geometry (25 percent; 12–13 items)

These items ask you to work with the measurements of various objects. Key ideas in geometry include properties of geometric figures; theorems of lines and triangles; and the perimeter, surface area, volume, lengths, and angles for geometric shapes. Look at the following example:

Mrs. Smith wants to make two baby blankets to give to her daughter as a baby shower gift. Each blanket is made from a fabric square that measures 36 inches × 36 inches. How many square yards of fabric will she need to make the blankets?

**A.** 1
**B.** 2
**C.** 9
**D.** 18
**E.** 2,592

## d. Data Analysis: Probability and Statistics (25 percent; 12–13 items)

These items ask you to use the basic concepts of probability, linear relationships, and measures of central tendency and variability to solve problems. Items may ask you to explain relations among events and data. Look at the following example:

Yesterday, five students took a math quiz. The teacher calculated the mean (average) score as 18; however, she wrote down only four of the students' scores in her grade book. If the four students' scores are 13, 15, 19, and 21, what is the value of the missing score?

**A.** 12
**B.** 17
**C.** 18
**D.** 20
**E.** 22

# 2. Process Categories

Regardless of item type, items may ask you to calculate the answer to the problem, choose an estimate, or choose an expression or equation that can be used to solve the problem. In addition, individual items may address one or more of these process categories:

- Understand mathematical concepts and procedures
- Analyze and interpret information
- Synthesize data and solve problems

## a. Understand Mathematical Concepts and Procedures

You will demonstrate your ability to solve equations and perform complex computations. Look at the following example:

Compute: $\dfrac{45+9^2-1}{7^2-6\times4}$

A. $-9$
B. $-5$
C. $5$
D. $9$
E. $25$

## b. Analyze and Interpret Information

You are given information from a variety of sources and asked to use this information to arrive at an answer. Look at the following example:

The chart shows the amount of surface area for each of the five oceans and all the land masses.

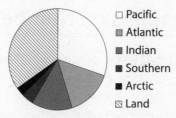

- □ Pacific
- ■ Atlantic
- ■ Indian
- ■ Southern
- ■ Arctic
- ▨ Land

If the total surface area of Earth is 196.9 million square miles, which of the following is the best estimate, in millions of square miles, for the surface area of the Pacific Ocean?

A. 50
B. 60
C. 80
D. 90
E. 100

## c. Synthesize Data and Solve Problems

You are asked to apply your knowledge of mathematics to solve problems from scenarios given to you. Look at the following examples:

---

Alysha claims to have 23 coins in her purse. She also claims that the coins are only quarters and dimes and that the total value of the coins is \$4.55. How many of each coin does Alysha have in her purse?

**A.**   13 quarters and 10 dimes
**B.**   15 quarters and 8 dimes
**C.**   17 quarters and 6 dimes
**D.**   19 quarters and 4 dimes
**E.**   21 quarters and 2 dimes

---

A 25-foot ladder leans against a vertical wall so that the bottom of the ladder is 7 feet from the base of the wall. If the bottom of the ladder slides away from the wall another 8 feet, how far down the wall does the top of the ladder slide?

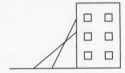

**A.**   4 feet
**B.**   8 feet
**C.**   14 feet
**D.**   20 feet
**E.**   24 feet

---

# B. Numbers and Operations on Numbers

## 1. Computation and Estimation

### a. Order of Operations

When we solve a math problem, we do the calculations in a certain order. Look at the following example:

---

What is the value of $28 + (14 - 81 \div 27)^2 - 16 \times 4 \div 8$?

**A.**   42
**B.**   46
**C.**   67.5
**D.**   117
**E.**   141

---

A phrase that may help you remember the order of operations is <u>P</u>lease <u>E</u>xcuse <u>M</u>y <u>D</u>ear <u>A</u>unt <u>S</u>ally.

This phrase may sound a bit silly, but it is very helpful in remembering the order in which you should do the operations:

- <u>P</u>arentheses—combine any terms inside parentheses (or inside other grouping symbols, such as brackets and braces) first.
- <u>E</u>xponents—evaluate any terms with exponents (or powers) next.
- <u>M</u>ultiplication and <u>D</u>ivision have equal priority and should be performed from left to right as they occur in the problem.
- <u>A</u>ddition and <u>S</u>ubtraction have the lowest priority. They, too, should be performed from left to right as they appear in the problem.

TIP: Exponents (powers) take the form base$^{power}$. An example is $5^2$. The power (or exponent) shows how many times the base should be multiplied. So $5^2$ means that 5 should be multiplied twice, that is, $5^2 = 5 \times 5 = 25$. The expression $4^3 = 4 \times 4 \times 4 = 64$.

To say a number with an exponent,

$5^2$ is read "five squared"

$5^3$ is read "five cubed"

$5^4$ is read "five raised to the fourth power" (or "five raised to the fourth")

Look at the example again:

$$28 + (14 - 81 \div 27)^2 - 16 \times 4 \div 8$$

The first step is grouping. Within the grouping, division is done first: $81 \div 27 = 3$, so the term within the parentheses is now $14 - 3$, or 11. The expression is now $28 + (11)^2 - 16 \times 4 \div 8$.

The second step is to compute exponents (powers). Computing the power, $(11)^2 = 121$, makes the expression $28 + 121 - 16 \times 4 \div 8$.

The third step is to perform the multiplication and division (from left to right). Multiply $16 \times 4$ to get 64. Then divide: $64 \div 8 = 8$.

The expression now reads $28 + 121 - 8$.

Finally, adding and subtracting (again, from left to right) gives $149 - 8$, or 141. The correct answer is Option E.

Try this example:

Compute: $32 \times (21 - 17)^2 \div 8 + 4 \times 3$

A. 44

B. $45\dfrac{2}{3}$

C. 76

D. 195

E. 288

If you said the answer is Option C, you are correct. To figure out this answer, follow order of operations.

First, perform the arithmetic inside the parentheses: $21 - 17 = 4$. The expression is now $32 \times (4)^2 \div 8 + 4 \times 3$.

Second, evaluate the exponent (power): $4^2 = 16$. The expression now reads $32 \times 16 \div 8 + 4 \times 3$.

Third, do the multiplication and division from left to right

$$32 \times 16 = 512 \qquad 512 \div 8 + 4 \times 3$$
$$512 \div 8 = 64 \qquad 64 + 4 \times 3$$
$$4 \times 3 = 12 \qquad 64 + 12$$

Finally, do the addition and subtraction from left to right :     76

Look at this example:

Compute: $\dfrac{45 + 9^2 - 1}{7^2 - 6 \times 4}$

To answer this problem, you need to keep in mind that this problem is the same as $(45 + 9^2 - 1) \div (7^2 - 6 \times 4)$. The parentheses are used to separate the **numerator** (the upper part of the fraction) from the **denominator** (the lower part of the fraction) in the problem. The answer is 5.

Working with terms grouped together are two important areas where use of a four-function calculator can be tricky. The example above, $\dfrac{45 + 9^2 - 1}{7^2 - 6 \times 4}$, was rewritten as $(45 + 9^2 - 1) \div (7^2 - 6 \times 4)$. The calculator you will use on the test will not have a set of parentheses, so you need to follow the order of operations as you work.

To determine the value of this expression using your calculator, first evaluate the numerator. First, type $9 \boxed{\times} 9 \boxed{=}$ to get 81. Then type $\boxed{+} 45 \boxed{-} 1 \boxed{=}$ to get 125. **Write** this number down on your scratch paper! Then evaluate the denominator: Type $7 \boxed{\times} 7 \boxed{=}$ to get 49. Write this number down on your scrap paper. Then type $6 \boxed{\times} 4 \boxed{=}$ to get 24. Then type $\boxed{+/-}$ to change 24 to –24. Then type $\boxed{+} 49 \boxed{=}$ to get 25. You can now divide 125 by 25 to get the answer: 5.

> TIP: You can use the memory in your calculator to simplify calculations. For example, after you multiply $7 \times 7$ $\left( 7 \boxed{\times} 7 \boxed{=} \right)$ you can store the answer in your calculator's memory by pressing $\boxed{M+}$. Then you can type $\boxed{MRC}$ to recall the answer later in the problem. While the memory function on your calculator can help you work more quickly, be careful when using it. One of the most common mistakes with calculator memory is using a value stored in memory that is from a previous problem. A good way to avoid this problem is to always clear the memory before starting a new problem: Press $\boxed{MRC}$ to recall the number in memory, and then press $\boxed{M-}$ or press $\boxed{MRC}$ again to clear it.

# b. Estimation

Some items ask you to choose an estimated answer, rather than to calculate the answer. Moreover, estimating and choosing the answer closest to your estimate may help you work more quickly on test day. Look at the following example:

---

One liter of gasoline is equivalent to approximately 0.264 gallons. Which of the following is a good approximation for the number of gallons in 11.8 liters?

A.  2
B.  2.5
C.  3
D.  3.5
E.  4

---

For the purposes of estimation, round the conversion from liters to gallons to 0.25 and the number of liters from 11.8 to 12. Multiply these approximations together to get 3 gallons, or Option C: $0.25 \times 12 = 3$.

---

TIP: The key to estimation is to use easy but reasonable numbers. Working with 10's, or multiples of 10's, is especially useful. Some rules that will help with estimations are

- When multiplying a number by 10, add a zero to the right of the number. When multiplying by 100, add two zeroes. For example, $36 \times 10 = 360$ and $36 \times 100 = 3,600$.

- Multiplying by 15 is most easily done by first multiplying the number by 10, taking half the answer, and adding. For example, $36 \times 15$ can be found by first multiplying $36 \times 10$ to get 360, taking half of 360 to get 180, and adding $360 + 180$ to get 540.

- There are two ways to think about multiplying by 25. One is to first multiply by 100 and then divide by 4 (or divide by 2 twice). Another way to think about multiplying by 25 is to think of quarters. There are 4 quarters in a dollar so think of the problem as how much money you have. For example, multiply $25 \times 36$. Using the first method, multiply $36 \times 100 = 3,600$ and then divide 3,600 by 4 to get 900. Using this "method of quarters," there are 4 quarters in a dollar and $36 \div 4 = 9$ so you have the equivalent of 9 dollars, or 900 cents.

---

Try this example:

---

Alice worked 28 hours last week. If Alice earns $12.70 per hour, what is a reasonable estimate for the amount of money she earned last week before taxes?

A.  $280
B.  $308
C.  $360
D.  $390
E.  $420

---

To answer this item, round to 10: Round up the number of hours Alice worked to 30 and round down the hourly rate to $12 to get an estimate of $360 (as compared to the actual amount of $355.60), making Option C the best choice. Be careful not to round up both values since that will give an estimate that is too high. For example, if you round Alice's hours up to 30 and round her hourly rate up to $13, the estimate would be $390, which would lead you to an incorrect answer, Option D.

## 2. Practice 1

### a. Items

1. Calculate: $81 + 45 \div 9 + 6 \times 2$

   A. 26
   B. 40
   C. 87
   D. 98
   E. 103

2. Compute: $\dfrac{78 + 18 \div 6}{5^2 - 4^2}$

   A. $1\dfrac{7}{9}$
   B. 8
   C. 9
   D. $40\dfrac{1}{2}$
   E. 80

3. Michael worked 37.5 hours last week. If Michael earns $19.80 per hour, which of the following would give Michael an estimate of his pre-tax earnings for last week?

   A. $40 \times 20$
   B. $40 \times 19$
   C. $40 \times 15$
   D. $35 \times 19$
   E. $30 \times 20$

4. One pound of meat is equivalent to approximately 0.454 kilograms. Which of the following is the best estimate for the number of kilograms of meat equivalent to 73.6 pounds of meat?

   A. 25
   B. 30
   C. 35
   D. 40
   E. 45

5. One liter of milk is approximately equal to 0.264 gallons. What is the best estimate for the number of liters of milk equivalent to 18.2 gallons of milk?

   A. 4.5
   B. 5
   C. 20
   D. 72
   E. 80

## b. Answer Explanations

1.  **D. 98 (Order of Operations)** Following the order of operations, perform the division and multiplication first; $81 + 45 \div 9 + 6 \times 2$ becomes $81 + 5 + 12$. Add these to get 98.

2.  **C. 9 (Order of Operations)** The problem $\dfrac{78+18\div6}{5^2-4^2}$ becomes $\dfrac{78+3}{25-16}$, which simplifies to $\dfrac{81}{9}=9$.

3.  **B. 40 × 19 (Estimation)** Rounding the hours to 40 is not a large increase, while dropping the wage to $19 per hour is not a large decrease. Multiplying these will result in an accurate estimate. ***Reminder:*** When estimating, don't round both numbers up; that will result an estimate that is too large.

4.  **C. 35 (Estimation)** Round the conversion to 1 pound = 0.5 kilograms, and round the weight of the meat to 70 pounds. Half of 70 is 35.

5.  **D. 72 (Estimation)** Round the conversion to 1 liter = 0.25 gallons. This is equivalent to 4 liters = 1 gallon. Multiply this conversion by 18 gallons to get 72 liters.

# 3. Ratios, Proportions, and Percents

## a. Ratios

Ratios are used to compare two values. Sometimes those values have the same units and at other times they do not. For example, the ratio of the wage earned when working overtime to one's normal wage is 3:2 (also written as the fraction $\frac{3}{2}$, time and a half). The rate 65 mph compares the distance traveled to the time traveled. A map scale might be 1 inch represents 25 miles.

Try this example:

---

A review of the voting records for those who voted in a particular district on a particular day showed that 1,250 registered Democrats voted. Of these voters, 500 were women. What is the ratio of the number of men to the number of women who are registered as Democrats and who voted on that day?

A. 2:5
B. 2:3
C. 1:1
D. 3:2
E. 5:2

---

The answer is Option D. If 500 of the 1,250 Democrats who voted that day were women, then 750 were men: 1,250 – 500 = 750. Because the item asks for the ratio of men to women, the correct ratio is 750:500. Divide each of these numbers by 250 to get the lowest possible denominator: 3:2. Therefore, Option D is correct.

# b. Proportion

When two ratios are set as equal, the resulting equation is called a **proportion.** Look at the following example:

---

If the scale drawing for a floor plan is 1 inch = 4 feet, what are the true dimensions of a room if the floor plan measures $3\frac{1}{2}$ inches by 3 inches?

A.  $12\frac{1}{2}$ feet by 12 feet

B.  14 feet by 12 feet
C.  16 feet by 12 feet
D.  18 feet by 12 feet
E.  26 feet by 12 feet

---

The answer is Option B. To answer this item, multiply 4 feet by $3\frac{1}{2}$ to find the dimension of the first wall: $4 \times 3\frac{1}{2} = 14$. The other wall will be 12 feet long: $4 \times 3 = 12$. Option A merely adds $\frac{1}{2}$ to $4 \times 3$, instead of including the fraction in the multiplication. Option C first rounds $3\frac{1}{2}$ to 4 and then multiplies by the scale value. Option D takes half of $4 \times 3$ and adds it to 12. Option E takes 14 and 12 and adds them together.

The proportion for the $3\frac{1}{2}$ wall is $\dfrac{1 \text{ inch}}{4 \text{ feet}} = \dfrac{3\frac{1}{2} \text{ inches}}{x \text{ feet}}$. The units are written in this example to emphasize that you need to put items with the same meaning in the same positions in the ratios. In this case, the scale measurements are in the numerators. Solve the proportion by cross-multiplying: $1x = 4 \times 3\frac{1}{2} = 14$ feet.

---

TIP: When solving a proportion such as $\dfrac{a}{b} = \dfrac{c}{d}$, you can cross-multiply to find the answer. Multiply the numerator of the first fraction with the denominator of the second fraction: *ad*. Then multiply the denominator of the first fraction by the numerator of the second fraction: *bc*. That is, the numbers that are diagonally opposite each other are multiplied together. When this is done, the equation becomes *ad* = *bc*. (Did you notice how the terms for multiplying *a* and *d* were written *ad*? This is normal in algebra—there can be some confusion when using the *x* to represent a number and then using the multiplication symbol × with it.)

---

## c. Percent

Percents may be the single most used mathematical concept aside from the four operations of addition, subtraction, multiplication, and division. Percents are used to compute discounts, taxes, raises, and as a representation of how the economy is performing (e.g., unemployment rates, growth in the Gross National Product or GNP, and inflation rates).

Look at the following example:

> Andrea is showing Tammy the new coat she just purchased. When Tammy asked how much it cost, Andrea said, "I paid $136 for it, but that was after a 20% discount." What was the original price of the coat?
>
> **A.** $156
> **B.** $163.20
> **C.** $165.60
> **D.** $170
> **E.** $180

Before we look at how to solve this problem, let's take a look at some of the properties of numbers starting with the order of operations. (If you are wondering, $156 is not the answer to the coat problem.)

The word percent means "out of a 100" (per cent). "What percent of 85 is 34?" Translating this in the language of proportions, the sentence becomes "What part out of 100 is 34 out of 85?" The proportion becomes $\dfrac{x}{100} = \dfrac{34}{85}$. Cross-multiply to get $85x = 3,400$, and then divide 3,400 by 85 to get 40. That is, 34 is 40% of 85.

Try this example:

> Find 60% of 190.
>
> **A.** 19
> **B.** 95
> **C.** 114
> **D.** 316.67
> **E.** 1,140

Since 190 represents the "entire amount" (or 100%), we know that 190 and 100 should both be in the denominators of the ratios. The proportion is $\dfrac{60}{100} = \dfrac{x}{190}$. Cross-multiply to get $100x = 11,400$, and then divide 11,400 by 100 to get 114, Option C.

> **TIP:** To make proportion problems easier to solve, simplify the proportions to a lower denominator. For example, simplify $\dfrac{60}{100}$ to $\dfrac{6}{10}$. Cross-multiply to get $10x = 1,140$, and then divide 1,140 by 10 to get 114. Another shortcut is to simplify $\dfrac{60}{100}$ to 0.6 and then multiply 0.6 and 190 ($0.6 \times 190 = 114$).

Try this example:

> 75% of what number is 36?
>
> A.   9
> B.   27
> C.   45
> D.   48
> E.   144

The phrase "of what number" tells us that we do not know what the full amount, or 100%, is for this problem. Therefore, 75 and 36 both represent parts of the whole and appear in the numerators of the ratios. The proportion is $\frac{75}{100}=\frac{36}{x}$. Cross-multiply to get $75x = 3,600$. Divide 3,600 by 75 to get 48, Option D. If you use decimals for this problem, the equation becomes $0.75=\frac{36}{x}$. Cross-multiplying gives $0.75x = 36$, and dividing 36 by 0.75 gives the correct answer, 48.

Let's look back to the example item of Andrea's new coat. Andrea paid $136 for the coat, and this number represents a 20% discount. You read earlier that when you set up a proportion, you need to put similar items in the same position of each ratio in the proportion. To solve this problem, you need to ask yourself a very important question: "What does the $136 represent?" Is it the amount of the discount? No, it is not. In fact, the $136 represents the cost of the coat *after* the discount has been subtracted from the original price. The next question you need to ask is, "What percent of the original price of the coat did Andrea pay?" The answer is 80% (100% represents the full price of the coat and 20% has been removed). Andrea paid $136, or 80% of the price of the coat. The proportion used to solve this problem is $\frac{80}{100}=\frac{136}{x}$. The 80 and 136 are the sale numbers, and the 100 and $x$ represent the full price of the coat. Cross-multiply to get $80x = 13,600$, and then divide by 80 to find that the original price of the coat: $13,600 \div 80 = $170, Option D. (Using decimals as in the previous paragraph, the problem becomes $0.8=\frac{136}{x}$ and then $0.8x = 136$. Divide by 0.8 to get the correct answer.)

Sales tax is a common example of the use of percents. The tax paid is in addition to the money owed for the goods purchased. For example, if the tax rate is 6%, the amount of money that must be paid is 100% of the cost of the goods plus 6% of the cost of the goods. That is, the final amount due after tax is 106% of the cost of the goods.

Try this example:

> Marjorie lives in an area where the sales tax on new and used cars is 5%. If the total cost of a car she bought is $13,020 after tax, what was the cost of the car before taxes?
>
> A.   $651
> B.   $12,369
> C.   $12,400
> D.   $12,955
> E.   $13,000

The final price, $13,020, represents 105% of the cost of the car. The proportion for this problem is $\frac{105}{100} = \frac{13,020}{x}$. Cross-multiply to get $105x = 1,302,000$, and then divide by 105 to determine the price of the car, which is $12,400, Option C.

The last example of percents for this section involves multiple discounts:

A store advertises that all items are on sale at a 30% discount from the marked prices. While at the store, a shopper sees an item with a tag indicating an additional discount of 10% will be taken at the cash register. If the price tag on the item shows a price of $100, how much will the shopper pay for the item?

A. $27
B. $30
C. $60
D. $63
E. $70

The answer is not $60; it is a common error to believe that the rate of discount is the sum of the two discounts, 30% and 10%. Actually, the store will take the 10% discount from the sale price, not the full original price. The final price of the item with both discounts can be found by multiplying $100 (the original price) times 70% (the percent left on the tagged price after the first discount) times 90% (the percent left on the sale price after the second discount). The final sale price is $100 \times 0.7 \times 0.9 = \$63$. Therefore, the correct answer is Option D.

TIP: On problems that involve multiple discounts, read the item carefully. On most items, you should calculate the discounts separately. Apply the first discount to the full price. Then apply the second discount to the discounted price.

## 4. Practice 2

### a. Items

1. The scale on a map reads 1 inch = 50 miles. How many miles correspond to $3\frac{3}{4}$ inches?

   A. 37.5
   B. 150
   C. 175
   D. 187.5
   E. 200

2. A recipe that serves 8 calls for 2 cups of flour. Which proportion shows how to determine the amount of flour needed if the recipe is to be adapted to serve 6 people?

   A. $\frac{2}{6} = \frac{8}{x}$
   B. $\frac{2}{8} = \frac{6}{x}$
   C. $\frac{2}{8} = \frac{x}{6}$
   D. $\frac{2}{6} = \frac{x}{8}$
   E. $\frac{2}{x} = \frac{6}{8}$

3. Serena read in an online article that 18% of the population of the high school students in her state enter the military after leaving high school. She read further in the article that 1,340 students entered the military from her state last year after leaving high school. Which equation could Serena use to determine the number of students who left high school in her state last year?

A. $\dfrac{18}{100} = \dfrac{x}{1{,}340}$

B. $\dfrac{82}{100} = \dfrac{x}{1{,}340}$

C. $\dfrac{18}{100} = \dfrac{1{,}340}{x}$

D. $\dfrac{82}{100} = \dfrac{1{,}340}{x}$

E. $\dfrac{18}{1{,}340} = \dfrac{x}{100}$

4. Approximately 32% of the money earned (gross pay) by an employee is taken for taxes. The net pay (the amount of pay that remains after taxes are deducted) for Marcus' last check was $544.72. What was the amount of the gross pay Marcus earned during this pay period?

A. $174.31
B. $370.41
C. $719.03
D. $801.06
E. $915.13

5. Shawn sees that a coat she has been looking at in a store is on sale at a 40% discount. Since Shawn has a coupon entitling her to an additional 10% discount on the sale price, she decides to purchase the coat. To her surprise, she learns that the store is offering an additional 15% discount, after all other discounts, to anyone who shops at the store this Thursday. Shawn goes to the store on Thursday and buys the coat. If the original price of the coat was $270, which expression can be used to show the final sale price that Shawn paid for the coat?

A. $270 \times 0.35$
B. $270 \times 0.65$
C. $270 \times 0.4 \times 0.1$
D. $270 \times 0.4 \times 0.1 \times 0.15$
E. $270 \times 0.6 \times 0.9 \times 0.85$

6. A training class for new employees contains 60 employees, 25 of whom are men. What is the ratio of women to men in the class?

A. 5:12
B. 12:5
C. 5:7
D. 7:5
E. 7:12

## b. Answer Explanations

1. **D. 187.5 (Proportion)** The proportion is $\dfrac{3\frac{3}{4}}{x}=\dfrac{1}{50}$. Cross-multiply to get $x=3\frac{3}{4}\times 50=187.5$. To simplify the calculations or to use your calculator on this problem, convert $3\frac{3}{4}$ to 3.75: $x = 3.75 \times 50 = 187.5$.

2. **C. $\dfrac{2}{8}=\dfrac{x}{6}$ (Proportion)** The number of cups is in the numerator and the number of servings is in the denominator. The ratio on the left has the corresponding number of cups and servings.

3. **C. $\dfrac{18}{100}=\dfrac{1{,}340}{x}$ (Percent)** Both 18 and 1,340 represent a part of the entire piece, so they should both be in the numerators of the ratios.

4. **D. $801.06 (Percent)** Net pay is the money left after 32% has been removed. The $544.72 represents the 68% that remains. Use the proportion $\dfrac{68}{100}=\dfrac{544.72}{x}$ to solve this problem. Cross-multiply and solve for $x$: $68x = 54{,}472$; $54{,}472 \div 68 = \$801.06$

5. **E. $270 \times 0.6 \times 0.9 \times 0.85$ (Percent)** Each discount is computed separately, and the price after discount uses the percent paid (not the percent removed) to compute the new sale price.

6. **D. (Ratios)** There are 35 women in the class: $60 - 25 = 35$. The ratio of women to men is 35:25, which reduces to 7:5, Option D. Option A is the ratio of men to the entire class, and Option B represents the ratio of the entire class to the men. Option C is the ratio of men to women, and Option E is the ratio of women to the entire class.

# C. Algebraic Concepts Part 1: Combining Terms

## 1. Number Properties

There are a handful of number properties that are so simple and straightforward that we often take them for granted. For example, most people realize that $2 + 3$ and $3 + 2$ give the same answer but $3 - 2$ and $2 - 3$ do not. Three key number properties are detailed in this section: commutative, associative, and distributive. Knowing the names of the properties is not as important as understanding when the properties apply and what they do.

### a. Commutative Property

**In addition:** The order in which two numbers are written does not change the answer to the problem. For example, $2 + 3 = 3 + 2$.

**In multiplication:** The order in which two numbers are written does not change the answer to the problem. For example, $2 \times 3 = 3 \times 2$.

Subtraction and division are not commutative.

## b. Associative Property

**In addition:** When adding three or more numbers, the grouping does not change the answer to the problem. For example, $2 + (3 + 4) = (2 + 3) + 4$.

**In multiplication:** When multiplying three or more numbers, the grouping does not change the answer to the problem. For example, $2 \times (3 \times 4) = (2 \times 3) \times 4$.

Subtraction and division are not associative.

## c. Distributive Property of Multiplication Over Addition

This property, often just referred to as the distributive property, is extremely important in understanding how algebraic terms are added and subtracted. When one of the terms in a multiplication problem is a grouping with addition (or subtraction) in it, such as $a(b + c)$, the answer can be found by adding the terms in the grouping and then multiplying (that is, follow the order of operations): $a(b + c) = ab + ac$.

For example, the expression $5(8 + 4)$ can be simplified two ways. One way is to add the numbers in parentheses and then multiply: $5 \times 12 = 60$. The answer can also be found by multiplying the factor outside the grouping, 5, with each term in the group and then adding the resulting products: $5 \times 8 + 5 \times 4 = 40 + 20 = 60$.

## d. Other Important Number Properties

**Additive Identity:** Adding zero to a number does not change the value. (Hopefully, your reaction to this is, "Of Course!") This is an important property and is used when solving equations. That is, for any number $n$, $n + 0 = n$.

**Multiplicative Identity:** Multiplying a number by 1 does not change the value. That is, for any number $n$, $(n)(1) = n$.

**Additive Inverse:** The additive inverse is defined as the number that must be added to a value to get zero. Normally, this is thought of as the negative of a positive number or the positive of a negative number. The additive inverse of 5 is –5 because $5 + -5 = 0$, and the additive inverse of –7 is 7 because $-7 + 7 = 0$.

**Multiplicative Inverse:** The multiplicative inverse is defined as the number that a value must be multiplied by to get 1. Normally, this is thought of as the reciprocal of the number. The multiplicative inverse of 5 is $\frac{1}{5}$, and the multiplicative inverse of –7 is $-\frac{1}{7}$. (The reciprocal of the number $\frac{a}{b}$ is $\frac{b}{a}$. When integers, such as 5, are written as a fraction $\left(\frac{5}{1}\right)$, the denominator is a 1, so the reciprocal of 5 is $\frac{1}{5}$. *Note:* The number zero does not have a multiplicative inverse.)

# 2. Combining Terms and Factors

Adding and subtracting algebraic terms makes use of the distributive property. If asked the question, "What is the sum of 5 apples and 4 apples?" you would simply answer 9 apples. When asked, "What is the sum of 5 apples and 4 oranges?" you might answer 9 pieces of fruit. There is no clear indication of what type of fruit. If clarity were needed, you would have to answer 5 apples and 4 oranges.

The same reasoning applies when adding $5x$ and $4x$. Instead of the characteristic being apples, it is $x$'s. In terms of the properties of mathematics, use the distributive property to rewrite $5x + 4x$ as $(5 + 4)x = 9x$. When adding $5x + 4y$, there is no common factor that can be used to apply the distributive property. (It is common to say that $5x$ and $4x$ are "like" terms and $5x$ and $4y$ are "unlike" terms.)

Try the following example:

---

Simplify: $(4x^3 + 3x^2 + 4) + (5x^2 - 3x + 7)$

A.  $4x^3 + 8x^2 - 3x + 11$
B.  $9x^3 + 3x^2 - 3x + 11$
C.  $4x^3 + 5x^2 + 11$
D.  $4x^3 + 11x^2 + 11$
E.  $9x^3 + 11$

---

There are only two pairs of like terms from each of the expressions in parentheses: $3x^2$ and $5x^2$ and 4 and 7. Therefore, the sum is Option A, $4x^3 + 8x^2 - 3x + 11$. In Options B and E, two unlike terms are added incorrectly, $4x^3$ and $5x^2$. In Option C, the error is adding two unlike terms, $3x^2$ and $-3x$, together to be 0. In Option D, the error is adding $3x^2$, $5x^2$ and $3x$ (ignoring the negative and adding unlike terms) to get $11x^2$.

Try this example:

---

Simplify: $(12x + 10y) - (8x - 3y)$

A.  $4x + 7y$
B.  $4x + 13y$
C.  $20x + 7y$
D.  $20x + 13y$
E.  $17xy$

---

Subtracting terms can cause many errors. It is worthwhile to rewrite the problem (even if only in your mind) as $(12x + 10y) + (-1)(8x + (-3)y)$. When the distributive property is applied, the expression becomes $12x + 10y + (-1)(8x) + (-1)(-3y) = 12x + 10y - 8x + 3y = 4x + 13y$. Therefore, the answer is Option B.

## a. Multiplication with Powers: $(x^m)(x^n) = x^{m+n}$

Multiplication with powers requires a different analysis. In the same way that $5^2$ means $5 \times 5$, $x^2$ means $x \times x$. What is the product of $5^2$ and $5^4$? The problem becomes a matter of counting the number of times 5 is used as a factor. $5^2 \times 5^4 = (5 \times 5) \times (5 \times 5 \times 5 \times 5)$. Since 5 is used as a factor 6 times, the answer must be $5^6$.

In the same way, the product of $x^2$ and $x^4$ must be $x^6$. From this, we can infer a simple rule: $(x^m)(x^n) = x^{m+n}$.

The rule states that when you multiply terms with the same base, rewrite the base and add the exponents. The sum of $5x^2$ and $4x^2$ is $9x^2$ (because $x^2$ is the common factor). What is the product of $5x^2$ and $4x^2$? The process involves a combination of the commutative and associative properties of multiplication.

$$(5x^2)(4x^2) = (5 \times 4)(x^2)(x^2) = 20x^4$$

An important difference between addition or subtraction and multiplication is that in multiplication, unlike terms can be combined. The product $(5x)(4y) = 20xy$. The product $(5xy)(6y) = (5 \times 6)[(x)][(y)(y)] = 30xy^2$.

## b. Powers of Powers: $(x^m)^n = x^{mn}$

When working with powers of powers, you multiply the exponents. Try this example:

Simplify: $(6x^3y^4)^3$

The power 3 outside the parentheses means you should write the base 3 times:

$$(6x^3y^4)^3 = (6x^3y^4)(6x^3y^4)(6x^3y^4)$$
$$= (6 \times 6 \times 6)(x^3 \times x^3 \times x^3)(y^4 \times y^4 \times y^4)$$
$$= (6)^3(x^3)^3(y^4)^3$$

You can compute $6^3 = 216$. What about $(x^3)^3$ and $(y^4)^3$? $(x^3)^3$ means to take the three factors of $x$ in the parentheses and write them down 3 times for a total of 9 factors of $x$. That is, $(x^3)^3 = x^9$. In the same way, $(y^4)^3$ results in 12 factors of $y$ so $(y^4)^3 = y^{12}$. Therefore, the answer further simplifies as follows:

$$(6)^3(x^3)^3(y^4)^3 = (216)(x^9)(y^{12})$$

## c. Division with Powers: $\dfrac{x^m}{x^n} = x^{m-n}$

Division of terms is similar. Try this example:

Simplify: $\dfrac{5^7}{5^4}$

The quotient $\dfrac{5^7}{5^4}$ contains seven factors of 5 in the numerator and four factors of 5 in the denominator,

$\dfrac{5 \times 5 \times 5 \times 5 \times 5 \times 5 \times 5}{5 \times 5 \times 5 \times 5}$. Four of the factors in the numerator will cancel with the four factors in the

denominator, leaving three factors of 5 in the numerator.

$$\frac{\cancel{5} \times \cancel{5} \times \cancel{5} \times \cancel{5} \times 5 \times 5 \times 5}{\cancel{5} \times \cancel{5} \times \cancel{5} \times \cancel{5}}$$

Consequently, $\dfrac{5^7}{5^4} = 5^3$. In the same way, $\dfrac{x^9}{x^5} = x^4$.

Try another example:

Simplify: $\dfrac{35x^7y^5}{15x^2y^9}$

Separate the fraction into factors: $\left(\dfrac{35}{15}\right)\left(\dfrac{x^7}{x^2}\right)\left(\dfrac{y^5}{y^9}\right)$. The numerator and denominator in the first fraction have

5 as a common factor. The second fraction has $x$ as a common factor twice, eliminating all the $x$ terms in the denominator and leaving 5 in the numerator, and the third fraction has $y$ as a common factor five times, eliminating all the factors of $y$ in the numerator and leaving 4 factors of $y$ in the denominator. Therefore,

$$\frac{35x^7y^5}{15x^2y^9}=\left(\frac{35}{15}\right)\left(\frac{x^7}{x^2}\right)\left(\frac{y^5}{y^9}\right)=\left(\frac{7}{3}\right)\left(\frac{x^5}{1}\right)\left(\frac{1}{y^4}\right)=\frac{7x^5}{3y^4}$$

*Note:* If the division rule for powers is strictly applied to $\dfrac{y^5}{y^9}$, the result would be $y^{-4}$ because $5-9=-4$.

Because of this, negative exponents have the rule $x^{-n}=\dfrac{1}{x^n}$.

Try this example:

Simplify: $\dfrac{\left(4k^5m^2\right)^3}{32k^{10}m^6}$

Simplify the numerator using the Powers of Powers rule to get $\dfrac{64k^{15}m^6}{32k^{10}m^6}$:

$$\frac{\left(4k^5m^2\right)^3}{32k^{10}m^6}=\frac{(4\times4\times4)\times(k^5\times k^5\times k^5)\times(m^2\times m^2\times m^2)}{32k^{10}m^6}=\frac{64\times(k^{5+5+5})\times(m^{2+2+2})}{32k^{10}m^6}=\frac{64k^{15}m^6}{32k^{10}m^6}$$

Use the common factors to reduce this to $2k^5$, remembering to subtract exponents when dividing:

$$\frac{64k^{15}\,m^6}{32k^{10}\,m^6}=\frac{^2\,\cancel{64}k^{15}}{\cancel{32}k^{10}}=\frac{2k^{15}}{k^{10}}=2k^5$$

(*Note:* If the division rule for powers is applied to $\dfrac{m^6}{m^6}$, the answer should be $m^0$. For this reason, so long as $x\neq0$, $x^0=1$.)

# 3. Practice 3

## a. Items

1. Simplify: $(7x^3+4x-5)+(3x^3-5x^2-9x)$

   A. $-5$
   B. $10x^3-5x^2-5x-5$
   C. $10x^3-5x^2+5x-5$
   D. $10x^3-10x^2-5$
   E. $10x^6-5x^4-5x^2-5$

2. Simplify: $(18v^3w^4)(4vw^5)$

   A. $22v^3w^9$
   B. $22v^4w^9$
   C. $72v^3w^9$
   D. $72v^4w^9$
   E. $72v^3w^{20}$

3. Simplify: $\dfrac{\left(4p^4r^2\right)^3}{\left(8p^6r^3\right)^2}$

A. 1

B. $\dfrac{3}{4}$

C. $\dfrac{1}{p}$

D. $\dfrac{1}{2p}$

E. $\dfrac{3}{4p}$

4. $(5x + 3)(3x - 8) =$

A. $15x - 24$
B. $15x^2 - 24$
C. $15x^2 - 31x - 24$
D. $15x^2 - 49x - 24$
E. $15x^2 + 31x - 24$

5. $(7x + 3)^2 =$

A. $14x + 6$
B. $49x^2 + 9$
C. $14x^2 + 42x + 9$
D. $49x^2 + 42x + 9$
E. $49x^2 + 21x + 9$

# b. Answer Explanations

1. **B. $10x^3 - 5x^2 - 5x - 5$ (Combining Terms and Factors)** Combine the like terms, $7x^3 + 3x^3 = 10x^3$. There is only one term with $x^2$, $4x - 9x = -5x$, and there is only one constant, $-5$.

$$(7x^3 + 4x - 5) + (3x^3 - 5x^2 - 9x) = 10x^3 - 5x^2 - 5x - 5$$

2. **D. $72v^4w^9$ (Multiplication with Powers)** $18 \times 4 = 72$. The product of $v^3$ and $v$ contains 4 factors of $v$, so $(v^3)(v) = v^4$, and $(w^4)(w^5) = w^9$.

$$(18v^3w^4)(4vw^5) = 72v^4w^9$$

3. **A. 1 (Division with Powers)** To simplify, take each term of the numerator to the third power and each term of the denominator to the second power. In this particular problem, the expressions in the numerator and denominator are equal once taken to the third and second powers and thus simplify to 1:

$$\frac{\left(4p^4r^2\right)^3}{\left(8p^6r^3\right)^2} = \frac{64p^{12}r^6}{64p^{12}r^6} = 1$$

4. **C. $15x^2 - 31x - 24$ (Distributive Property)** Use the distributive property to solve this problem.

$$(5x + 3)(3x - 8) = 5x(3x - 8) + 3(3x - 8) = 15x^2 - 40x + 9x - 24 = 15x^2 - 31x - 24$$

5. **D. $49x^2 + 42x + 9$ (Distributive Property)** Use the distributive property to solve this problem.

$$(7x + 3)^2 = (7x + 3)(7x + 3) = 7x(7x + 3) + 3(7x + 3) = 49x^2 + 21x + 21x + 9 = 49x^2 + 42x + 9$$

# D. Algebraic Concepts Part 2: Solving Equations and Inequalities

## 1. Solving Linear Equations

Two analogies are worth noting when it comes to solving equations. The first is that solving linear equations is like removing objects from a pile, trying to get to the bottom. You start with the last piece put on the pile and work back to the first item that was put down. In solving equations, the pile is built using the order of operations. To get back to the beginning, apply the order of operations in reverse order. The second analogy is that an equation is a balanced scale. Whatever is done to one side of the equation must be done to the other side as well so that the scale remains balanced.

Try this example:

Solve for $x$: $2x + 37 = 75$

The order of operations states that multiplication has a higher priority than addition. Consequently, you need to work backward and remove the addition first. Use the additive inverse of 37 to remove it, remembering to subtract from both sides of the equation.

$$2x + 37 + -37 = 75 + -37$$
$$2x = 38$$

Divide both sides of the equation by 2.

$$\frac{2x}{2} = \frac{38}{2}$$
$$x = 19$$

Look at this example:

Alysha claims to have 23 coins in her purse. She also claims that the coins are only quarters and dimes and that the total value of the coins is $4.55. How many of each coin does Alysha have in her purse?

A.  13 quarters and 10 dimes
B.  15 quarters and 8 dimes
C.  17 quarters and 6 dimes
D.  19 quarters and 4 dimes
E.  21 quarters and 2 dimes

Alysha has 23 coins, and the value of the coins is $4.55. Paying attention to the units of a problem is often a great help in determining how to solve a problem. How many quarters does Alysha have in her purse? This is the classic "unknown." Let's call this number $q$.

The rest of the coins, $23 - q$, represents the number of dimes. The equation for this problem is now based on the **value** of the money in the purse. Each quarter is worth 25 cents, each dime is worth 10 cents, and the total value of the money in the purse is 455 cents (keep the units the same). The equation that can be used to solve this problem is $25q + 10(23 - q) = 455$:

$$25q + 10(23 - q) = 455$$

| | |
|---|---|
| Apply the distributive property: | $25q + 230 - 10q = 455$ |
| Combine like terms: | $15q + 230 = 455$ |
| Subtract the 230 from both sides: | $15q = 225$ |
| Divide both sides by 15: | $\dfrac{15q}{15} = \dfrac{225}{15}$ |
| | $q = 15$ |

Alysha has 15 quarters and $23 - q$ dimes, or $23 - 15 = 8$ dimes in her purse. Therefore, the answer is Option B. Look at the following example:

Solve for $x$: $47x + 237 = 22x - 363$

The equation has variables on both sides of the equal sign. Because the goal is to determine the value of $x$, we need to gather the common terms together. This can be accomplished by subtracting $22x$ from both sides of the equation and subtracting 237 from both sides of the equation. **Note:** It might be worth your while to think of the right side of the equation as $22x + (-363)$ so that you get the subtraction correct.

$$47x + 237 - 22x - 237 = 22x - 363 - 22x - 237$$
$$25x = -600$$

Divide both sides by 25 to solve for $x$:

$$\frac{25x}{25} = \frac{-600}{25}$$
$$x = -24$$

## a. Absolute Value Equations

The absolute value of a number is the distance that number is from the 0 on a number line. The absolute value of 5, written as $|5|$, is 5. The absolute value of $-5$, written as $|-5|$, is also 5.

Look at the following example:

Solve for $x$: $|x| = 6$

There are two numbers that are 6 units from the 0 on a number line: 6 and $-6$. Therefore, $x = \pm 6$.

Try this example:

> Solve for $p$: $|2p + 3| = 7$

There are two numbers that are 7 units from 0 on a number line: 7 and –7. Therefore, $2p + 3 = 7$ or $2p + 3 = -7$. Solve each equation to get $p = 2$ or $p = -5$.

# 2. Solving Inequalities

When comparing two numbers, $a$ and $b$, one of three relationships must be true: $a$ is equal to $b$, $a$ is less than $b$, or $a$ is greater than $b$. The two scenarios where $a$ and $b$ are not equal are referred to as inequalities.

Solving algebraic inequalities is just like solving linear equations, but with one very important difference: Whenever both sides of an inequality are multiplied (or divided) by a negative number, the direction of the inequality is reversed. That is, for the inequality $-2x > 8$, the result after dividing by $-2$ is $x < -4$. (Don't confuse this with the solution to the inequality $2x > -4$ being $x > -2$. In this case, both sides of the inequality are divided by 2.)

A second important aspect of inequalities is the difference between inclusion and exclusion of the endpoint. That is, the inequality $x > 2$ does not include 2 as part of the solution, while the inequality $x \geq 2$ does include 2 as part of the solution. The difference is represented graphically on a number line by whether the endpoint on the segment (or ray) is open or closed.

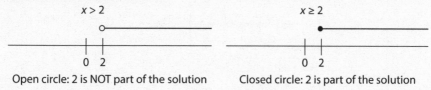

Look at the following example:

> Solve for $n$: $4n - 3 \leq 2n + 11$

Combine the like terms as you would with a linear equation by subtracting $2n$ from each side and adding 3 to each side of the inequality, and then divide both sides by 2 to solve for $n$:

$$4n - 3 \leq 2n + 11$$
$$4n - 3 - 2n + 3 \leq 2n + 11 - 2n + 3$$
$$2n \leq 14$$
$$\frac{2n}{2} \leq \frac{14}{2}$$
$$n \leq 7$$

**TIP:** Translating written statements to mathematical inequalities can be tricky. The phrase "more than" is the inequality > but "no more than" or "at most" means ≤. "At least" translates to ≥.

Try this example:

> Solve for $x$: $-17 < 4x + 3 \leq 27$

This compound inequality represents the two statements $-17 < 4x + 3$ and $4x + 3 \leq 27$. Both statements are solved by subtracting 3 and dividing by 4. Doing this all at once with both statements gives $-5 < x \leq 6$:

$$-17 < 4x + 3 \leq 27$$
$$-17 - 3 < 4x + 3 - 3 \leq 27 - 3$$
$$-20 < 4x \leq 24$$
$$\frac{-20}{4} < \frac{4x}{4} \leq \frac{24}{4}$$
$$-5 < x \leq 6$$

## a. Absolute Value Inequalities

Absolute value inequalities are a bit trickier. An effective way of solving absolute value inequalities is to picture the number and remember that the definition of absolute value is based on distance. For example, if $|x| = 5$ means that $x = \pm 5$ because both 5 and $-5$ are 5 units from 0 on a number line, then the solution to $|x| < 5$ must be $-5 < x < 5$ because all these points are less than 5 units from 0 on a number line. Then the solution to $|x| \geq 5$ must be $x \leq -5$ or $x \geq 5$ because these points are at least 5 units from 0 on a number line.

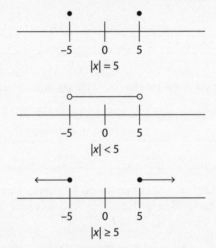

When solving absolute value inequalities, first solve the equation and then determine the nature of the inequality based on the distance from 0 on a number line.

> Solve for $x$: $|3x - 4| > 5$

Solve the corresponding equation, $|3x - 4| = 5$.

$$3x - 4 = 5 \qquad 3x - 4 = -5$$
$$3x = 9 \qquad 3x = -1$$
$$x = 3 \qquad x = -\frac{1}{3}$$

The values $x = 3$ and $x = -\frac{1}{3}$ represent those points for which the expression $3x - 4$ is exactly 5 units from 0 on a number line. This problem requires that the distance from 0 be more than 5 units so the solution to this problem is $x < -\frac{1}{3}$ or $x > 3$.

Here's another example:

> A manufacturer of ball bearings works under the specifications that the diameter of the bearings should be no more than 0.3 mm from the expected diameter of 2.5 mm. Determine the range of diameter measurements that are acceptable to the manufacturer.
>
> **A.** $d < 2.8$
> **B.** $d \leq 2.8$
> **C.** $d > 2.2$
> **D.** $2.2 < d < 2.8$
> **E.** $2.2 \leq d \leq 2.8$

The acceptable measurements may be less than 2.5 mm or more than this amount, but must be within 0.3 mm. The inequality that describes the length of all possible diameters is $|d - 2.5| \leq 0.3$, and the solution is $2.2 \leq d \leq 2.8$. Therefore, the correct answer is Option E.

## b. Zero Product Property

If you multiply any number by 0, the product will be 0. The Zero Product Property states that if the product of two or more numbers is 0, *at least* one of the numbers multiplied must be 0.

Look at the following example:

> Solve for $x$: $(3x - 4)(5x + 9)(2x + 8) = 0$
>
> **A.** $-4$
> **B.** $0$
> **C.** $\frac{4}{3}$ or $-4$
> **D.** $\frac{4}{3}$ or $\frac{-9}{5}$ or $-4$
> **E.** $0$ or $\frac{4}{3}$ or $\frac{-9}{5}$ or $-4$

The Zero Product Property states that at least one of the factors $3x - 4$, $5x + 9$, or $2x + 8$ must equal 0. Set each factor to 0 and solve.

$$3x - 4 = 0 \qquad 5x + 9 = 0 \qquad 2x + 8 = 0$$
$$3x - 4 + 4 = 0 + 4 \qquad 5x + 9 - 9 = 0 - 9 \qquad 2x + 8 - 8 = 0 - 8$$
$$3x = 4 \qquad 5x = -9 \qquad 2x = -8$$
$$x = \frac{4}{3} \qquad x = \frac{-9}{5} \qquad x = -4$$

Therefore, the solution is $x = \frac{4}{3}$ or $x = \frac{-9}{5}$ or $x = -4$ since all three of these values will cause the product to equal 0. Therefore, Option D is the answer.

# 3. Practice 4

## a. Items

1.  Solve for $x$: $17x + 27 = 9x + 179$

    A.  $\dfrac{76}{13}$

    B.  $\dfrac{103}{13}$

    C.  $\dfrac{103}{4}$

    D.  19

    E.  25

2.  Solve for $x$: $ax + b = cx + d$

    A.  $d - b$

    B.  $\dfrac{d - b}{a - c}$

    C.  $\dfrac{d - b}{a + c}$

    D.  $\dfrac{d + b}{a + c}$

    E.  $\dfrac{d + b}{a - c}$

3.  Michael has 25 bills in his wallet. Some of them are five-dollar bills and the rest are one-dollar bills. The total value of the money in his wallet is \$57. If $F$ represents the number of five-dollar bills in his wallet, which equation can be used to determine the number of each type of bill in Michael's wallet?

    A.  $F + 1 = 25$
    B.  $F + 1 = 57$
    C.  $5F + 25 = 57$
    D.  $5F + 1(25 - F) = 57$
    E.  $5F + 1(57 - F) = 25$

4.  As part of her chemistry lab, Inez must add pure, distilled water to 20 mm of an acid solution that is 20% acid to create an acid solution that is 15% acid. If $w$ represents the number of millimeters of water added, which equation can be used to solve the problem?

    A.  $0.20(20) + w = 0.15(20 + w)$
    B.  $0.20(20) = 0.15(20 + w)$
    C.  $20(20) + w = 15(20 + w)$
    D.  $20(20) = w + 15(20 + w)$
    E.  $0.20(20 + w) = 0.15(20)$

5. Solve for $x$: $-19 \le 6x - 1 < 31$

   A. $-3 \le x < 5$

   B. $-3 \le x < \dfrac{16}{3}$

   C. $\dfrac{-10}{3} \le x < \dfrac{16}{3}$

   D. $\dfrac{-10}{3} \le x < 5$

   E. $-5 \le x < 3$

6. Solve for $x$: $(5x + 12)(3x - 9)(2x + 7) = 0$

   A. 3
   B. $-3.5$
   C. 2.4
   D. 2.4 or 3 or $-3.5$
   E. $-2.4$ or 3 or $-3.5$

7. Solve for $x$: $x(4x - 2)^2 = 0$

   A. 0

   B. $\dfrac{1}{2}$

   C. $-\dfrac{1}{2}$

   D. 0 or $\dfrac{1}{2}$

   E. 0 or $\dfrac{1}{2}$ or $-\dfrac{1}{2}$

8. Solve for $w$: $|4w - 1| = 23$

   A. $-5.5$
   B. $5.5$
   C. 6
   D. 6 or $-5.5$
   E. 6 or 5.5

9. Which graph represents the solution to $|5x - 3| < 7$?

   A.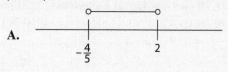

   B.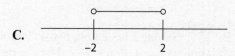

   C.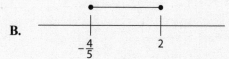

   D.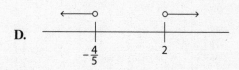

   E.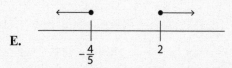

10. A security company requires that all its male security guards have a height, $h$, within 2 inches of 6 feet. Which inequality correctly represents this requirement?

    A. $|h - 2| \le 72$
    B. $|h - 2| \ge 72$
    C. $|h - 72| \le 2$
    D. $|h - 72| \ge 2$
    E. None of the above correctly represent the height requirement.

# b. Answer Explanations

1. **D. 19 (Solving Linear Equations)** Combine like terms by subtracting $9x$ and 27 from both sides of the equation and then divide by 8 to solve for $x$:

$$17x + 27 = 9x + 179$$
$$17x + 27 - 9x = 9x + 179 - 9x$$
$$8x + 27 - 27 = 179 - 27$$
$$8x = 152$$
$$\frac{8x}{8} = \frac{152}{8}$$
$$x = 19$$

2. **B. $\dfrac{d-b}{a-c}$ (Solving Linear Equations)** Combine like terms by subtracting $cx$ and $b$ from both sides of the equation to get $ax - cx = d - b$. Use the distributive property on the left side of the equation to get $(a - c)x = b - d$. Divide by $a - c$ to solve for $x$:

$$ax + b = cx + d$$
$$ax + b - cx = cx + d - cx$$
$$ax + b - cx - b = d - b$$
$$ax - cx = d - b$$
$$(a - c)x = d - b$$
$$\frac{(a - c)x}{a - c} = \frac{d - b}{a - c}$$
$$x = \frac{d - b}{a - c}$$

3. **D. $5F + 1(25 - F) = 57$ (Solving Linear Equations)** The value of the five-dollar bills is $5F$ and the value of the one-dollar bills is $1(25 - F)$. Added together, $5F + 1(25 - F)$, they represent the $57 in his wallet.

4. **B. $0.20(20) = 0.15(20 + w)$ (Solving Linear Equations)** The units in this problem are millimeters of acid. The original solution of 20 mm contains 20% acid, so the amount of acid in the original solution is $0.20(20)$. There is no acid in the pure water. The final 15% solution will contain $20 + w$ mm and the amount of acid will be $0.15(20 + w)$. Writing the equation $0.20(20) = 0.15(20 + w)$ gives the correct statement about the amount of acid.

5. **B. $-3 \le x < \dfrac{16}{3}$ (Solving Inequalities)** Add 1 to all terms to get $-18 \le 6x < 32$. Then divide by 6 to isolate $x$:

$$-19 \le 6x - 1 < 31$$
$$-19 + 1 \le 6x - 1 + 1 < 31 + 1$$
$$-18 \le 6x < 32$$
$$\frac{-18}{6} \le \frac{6x}{6} < \frac{32}{6}$$
$$-3 \le x < \frac{16}{3}$$

6. **E. −2.4 or 3 or −3.5 (Zero Product Property)** Set $5x + 12 = 0$, $3x - 9 = 0$, and $2x + 7 = 0$ and solve for $x$:

$$
\begin{array}{lll}
5x + 12 = 0 & 3x - 9 = 0 & 2x + 7 = 0 \\
5x + 12 - 12 = 0 - 12 & 3x - 9 + 9 = 0 + 9 & 2x + 7 - 7 = 0 - 7 \\
5x = -12 & 3x = 9 & 2x = -7 \\
x = \dfrac{-12}{5} & x = \dfrac{9}{3} & x = \dfrac{-7}{2} \\
x = -2.4 & x = 3 & x = -3.5
\end{array}
$$

7. **D. 0 or $\dfrac{1}{2}$ (Zero Product Property)** After applying the meaning of squaring, the equation becomes $x(4x - 2)(4x - 2) = 0$. Set each factor to 0 and solve for $x$:

$$
\begin{array}{lll}
x = 0 & 4x - 2 = 0 & 4x - 2 = 0 \\
& 4x - 2 + 2 = 0 + 2 & 4x - 2 + 2 = 0 + 2 \\
& 4x = 2 & 4x = 2 \\
& x = \dfrac{2}{4} & x = \dfrac{2}{4} \\
& x = \dfrac{1}{2} & x = \dfrac{1}{2}
\end{array}
$$

Therefore, $x = 0$ or $x = \dfrac{1}{2}$. (*Note:* You do not need to write $\dfrac{1}{2}$ as a possible solution twice.)

8. **D. 6 or −5.5 (Absolute Value Equations)** Solve both equations $4w - 1 = 23$ and $4w - 1 = -23$ for $w$:

$$
\begin{array}{ll}
4w - 1 = 23 & 4w - 1 = -23 \\
4w - 1 + 1 = 23 + 1 & 4w - 1 + 1 = -23 + 1 \\
4w = 24 & 4w = -22 \\
w = \dfrac{24}{4} & w = \dfrac{-22}{4} \\
w = 6 & w = -5.5
\end{array}
$$

9. **A. (Absolute Value Inequalities)** Solve $|5x - 3| = 7$:

$$
\begin{array}{ll}
5x - 3 = 7 & 5x - 3 = -7 \\
5x = 10 & 5x = -4 \\
x = 2 & x = -\dfrac{4}{5}
\end{array}
$$

Because the distance is "less than," the correct solution is $-\dfrac{4}{5} < x < 2$, and the correct graph is Option A.

10. **C. $|h - 72| \leq 2$ (Absolute Value Inequalities)** All heights must be within 2 inches of 6 feet (or 72 inches). This means acceptable heights are from 70 to 74 inches. The inequality that properly represents the height requirement is $|h - 72| \leq 2$, Option C.

# E. Algebraic Concepts Part 3: Graphs and Functions

## 1. Coordinate Plane

The rectangular coordinate plane system consists of two lines, the **x-axis** and **y-axis**, which are perpendicular to each other. The lines form four regions, called **quadrants**. Look at the following example:

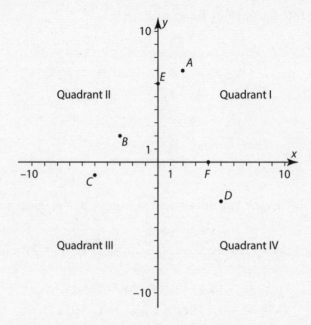

The point of intersection of the axes is called the **origin.** Each axis is marked in equal increments. Positive numbers are to the right of the origin on the x-axis, while the negative numbers are to its left. Positive numbers are above the origin on the y-axis, and negative numbers are below it.

Each point in the coordinate plane is identified by counting horizontally from the origin and then vertically until the point is reached. Since no counting is needed to reach the origin, the coordinates of the origin are (0, 0). Point A has coordinates (2, 7) since you go two units to the right and then seven units up. Point B has coordinates (–3, 2) because it is located to the left of the origin and above the y-axis. Point C has coordinates (–5, –1), point D is at (5, –3), point E is at (0, 6), and point F has coordinates (4, 0).

# a. Relations and Functions

A mathematical relation is any set of ordered pairs. The set of all first elements in the ordered pairs is called the **domain,** while the set of all second elements is called the **range.** For example, given the relation A = {(2, 1), (2, 3), (0, 4), (–2, 5), (3, –1)}, the domain of A is {2, 0, –2, 3} and the range is {1, 3, 4, 5, –1}.

A special type of relation is called a **function.** A function requires that each element in the domain be associated with exactly one element in the range. The relation A in the previous paragraph does not represent a function because the value 2 in the domain is associated with both 1 and 3 in the range. (When you think of the elements of the domain as the input and the elements of the range as the output, a function can be defined as a relation in which each input has exactly one output.)

Mathematical relations are often represented by graphs. An easy way to determine if the graph represents a function is the *vertical line test*. Hold your pencil on the paper so that it is perpendicular to the $x$-axis. Slide your pencil left and right. If the pencil ever crosses the graph at two different points, the graph does **not** represent a function.

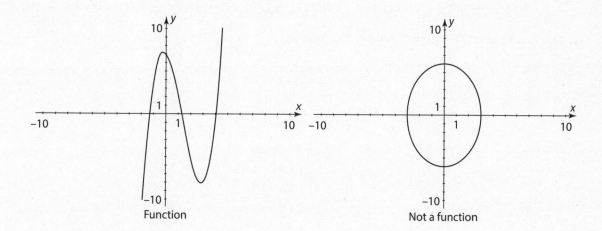

Function                                  Not a function

# b. Function Notation

It is common for a function to be written so it identifies or names the function. For example, it is possible that two functions can be written two ways: $f(x) = 3x + 2$ and $g(x) = 5x - 1$. One of the advantages of writing functions in this manner (as opposed to $y = 3x + 2$ and $y = 5x - 1$) is that it is easier to reference the function by the name ($f$ or $g$, in this case) than having to spell it all out.

Determining the inputs and outputs of functions is done through substitution. That is, the output for the function $f$ when the input is 4 would be written as $f(4) = 14$. (Notice how this works: With the input 4, replace $x$ with 4 on both sides of the equal sign: $f(4) = 3(4) + 2 = 14$. $f(4) = 14$ is read as "$f$ of 4 is 14".) The output of $g$ when the input is 4 is 19, i.e., $g(4) = 5(4) - 1 = 19$.

The input for $f$ when the output is 17 is written $f(x) = 17$. Because the **rule** for $f(x)$ is $3x + 2$, this equation becomes $3x + 2 = 17$. Solve this equation to determine that $x = 5$. The input for $f$ when the output is 17 is 5.

Look at the following example:

Given $f(x) = 3x^2 + 9x - 7$, determine $f(-2)$ and $f(4)$.

$$f(-2) = 3(-2)^2 + 9(-2) - 7 = 3(4) - 18 - 7 = 12 - 25 = -13$$
$$f(4) = 3(4)^2 + 9(4) - 7 = 3(16) + 36 - 7 = 48 + 29 = 77$$

Try this example:

Given $f(x) = \dfrac{3x+2}{2x-3}$, find the value of $x$ for which $f(x) = 2$.

Set $\dfrac{3x+2}{2x-3} = 2$. Multiply by $2x - 3$ to get $3x + 2 = 2(2x - 3)$. Distribute the 2 to get $3x + 2 = 4x - 6$. Subtract $3x$ from both sides and add 6 to both sides of the equation to get $x = 8$:

$$\frac{3x+2}{2x-3} = 2$$
$$\frac{3x+2}{\cancel{2x-3}} \cdot \frac{\cancel{2x-3}}{1} = 2(2x-3)$$
$$3x+2 = 4x - 6$$
$$3x + 2 - 3x = 4x - 6 - 3x$$
$$2 = x - 6$$
$$2 + 6 = x - 6 + 6$$
$$8 = x$$

## c. Slopes and Lines

Slope of a line measures the steepness (the degree of rise or fall) of the line relative to the $x$-axis. Slope shows how many units the $y$-coordinate rises or falls for each change of 1 unit of the $x$-coordinate.

The slope-intercept form of the equation of a line is $y = mx + b$, where $m$ represents the slope of the line and $b$ represents the $y$-intercept, the point where the line crosses the $y$-axis. The role of the $x$ and $y$ in the equation is to represent the coordinates of any point that lies on the line.

For example, if the slope of the line is 3, then the $y$-coordinate will increase by 3 units each time the $x$-coordinate increases by 1 unit. The equation for computing the slope of a line that passes through the points $(x_1, y_1)$ and $(x_2, y_2)$ is $m = \dfrac{y_2 - y_1}{x_2 - x_1}$. The subscripts 1 and 2 simply indicate the first set of values for $x$ and $y$ and the second set of values for $x$ and $y$. Try this example:

---

Compute the slope of the line that passes through the points $(-3, 4)$ and $(2, -6)$.

A.   $-10$

B.   $-2$

C.   $-\dfrac{1}{2}$

D.   $2$

E.   $10$

---

To solve, use the formula for slope, $m = \dfrac{y_2 - y_1}{x_2 - x_1}$: $m = \dfrac{-6 - 4}{2 - (-3)} = \dfrac{-10}{5} = -2$. Therefore, Option B is the correct answer. Option C is the result of treating slope as the ratio of the change in the $x$ coordinates to the change in the $y$ coordinates. The other options are the results of subtracting the numbers incorrectly.

**TIP: A line with a positive slope moves upward from the lower left to the upper right on the coordinate plane. A line with a negative slope moves downward from the upper left to lower right on the coordinate plane.**

Look at the following example:

---

Write the equation of the line that passes through the points $(-3, 4)$ and $(2, -6)$.

---

First, compute the slope as you did in the previous example: $m = \dfrac{-6 - 4}{2 - (-3)} = \dfrac{-10}{5} = -2$. Next, substitute this value for $m$ in $y = mx + b$: $y = -2x + b$. Then select one of the two points that you know lies on this line and substitute the coordinates for $x$ and $y$ to solve for $b$. For example, using the point $(-3, 4)$,

$$4 = -2(-3) + b$$
$$4 = 6 + b$$
$$-2 = b$$

Therefore, the equation of the line is $y = -2x - 2$.

**TIP: A horizontal line has a slope of zero because the difference in the $y$-coordinates is 0 when computing the slope. The equation of a horizontal line is $y = c$, where $c$ is the value of the $y$-coordinate for every point on the line. The slope of a vertical line is undefined because there is no change in the $x$-coordinates, making the denominator of the slope fraction 0. The equation of a vertical line is $x = c$, where $c$ is the value of the $x$-coordinate for every point on the line.**

Try this example:

For what value of $x$ will the line $y = 4x - 14$ intersect the $x$-axis?

A. −14
B. −3.5
C. 0
D. 3.5
E. 14

All points on the $x$-axis have a $y$-coordinate of 0. Set $y = 0$ and solve for $x$:

$$0 = 4x - 14$$
$$14 = 4x$$
$$x = 3.5$$

Therefore, Option D is correct answer.

Look at the following example:

The graph below represents the motion of a car on a trip

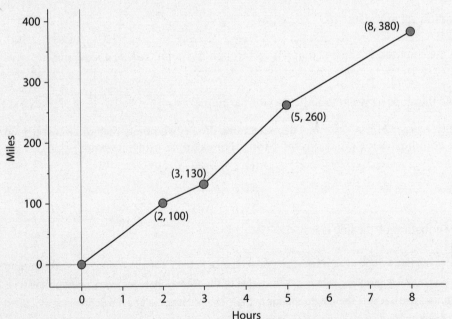

What is the average speed of the car (in miles per hour) from time 2 hours to time 3 hours?

What is the average speed of the car from time 2 hours to time 5 hours?

What was the average speed of the car over the entire trip?

The $y$-coordinates for each point in the graph represent the cumulative number of miles traveled, and each $x$-coordinate represents the number of hours that have passed by. Therefore, the slope of each segment is $\frac{\text{miles}}{\text{hours}}$, which are the units for speed. From the second hour to the third hour, the slope is $\frac{30 \text{ miles}}{1 \text{ hour}}$, or 30 mph. From the second hour to the fifth hour, the slope is $\frac{160 \text{ miles}}{3 \text{ hours}}$, or $53\frac{1}{3}$ mph. The entire trip covered 380 miles in 8 hours so the average speed is $\frac{380 \text{ miles}}{8 \text{ hours}}$, or 47.5 mph.

## 2. Practice 5

### a. Items

1. Which of the following sets of ordered pairs represents a function?

   **A.** {(1, 2), (3, 4), (3, 5), (4, 2), (6, 1)}
   **B.** {(1, 2), (3, 4), (4, 5), (5, 2), (6, 1)}
   **C.** {(1, 2), (–3, 4), (–3, 5), (4, 2), (6, 1)}
   **D.** {(1, 2), (1, 4), (3, 5), (4, 2), (6, 1)}
   **E.** {(–1, 2), (1, 4), (3, 5), (6, 2), (6, 1)}

2. If $f(x) = 5x - 19$, $f(7) + f(-7) =$

   **A.** –54
   **B.** –38
   **C.** 0
   **D.** 16
   **E.** 38

3. $f(x) = 5x - 19$. If $f(a) = 6$ and $f(b) = -1$, then $a + b =$

   **A.** –1
   **B.** 1.4
   **C.** 5
   **D.** 8.6
   **E.** 9

*The graph at the top of the next column shows the revenue earned (in millions of dollars) corresponding to the number of units sold (in lots of a thousand) for products labeled J, K, L, M, and N. Use the graph to answer items 4 and 5.*

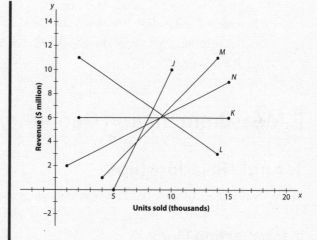

4. Which product showed the greatest rate of increase?

   **A.** J
   **B.** K
   **C.** L
   **D.** M
   **E.** N

5. An equation for the revenue of product $J$ is

   **A.** Revenue = 2(units sold) – 10
   **B.** Revenue = 2(units sold) – 5
   **C.** Revenue = 2(units sold)
   **D.** Revenue = 2(units sold) + 5
   **E.** Revenue = 2(units sold) + 10

## b. Answer Explanations

1. **B. {(1, 2), (3, 4), (4, 5), (5, 2), (6, 1)} (Relations and Functions)** {(1, 2), (3, 4), (4, 5), (5, 2), (6, 1)} is the only set in which none of the first coordinates are repeated.

2. **B. –38 (Function Notation)** $f(7) = 5(7) – 19 = 35 – 19 = 16$ and $f(–7) = 5(–7) – 19 = 5 – 19 = –54$; $16 + (–54) = –38$.

3. **D. 8.6 (Function Notation)** $f(a) = 6$ gives the equation $5a – 19 = 6$. Solve: $5a = 25$; $a = 5$. $f(b) = –1$ gives the equation $5b – 19 = –1$. Solve: $5b = 18$; $b = 3.6$. $a + b = 5 + 3.6 = 8.6$.

4. **A. J (Slopes and Lines)** The slopes are J: $\frac{10-0}{10-5} = \frac{10}{5} = 2$, K: $\frac{6-6}{15-2} = \frac{0}{13} = 0$, L: $\frac{3-11}{14-2} = \frac{-8}{12} = \frac{-2}{3}$; M: $\frac{11-1}{14-4} = \frac{10}{10} = 1$; and N: $\frac{9-2}{15-1} = \frac{7}{14} = \frac{1}{2}$. Therefore, J should the greatest increase, at a rate of 2.

5. **A. Revenue = 2(units sold) – 10 (Slopes and Lines)** To answer this item, first find the slope of the line and then use the formula for a line. The slope of the line is 2: $\frac{10-0}{10-5} = \frac{10}{5} = 2$. Use the point (5, 0) to determine $0 = 2(5) + b$ so that $b = –10$.

# F. Measurement and Geometry

## 1. Angle Relationships

There are a number of important angle relationships in plane geometry.

### a. Intersecting Lines

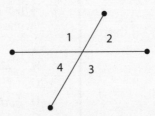

When two lines cross one another, they are said to **intersect**. The opposite angles of intersecting lines are called **vertical angles**. The measures of vertical angles are always equal. In the figure above, $m\angle 1 = m\angle 3$ and $m\angle 2 = m\angle 4$.

The sum of each pair of non-vertical angles is always 180°: $m\angle 1 + m\angle 2 = 180°$

### b. Parallel Lines

Parallel lines are lines that run alongside one another, staying a constant distance apart and never intersecting. When another line crosses two parallel lines, corresponding vertical angles will have the same measures.

$$m\angle 5 = m\angle 8 = m\angle 9 = m\angle 12$$
$$m\angle 6 = m\angle 7 = m\angle 10 = m\angle 11$$

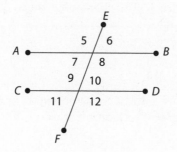

## c. Triangles

The sum of the measures of the interior angles of a triangle is always 180°.

# 2. Polygons

A polygon is an enclosed figure with three or more sides. Triangles, squares, rectangles, pentagons, and so on are all polygons. Every polygon with $n$ sides can be divided into $n - 2$ triangles. For example, a square or rectangle can be divided into two triangles (4 sides – 2 = 2).

The sum of the interior angles of the polygon is $180(n - 2)°$. Therefore, the sum of the interior angles of a triangle is 180°: $180(3 - 2) = 180°$. The sum of the interior angles of a square or rectangle is 360°: $180(4 - 2) = 360°$.

The sum of the exterior angles of a polygon is always 360°.

Look at the following example:

If two angles of a triangle measure 49° and 77°, what is the measure of the third angle?

Subtract the sum of 49 and 77 from 180 to get 54°: $49 + 77 = 126$; $180 - 126 = 54°$.

Try this example:

Three of the interior angles of a five-sided polygon have measures 68°, 77°, and 115°. The remaining two angles have the same measure. What is the measure of each of the remaining angles?

A.   50°
B.   100°
C.   130°
D.   140°
E.   260°

If there are five sides in the polygon, then there are three triangles that can be formed. The sum of the measures of the interior angles of the polygon is $3 \times 180° = 540°$. The measures of the three angles given in the problem add to 260°: $68° + 77° + 115° = 260°$. Subtract this from 540° to get 280°: $540° – 260° = 280°$. Then divide by 2 to get the measure for each of the remaining angles: $280° \div 2 = 140°$.

The answer is Option D.

## a. Triangles

An **isosceles triangle** is a triangle with two sides of the same length, or congruent. The angles opposite the sides with equal measures are also congruent with one another.

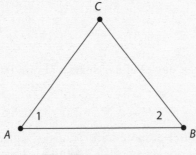

$\overline{AC} \cong \overline{BC}$ and $m\angle 1 \cong m\angle 2$

An **equilateral triangle** is a triangle with three equal angle measures: All the angles measure 60°. The sides of an equilateral triangle are always congruent.

A **right triangle** is a triangle with a 90° (or right) angle. The side opposite the right angle is called the **hypotenuse** and is always the longest side of the triangle. The other two sides of the right triangle are called the **legs.**

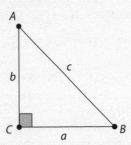

## b. Pythagorean Theorem

The **Pythagorean theorem** always applies to right triangles. The Pythagorean theorem states that $a^2 + b^2 = c^2$, where $c$ is the measure of the hypotenuse.

Look at the following example:

If $\triangle ABC$ is a right triangle with right angle at $C$, $AB = 13$, and $AC = 12$, how long is $BC$?

Use the Pythagorean theorem to solve this problem. The segment $\overline{AB}$ is the hypotenuse for this triangle, so the equation is $12^2 + BC^2 = 13^2$. Square both 12 and 13 to get $144 + BC^2 = 169$ and then subtract 144 from both sides of the equation. $BC^2 = 25$, so $BC = 5$.

Try this example:

A 25-foot ladder leans against a vertical wall so that the bottom of the ladder is 7 feet from the base of the wall. If the bottom of the ladder slides away from the wall another 8 feet, how far down the wall does the top of the ladder slide?

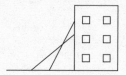

**A.**    4 feet
**B.**    8 feet
**C.**    14 feet
**D.**    20 feet
**E.**    24 feet

The ladder represents the hypotenuse of the right triangle. The height of the ladder (the height is the point where the top of the ladder touches the building) can be computed using the Pythagorean theorem.

$$7^2 + \text{height}^2 = 25^2$$
$$49 + \text{height}^2 = 625$$
$$\text{height}^2 = 576$$
$$\text{height} = 24$$

The bottom of the ladder slides another 8 feet from the wall so that it is now 15 feet from the wall. Use the Pythagorean theorem again to determine the new height of the ladder against the building.

$$15^2 + \text{height}^2 = 25^2$$
$$225 + \text{height}^2 = 625$$
$$\text{height}^2 = 400$$
$$\text{height} = 20$$

You can now determine that the top of the ladder slid down the wall 4 feet: $24 - 20 = 4$. Option A is the correct answer.

# 3. Circles

There are 360° in a circle.

**Chords** are segments that join two points on a circle. If the chord passes through the center of the circle, it is called the **diameter** (*d*).

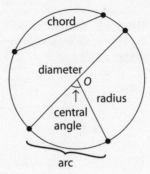

A **radius** (*r*) of a circle joins the center of the circle to a point on the circle. The plural of radius is *radii*.

A **central angle** of a circle has its vertex at the center of the circle and the sides of the angle are radii of the circle.

The part of the circle contained with a central angle is called an **arc** of the circle. The degree measure of the arc is equal to the measure of the central angle.

The interior part of the circle formed by a central angle is called a **sector** of the circle.

# 4. Area and Perimeter

The **perimeter** of any polygon is the sum of the lengths of the sides of the polygon. For circles, the distance around the figure is called the **circumference** and the formula is $C = \pi d = 2\pi r$. Pi ($\pi$) is a constant and is defined as the ratio of the circumference to the diameter of a circle. The approximate value of $\pi$ is 3.14.

The length of an arc of a circle is proportional to the measure of the central angle:

$$\frac{\text{measure of angle}}{360} = \frac{\text{length of arc}}{2\pi r}$$

## a. Area Formulas

**Square:** $A = s^2$, where $s$ is the length of one side of the square.

**Rectangle:** $A = b \times h$, where $b$ is the base of the rectangle and $h$ is the height.

**Triangle:** $A = \frac{1}{2}b \times h$

**Parallelogram:** $A = b \times h$ (see figure below to find height)

**Trapezoid:** $A = \frac{1}{2}h \times (b_1 + b_2)$ (see figure below to find height)

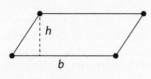

Parallelogram: $A = b \times h$

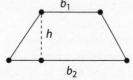

Trapezoid: $A = \dfrac{1}{2} h \times (b_1 + b_2)$

**Circle:** $A = \pi r^2$

**Sector of a circle:** $\dfrac{\text{measure of angle}}{360} = \dfrac{\text{area of sector}}{\pi r^2}$

Look at the following example:

> A window in a house, as shown in the accompanying diagram, is in the shape of a rectangle with a semicircle above it. Determine the area of the window, to the nearest tenth of a square foot.
>
>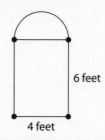
>
> 6 feet
>
> 4 feet

The area of the rectangular portion of the window is 24 square feet. The diameter of the semicircular portion of the window must be 4 feet, so the radius is 2 feet. The area of the semicircle is half the area of the circle, $A = \dfrac{1}{2}\pi\left(2^2\right) = \dfrac{1}{2} \times 3.14 \times 4 = 6.28$. The area of the window, to the nearest tenth of a square foot, is $24 + 6.28 = 30.28$ or approximately 30.3 square feet.

## b. Volume of a Cube or Rectangular Prism

A rectangular prism is a three-dimensional figure whose top and bottom (called the bases) are identical figures and whose sides are rectangles. A cube is a three-dimensional figure whose sides are identical squares. The **lateral surface area, LSA,** (the area along the sides) is equal to the sum of the areas of four sides. The **total surface area** is equal to the sum of the lateral surface area and the area of the two bases. The **volume** of a cube or rectangular prism is equal to the product of the area of the base ($B$) and the height of the solid ($h$): $V = Bh$.

Try this example:

> Construction workers refer to the amount of concrete they use in cubic yards. A sidewalk is being constructed in rectangular patches. Each patch measures 3.5 feet across and 6 feet long. The depth of the concrete is 4 inches. How many cubic yards of concrete, rounded to the nearest tenth, are needed to construct 24 of these patches?
>
> **A.** 6.2
> **B.** 7.0
> **C.** 54.0
> **D.** 168.0
> **E.** 2,916.0

There are 3 feet in a yard, so the width and length of each patch is $\dfrac{3.5}{3}$ yards and 2 yards, respectively. There are 36 inches in a yard, so the depth of a patch of concrete is $\dfrac{4}{36} = \dfrac{1}{9}$ of a yard. The volume of one patch is $\dfrac{3.5}{3} \times 2 \times \dfrac{1}{9}$ cubic yards, and the volume of concrete needed for all 24 patches is $24 \times \dfrac{3.5}{3} \times 2 \times \dfrac{1}{9} = \dfrac{168}{27} = 6.222... \approx 6.2$ cubic yards of concrete (rounded to the nearest tenth). Therefore, Option A is the correct answer.

Try this example:

> John and Lisa plan to paint the walls of their bedroom and realize they will need two coats of paint to do so. Their bedroom is a rectangular-shaped room measuring 15 feet by 12 feet with 8-foot ceilings. The research they have done shows that a gallon of paint covers approximately 400 square feet. How many gallons of paint will they use?
>
> **A.** 0.9
> **B.** 1.08
> **C.** 1.18
> **D.** 2.16
> **E.** 7.2

Two of the walls of the bedroom that will be painted have an area of 15 × 8 = 120 square feet, while the other two walls have an area of 12 × 8 = 96 square feet for a total of 2(120 + 96) = 432 square feet. Because they are planning to put two coats of paint on the wall, they need to cover 432 × 2 = 864 square feet. Since 1 gallon covers 400 square feet, John and Lisa will use $\dfrac{864}{400} = 2.16$ gallons of paint, Therefore, Option D is the correct answer.

# 5. Practice 6

## a. Items

1. Marcia and Alonzo had 7 cubic yards of mulch delivered to their client's home. They plan to lay the mulch 6 inches deep around the flowerbeds. Which expression shows the number of square feet of surface area they will be able to mulch?

   A. $7 \times 6$

   B. $7 \times 36$

   C. $\dfrac{7 \times 3}{\frac{1}{6}}$

   D. $\dfrac{7 \times 27}{\frac{1}{2}}$

   E. $\dfrac{7 \times 36}{\frac{1}{6}}$

2. A vacant rectangular lot has dimensions of 120 feet by 50 feet. Many people walk diagonally across the lot to get from one corner to the opposite corner of the lot. How many feet less is it to walk along the diagonal than it is to walk around two sides of the lot?

   A. 40
   B. 50
   C. 130
   D. 170
   E. 340

3. In $\triangle DEF$, $DE = EF = 8$ inches and the measure of angle $E$ is 40°. What is the measure of angle $D$?

   A. 40°
   B. 70°
   C. 90°
   D. 110°
   E. 140°

4. Squares *TRIG* and *ROSY* have areas 400 square meters and 256 square meters, respectively, and $\triangle TRY$ is a right triangle. What is the length of a side of square *KATY*?

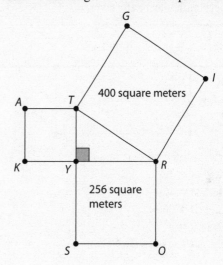

   A. 12
   B. 16
   C. 144
   D. 256
   E. 656

5.  A farmer needs to fence off a rectangular pasture with one side of the rectangle bordering a river. The side by the river does not need fencing. The fencing for the remaining three sides of the rectangle costs $3 per foot. If the fence will cost $120, which of the following represents the area of the rectangle in terms of the length of the side perpendicular to the river, $w$?

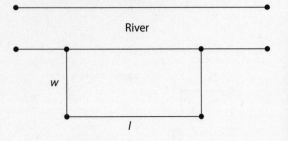

A.  $A = 3w$

B.  $A = 120w$

C.  $A = 360w$

D.  $A = w^2$

E.  $A = w(40 - 2w)$

# b. Answer Explanations

1. D.  $\dfrac{7 \times 27}{\dfrac{1}{2}}$  (**Volume of a Cube or Rectangular Prism**) The volume of a cube that measures 1 yard by 1 yard by 1 yard is one cubic yard. The dimensions of this same cube can also be thought of as 3 feet by 3 feet by 3 feet, making the volume 27 cubic feet. Therefore, the conversion between cubic yards and cubic feet is to multiply the number of cubic yards by 27. The number of cubic feet of mulch delivered is $7 \times 27$. Divide this by the number of feet in depth to get the surface area.

The formula for the volume of a box is $V = lwh$, with $h$ being the height of the box and $lw$ being the area of the base of the box. In general, the formula for the volume of an object in which the height is always the same number is $V = Bh$, where $B$ is the area of the base. For this problem, $V = 7 \times 27$ and the height is $\dfrac{1}{2}$ foot (because 6 inches is $\dfrac{1}{2}$ foot). Therefore, to find the number of square feet of surface area that Marcia and Alonzo will be able to mulch, solve the equation $7 \times 27 = B \times \dfrac{1}{2}$ to get $B = \dfrac{7 \times 27}{\dfrac{1}{2}}$.

2. **A. 40 (Pythagorean Theorem)** The distance around two edges of the lot is $120 + 50 = 170$ feet. Use the Pythagorean theorem to determine the distance across the diagonal path:

$$a^2 + b^2 = c^2$$
$$120^2 + 50^2 = c^2$$
$$14,400 + 2,500 = c^2$$
$$16,900 = c^2$$
$$\sqrt{16,900} = c$$
$$130 = c$$

The difference is $170 - 130 = 40$ feet.

3. **B. 70° (Angle Relationships)** With $DE = EF$, then angles $D$ and $F$ must have the same measure. *Remember:* The sum of the interior angles of a triangle is always 180°. Therefore, $40 + x + x = 180$. Solve for $x$:

$$40 + x + x = 180$$
$$40 + 2x = 180$$
$$40 + 2x - 40 = 180 - 40$$
$$2x = 140$$
$$x = 70$$

The measure of angle $D$ is 70°.

4. **A. 12 (Pythagorean Theorem)** The area of square $KATY$ is 144, which is determined by the Pythagorean theorem: $TY^2 + YR^2 = TR^2$. Since the area of square $TRIG$ is 400 square meters, $TR^2 = 400$ (each side is 20 meters; $20 \times 20 = 400$. Since the area of square $ROSY$ is 256 square meters, $YR^2 = 256$ (each side is 16 meters; $16 \times 16 = 256$). Substitute these values into $TY^2 + YR^2 = TR^2$ to find the length of $TY$:

$$TY^2 + YR^2 = TR^2$$
$$TY^2 + 256 = 400$$
$$TY^2 + 256 - 256 = 400 - 256$$
$$TY^2 = 144$$
$$TY = \sqrt{144}$$
$$TY = 12$$

Therefore, the length of a side in square $KATY$ is 12.

5. **E. $A = w\,(40-2w)$ (Area and Perimeter)** The farmer has to fence three sides of the rectangle, $w$, $w$, and $l$. Because the farmer will spend \$120 and the fence costs \$3 per foot, the farmer will buy 40 feet of fencing: $120 \div 3 = 40$. Therefore, $2w + l = 40$ or $l = 40 - 2w$. The area of the rectangle is $lw$. Substitute $40 - 2w$ for $l$ for the proper equation: $A = w(40 - 2w)$.

# G. Data Analysis: Probability and Statistics

## 1. Probability

Probability is the measure of the likelihood that an event will occur. The "likelihood" is calculated by examining the ratio of favorable outcomes to the set of all possible outcomes. For example, when drawing a number from a set of 10 cards numbered 1 through 10, the probability of randomly selecting a 3 is one out of ten, or $\frac{1}{10}$, while the probability of selecting a number greater than 7 is three out of ten, or $\frac{3}{10}$, since the only favorable outcomes are 8, 9, and 10.

To compute probabilities, you need to learn how to count the number of favorable and possible outcomes for a given problem.

### a. Counting Principle

The **Fundamental Theorem of Counting** tells us that when a series of steps are needed to complete a process, then the number of possible processes is equal to the product of the number of ways each step can be performed.

Look at the following example:

> A lunch menu consists of a sandwich, a drink, and a side. The sandwich choices are roast beef, turkey, tuna, veggie, or cheese. The drink choices are iced tea, cola, diet cola, milk, or coffee. The side choices are salad, fruit salad, or potato chips. How many different lunch combinations are possible if you pick one sandwich, one drink, and one side?

In selecting a lunch from the given menu, there are 5 possible sandwiches, 5 drink choices, and 3 sides options. The number of possible lunch combinations is $5 \times 5 \times 3 = 75$.

Try this example:

> A non-personalized license plate for an automobile consists of 3 letters of the alphabet (2 letters, I and O, are excluded) followed by 3 digits from 0 to 9. How many different non-personalized license plates can be made? Duplication of letters and numbers is allowed.

How many ways can the first step (picking a letter) be performed? Because the letters I and O are not available, there are 24 letter possibilities: $26 - 2 = 24$. The same is true for selecting the second letter and the third letter. The fourth step is to pick a digit. Because there are no restrictions, there are 10 possibilities for the first digit picked, as well as for the second and third digits. Therefore, the number of possible personalized license plates is $24 \times 24 \times 24 \times 10 \times 10 \times 10 = 13,824,000$.

Look at the following example:

> A gym lock's combination is a 3-number code selected from the numbers 1 to 36 with no repetition of numbers allowed. (That is, the same number cannot be used twice in the combination.) How many possible combinations are there?

There are 36 possible numbers for the first number but only 35 for the second number in the combination (whatever the first number of the combination is, it cannot be used for the second number), and 34 possibilities for the third number in the combination. Therefore, the locker has $36 \times 35 \times 34 = 42,840$ possible combinations.

## b. Venn Diagrams

The Venn diagram is an efficient method for displaying information that comes from a survey. The diagram below shows the results of survey done to compare gender and political affiliation.

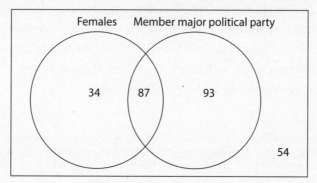

Reading the diagram, the two characteristics identified in the diagram are females and member of a major political party. The overlap of the two circles shows 87, meaning these 87 responses represent females who are members of a major political party. The diagram shows there are 34 responses within the category females, but outside the member major political party; therefore, there are 34 responses from females who are not members of a major political party. The 93 responses within the major political party and outside the category females represent 93 males who are members of a major political party, while the 54 outside the two circles represent the number of males who are not members of a major political party. You can conclude that 268 people answered the survey ($34 + 87 + 93 + 54 = 268$). Of these 268 people, 121 are female ($87 + 34 = 121$), and 180 are members of a major political party ($87 + 93 = 180$).

Look at the following example:

> The diagram shows the results of a survey of people who passed by the corner of Main Street and Broadway on a Saturday afternoon.

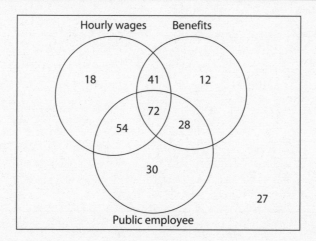

Responders were asked to indicate if they were public employees, if they had benefits, and if they earned an hourly wage (as opposed to some other payment schedule). A different breakdown of the results shows:

- The total number of responders is 282 (18 + 41 + 12 + 54 + 72 + 28 +30 + 27 = 282).
- 184 responders were public employees (30 + 54 + 72 + 28 = 184).
- 153 responders had benefits (28 + 72 + 41 + 12 = 153).
- 185 responders earned an hourly wage (18 + 54 + 72 + 41 = 185).
- 28 responders are public employees and have benefits, but do not earn an hourly wage.
- 54 responders are public employees and earn an hourly wage, but do not have benefits.
- 41 responders earn an hourly wage and have benefits, but are not public employees.
- 72 responders are public employees with benefits and earn an hourly wage.
- 27 of the responders do not have any of these characteristics.

Look at the following example:

> What is the probability that a responder from the above survey is a public employee?

Since the total number of responders to this survey is 282 and there are 184 public employees, the probability that a responder is a public employee is $\dfrac{184}{282}$.

Try this example:

> What is the probability that a responder to the survey above is a public employee and has benefits?

There are 100 responders who are public employees and have benefits (28 + 72 = 100). Therefore, the probability is $\dfrac{100}{282}$.

Try this example:

> What is the probability that a responder to the survey above is a public employee given that the responder has benefits?
>
> A. $\dfrac{28}{282}$
>
> B. $\dfrac{100}{153}$
>
> C. $\dfrac{141}{153}$
>
> D. $\dfrac{153}{282}$
>
> E. $\dfrac{184}{282}$

The phrase "given that the responder has benefits" changes the number of possible outcomes. The group under discussion is no longer anyone who responded to the survey but only those who identified that they had benefits. Of the 153 responders who stated they had benefits (12 + 41 + 72 + 28 = 153), 100 are public employees (72 + 28 = 100). Therefore, the probability is $\dfrac{100}{153}$; Option B is the correct answer.

Try this example:

---

What is the probability that a responder earns an hourly wage or is a public employee?

A. $\dfrac{48}{282}$

B. $\dfrac{126}{282}$

C. $\dfrac{167}{282}$

D. $\dfrac{225}{282}$

E. $\dfrac{243}{282}$

---

Do not be deceived from the summary that there are 184 public employees and 185 responders who earn an hourly wage. The sum of these numbers, 369, is more than the total number of responders. Looking at the Venn diagram again, you can see that there are 126 responders who are public employees and earn an hourly wage (54 + 72 = 126). Subtract this number from 369 to get the 243 people who meet the criteria of the question (369 – 126 = 243). The probability is $\dfrac{243}{282}$; Option E is the correct answer. You can also add the numbers from the diagram to get 243 (18 + 41 + 72 + 54 + 30 + 28 = 243).

# 2. Statistics

The average cost of a home, the percent of the population who are unemployed, and the results of public opinion polls are statistics that are regularly featured in the news. The information is often displayed graphically to give "a big picture," with key numbers often used to summarize.

## a. Charts

A chart is one way to present statistical data. Look at the following example:

The chart shows the amount of surface area for each of the five oceans and all the land masses.

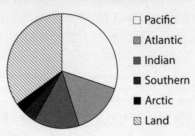

☐ Pacific
■ Atlantic
■ Indian
■ Southern
■ Arctic
▨ Land

If the total surface area of Earth is 196.9 million square miles, which of the following is the best estimate, in millions of square miles, for the surface area of the Pacific Ocean?

A. 50
B. 60
C. 80
D. 90
E. 100

The pie chart indicates that the Pacific Ocean occupies more than 25% of Earth's surface area but less than half; a fair estimate is one-third. One-third of 196.9 is approximately 65.6, so the best guess for the surface area of the Pacific Ocean is Option B, 60 million square miles.

## b. Central Tendency

Finding the center of a set of data provides a sense of where the typical data point is located; this is called the **average.** For most people, when they think of the average, they imagine adding a set of numbers and dividing by the number of data points. Statistically, this measure of center is called the **mean** and is the measure of average most often used.

There are two other measures of central tendency: the median and the mode. As with driving, where the median is a place in the center of the road dividing the traffic going one way from the other, the **median** is the number in the middle, once the numbers are arranged from increasing to decreasing or decreasing to increasing order. If there are an odd number of data points, the median will be the middle number. For example, given the data set (4, 5, 7, 8, 19, 21, 30), there are three numbers to the left of 8 and three numbers to the right of 8, so 8 is the median. If there is an even number of data points, the median is the mean of the two middle points. For example, given the data set (4, 5, 7, 8, 19, 21, 30, 50), the data can be split 4, 5, 7, 8 and 19, 21, 30, 50. The median for this data then is the mean of 8 and 19, or 13.5 $\left( \dfrac{8+19}{2} = 13.5 \right)$.

The **mode** is the data value that occurs with the highest frequency. The data set (4, 5, 7, 8, 19, 21, 30, 50) has no mode because none of the values occurs more than any other, while the data set (4, 4, 5, 7, 8, 19, 21, 30, 50) has a mode of 4.

Look at the following example:

> Given the data set (23, 45, 38, 29, 15, 52, 41, 23), find the mean, median, and mode.

First arrange the data in increasing order: (15, 23, 23, 29, 38, 41, 45, 52).

The mean is the sum of the data values divided by 8: $\dfrac{15+23+23+29+38+41+45+52}{8} = \dfrac{266}{8} = 33.25$

There are 8 data values, so the median is midway between the fourth and fifth data points, 29 and 38: $\dfrac{29+38}{2} = \dfrac{67}{2} = 33.5$

The value 23 appears twice in the data set, while all the others appear just once; 23 is the mode.

The mean is the most volatile of the central tendency measures because it is the measure that is most affected when a number in a data set is drastically different from the others.

Try this example:

> Given the data set (23, 45, 38, 29, 15, 52, 41, 23, 320), find the mean, median, and mode.
>
> A.  mean = 23, median = 38, mode = 65.11
> B.  mean = 23, median = 65.11, mode = 38
> C.  mean = 38, median = 65.11, mode = 23
> D.  mean = 65.11, median = 38, mode = 23
> E.  mean = 65.11, median = 23, mode = 38

First arrange the data in increasing order: (15, 23, 23, 29, 38, 41, 45, 52, 320).

The mean is 65.11: 15 + 23 + 23 + 29 + 38 +41 + 45 + 52 + 320 = 586; $\dfrac{586}{9} = 65.11$ (rounded to two decimal places). There are 9 data points so the fifth data value, 38, is the median. The value 23 appears twice while all the others appear just once, so 23 is the mode. Therefore, Option D is the correct answer.

## c. Frequency Distribution

A frequency distribution is a table or chart that shows the number of times an event took place. With large sets of data in which data points are repeated, the representation of the data may be in the form of a frequency chart.

Look at the following example:

> The data for the number of days each employee has been absent during the past year are collected and displayed in the frequency chart. Find the mean (rounded to the nearest one-hundredth), median, and mode.
>
> | Days Absent | Frequency |
> |---|---|
> | 0 | 23 |
> | 1 | 45 |
> | 2 | 52 |
> | 4 | 23 |
> | 5 | 12 |
> | 7 | 8 |
> | 8 | 3 |
> | 10 | 1 |

The mean is found by setting up a third column and multiplying the number of days absent with the frequency and adding these together. Divide the sum by 167, the total number of data points in the frequency column.

$$\frac{0(23)+1(45)+2(52)+4(23)+5(12)+7(8)+8(3)+10(1)}{167}=\frac{45+104+92+60+56+24+10}{167}=\frac{391}{167}=2.34$$

The median is 2. Add the frequency column to determine the number of data points: 167. This tells you that the median is the 84th data point (one more than half of 166). The table shows that 68 employees have been absent 0 or 1 day (23 + 45 = 68). The 84th data point is one of the values in the group of 52 with 2 days absent; therefore, the median is 2. The mode for this data is also 2 since 2 occurs 52 times, more often than any other data point.

## 3. Practice 7

### a. Items

*A survey of teachers in a suburban school district was taken. A summary of the survey is provided. Use this data to answer items 1 and 2.*

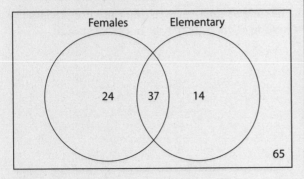

1. If a teacher from this survey is selected at random, what is the probability the teacher is female?

A. $\dfrac{24}{37}$

B. $\dfrac{24}{61}$

C. $\dfrac{24}{140}$

D. $\dfrac{37}{140}$

E. $\dfrac{61}{140}$

2. If a teacher from this survey is selected at random, what is the probability that the teacher is a female elementary school teacher?

A. $\dfrac{37}{61}$

B. $\dfrac{37}{140}$

C. $\dfrac{51}{140}$

D. $\dfrac{75}{140}$

E. $\dfrac{37}{75}$

*The librarian at the local branch conducted a survey of the number of books checked out by each patron during one day. The results of the survey are shown in the following frequency table. Use this summary to answer items 3 and 4.*

| Number of Books Checked Out | Frequency |
|---|---|
| 1 | 41 |
| 2 | 37 |
| 3 | 29 |
| 4 | 51 |
| 5 | 17 |
| 6 | 10 |

3. Which statement about the measures of central tendency is correct for this data?

A. Median < Mean < Mode
B. Mean < Median < Mode
C. Mode < Mean < Median
D. Mode < Median < Mean
E. Mean < Mode < Median

4. If a patron of the library is selected at random, what is the probability that the patron checked out more than 3 books?

A. $\dfrac{29}{185}$

B. $\dfrac{51}{185}$

C. $\dfrac{78}{185}$

D. $\dfrac{80}{185}$

E. $\dfrac{107}{185}$

5. The mean of the data set (23, 14, 19, 32, 27, x) is 20. Find the value of x.

A. 5
B. 10
C. 20
D. 115
E. 120

# b. Answer Explanations

1. **E.** $\dfrac{61}{140}$ **(Probability)** There are 61 female teachers in the survey (24 + 37 = 61) out of the 140 total teachers in the survey (27 + 37 + 14 + 65 = 140). Therefore, the probability that a teacher from this survey selected at random is female is $\dfrac{61}{140}$.

2. **B.** $\dfrac{37}{140}$ **(Probability)** There are 37 elementary teachers in the survey who are female. Therefore, the probability that the teacher is a female elementary school teacher is $\dfrac{37}{140}$.

3. **B. Mean < Median < Mode (Central Tendency)** You can easily identify the mode as 4 since it has the highest frequency. There are a total of 185 data values (41 + 37 + 29 + 51 + 17 + 10 = 185), so the median is the 93rd data point. The 92nd data point is 3 because that data point falls within the patrons

who checked out 3 books (41 + 37 +29 = 107). Therefore, median is 3, making median < mode. You can use the data to estimate the mean as being less than 3: The mean must be less than 3 because the number of patrons who took out 1, 2, or 3 books (41 + 37 + 29 = 107) is larger than the number of patrons who took out more than 3 books (51 + 17 + 10 = 78). Therefore, mean < median < mode.

You can check this answer by calculating the mean. First, calculate the total number of books checked out. Multiply each frequency value by the number of books checked out and add the results: 1(41) + 2(37) + 3(29) + 4(51) + 5(17) + 6(10) = 551. Next, calculate total number of patrons (41 + 37 + 29 + 51 + 17 + 10 = 185). Then divide: 551 ÷ 185 = 2.97.

4. **C.** $\dfrac{78}{185}$ **(Probability)** More than 3 books checked out means the patron checked out 4, 5, or 6 books (according to this table). There are a total of 78 patrons in this group (51 + 17 + 10 = 78). There are 185 total patrons surveyed. Therefore, the probability that a patron selected at random checked out more than 3 books is $\dfrac{78}{185}$.

5. **A. 5 (Central Tendency)** If the mean of the six-value data set is 20, then the sum of the six data points must be 6 × 20 = 120. The sum of the five known data points is 115 (23 + 14 + 19 + 32 + 27 =115), so the last value must be 120 – 115 = 5; $x = 5$.

# VII. Science

The HiSET Science section tests your ability to:

- Understand and use science content knowledge
- Apply principles of science inquiry (such as the scientific method)
- Interpret, analyze, evaluate, and apply scientific information

The HiSET Science section has 50 multiple choice items, and you will have 80 minutes to complete the section. The test items address the three main branches of science: physical science, earth and space science, and life science. You do not need specialized knowledge in these areas to answer the items; rather, the test asks you to read and interpret reading passages and graphic information (tables, graphs, maps, and diagrams) to answer the items.

# A. Test Format

The 50 multiple-choice items on the HiSET Science section are based on reading passages and/or graphic material. About 75 to 80% of the items will be based on longer passages and/or graphics, while the remaining 20 to 25% will be based on shorter passages and/or graphics. Longer passages usually have six to eight items (sometimes more), while shorter passages and/or graphics may have only one or two items.

There are four item types on the Science test:

- text-based
- table-based
- graph-based
- diagram-based

Examples of these four item types follow.

## 1. Text-Based Items

Here is an example of a longer reading passage and item:

Mobile phones and radios both use electromagnetic waves to transmit their signals. These waves can travel through the air, as well as through certain solid and liquid substances. Many electromagnetic waves can travel through insulators but not through conductors. A conductor, such as various kinds of metal, can conduct electricity. An insulator, such as plastic or ceramic, cannot conduct electricity. The reason that many electromagnetic waves cannot pass through conductors is relatively simple: Most of the waves are reflected back. The few waves that are not reflected back are absorbed into the conductor. Insulators, on the other hand, tend to let many, but not all, waves pass through. For example, radio waves can pass through most insulators. However, light rays can only travel through some materials, such as glass. The tinted glass used in many modern energy-efficient buildings tends to partially block light waves. These windows can also block or partially block some other waves, such as microwaves.

Though many waves can pass through insulators, some can do so more easily than others. Radio waves, which have a relatively long wavelength, can easily pass through many kinds of materials, such as concrete walls. However, microwaves, which have a much shorter wavelength, such as the ones used in microwave ovens and mobile phones, have a more difficult time passing through many insulators. Other waves cannot travel through certain insulators because of the molecular structure of the substances. This is why infrared waves cannot travel through glass, for example.

---

Tyrone notices that his mobile phone works well in his home, a small wood-frame house. However, at his workplace, which is located in an old steel-frame building with large, thick walls with many metal studs inside, his phone's reception is much worse. Which of the following is the most likely explanation for why his phone does not function well when he is at work?

A. The mobile phone uses radio waves, which are blocked by the building where he works.
B. The energy-efficient windows at his workplace do not let the phone's microwaves through.
C. Infrared waves cannot pass through the glass in his building.
D. Microwaves cannot travel through the old building's thick walls.

---

Option D is correct because the passage says that microwaves cannot pass through the thick walls of the building. The steel frame and heavy metal studs used in the construction also reduce the wave's ability to get through. Option A is incorrect because according to the passage, mobile phones use microwaves, not radio waves. In addition, radio waves can travel through thick walls. Option B is incorrect because the passage does not mention that his workplace has windows. In addition, Tyrone works in an older building that most likely does not have new energy-efficient windows. Moreover, Option B does not explain why the waves cannot travel through the building's walls. Option C is incorrect because mobile phones use microwaves, not infrared waves.

**TIP: A longer reading passage may have six or more items. When reading a longer passage, read the items first. Then skim the passage quickly. First read the title and any illustrations or graphic materials. Then read the first sentence of each paragraph. Then go back and read the entire passage quickly. After that, try to answer the items.**

Here is an example of a shorter passage and item. Shorter passages are typically combined into the item itself and do not appear separately before the related item(s).

---

A student wants to determine whether a certain houseplant will grow better indoors in full sunlight or partial sunlight. Which of these growing conditions should the student use?

A. Place one plant in a room that has bright sun all day, and place a second plant in a room with no windows and bright electric lights.
B. Place one plant in a dark closet, and place a second plant in a room that has sun half the day.
C. Place one plant in a room that has sun half the day, and place a second plant in a room that has bright sunlight most of the day.
D. Plant one of the plants outdoors in a part of the garden that gets sun all day, and place a second plant in a room that gets sunlight half the day.

---

Option C is correct because in this experimental design, the two plants will get different amounts of sunlight. The student can compare the growth of the plants to see which conditions result in more growth.

Option A is incorrect because the second plant needs to be in partial light, not artificial light. Option B is incorrect because the first plant needs to be in full sunlight, not darkness. Option D is incorrect because although the first plant is in bright sunlight, the student wants to find out about how the plants grow indoors, not outdoors.

# 2. Table-Based Items

Tables are frequently used to organize and present numeric and textual information. Tables may appear with textual information or alone. Look at the following example:

Each year, the "All About Wildlife" website publishes a list of the animals it considers the most endangered.

| Most Endangered Species | | |
|---|---|---|
| Animal | Habitat | Estimated Number Living in the Wild |
| 1. Ivory billed woodpecker | Southeastern United States and Cuba | Unknown; possibly extinct |
| 2. Amur leopard | Eastern Russia | 40 |
| 3. Java rhinoceros | Western tip of Java | 40–60 |
| 4. Northern sportive lemur | Northern Madagascar | 20 |
| 5. Northern right whale | Atlantic Ocean | 350 |

Source: www.allaboutwildlife.com/ten-most-endangered-animals

Which of the species has the smallest number of individuals living in the wild?

A. Ivory billed woodpecker
B. Amur leopard
C. Java rhinoceros
D. Northern sportive lemur

Option A is the correct answer because the table says that this animal is possibly extinct or almost extinct. Therefore, this animal has fewer individuals living in the wild than the other species in the list.

The northern sportive lemur is estimated to have 20 individuals living in the wild, and ranks number 4 on the list of endangered species. The java rhino ranks higher on the list, at number 3, but has a greater number of individuals living in the wild.

Which of these reasons is the most logical explanation of this apparent discrepancy?

A. There are more rhinos than lemurs in zoos around the world.
B. Rhinos are carnivores that eat lemurs.
C. The lemur's habitat is more threatened than the rhino's habitat.
D. It's more difficult for rhinos to reproduce than lemurs.

Option D is the only option that accounts for the apparent discrepancy. If rhinos have difficulty reproducing, then they would be more endangered than lemurs, even in larger numbers. (In fact, rhinos have difficulty reproducing because of the limited number of female rhinos of reproduction age in the wild and their long gestation period, the time it takes for them to reproduce.) Option A is incorrect because the item is asking about animals living in the wild, not in captivity. Option B is not a reason for lemurs being less endangered than rhinos, so it is incorrect. In addition, rhinos are plant eaters and do not live in the same habitat as lemurs. Option C does not explain the data because rhinos are considered more endangered than lemurs.

To interpret a table, do the following:

- Read the name of the table and the column and row heads. This will help you understand what information is in the table.
- Read any caption or accompanying text.
- Make sure you understand the value of the numbers in each column of the table. Are the values expressed in money (such as dollars), mass (such as grams), percentages, averages, or some other measure?
- To find information in a table, use the rows and columns. Find the row and column you are interested in. Trace the row from left to right with your left index finger and the column with your right index finger to find the cell of the table with the information you are looking for.

# 3. Graph-Based Items

Graphs are used to show data visually. There are three main kinds of graphs: line graphs, bar graphs, and pie charts. Like tables, graphs may appear alone or accompany text.

## a. Line Graphs

Line graphs are used to show the relationship between two variables. They are often used to show changes or trends in data. For example, this line graph was prepared by students studying the growth of plants. The following graph shows the relationship between the height of a bean plant and the number of days passed. Look at this example:

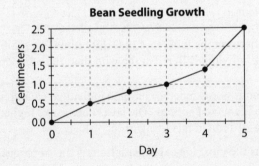

When did the plant experience the fastest growth?

**A.** Days 0–1
**B.** Days 1–2
**C.** Days 3–4
**D.** Days 4–5

Option D is correct because the line is the steepest in this interval of the graph. It rises by approximately 1 centimeter. Option A is incorrect because the plant only grew by 0.5 centimeters. Option B is incorrect because the plant grew by less than 0.5 centimeters. Option C is incorrect because it rises by slightly less than 0.5 centimeters.

To interpret a line graph, do the following:

- Read the title of the graph and the labels for each axis. Make sure you understand the units used on each axis. In this line graph, the x-axis (horizontal axis) shows the number of days, and the y-axis (vertical axis) shows the height in centimeters.

- Decide which of the variables in the graph is being affected. That is, one of the variables is affected by the other. In this case, height is affected by time (number of days).

- Look at the line. What is the relationship between the two variables? This graph shows a positive relationship: Over time, the plant continues to grow taller.

## b. Bar Graphs

A bar graph uses horizontal or vertical bars to compare numbers. The following graph was prepared by environmentalists studying pollution at a local beach. As they cleaned the beach, the team of researchers logged each kind of trash they picked up. Look at this example:

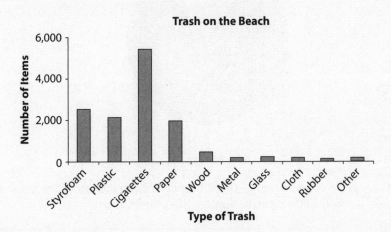

Which of these items was found <u>most frequently</u> on the beach?

A. Plastic
B. Glass
C. Wood
D. Metal

Of the four options given, Option A, plastic, has the highest bar, so it was the item most frequently found on the beach. The other options have shorter bars, so they are incorrect.

To interpret a bar graph, do the following:

- Read the title of the graph and the labels for each axis. Make sure you understand the units used on each axis. In this line graph, the *x*-axis (horizontal axis) shows the kinds of items, and the *y*-axis (vertical axis) shows the number of each kind of item.

- Look at the height of each bar. Which one is the highest? Which one is the lowest?

## c. Pie Charts

A pie chart is used to show data as parts of a whole. Each "slice" of the pie shows the proportion of the whole that the data represents. Look at the following example:

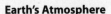

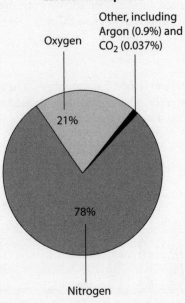

In this case, the "whole" is the composition of the atmosphere. Each section of the graph shows the percentage of a certain gas in the atmosphere. Now try this example item:

> What percentage of Earth's atmosphere consists of nitrogen?
>
> **A.** 78%
> **B.** 21%
> **C.** 0.9%
> **D.** 0.037%

Option A is correct. According to the pie chart, the largest proportion of gas in the atmosphere is nitrogen, which makes up 78 percent of the atmosphere. Option B is the percentage of oxygen in the atmosphere. Option C is the percentage of argon in the atmosphere. Option D is the percentage of $CO_2$ (carbon dioxide) in the atmosphere.

To interpret a pie chart, do the following:

- Read the title of the chart and the labels of each section. Make sure you understand what the pie chart represents.
- Look at the values in the chart. Do they represent percentages or something else, such as a number?
- Look at the slices of the pie. Which ones are larger? Which ones are smaller?

TIP: It is often easy to estimate visually which section of a pie chart is the largest or the smallest, but if slices of the pie are very small, visual estimation of the size or quantity represented is difficult. Use the labels and numbers in the chart, if any, to help you figure out the proportion represented by each section of the pie.

# 4. Diagram-Based Items

A diagram is a drawing or sketch used to depict information visually. A diagram can be simple or complex. Look at the following example:

A simple machine has few or no moving parts, and does not use a power source. Simple machines can change the direction or strength of a force. Six of the most common simple machines are levers, inclined planes, wedges, pulleys, screws, and wheel and axle.

**Simple Machines**

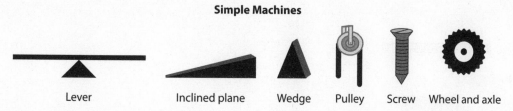

Lever      Inclined plane    Wedge    Pulley    Screw    Wheel and axle

Now try these example items:

A worker needs to move some heavy boxes from the floor of the auditorium to the stage, a height of about 4 feet, using a dolly (a cart with wheels). Which of these simple machines could the worker use to make the task easier?

A. Screw
B. Lever
C. Inclined plane
D. Wedge

Option C is correct. An inclined plane directs a horizontal force upward. By using an inclined plane, the worker can easily carry or push the boxes up to the level of the stage. Option A is incorrect because a screw directs the force into a spiral. Option B is incorrect because while a lever can raise an object, it would not work with a dolly. Option D is incorrect because a wedge is used to direct a force outward. A wedge is often used with a hammer or mallet to split things, such as wood for building a fire.

What kind of simple machine is a crowbar?

A. Screw
B. Lever
C. Inclined plane
D. Wedge

A crowbar is a kind of lever, Option B.

Some items have art in each answer option, as in the following example:

Which of the following items is NOT an example of an inclined plane?

A.

B.

C.

D.

Option A is correct. A crowbar is a lever, not an inclined plane. Options B and C are both special kinds of inclined planes. Each one breaks the plane into steps. Option D is a ramp, a kind of inclined plane.

To interpret a drawing, do the following:

- Read the figure title and labels, if any. Make sure you understand what the drawing represents.
- Read any accompanying text. Use the information in the text to help you understand the drawing.

# B. Types of Items: A Detailed Look

HiSET Science items are divided into three types:

- Interpret and apply
- Analyze
- Evaluate and generalize

This section gives detailed information on how to answer each type of item.

# 1. Interpret and Apply

## a. Interpreting Information

Interpreting information involves reading and understanding the main idea and details, identifying implications, and making inferences. The items about endangered species you saw on page 221 are examples of interpreting information items.

Now look at this sample reading passage and item about producers and consumers:

Green plants are organisms that can make their own food using photosynthesis. They use energy from the sun, along with water and carbon dioxide, to create their own food, usually in the form of simple sugars. Green plants are considered producers. Most producers are green plants, but there are a few exceptions. A few rare bacteria, called cyanobacteria, produce their own food using oxidation, not photosynthesis.

Animals, on the other hand, are consumers. Consumers eat plants or other animals to get their food. Animals that eat only plants are called primary consumers. Secondary consumers eat primary consumers. Some secondary consumers can eat plants as well. The third type of consumer is an apex consumer. An apex consumer is at the top of a food chain and can eat plants as well as primary consumers, and/or secondary consumers. Generally, apex, or tertiary predators, have few or no known predators. Human beings are one kind of apex consumer.

> How do <u>most</u> producers create their own food?
>
> **A.** They use oxidation to create food.
> **B.** They eat small insects.
> **C.** They convert energy from the sun into food.
> **D.** They decompose dead plant material and use it to create new food.

Option C correctly paraphrases information stated directly in the passage. Option A is true of only a tiny number of producers, cyanobacteria. Option B is not correct. All green plants make their own food using photosynthesis. Even carnivorous plants, such as Venus flytraps, only use prey as a secondary source of nutrients that they cannot get from the soil. Option D is about decomposers, not producers.

## b. Applying Information

When you apply scientific information, you use the information to complete a specific task or answer a specific question. Sometimes, these questions are related to life skill applications. For example, the item you saw earlier in this chapter about mobile phones (page 220) asks you to apply information about wave theory to figure out why mobile phone reception can vary inside different kinds of buildings. Two of the simple machine items (page 226) were application items, too. They asked you to apply information about simple machines to determine the kind of machine a crowbar is and to determine which simple machine is not an inclined plane.

Here is another example of an application item. It refers to the passage on producers and consumers:

> Which of the following is an example of an apex consumer?
>
> **A.** A plant-eating rhino
> **B.** A grizzly bear that eats fruit, fish, deer, eagles, and black bears
> **C.** A snake that catches and eats smaller animals such as mice and rabbits
> **D.** A fungus that obtains its food by decomposing dead plant and animal material

In this application item, you need to use information from the passage to determine which of the options is an apex consumer. Option B is correct because a grizzly bear eats plants (such as fruit) as well as primary consumers (such as fish and deer) and secondary consumers (such as eagles). Option A (rhinos) is not correct because plant-eating rhinos are primary consumers. Snakes (Option C) that eat mice and rabbits, which are primary consumers, are examples of secondary consumers. A fungus is not an example of a consumer, but of a decomposer. Decomposers get their food not by eating it, but by decomposing it.

## c. Applying the Scientific Method

On each administration of the HiSET, items will ask you to understand, design, use, and evaluate experiments. Experiments follow the scientific method. The example item you saw previously about houseplants (page 220) asked you to use knowledge of the scientific method to design an experiment. The scientific method consists of these steps:

1. You make observations on some aspect of the world around you. For example, you observe that ice melts when it is left in a glass on the kitchen counter at room temperature.
2. You formulate a research question based on your observation. You ask, "At what temperature does water change from a solid (ice) to a liquid?"

3. You formulate a hypothesis that you can test: Ice will melt at a specific temperature.

4. You design an experiment to test the hypothesis. For example, to test this hypothesis, you can place ice in a beaker over a source of heat. Insert a lab thermometer into the middle of the ice. Heat the ice and take note of the time and temperature every minute as you stir the ice. (Stirring the ice keeps it at a constant temperature.) Take note of the temperature when it begins to melt.

5. You analyze the data. In this case, your data showed that the ice began to melt when it reached 100°C. You conclude that the melting point of water is 100°C.

Now try this sample item.

---

Jennifer notices that bread she buys gets moldy after a few days. She wants to figure out where in her kitchen she should store her bread so it will stay fresh the longest: the refrigerator, the counter, or a dark cabinet. What procedure should she follow?

A. Place a loaf of bread in her refrigerator for 3 days, then move it to the counter for 3 days, and then place it in the cabinet for 3 days.

B. Put several slices of bread in small plastic bags, and place them in the three different places in her kitchen (refrigerator, counter, and dark cabinet); check them daily.

C. Place unwrapped slices of bread in the three different places in her kitchen (refrigerator, counter, and dark cabinet) and check them daily.

D. Keep all of her bread in the freezer, since it gets moldy too fast in the other places in her kitchen.

---

This is an example of an item that has a life skill application. To answer this item, you need to figure out which of the proposed experiment designs will answer Jennifer's research question: In which location will bread stay fresh the longest? Only Option B will let her evaluate and compare the results from the three locations while just changing one variable in the experiment.

# 2. Analyze

When you analyze information, you explore the relationships between ideas such as cause-effect, part-whole, distinguishing fact from opinion, and understanding steps in a process. Try these sample analysis items.

| Property Damage Caused by Earthquakes | | | | | |
|---|---|---|---|---|---|
| Rank | Name | Year | Magnitude | Casualties (Number of Deaths Confirmed) | Property Damage |
| 1 | Tohoku earthquake and tsunami, Japan | 2011 | 9.0 | 15,787 | $235 billion |
| 2 | Great Hanshin earthquake, Japan | 1995 | 6.9 | 6,434 | $100 billion |
| 3 | Sichuan earthquake, China | 2008 | 8.0 | 69,195 | $75 billion |
| 4 | Christchurch earthquake, New Zealand | 2011 | 6.3 | 185 | $30 billion |
| 5 | Chile earthquake | 2010 | 8.8 | 525 | $15–30 billion |

*Source: http://en.wikipedia.org/wiki/Lists_of_earthquakes#Property_damages_caused_by_earthquake*

Using the information in the table, which of the following statements can be proved to be true?

A. Earthquakes are getting stronger from year to year.

B. Earthquakes are getting less deadly from year to year.

C. The value of the damage caused by an earthquake is directly related to its magnitude.

D. A tsunami increased the deadliness of the Tohoku earthquake.

This item asks you to determine which conclusion can be drawn from this information. Option D is correct. The Tohoku earthquake triggered a tsunami, a giant wave of water that causes great damage when it strikes land. The table does not contain enough information to support Options A or B because this table only gives data of the five most destructive earthquakes, not the strongest (Option A) or most deadly (Option B). Option C is contradicted by the data in the table. The Hanshin earthquake caused $100 billion in damages and had a magnitude of 6.9, while the Sichuan earthquake caused $75 billion in damages, but was much stronger (8.0).

The Tohoku earthquake happened off the east coast of Japan and triggered a large tsunami wave. Which of the following is the most likely result of the earthquake and tsunami, according to the information in the table?

A. The tsunami wave caused damage along the coast of Japan.

B. The Tohoku earthquake triggered the Christchurch earthquake.

C. More people died from collapsing buildings than from the tsunami wave.

D. People in the affected areas will not rebuild in those locations, but move to safer locations inland.

This item asks you to analyze cause-effect relationships and choose the most likely effect. Option A is correct. The tsunami wave in fact caused huge damage along the coast of Japan. There is no reason to think that there is a cause-effect relationship between the Tohoku earthquake and the Christchurch earthquake (Option B). It is impossible to reach the conclusions in Options C and D using the information in the table.

Which of the following statements is an opinion about the information in the table?

A. Earthquakes can cause massive damage and death in a very short amount of time.

B. People should not live in earthquake-prone areas.

C. One of the risks of an undersea earthquake is a massive tsunami.

D. There is no direct relationship between the damages and number of deaths caused by an earthquake.

This item asks you to distinguish fact from opinion. While Option B may seem like good advice, it is not a fact, but merely an observation about choices people make, so it is therefore correct. Option A is a fact that is proven by the table; earthquakes strike for seconds, yet can cause considerable damage. Option C is a fact, since the Tohoku earthquake caused a destructive tsunami. Option D is a fact supported by information in the table; a small earthquake can cause more damage or deaths than some larger ones, depending on the location, population density, and other factors.

# 3. Evaluate and Generalize

## a. Evaluating Information

When you evaluate information, you make a judgment about the accuracy, usefulness, or importance of the information. You might decide whether information makes sense, is logical, or supports a generalization. For instance, in the example item about storing bread on page 229, Jennifer could use the results of her study to make a decision about where to store bread in her kitchen. Now try this item:

Friction occurs when objects rub together. Friction creates heat. For example, if you rub your hands together very quickly, friction will cause your hands to feel warm.

---

When is friction helpful to people?

A. Friction on the brake pads of a car causes the brakes to overheat.
B. Friction between tires and a road helps a car avoid going into a skid.
C. A worker is having difficulty pushing a large, heavy box a few feet to a storage room.
D. Excessive friction inside the axles of a skateboard helps the skateboarder to do tricks.

---

This item integrates application and evaluation. Each of the options is an application of the concept of friction. Your task is to make a judgment about when friction is helpful. Option B is correct; friction is helping the car stay safely on the road. Option A is incorrect because overheating causes damage to the brakes and makes the car unsafe to drive. Option C is incorrect because friction between the box and the floor make the box harder to push. Option D is incorrect because excessive friction prevents the skateboard from going fast enough to do tricks.

## b. Generalizing

When you generalize, you use the information you have to make a broader or more general inference or conclusion. For example, from the information Jennifer gathered in her bread experiment (page 229), she could make generalizations about the best places to store other kinds of baked goods, such as muffins. Now try this example:

---

Which of the following statements is TRUE of friction?

A. Friction is always a problem.
B. Friction is both beneficial and harmful.
C. The heat created by friction is causing global warming.
D. Loss of friction is not a problem for drivers.

---

This item asks you to find a generalization about friction that is supported by the information. In this case, Option B is correct. Friction can cause problems, such as damage to brakes, but also helps us move about. For this reason, Option A is incorrect. Option C is incorrect because it is not supported by information in the passage. Option D is incorrect; loss of friction can cause a car to go into a skid or a truck to jackknife.

# C. Science Review

This section will help you refresh your understanding of reading and interpreting scientific information in the three main areas of science: physical science, earth and space science, and life science. This section will also help you learn to use your scientific knowledge and understanding on science items.

## 1. Physical Science

The physical sciences study **matter**—all the material in the world around us. The physical sciences include chemistry and physics. **Chemistry** studies composition, structure, properties, and changes of matter. It studies the properties of matter, atoms and molecules, and chemical reactions. Some people say that chemistry is the "central science" because other branches of science use its knowledge. **Physics** studies the atomic structure of matter and its motion through space and time.

### a. Atoms and Molecules

*Items 1 through 3 are based on the information below.*

    **Atoms** are the basic building blocks of matter. They are the smallest particle of an element that has the properties of that element. Atoms consist of a tightly packed center, the **nucleus,** and some orbiting particles. The nucleus consists of **protons,** positively charged particles, and **neutrons,** neutral particles (having neither a positive nor a negative charge). The role of the neutrons is to keep the positively charged protons in the nucleus together. Otherwise, the protons would repel each other, and the atom would disintegrate. Negatively charged **electrons** circle the nucleus in an **electron cloud.** In a stable atom, the number of protons and electrons is equal. As a result, the atom is neutrally charged because the equal number of positive protons and negative electrons keep one another in balance. The electromagnetic force between the positive protons and negative electrons creates an attraction that holds the atom together. The following illustration shows a helium atom:

**Structure of a Helium Atom**

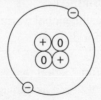

    A **molecule** consists of two or more atoms chemically bonded together into a single unit. The atoms of some elements generally occur in nature as two atoms bound tightly together. These are called **diatomic elements.** Some common diatomic elements are hydrogen ($H_2$), oxygen ($O_2$), nitrogen ($N_2$), and chlorine ($Cl_2$). **Compounds** occur when different atoms are bound together and form a new substance. For example, water molecules are composed of two hydrogen atoms and one oxygen atom. The chemical formula for water is $H_2O$. The **molecule** is the smallest particle of a compound that has the properties of the compound. While the particles of an atom are held together by electromagnetic bonds, the atoms in a molecule are held together by chemical bonds. Molecules have different properties than their constituent atoms. For example, both hydrogen and oxygen are gases at room temperature. Water is a liquid at room temperature.

---

1. Which of the following statements is true of molecules?

    **A.** They are formed by mixing together atoms of different types.
    **B.** They are composed of two or more atoms.
    **C.** They are held together by electromagnetic bonds.
    **D.** They have the properties of their constituent atoms.

---

This is an example of an interpreting information item. Option B is correct and is directly stated in the passage. Option A is not correct because a molecule is not formed by mixing atoms, but by having the atoms join together through a chemical process. Option C is a property of atoms, not molecules. Option D is contradicted by the passage; molecules and atoms have different properties.

---

2. Which of the following is TRUE about an atom of helium, according to the diagram?

    **A.** It has four electrons.
    **B.** It has four neutrons.
    **C.** Its nucleus has four particles.
    **D.** It is composed of a total of four particles.

---

This is an example of an interpreting information item. You need to use information from paragraph 1 and the diagram to answer the item. The information in paragraph 1 explains the labels in the diagram. According to the information and the diagram, the nucleus of a helium atom contains two protons and two neutrons, for a total of four particles. Therefore, Option C is the correct answer. Option A is incorrect because the diagram shows that a helium molecule has two negatively charged electrons. Option B is incorrect because the diagram shows that a helium molecule has two neutrons. Option D is incorrect because the diagram shows that the molecule has a total of six particles: two protons, two neutrons, and two electrons.

**TIP: When an item references a specific chart, table, or diagram, read the item. Then look at the diagram. Study the labels, and ensure you know what each one means. If necessary, find the paragraph that refers to the diagram. In this case, the first few sentences of paragraph 1 explain the labels in the diagram.**

---

3. The structure of an atom <u>most closely</u> resembles

    **A.** the solar system.
    **B.** a laptop computer.
    **C.** a cell.
    **D.** Earth's structure.

---

This is an example of an applying information item. In this case, you need to figure out which of the items in the options has a structure most similar to the structure of an atom. The diagram looks similar to diagrams of the solar system, with the sun (the nucleus) at the center and planets (electrons) in orbit around it. Therefore, Option A is correct. Option B is incorrect because a laptop computer does not have a central nucleus with objects in orbit around it. Option C is incorrect because while a cell has a nucleus, other cell components are not in orbit around the cell. Earth (Option D) is composed of a succession of layers around a molten core, but the layers are not in orbit.

## b. States of Matter

*Items 4 through 6 are based on the information in the table below.*

| Fundamental States of Matter | | |
|---|---|---|
| **State** | **Volume and Shape** | **Characteristics** |
| **Solid** | Fixed volume and shape | Atoms and molecules are packed closely together and cannot move about freely. |
| **Liquid** | Fixed volume but variable shape<br>Adapts its shape to fill its container | Atoms or molecules are close together but can move about freely. |
| **Gas** | Variable volume and shape<br>Adapts its shape and volume to fill its container | Atoms and molecules are not close together or fixed in place. |
| **Plasma** | Variable volume and shape | Contains ions and electrons that can move about freely. The most common form of visible matter in the universe. |

4. Which of the following shows that a gas adapts its shape and volume to fill a container?

    **A.** A chunk of dry ice quickly evaporates into gas when it is removed from the special freezer where it is made.

    **B.** A small amount of the water in a swimming pool evaporates and has to be replaced with fresh water.

    **C.** On summer mornings, the grass in the park is covered with dew.

    **D.** A few drops of perfume placed on a plate fill a room with a nice smell.

Option D is correct. The perfume changed to a gas and then filled the room with scent. This shows that the gas filled its container, in this case, the room. Option C is incorrect because dew is a liquid, not a gas. Options A and B are incorrect because though they are about gases, they do not demonstrate that a gas will fill its container.

5. Other states of matter have been discovered by scientists. These include such states as Bose-Einstein condensates. What is the <u>most likely</u> reason these states of matter are not in the table?

    **A.** They do not really exist.

    **B.** They are only scientific speculation, not proven fact.

    **C.** They are rare or occur only in unusual conditions.

    **D.** They only exist in space and not on Earth.

Option C is correct . The title of the table includes the word Fundamental, which indicates that these are the basic states of matter. This implies that other states of matter are less basic, which makes them rare or unusual.

6. A scientist is investigating a pure substance that is a liquid at room temperature. The scientist places a sample of 20 centiliters (cl) of the substance in a beaker and then places a piece of the same material in solid form in the beaker. The total volume is 30 cl. After the solid has changed state to liquid form, the scientist measures the volume again and notices that it has increased. What is the best explanation of why the volume of the sample increased?

A. The mass of the substance increased as the substance changed from solid to liquid.

B. A chemical reaction changed the physical properties of the substance.

C. The molecules that compose the substance are less tightly packed in liquid state than in solid state.

D. The particles in the atoms that compose the substance are less tightly packed in liquid form than solid form.

Option C is correct. According to the information, the particles in a solid are tightly packed and less able to move around than when in liquid form. For this reason, a liquid will generally have greater volume than the same amount of the substance in solid form. Option A is incorrect because more matter was not added to the beaker; the matter in the beaker just changes state. Option B is incorrect because changes of state are not chemical reactions. Option D is not supported by the information.

## c. Force and Motion

*Items 7 and 8 refer to the following information.*

Objects in the universe can move about. Nearly all objects are moving or can move, even if the motion is nearly undetectable. Even the continents on Earth's surface are in motion, though very slowly. When we apply **force** to an object, we make it move. **Velocity** is the speed of an object in a direction. **Acceleration** is a change in speed and/or direction. For an object to accelerate, a force needs to be applied. Newton's Three Laws explain the operations of force and motion.

### Newton's Laws

1. An object at rest tends to stay at rest, and an object in motion tends to stay in motion, unless another force acts on it to make it stop. For this reason, if you throw an object, such as a ball, the ball will eventually slow down, fall to the ground, and roll to a stop. A number of forces act on the ball to make it stop: gravity pulls it down, friction from the air slows it down, and friction from the ground causes it to roll to a stop.

2. Acceleration happens when a force acts on an object. The greater the force, the greater the acceleration. The greater the mass of the object, the more force required to move it. For example, it takes more force to pick up a 5 kilogram box than a 1 kilogram box.

3. For every action, there is an equal and opposite reaction. Forces always occur in pairs, an action force and a reaction force. So when a firework is lit, for example, there is an action force—thrust pushing down against the ground. There is also a reaction force—the firework flying into the air.

7. According to a popular myth, Sir Isaac Newton discovered which of these things when an apple fell from a tree onto his head?

   **A.**   Velocity
   **B.**   Newton's Third Law
   **C.**   Friction
   **D.**   The force of gravity

In this application item, you need to figure out which of the options could explain why an apple falls to the ground. Only the force of gravity, Option D, which pulls objects toward the center of the earth, can account for an apple falling to the ground.

8. What is the difference between velocity and acceleration?

   **A.**   Velocity is the action force, and acceleration is the reaction force.
   **B.**   Force is the cause of acceleration, and gravity is the cause of velocity.
   **C.**   Velocity is the speed of movement of an object in a certain direction, and acceleration is an increase in the speed of the object.
   **D.**   Velocity is the speed of movement of an object in a certain direction, and acceleration is a change in speed or direction.

The correct answer is Option D. This information is stated directly in the passage. Options A and B are not supported by the information in the passage. Option C is only partially correct, so it cannot be the answer (the definition of velocity is correct, the definition of acceleration is misstated).

> **TIP:** Beware of contradictory answer options or answer options that are only partially correct. In this example, Option C is partially correct and contradicts Option D. To avoid choosing the wrong answer, always read all the options and read them completely through. If two items contradict, as in the case of C and D, consider those two options carefully. It's highly likely one of them is correct. Find the difference between the two options and choose the one that is correct.

# 2. Earth Science

Earth science studies the structure of planet Earth as well as the structure and workings of the solar system and universe. It includes subjects such as these:

- **Geology:** the rocks and minerals that are found on Earth
- **Geography:** the study of Earth's land and water formations, atmosphere, etc.
- **Ecology:** the study of interaction between living things and the environment they live in
- **Astronomy:** The study of the solar system and space and the stars, planets, and other bodies found there
- **Meteorology:** The study of weather and climate

# a. The Solar System

*Items 1 and 2 are based on the following illustration.*

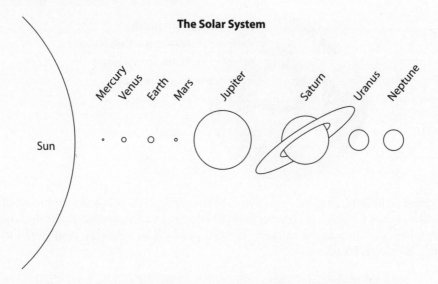

**The Solar System**

1. According to the illustration, which planet would <u>most likely</u> be the coldest?

   A.  Mercury
   B.  Earth
   C.  Jupiter
   D.  Neptune

Option D is correct. Of the four planets in the answer options, Neptune is farthest from the sun, so it would most likely be the coldest.

2. How many planets are in the solar system in total?

   A.  one
   B.  three
   C.  eight
   D.  nine

Option C is correct. There are eight planets in the solar system. This information can be determined by counting the number of planets in the illustration.

**TIP:** When answering an item, base your answer only on the information in the accompanying passage or illustration(s). In this item, outdated background knowledge from when Pluto was considered a planet could cause you to choose Option D, nine. The correct answer, Option C, can be determined by using information shown directly in the illustration.

## b. Earth's Crust

*Items 3 and 4 refer to the following information , diagram, and map.*

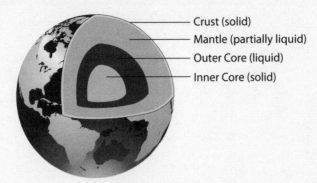

— Crust (solid)
— Mantle (partially liquid)
— Outer Core (liquid)
— Inner Core (solid)

Earth's **crust** is the hard, thin outermost shell of the planet. It is primarily composed of various kinds of rocks and minerals. Earth's crust on average is 25 kilometers deep, and ranges from about 10 kilometers deep to 50 kilometers deep at the thickest, in most places. The following map shows the thickness of Earth's crust in various locations.

3. According to the information and the diagram of Earth, which layers of Earth are solid?

   A. Mantle and inner core

   B. Mantle and crust

   C. Crust and inner core

   D. Inner core and outer core

Option C is correct. The crust and inner core are solid, according to the diagram.

4. According to the map, where is Earth's crust thinnest?

   A.   Along the edges of continents
   B.   Under the oceans
   C.   Under central continental mountain ranges
   D.   Under Africa

According to the map, the thickness of the crust under the ocean (Option B) is 10 kilometers deep. Other areas of the map have crust as thick as 30 kilometers or more. Option A is incorrect because the map shows that the crust is usually about 30 kilometers deep in these locations. Central continental mountain ranges are in areas with the thickest crust. Thicknesses as high as 70 kilometers deep are indicated for some of these mountain ranges. Option D is incorrect because values in the map for Africa range from 30 to 40 kilometers.

## c. Plate Tectonics

*Items 5 and 6 refer to the following information.*

According to the theory of **plate tectonics,** the **lithosphere** (Earth's crust, the top layer of the mantle), is composed of seven to eight major plates and numerous smaller ones that "float" or move about on the molten rock deeper in the mantle. These plates are not fixed and are able to move about as they float. The movement of the plates results in many kinds of events such as earthquakes, volcanic eruptions, and mountain formation.

5. According to the information, where in Earth's crust would you most likely find a volcano?

   A.   Where earth's crust is thickest
   B.   Where tectonic plates meet together
   C.   In the middle of tectonic plates
   D.   Along the equator, where temperatures are hottest

Option B is correct. At plate boundaries, molten rock from Earth's mantle can rise to the surface. Therefore, Option C is incorrect. Option A is not likely because it would be very difficult for molten rock to rise to the surface in places where the crust is very thick. There is nothing in the information given to support Option D.

6. Which of the following CANNOT be explained by plate tectonics?

   A.   A new volcano is discovered deep in the Pacific Ocean.
   B.   The face of a cliff alongside the ocean collapses.
   C.   A massive earthquake strikes in Taiwan.
   D.   A new island begins to appear in the Pacific Ocean.

Option B is correct. The collapse of the cliff is most likely caused by erosion and/or weathering from the ocean water below the cliff, not by the movement of tectonic plates. The other options are related to the earthquakes, volcanos, and mountain formation discussed in the information as consequences of movement of Earth's tectonic plates.

# 3. Life Science

Life science studies living things from microorganisms to plants to animals.

## a. The Cell

*Items 1 and 2 refer to the following information.*

All organisms consist of microscopic units called **cells.** The simplest organisms are **unicellular**—composed of a single cell. Other organisms are made up of many cells. Basic life functions take place within cells. Cells take in food, break it down into energy, and dispose of waste products. In complex organisms, cells can have specialized functions. Cells in the pancreas, for example produce a certain chemical needed by our bodies. **Red blood cells** specialize in transporting gases throughout the body. **White blood cells** specialize in fighting illness. **Fat cells** specialize in storing energy in the body in the form of fat.

While cells may have different specializations, they have similar structures. Each cell is surrounded by a **membrane** that lets substances enter or leave the cell and protects the cell from harmful substances. The interior of a cell is divided into two parts:

- The **nucleus** contains the cell's genetic material and regulates the operation of the cell. The nucleus is enclosed in a **nuclear membrane.**

- The **cytoplasm** contains **organelles**—cell structures with certain defined functions. Following are some key organelles:

  - **Mitochondria**—these organelles produce energy for the cell by breaking down food.
  - **Vacuoles**—these organelles are storage structures. Some vacuoles store substances the cell needs such as water or food. Other vacuoles store waste materials.
  - **Endoplasmic reticulum**—the function of these bandlike structures is to transport substances throughout the cell.

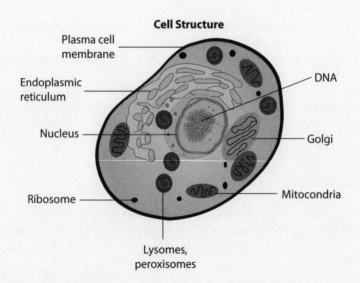

**Cell Structure**

Plasma cell membrane

Endoplasmic reticulum

Nucleus

Ribosome

DNA

Golgi

Mitocondria

Lysomes, peroxisomes

1. Which part of a cell is responsible for breaking down food for use by the cell?

   A.  Mitochondria
   B.  Membrane
   C.  Nuclear membrane
   D.  Endoplasmic reticulum

Option A, mitochondria, is correct; it is stated directly in the passage. The membrane (Option B) is responsible for letting substances enter and leave the cell and preventing harmful substances from hurting the cell. The nuclear membrane (Option C) is responsible for enclosing the nucleus. The endoplasmic reticulum (Option D) is responsible for transporting materials throughout the cell.

2. Which of the following is TRUE of all cells?

   A.  They all have a nucleus.
   B.  They all make food for the organism.
   C.  They all carry oxygen throughout the body.
   D.  They all have specialized functions.

Option A is correct. According to the information, all cells have a nucleus. Only certain cells in green plants make food for the organism, almost always using a process called photosynthesis, so Option B is incorrect. Option C is incorrect because only red blood cells carry oxygen throughout the body. Option D is incorrect because only the cells of multicellular organisms are specialized.

# b. Plant Parts

*Items 3 and 4 refer to the following illustration and information.*

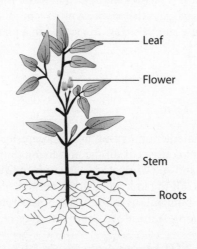

Each part of a plant helps the plant stay alive. In the **leaves,** plants make their own food using a process called **photosynthesis.** Leaves also have special openings, called **stomata,** which let gases, water vapor, and other materials in and out of the plant. These materials are the waste products and some of the raw materials of photosynthesis. The **roots** bring in water and essential nutrients into the plant from the ground. The roots also help hold the plant in the ground. In addition, food produced by the plant is stored in the roots as simple sugars. **Stems** hold the plant upright so that leaves can get sunlight needed for photosynthesis. The stems also help transport materials throughout the plant. They allow water to rise to leaves and transport food to cells in the plant that need it. Many, but not all, plants use flowers to reproduce.

---

3. In which part of the plant are simple sugars made?

   A. Flowers
   B. Roots
   C. Stems
   D. Leaves

---

Option D is correct and is stated indirectly in the passage. In one place the passage says that plants produce their own food in their leaves, and in another place the text says the food consists of simple sugars. Plants use flowers (Option A) to reproduce; roots (Option B) to obtain water, store food, and keep the plant in the ground); and stems (Option C) transport materials and keep the plant upright.

---

4. Which of the following can be inferred about photosynthesis?

   A. Photosynthesis takes place in plant stems.
   B. Photosynthesis does not produce waste products.
   C. The nectar in flowers is stored food for the plant.
   D. Water is used in photosynthesis.

---

Option D is correct and can be inferred from information in the passage. While the passage does not directly state that water is used, it says that water, a necessary nutrient, is transported to the leaves, where photosynthesis takes place. Therefore, it is possible to infer that water is used in photosynthesis. Option A is contradicted by the passage. The passage says that photosynthesis produces waste materials, so Option B is incorrect. Option C is incorrect because simple sugars are stored in a plant's roots. The passage also says that flowers help plants reproduce.

## c. Ecosystems

*Items 5 and 6 refer to the following information.*

   **Ecology** is the study of the interaction among living organisms and things in the environment that surround them. The environment consists of all the non-living things that surround the organism, such as water, soil, land formations, and so on. Ecology can study **individuals** (a single living organism, such as a single animal), **populations** (all the individuals of a certain species living in an area), **communities** (the interactions of some of the populations in the area), or **ecosystems** (the interactions of all the living and non-living things in a location). A meadow, pond, forest, or beach can be defined as an ecosystem.

---

5. Which of the following would NOT be considered part of a North American forest ecosystem?

   A. Trees
   B. Foxes
   C. Fish
   D. Soil

---

Option C is correct; fish would not be found in a forest ecosystem. The remaining options are all examples of things that would be found in a forest ecosystem.

---

6. A scientist is observing the reproduction of a unique species of ant that only lives in certain prairielands in central Indiana. These ants build large mounds that can reach 1 meter in height. What is the scientist studying?

   **A.** An individual
   **B.** A population
   **C.** A community
   **D.** An ecosystem

---

Option B is correct. The scientist is studying a group of individuals of the same species, which is a population. Therefore, Option A is incorrect. Option C is incorrect because to study a community, the scientist would have to study more than one species. Option D is incorrect because to study an ecosystem, the scientist would study all the living and non-living things in the prairielands, not just one species.

# D. Practice

## 1. Items

*Items 1 through 6 refer to the following information.*

**Life Cycle of Monarch Butterfly**

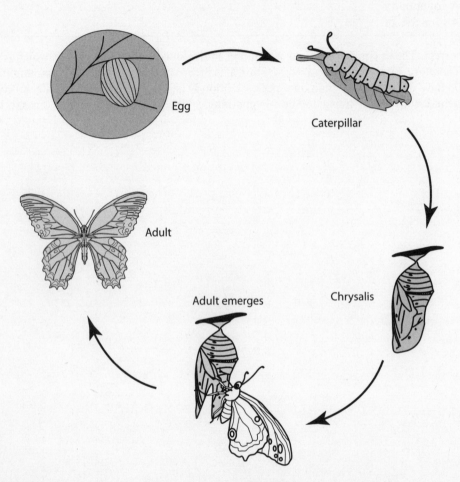

The Monarch butterfly is one of the most common butterflies in North America. Like all insects, its body has three main sections: head, thorax, and abdomen. Each of these sections has different body parts that the butterfly uses to live.

### Head

A butterfly's head contains sensory organs and a special organ used to take in food. Antennae are used to sense chemicals in the air. With their antennae, butterflies can sense the smell of flowers or other insects or even other butterflies. They can also sense the smell of a potential mate. Butterflies can also sense motion with their antennae, such as the movement of a camouflaged predator. A butterfly's head also contains compound eyes. A butterfly's compound eye contains many lenses that let it see in many directions at once. Thus, butterflies have a much larger field of vision than many other organisms, such as humans, whose eyes have only one lens. Butterflies take in food through a special feeding tube called a proboscis. Similar to a straw, a proboscis is a thin, hollow tube that the butterfly can use to drink nectar, water, or other liquids. The proboscis cannot bite or sting.

## Thorax

Attached to the thorax are key body parts such as legs and wings. Like all insects, butterflies have six legs. On some butterflies, the first pair of legs has lost its function, and the legs are very small. These small vestigial legs are not used for walking. This is because butterflies depend on flying, not walking, to move about. They use their legs mainly for grip when landing on something, such as a flower or plant. A butterfly's wings have two parts, a pair of forewings and a pair of hind wings. These two-part wings help butterflies be more aerodynamic in flight. Some butterflies can fly as fast as 30 miles per hour, which helps them travel long distances and escape from predators. The marking of the wings helps the butterfly in many ways. Markings can act as camouflage so that the butterfly can hide from predators. Markings can also alert predators that the butterfly is poisonous for predators to eat. Often, the toxins that make a butterfly poisonous to predators are stored in the wings. Predators know that the poisons in a Monarch butterfly or other poisonous species will taste bad or even kill them, so they avoid preying on these species. The amount of poison in these butterflies is so small that it is not a real danger to larger predators, but they will still avoid these butterflies because the poison makes the butterflies taste bad.

## Abdomen

The abdomen contains vital internal organs, such as the digestive tract and reproductive organs.

1. Which of the following is a function of the antennae of a butterfly?

    A. Seeing potential predators
    B. Drinking nectar
    C. Sensing the scent of flowers
    D. Hearing other butterflies

2. Which of the following body parts do some butterfly species use to defend against predators?

    A. Abdomen
    B. Legs
    C. Proboscis
    D. Wings

3. Which part of a butterfly is most like a human nose?

    A. Proboscis
    B. Antennae
    C. Compound eyes
    D. Abdomen

4. A poisonous Monarch butterfly senses a potential predator nearby. What will the butterfly most likely do?

    A. Show its wing coloration so the predator knows it is poisonous.
    B. Use its six legs to run away from the predator and hide under a leaf.
    C. Use its proboscis to bite the predator and inject it with poison.
    D. Use its antennae to fight off the predator.

5. Which of the following statements is TRUE?

   A. Butterflies cannot defend themselves against predators.
   B. Butterflies have a well-developed sense of hearing.
   C. Poisonous butterflies cannot harm humans.
   D. Butterflies are not true insects because they only have four legs

6. The Viceroy butterfly is non-poisonous and lives in the same geographic region as the Monarch butterfly. The orange and black markings of the Viceroy are similar to those of the Monarch. The predators of most butterflies are birds. Which of the following will <u>most likely</u> happen if a bird sees a Viceroy?

   A. The Viceroy butterfly will use its markings to blend into a gray tree trunk.
   B. The Viceroy butterfly will fly to an area with many Monarchs to blend in with them.
   C. The bird will not eat the Viceroy butterfly because the bird confuses it with a Monarch butterfly.
   D. The bird will not eat the Viceroy butterfly because the bird knows the butterfly is poisonous.

*Items 7 through 9 refer to the following information.*

A student is studying the solubility of certain chemical substances in distilled water. In one experiment, the student dissolved common table salt (NaCl) in 100g of distilled water at different temperatures until the water was saturated, and then calculated the amount of salt dissolved. The student summarized the data in this table.

| Solubility of Salt (NaCl) in Water | |
| --- | --- |
| Temperature (°C) | Salt Dissolved (g/100g of water) |
| 0 | 35.65 |
| 10 | 35.72 |
| 20 | 35.89 |
| 30 | 36.09 |
| 40 | 36.37 |
| 50 | 36.69 |
| 60 | 37.04 |

7. How much NaCl, in grams, can be dissolved in 100g of distilled water at 20°C?

   A. 35.65
   B. 35.72
   C. 35.89
   D. 36.09

8. What is the lowest temperature at which the student can dissolve 36.69g of salt in 100g of water?

   A. 30°C
   B. 40°C
   C. 50°C
   D. 60°C

9. The student dissolves 36.09g of salt in 100g of water at 30°C, and then cools the solution to 0°C. Based on the information in the table, which of these predictions can you make?

   A. 0.44g of salt will come out of the solution as a solid.
   B. The amount of salt that can be dissolved in the solution will not change.
   C. The water will change from liquid to solid and all of the salt will come out of the solution as a solid.
   D. The student can dissolve an additional 0.44g of salt in the solution.

*Items 10 through 12 refer to the following information.*

| Renewable and Non-Renewable Energy Sources | | |
|---|---|---|
| **Energy Source** | **Definition** | **Examples** |
| Renewable | The source can be easily replaced or renewed immediately or in a short period of time. | Wind power, solar power, water power, geothermal power |
| Non-Renewable | The source cannot be easily replaced or renewed in a short period of time. | Petroleum, natural gas, coal |

10. Which of the following is NOT an example of a non-renewable energy source?

    A. Petroleum
    B. Coal
    C. Water power
    D. Natural gas

11. Biomass (dead plant material, such as cornstalks and leaves) can be used to make a clean-burning fuel that can be used to power many machines, sometimes in combination with gasoline. Which of the following is true of biomass?

    A. Fuel from biomass is not a renewable energy source because it is often mixed with gasoline.
    B. Biomass is a renewable energy source because it quickly regrows.
    C. Biomass cannot be used to make fuel because the fuel is too expensive.
    D. Biomass is non-renewable because farmers can only grow one crop of corn per year.

12. A farming community is considering building a new coal-fired power plant. A community group is proposing that the town explore renewable energy sources. The community is located near a large lake and experiences strong winds year-round. The weather is sunny in summer, but overcast throughout much of the winter. Which of the following renewable energy sources should the town consider before building the coal-fired power plant?

    A. Use solar power to provide electricity year-round.
    B. Use wind power by erecting large wind turbines on unused farmland.
    C. Build a hydropower dam to generate electricity.
    D. Use abundant natural gas from a neighboring state to run the power plant.

## 2. Answer Explanations

1. **C. Sensing the scent of flowers (Interpreting Information/Life Science)** This answer is stated directly in the passage. Butterflies use eyes, not antennae (Option A) to see potential predators. A butterfly uses its proboscis (Option B), not its antennae, to drink nectar. Option D is not supported by information in the passage.

2. **D. Wings (Interpreting Information/Life Science)** Option D is correct because the wings of some butterfly species are poisonous, while the wing markings of other butterfly species provide camouflage. Option A is incorrect because the abdomen contains internal organs for functions such as digestion and reproduction. Option B is not supported by information in the passage. The proboscis (Option C) is used to drink liquids, not to defend the butterfly.

3. **B. Antennae (Applying Information/Life Science)** The passage says that the butterfly can use its antennae to sense chemicals in the air. This is similar to the way human noses work, so Option B is the best answer. Option A is incorrect because the proboscis is used for feeding, so it is similar to the human mouth. Options C and D do not make sense.

4. **A. Show its wing coloration so the predator knows it is poisonous. (Analyzing Information/Life Science)** Option A is correct because the Monarch's noticeable coloration signals that it is poisonous. Option B is not supported by information in the passage. Option C is contradicted by information in the passage. A butterfly only uses its proboscis to drink. Option D is not supported by information in the passage.

5. **C. Poisonous butterflies cannot harm humans. (Generalizing/Life Science)** Option C is correct because butterflies cannot bite or sting people, and the amount of poison in poisonous species is not enough to harm humans. Option A is contradicted by the passage, which makes clear that butterflies have defense mechanisms. Option B is not supported by information in the passage. Option D is incorrect because all butterflies have six legs. Certain species appear to have only four legs, but these species have an additional pair of non-functioning legs that are very small and difficult to see.

6. **C. The bird will not eat the Viceroy butterfly because the bird confuses it with a Monarch butterfly. (Evaluating Information/Life Science)** Option C is correct because the Viceroy butterfly is using a kind of mimicry to confuse the bird. Option A does not make sense because an orange and black butterfly will not blend into a gray tree trunk. Option B is not correct because nothing in the passage indicates that Viceroy butterflies have the ability to track and follow other butterfly species. Option D does not make sense because the Viceroy butterfly is not poisonous.

7. **C. 35.89 (Interpreting Information/Physical Science)** This answer is stated directly in the table. Find the 20 in the temperature column and then read across to the second column. The amount of NaCl that can be dissolved in water at 20°C is 35.89g.

8. **C. 50°C (Interpreting Information/Physical Science)** This answer is stated directly in the table. Find 36.69 in the Salt Dissolved column, and then read left to the temperature column. The lowest temperature at which 36.69g of salt can be dissolved in water is 50°C. When the water is below this temperature, less than 36.69g can be dissolved.

9. **A. 0.44g of salt will come out of the solution as a solid. (Analyzing Information/Physical Science)** Option A is correct because at 0°C, only 35.65 can be dissolved in the water. That is less than how much was dissolved before cooling the solution. To find the amount of salt that will precipitate, you subtract: $36.09 - 35.65 = 0.44$. For this reason, Option B is incorrect. Option C is incorrect because the water is at its freezing point but has not frozen yet. At this temperature, only 0.44g will precipitate even if the solution then becomes solid. The freezing point of the water also changes with the addition of salt. Option D does not make sense because you subtract, not add, to find the answer, since less salt can be dissolved at the lower temperature.

10. **C. Water power (Interpreting Information/Earth Science)** Option C is correct because the item asks you to identify which energy source is NOT non-renewable. All of the options are non-renewable except water power.

11. **B. Biomass is a renewable energy source because it quickly regrows. (Applying Information/Earth Science)** Option B is correct because biomass such as cornstalks quickly regrows, unlike non-renewable energy sources that were formed over millions of years. For this reason, Option D is incorrect. Option A is incorrect because biomass itself comes from a renewable source. Option C may be true, but is not supported by the information.

12. **B. Use wind power by erecting large wind turbines on unused farmland. (Applying Information/Earth Science)** Option B is correct because the community is located in an area that is windy year-round and has vacant land. Therefore, erecting wind turbines is the most logical option for the community. Option A is not the best answer because the community gets abundant sunlight for solar power only in summer. Option C is incorrect because running water, such as a river, is needed to build a hydropower dam. According to the information, the town is near a lake, not a river. Option D is incorrect because natural gas is a non-renewable source, and the community group is proposing using a renewable source.

# VIII. Social Studies

The HiSET Social Studies section tests your ability to:

- Understand and use social studies content knowledge
- Understand and apply research methods used in social studies
- Interpret, analyze, evaluate, and apply social studies information

The HiSET Social Studies section has 50 multiple-choice items, and you will have 70 minutes to complete the section. The items address four main branches of social studies:

- History (45%)
- Civics/Government (30%)
- Economics (15%)
- Geography (10%)

You do not need any specialized knowledge in these areas to answer the items; rather, the test asks you to read and interpret reading passages, primary documents (including political cartoons, historical documents, and other materials), maps, graphs, and charts. Items will ask you to find main ideas, identify cause-effect relationships, recognize bias, distinguish fact from opinion, make inferences, distinguish main idea and detail, evaluate the relevance of information, solve problems, draw conclusions, and find support for ideas.

## A. Test Format

The 50 multiple-choice items on the HiSET Social Studies section are based on reading passages, primary sources, and other documents. About 80% of the items will be based on longer passages and/or materials, while the remaining 20% will be based on shorter selections. Longer passages usually have six to eight, or more, items, while shorter passages and/or materials may have only one to three items. Of the items in the Social Studies section, about half will be based on primary source documents and materials, political cartoons, graphic information (tables, graphs, timelines, and charts), maps, posters, and timelines.

## 1. Passage-Based Items

Here is an example of a longer reading passage and item:

> The **Freedom of Information Act** is a law designed to give people open access to government information. The purpose of the law is to ensure free and open access to information in federal, executive branch departments. Many states have enacted similar laws of their own, often modeled on the federal law.
>
> The Freedom of Information Act was designed to balance citizens' right to know information with the needs of the government to protect national security. Therefore, the Act defines the kinds of information that people can obtain. In addition to documents and information related to defense and foreign policy that are classified as secret, the law does not allow disclosure of personal information, trade

secrets, and information about criminal investigations that could compromise the investigations. The law has been updated periodically. One recent amendment was designed to improve access to online and electronic information.

Freedom of Information Act requests need to be filed according to certain rules and procedures. Many, but not all, Freedom of Information Act requests are filed by journalists. But companies, not-for-profit organizations, and individual citizens file requests, too. For the most recent year available, the U.S. government received 704,394 Freedom of Information Act requests in total. The three agencies receiving the most requests were the Department of Homeland Security, the Department of Justice, and the Department of Defense. Of all requests filed, approximately 49% were approved in full, 42% were approved in part, and 9% were denied in full.

---

What is the purpose of the Freedom of Information Act?

**A.** To allow access to information on criminal investigations
**B.** To allow access to top secret information
**C.** To provide free access to important government information
**D.** To protect classified information

---

Option C is correct because the passage says the purpose of the law is to "give people open access to government information." Option A is contradicted by the information; citizens cannot get information on criminal investigations under the Act. Option B contradicts the national security goals of the Act and is therefore incorrect. Option D is incorrect because laws about how secret information is classified as secret protect classified information. The purpose of the Freedom of Information Act is to allow maximum public access to non-classified information.

TIP: A longer reading passage may have six or more items. When reading a longer passage, read the items first. Then skim the passage quickly. First read the title, any heads, and any illustrations or graphic materials. Then read the first sentence of each paragraph. Then go back and read the entire passage quickly. After that, try to answer the items.

Here is an example of a shorter passage and item:

The **Elementary and Secondary Education Act (ESEA)** is an important federal law that affects the nation's public schools. Like many federal laws, it expires periodically and needs to be reauthorized by Congress. The ESEA expired in 2007, but despite the efforts of many political leaders and members of Congress, it still had not been reauthorized 7 years later, in 2014.

---

Which of the following statements is the <u>most likely</u> reason that the law was not reauthorized during this period?

**A.** Major political parties in Congress disagreed so strongly that gridlock caused reauthorization to fail.
**B.** Political parties agreed that the bill should not pass because education is a local responsibility, not a federal matter.
**C.** Leaders in Congress decided that other matters are more important than education.
**D.** No one in Congress took responsibility for ensuring that the reauthorization passed in Congress.

---

Only Option A gives an explanation that accounts for all the information about ESEA in the item. The remaining options are contradicted by the information: Many leaders worked to support the bill, so they must have believed the federal government had a role in education (Option B), thought education was important (Option C), and took leadership roles to ensure it passed (Option D).

> TIP: To help you focus your reading on shorter passages, read the item first and then go back and read the passage.

# 2. Primary Source–Based Items

**Primary sources** are documents and other materials that were created during the time under study. A well-known example of a primary-source document about the American Revolution is the Declaration of Independence. However, many other items could also be considered primary sources, including letters from soldiers in the Revolutionary War, newspaper articles from the time, works of literature (novels, short stories, and poems), the lyrics of popular songs, and original maps from the time. Primary sources can also include physical objects such as Native American weavings and pottery, tools from the time, and even old or classic cars.

Look at the following example:

> In 1775, American patriot Patrick Henry made a speech to the Virginia legislature to convince it to use its militia to support the fight against England. In the speech, Henry said, "Gentlemen may cry, Peace, Peace—but there is no peace. The war is actually begun! The next gale that sweeps from the north will bring to our ears the clash of resounding arms! Our brethren are already in the field! Why stand we here idle? What is it that gentlemen wish? What would they have? Is life so dear, or peace so sweet, as to be purchased at the price of chains and slavery? Forbid it, Almighty God! I know not what course others may take; but as for me, give me liberty or give me death!"

> What was Patrick Henry's attitude toward the Revolutionary War?
>
> **A.** He wanted to stop the war.
> **B.** He opposed involvement in the war.
> **C.** He was a fervent supporter.
> **D.** He felt that caution was warranted.

Option C is correct. The last line of the speech was a clear indication that he believed that going to war was necessary in order to secure freedom. For this reason, the other options (A, B, and D) are incorrect.

> Which of the following can be inferred about the attitude of other members of the Virginia legislature from the excerpt from Patrick Henry's speech?
>
> **A.** They opposed the war.
> **B.** They wanted Virginia to get involved in the war.
> **C.** They were not certain that freedom was worth the risk of losing their lives.
> **D.** They were bigger supporters of the war than Henry.

Option C is correct. In his speech, Patrick Henry says, "What would they have? Is life so dear, or peace so sweet, as to be purchased at the price of chains and slavery?" The option closest in meaning to this statement is Option C. For this reason, Options B and D are incorrect. Option A is not supported by the information.

Though not a primary-source document about the American Revolution itself, Ralph Waldo Emerson's poem "Concord Hymn" (1836) shows how American patriotism developed as the United States strengthened and grew early in its history. This poem is another example of a primary source. Following is an excerpt from Emerson's poem with two example items:

**The "Concord Hymn" is a poem written in 1836 by Ralph Waldo Emerson, a leading American poet, about the Battle of Concord. It was written to commemorate the 1837 dedication of a monument to the Battle of Concord.**

> By the rude bridge that arched the flood,
> Their flag to April's breeze unfurled,
> Here once the embattled farmers stood,
> And fired the shot heard round the world.
>
> On this green bank, by this soft stream,
> We set to-day a votive stone;
> That memory may their deed redeem,
> When, like our fathers, our sons are gone.

---

With which of these statements would the author <u>most likely</u> agree?

- **A.** It's very strange that local farmers could have such a big effect on history.
- **B.** The American colonists were not justified in rebelling against the King of England.
- **C.** American colonists did not make very good soldiers.
- **D.** The Battle of Concord was a small event with global consequences.

---

Option D is correct. The poem makes clear that the rebellion that was started by simple, rural farmers was a "shot heard round the world" that had global consequences. Emerson is not surprised, so Option A is incorrect. Options B and C are not supported by the information.

---

In 1837, the Fourth of July was not yet a federal holiday. What do the poem and monument indicate about the importance of this holiday?

- **A.** The importance of this celebration was growing.
- **B.** People did not appreciate the sacrifices of the participants in the battle.
- **C.** People had completely forgotten the battle and needed to be reminded.
- **D.** Little by little, people were forgetting their history.

---

Option A is correct. The construction of the monument and a poem about it by a major writer are both evidence that the importance of July Fourth as a national holiday was growing. Therefore, Option C is incorrect. The reverent tone of the poem contradicts Option B. Option D is contradicted by the poem. People remembered the battle and wanted to ensure it was remembered in the future.

Many flags were produced during the American Revolution. These flags are examples of primary sources. Look at the following example:

Source: HistoryImages.com

The Gadsden flag was designed in 1775 by Christopher Gadsden. Gadsden presented his flag to the commander in chief of the Navy so it could be flown on the commander's flagship.

---

What does the Gadsden flag indicate about the Revolutionary War?

A.  The new country was developing its own identity and traditions.
B.  Support for the revolution was decreasing.
C.  The Revolutionary War was not going well.
D.  A revolution of mostly agrarian colonists could not succeed.

---

Option A is correct. The new flag shows increasing pride, identity, and strength. Option B is therefore incorrect. Options C and D are not supported by the information.

# 3. Political Cartoon–Based Items

**Political cartoons** are a kind of primary source that frequently appears on the HiSET Social Studies section. Though they are commonly called political cartoons, because they are often about political issues, these cartoons can address important matters relating to society, the economy, ecology, and other topics that concern people. In the past, these cartoons frequently appeared on the editorial and opinion pages of newspapers and in some magazines, but now are found online, too. Look at the following example:

At the beginning of the twentieth century, the power and influence of large companies, many of them monopolies, was decried by social reformers. The cartoon shows one cartoonist's point of view about the power of one of the biggest companies in the United States, Standard Oil.

What does the octopus show about the cartoonist's attitude toward the company?

A. The company is hiding important information, like an octopus uses its ink to hide in the sea.

B. The company is uniquely adapted to its environment, just as an octopus is adapted to live in the sea.

C. The company is grabbing too much power with its many arms, similar to a sea monster.

D. The company is helpful because the long reach of the arms shows that people can get the company's products across the country.

Option C is correct. The octopus's aggressive expression and the people and government buildings in its many arms show that the cartoonist believes that the company has too much power and influence. Option A is incorrect because octopus ink is not visible in the cartoon. Option B is contradicted by the cartoon. The aggressive expression and grabbing arms show that the cartoonist is critical of the company. Option D is contradicted by the cartoon. The people in the cartoon do not look like happy customers, but rather victims of the company's excessive power.

Which of the following positions would the cartoonist <u>most likely</u> adopt toward Standard Oil?

A. Give in to the company's demands so it stops trying to control the government.

B. Break the company into smaller companies.

C. Let the company continue operating as it had been operating.

D. Close the company completely.

Option B is correct. Only Option B would solve the problem of the company's excessive power. For this reason, Option A is incorrect. Option C is contradicted by the information. Someone so opposed to the company would not advocate for business as usual. Option D does not make sense, because the company provided vital products and services. The problem with the company is its excessive power and size.

TIP: To understand a political cartoon, first look at the cartoon and decide the issue that it's about. Then use the information to figure out the cartoonist's opinion about the matter. The opinion may not be stated directly and will most likely be expressed with humor. Therefore, try to figure out why the cartoon is humorous. Use the characters' words, facial expressions, and actions to help you.

# 4. Graphic Information Items

Many kinds of tables and graphs can appear on the HiSET Social Studies section. Tables are the most common, but sometimes items will be based on a graph of some kind.

## a. Tables

Tables are frequently used to organize and present both text-based and numeric information. Tables may appear with accompanying information or alone. Look at the following example of a text table:

| Branches of Government | | |
|---|---|---|
| Executive | Legislative | Judicial |
| Enforces the laws | Makes the laws | Interprets the laws |

Which of the following is a matter for the judicial branch?

A. A company president filed false tax returns.
B. A new law is needed to stop email spamming.
C. A state needs assistance because of flooding from a hurricane.
D. A driver is suing the city for damages to his car from a huge pothole.

Option D is correct. The role of the judicial branch is to interpret the law, which in this case is deciding whether the driver or the city should pay for the damages. The remaining options do not involve interpreting the law, so they are incorrect. Option A is a function of the executive branch. Option B is a function of the legislative branch. Option C is a function of the executive branch.

A data table sums up numerical information in a graphic format. Numeric data tables are used in all branches of social studies, but are especially important in economics. Look at the following table and two example items:

| Federal Minimum Wage Rates | |
|---|---|
| 1978 | $2.65 |
| 1979 | $2.90 |
| 1980 | $3.10 |
| 1981 | $3.35 |
| 1990 | $3.80 |
| 1991 | $4.25 |
| 1996 | $4.75 |
| 1997 | $5.15 |
| 2007 | $5.85 |
| 2008 | $6.65 |
| 2009 | $7.25 |

Source: U.S. Department of Labor, http://www.dol.gov/whd/minwage/chart.htm

When was the minimum wage $5.15 per hour?

A. 1996
B. 1997
C. 2007
D. 2008

Option B is correct. Find $5.15 in the second column. Then trace across to the year column. The answer is 1997. The minimum wage was $4.75 in 1996 (Option A), $5.85 in 2007 (Option C), and $6.65 in 2008 (Option D).

TIP: To find information in a table, find the row and column you are interested in and find the cell where they intersect. In long, complicated tables, trace down and across with your right and left index fingers.

How much was a worker making the minimum wage paid in 1995?

A. $3.80
B. $4.25
C. $4.50
D. $4.75

This item was less straightforward than the previous one. In this item, you need to determine the minimum wage for a year that was not listed in the table. The minimum wage was raised to $4.75 in 1996. Therefore, from 1991 to 1995, the minimum wage was $4.25 (Option B). For this reason, the other options are incorrect. Option C is a kind of trick, since it is between $4.25 and $4.75. However, since the table shows each time the government raised the minimum wage, the wage for 1995 must have not changed from 1991.

To interpret a table, do the following:

- Read the name of the table and the column and row heads. This will help you understand what information is in the table.
- Read any caption or accompanying text.
- Make sure you understand the value of the numbers in each column of the table. Are the values years, dollars, percentages, averages, or some other measure? Are the values expressed in large units, such as hundreds, thousands, or millions?

# b. Graphs

Graphs are used to show data visually. There are three main kinds of graphs: line graphs, bar graphs, and pie charts. All of these graphs are covered extensively in Chapter VII, "Science." See pages 222–225 for information on how to interpret graphs.

# 5. Map-Based Items

Several types of maps can appear on the HiSET Social Studies section. Maps are used in all branches of social studies, but are especially important in history and geography. There are many kinds of maps for different purposes:

- **Political maps** show features such as the boundaries of countries or states, capital cities, and so on.
- **Physical maps** show features of land and water such as the kind of land (desert, forest, mountain, etc.) and the bodies of water (rivers, lakes, seas, and oceans).
- **Topographic maps** show the elevation of the land using special lines called contour lines.
- **Climate maps** show what the weather is usually like in the places on the map, detailing mean or average temperatures, rainfall, or other weather features. Often, these maps use colors, shading, or patterns to show different kinds of weather.
- **Economic or resource maps** show different kinds of economic or natural resources. They can show locations of different kinds of natural resources such as the location of mines or the kinds of crops grown in certain areas.
- **Road maps** are familiar to most of us. These maps show streets, roads, or highways.
- **Thematic maps** give detailed information on a particular topic or subject. For example, a thematic map could show the gross national product (GNP) of various countries, birth rates in various locations, or other very specific kinds of information. Usually, a thematic map will have a political or physical map as the base to orient the reader.
- **Historical maps** show the world as it existed in the past. For example, a map of North America might show the regions controlled by the various colonial powers: England, France, and Spain. A map of the United States during the civil war might distinguish the states that belonged to the Union and those that belonged to the Confederacy.
- An **antique map** differs from a historical map in that the actual map was made in the past. Examples include the maps and atlases produced during the exploration of the Americas by Europeans.

Look at the following example:

The construction of the transcontinental railroad between Council Bluffs, Iowa, and California between 1863 and 1869 is a key event in American history. Until the construction of the railroad, travel to California was slow and hazardous. Before work even started, extensive research, exploration, and surveying were carried out. Construction began in 1863 in California and in 1865 in Iowa. Many problems had to be solved. For the western leg, rails and equipment had to be shipped from the east coast around the tip of South America. For the eastern leg, materials were shipped from the east coast to the Gulf of Mexico and then up the Mississippi and Missouri rivers. Finally, the two sections met with the driving of the Golden Spike on May 10, 1869, an event that was transmitted telegraphically to the world. Trains had already been traveling on completed sections of track since construction had started, so transcontinental railroad traffic started immediately. The hazardous trip west, which had taken weeks or months, was shortened to a week.

On a project of this magnitude, a few loose ends remained. The section between Oakland, California, and Sacramento was completed shortly after the driving of the Golden Spike. And trains had to cross the river between Council Bluffs, Iowa, and Omaha, Nebraska, by ferry until a railroad bridge was completed in 1873. Several other problems also had to be solved. For example, engineers had to find ways to keep snow from blocking trains while crossing the Rocky Mountains.

**TIP: When items refer to a passage and a map, look at the map first. Use information from the map to help you understand the passage. Then, as you read, refer to the map to help you understand.**

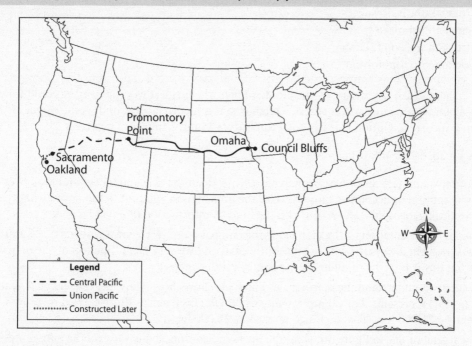

Which of the following locations is NOT on the route of the transcontinental railroad?

A.  San Francisco, California
B.  Omaha, Nebraska
C.  Council Bluffs, Iowa
D.  Oakland, California

This item can be answered directly from the map. San Francisco is the only city in the options that is not on the map. Therefore, Option A is correct.

Where did the two legs of the railroad come together?

A.  Promontory Point, Utah
B.  Council Bluffs, Iowa
C.  Sacramento, California
D.  Oakland, California

Option A is correct. This item can also be answered directly from the map. According to the map, the eastern and western legs meet at Promontory Point, Utah (Option A). Council Bluffs, Iowa, was the beginning of the Eastern leg, so it is incorrect (Option B). Sacramento is where construction of the western leg began (Option C). Oakland, California (Option D), is the endpoint of the railroad after the final leg between Sacramento and Oakland opened later in 1869.

According to the map and the information, what location is the point farthest west a train passenger starting in Omaha, Nebraska, could reach prior to May 10, 1869?

**A.** Council Bluffs, Iowa

**B.** Omaha, Nebraska

**C.** Promontory Point, Utah

**D.** Sacramento, California

Option C is correct. Until the driving of the Golden Spike, the farthest west passengers could travel was Promontory Point, Utah. Option A is east of Omaha, so it is incorrect. Option B is the origin of the passenger, so is incorrect. Option D is west of Promontory Point, Utah, so is incorrect.

To interpret a map, do the following:

- Make sure you understand what the map represents. Read the title and labels, and look over the map. Read any caption or accompanying text. Use the information you find to figure out what type of map it is (political, geographic, and so on) and the kind of information that will be on it.

- Figure out the orientation of the map using the compass rose. A **compass rose** may be simple or complex, but will always indicate north, south, east, and west. (Usually, the top of the map will be north, but this is not true of all maps, especially antique maps.)

- Make sure you understand the map's scale. The **scale** shows how many feet, meters, miles each unit in the map scale represents. For example, many walking maps (such as those carried by tourists) are frequently 1:25,000 feet. That is, 1 inch represents 25,000 feet.

- Use the **legend** or **key** to figure out what the lines, circles, dots, icons, etc., on the map represent. For example, different size dots may represent cities of different sizes, national and state capitals, etc. One type of line may represent a national border, while another type of line can represent a state border.

# 6. Timeline-, Diagram-, and Realia-Based Items

## a. Timelines

A timeline is a graphic representation of events in the order in which they occurred. A timeline is good for helping organize important information chronologically. This timeline shows events related to the construction of the transcontinental railroad.

TIP: Every administration of HiSET will most likely contain at least one, or possibly two, timelines.

| Construction of the Transcontinental Railroad | |
|---|---|
| 1853–1855 | Government surveyors examine possible routes |
| 1862 | Congress authorizes construction to begin |
| 1863 | Construction begins on the western leg of the railroad |
| 1865 | Construction begins on the eastern leg of the railroad |
| 1869 | The Golden Spike is driven in and the railroad opens |
| 1869 | November: The leg between Sacramento and Oakland is completed |
| 1873 | Railroad bridge between Council Bluffs and Omaha is completed. |

Now try these examples:

> What is the significance of the Golden Spike?
>
> **A.** It showed that the railroad would be expensive for travelers to use.
> **B.** It showed the importance of the new railroad and the pride of the builders.
> **C.** Special materials were needed to construct a railroad under such challenging circumstances.
> **D.** It lacks significance because the railroad was not actually finished then.

Option B is correct. The railroad was a massive engineering feat, and the companies were proud of their work. Option A is not supported by the timeline. Option C does not make sense; the Golden Spike was an object used in an important celebration. Option D is not supported by the timeline; the railroad was completed successfully and ready to begin transcontinental operations.

> What is the <u>most likely</u> reason small projects remained unfinished at both the eastern and western ends of the railroad?
>
> **A.** Those sections of the railroad posed special engineering challenges.
> **B.** The companies did not have enough money to complete the projects at the same time.
> **C.** The railroads lacked necessary U.S. government authorizations for construction in those places.
> **D.** The companies did not think that those sections of the railroad were very important.

Option A is correct. Those sections were hard to build because of special geographic challenges. Option B is incorrect because the companies were well financed and completed those projects as quickly as possible. Option C is contradicted by the timeline. The companies got federal authorization in 1862. Option D is contradicted by the information. The Sacramento-to-Oakland section was already under construction at the time of the driving of the Golden Spike, and the bridge was completed within a few years of the main project. This shows that these parts of the project were important to the companies.

To interpret a timeline, do the following:

- Read the title and make sure you understand what the timeline is about.
- Read the years and dates in chronological order.
- Read the events. Try to figure out the relationships among the events. Are they simply events in chronological order? Do they show causes and effects? Which ones are causes? Which ones are effects?

## b. Diagrams

A diagram is a drawing or sketch used to depict information visually. Diagrams can include a flow chart (which shows steps in a process such as how a bill becomes a law), an organizational chart (which shows a hierarchical structure such as the three branches of government), and a Venn diagram (which compares and contrasts ideas such as the commonalities and differences between a monarchy and a dictatorship). A diagram can be simple or complex.

Look at the following examples:

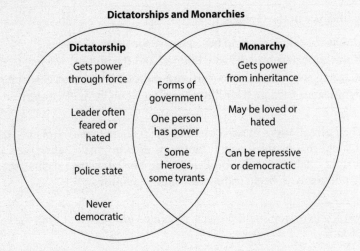

**Dictatorships and Monarchies**

**Dictatorship**

Gets power through force

Leader often feared or hated

Police state

Never democratic

Forms of government

One person has power

Some heroes, some tyrants

**Monarchy**

Gets power from inheritance

May be loved or hated

Can be repressive or democractic

---

Which of the following is a possible characteristic of a monarchy?

- **A.** The government has a powerful legislature that is freely elected.
- **B.** The leader took power when his soldiers jailed the elected representatives.
- **C.** The leader is elected in free elections every year.
- **D.** The leader killed the royal family in order to take power.

---

If you chose Option A, you are correct. According to the Venn diagram, Option A is a possible characteristic of a monarchy, which can be democratic. Dictatorships obtain power through force, and Options B and D are examples of ways this can happen, so are incorrect. Option C is a characteristic of a democracy, so is incorrect.

---

Which of the following is an example of a dictatorship?

- **A.** England, as ruled by the beloved Queen Elizabeth II
- **B.** Russia, as ruled by the tyrannical Czar Ivan the Terrible
- **C.** Spain, as ruled by the hard-fisted General Francisco Franco
- **D.** Germany, as ruled by elected Chancellor Angela Merkel

---

Option C is correct. As a general, Franco gained power by force. Options A and B are examples of monarchies. Option D is an example of a democracy.

To interpret a diagram, do the following:

- Read the title, labels, and other key words and make sure you understand what the diagram is about.
- Figure out whether the diagram shows organization, compares and contrasts, illustrates a process or a cycle, or something else.
- Examine the details in the diagram.

## c. Realia

**Realia** includes real-life graphic materials such as ads, posters, and announcements. Look at the following example:

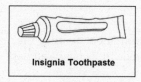

Insignia Toothpaste

Dentists report that 9 out of 10 their patients who use Insignia have fewer cavities than people who use another national brand.

This ad uses which of the following appeals to convince people to buy the brand of toothpaste?

A. Flavor—the toothpaste flavor encourages people to brush their teeth longer
B. Authority—dentists are experts, so people should take the dentists' advice and buy the product
C. Effectiveness—data show that the product works better than similar products
D. Attractiveness—people will find a boyfriend or girlfriend if they use the toothpaste

Option C is correct. The ad is telling people to buy the product because it prevents dental problems more effectively than other products. Option A is incorrect because flavor is not mentioned in the ad. Option B is incorrect because the ad is not citing the dentists' recommendations, but rather the results they observed. Option D is incorrect because attractiveness is not mentioned in the ad.

Which of the following statements can be <u>most reasonably</u> concluded from the ad?

A. 9 out of 10 dentists use Insignia themselves.
B. 1 out of 10 patients who use Insignia had similar or worse results than patients who use another national toothpaste brand.
C. 1 out of 10 people use another national brand instead of Insignia.
D. 9 out of 10 people brush their teeth twice a day.

Option B is correct. Since the information says that 9 out of 10 patients have better results when using Insignia, then 1 out of the 10 patients using Insignia had equal or worse results. Option A is incorrect because the ad is citing patients' results using the toothpaste. Option C is incorrect because the ad does not provide information on the number or proportion of people who use Insignia or another brand. Option D is not supported by the information in the ad.

# B. Types of Items: A Detailed Look

HiSET Social Studies items are divided into three types:

- Interpret and apply
- Analyze
- Evaluate and generalize

This section gives detailed information on how to answer each type of item.

# 1. Interpret and Apply

## a. Interpreting Information

Interpreting information involves reading and understanding the main idea and details, identifying implications, and making inferences and predictions based on data. Look at the following example:

*Example items 1 through 7 are based on the following realia.*

The Friends of the Flag Association prepared this information card to help members of the public fly flags correctly. This is a small card with information on when and how to fly the flag that might be carried by a boy scout or a city worker.

---

 **Basic Customs for Flying the U.S. Flag**

1. The U.S. flag should be flown only from sunrise to sunset, unless it is illuminated electrically.

2. When the U.S. flag is flown with the flags of other countries, all the flags should receive equal respect. Each flag should be of the same size and should be on a separate pole of the same height (except in international sporting competitions) and raised and lowered at the same time.

3. When the U.S. flag is displayed with state or local flags, those flags should be on shorter poles or the U.S. flag should be above all flags on the same pole.

4. The U.S. flag should be raised quickly and proudly and lowered slowly and ceremoniously.

5. If flags are ordered to be flown at half-staff, the flags should first be raised to the top of the flagpole and then lowered ceremoniously to half-staff. Flags should only be flown at half-staff upon order from the government. Many websites track this information, including the Association's.

6. Flags should be clean and in good condition. Once a flag is soiled, torn, or showing signs of wear, it should be disposed of in a dignified way. Check with your local government about proper procedures. The Association will properly dispose of flags at no charge.

---

1. Which of the following is the correct procedure for flying the flag at half-staff?

    **A.** Raise the flag slowly and ceremoniously to half-staff.

    **B.** Fly it half staff on a flag pole twice the height of the flagpoles of state and local flags that fly at full staff.

    **C.** Raise the flag to full staff and then lower it ceremoniously to half-staff.

    **D.** Light the flag with bright floodlights.

Option C correctly paraphrases information stated directly in the passage. Therefore, Option C is correct. Option A contradicts the information stated; item 5 clearly states that the flag should first be raised to the top of the pole and then lowered to half-staff. Option B is not supported by information in the passage. Option D is about flying the flag at night, not at half-staff.

## i. Vocabulary Items

Vocabulary items, a special type of HiSET item, ask you to determine the meaning of a word from the context. Look at the following example:

---

2. What is the meaning of the word "illuminated" in item 1?

    **A.** Enlightened

    **B.** Lit up

    **C.** Taught

    **D.** Darkened

---

Option B is correct You can figure out this meaning because the information points out that the flag should not be flown at night and uses the word *electrically*. From this we can figure out that *illuminate* means to shine light on something. *Illuminate* can also mean to teach someone or inform someone of some news or information (Options A and C), but these meanings do not make sense in the context of this passage. Option D has the opposite meaning of illuminated, so it is incorrect.

To answer a vocabulary item, do the following:

- If you already know the meaning of the word, read all the options and find that meaning in the list, and then plug it in to the original sentence in the passage to make sure that the meaning makes sense. If it has the same meaning, choose that option and go on to the next item.

> TIP: HiSET vocabulary items often use words with more than one meaning. For example, the word *illuminate* can mean "light up; shine light on something" or "provide valuable, insightful, or revealing information to someone." Therefore, do not choose the first option that you recognize as having the same meaning as the word, since the word may be used with another of its meanings in the information. Read all the options, and then insert the one you believe is correct into the original sentence in the information to double-check meaning.

- If you cannot find the correct answer, use clues in the sentence and surrounding sentences. For example, the indication that generally the flag should only be flown during the day and the word *electrically* are hints that the word *illuminated* is used to mean, "lit up."
- If you still cannot find the right answer, eliminate options you know to be incorrect and then choose one of the remaining options at random. For example, in this item, you can eliminate Option D as incorrect; *darkened* does not makes sense because the information indicates that the flag is not to be flown in the darkness of night.

## b. Applying Information

When you apply information, you use the information in a new context or situation. When you figured out which ruler—Elizabeth II, Czar Ivan the Terrible, Francisco Franco, or Angela Merkel—was an example of a dictator (page 262), you were applying the information about monarchies and dictatorships. Look at this example of an application item:

3. A small town in Texas on the border with Mexico is organizing a celebration of friendship between the two countries. How should they fly the flags of the two countries?

   A. Fly the Mexican flag at half-staff.
   B. Fly both flags on the same flagpole, with the U.S. flag at the top.
   C. Raise the Mexican flag first because guests are always first.
   D. Fly flags of equal sizes on flagpoles of equal heights.

Option D is correct. The second rule indicates that flags of different countries should receive this equal treatment. Options A and C violate this principle, so these options are incorrect. Option B applies to state and local flags flying with the U.S. flag, so it is incorrect.

# 2. Analyze

When you analyze information, you explore the relationships between ideas such as cause-effect, part-whole, distinguishing fact from opinion; identifying writers' values, biases, and assumptions; and identifying authors' main arguments and purposes for writing.

Try this example analysis item:

4. Which of the following is the most likely reason the association prepared the information card?

   A. No one cares about respecting flags.
   B. Many people have questions about proper flag etiquette.
   C. Rules for flying the flag changed recently.
   D. Rules for flying the U.S. flag vary from state to state.

This item asks you to determine the Association's purpose in preparing the information card. Option B is correct. People frequently have questions about proper flag display, especially around national holidays, so this is the most likely reason. Option A is contradicted by the information. If people did not respect the flag, the Association would not exist. Options C and D are not supported by the information. The word *customs* in the title of the card indicates that information did not change recently (Option C). Customs for the U.S. flag apply to the entire country (Option D).

> **TIP:** Answer options that contain absolute words such as *always, never, everyone,* and *no one* are usually incorrect. Look for an answer option that is less specific. Words such as *generally, usually,* etc., may signal this.

# 3. Evaluate and Generalize

## a. Evaluating Information

When you evaluate information, you make a judgment about the accuracy, usefulness, or importance of the information. You might decide whether information makes sense, is logical, or supports an inference or conclusion. Items also may ask you to evaluate the reliability or accuracy of information from different sources. Try this example item:

5.  Mr. Mitchell is responsible for raising and lowering the flag every day at the building where he works. One day, the wind blew the flag onto the ground. A co-worker told him that now he needs to burn the flag, but Mr. Mitchell is not sure what to do. Starting fires outdoors is illegal in the town. What should he do?

    A.  Throw the flag away.
    B.  Burn the flag anyway.
    C.  Contact the Association or his local government for information.
    D.  Continue using the flag, since it is clean and unharmed.

This item integrates application and evaluation. In this case, Mr. Mitchell needs to consider information from two sources, the card and his co-worker, and evaluate which one is better to follow. Option D is the correct answer because the card says that only worn and soiled flags should be disposed of. Therefore, Option C is an unnecessary step. Options A and B contradict both local laws and the information on the card, so they are incorrect.

## i. Evaluating Two Statements

A special type of HiSET item asks you to evaluate two statements and decide whether each one is correct. Look at this example:

6.  Consider the following two statements.

    I.  Mr. Mitchell and his co-worker lower the flag respectfully and fold it properly before storing it in a safe place.

    II. A sudden rainstorm drenches the flag just before sundown. The flag is lowered and hung up to dry in an appropriate place.

    In which of these statements, if either, are the people following the instructions in the information?

    A.  I only
    B.  II only
    C.  I and II
    D.  Neither I nor II

Option C is correct. Statements I and II are both consistent with the rules for displaying flags in the information.

TIP: When a HiSET item asks you to evaluate statements, consider each of the statements a true/false item. Write the numbers of the statements on your scratch paper. Write "T" or "F" next to each one. Then look for the answer option that reflects your answers. In this case, both statements are true. Therefore, Option C is correct.

## b. Generalizing

When you generalize, you use the information you have to make a broader or more general inference or conclusion. Items may ask you to decide whether a generalization is justified, identify supporting details for a generalization, or make a generalization. Try this example item.

7. The customs for flying the U.S. flag with the flags of other countries are based on which of these principles?

   **A.** People's pride in the United States
   **B.** Superiority of one country over others
   **C.** Consideration of individual rights and responsibilities
   **D.** Respect for all countries

This item asks you to find a generalization that is supported by the information. In this case, Option D is correct. The equal treatment of the flags shows respect for all countries. For this reason, Option B is incorrect. The respectful treatment of the U.S. flag in the information, not the information about other countries' flags, is a reflection of people's pride in the United States, so Option A is incorrect. Option C is not supported by the information in the passage.

## i. Evaluating Different Points of View

A special kind of passage involves two or more different points of view followed by several items. These items frequently ask you questions of different types. Answering textual comparison items involve some special test-taking skills. Look at the examples that follow:

*Example items 8 and 9 are based on the following information.*

**People in the small suburb of Park Heights are concerned about a new convenience store that wants to open in their town. Two neighbors wrote letters to the editor about the store.**

### Neighbor 1

I am writing as the mother of four growing sons. Our lovely town keeps standing in the way of progress. As a mother, I often run out of important products late at night. Last night, I had to drive an extra 5 miles to buy milk and bread for my family because all the stores in town close at 10 p.m. The new store would provide valuable convenience to all Park Heights families. In addition, the new store would create valuable jobs and sales tax revenue. Our taxes are already too high. Why should we have to drive to Shelbyville to shop for needed items late at night, and give the jobs and tax revenue to them?

### Neighbor 2

I am writing to express my opposition to this store. Convenience stores are an unattractive nuisance in a community like ours. We live in a beautiful park-like setting with many old and established businesses. We do not need a 24-hour convenience store to mar our neighborhood. These stores are unsightly, bring traffic and litter, and sell products like alcohol and cigarettes.

8. Which of the following is a reason Neighbor 1 cites to supports her opinion?

   **A.** Convenience stores make a town unattractive.
   **B.** The store will bring unneeded traffic to town.
   **C.** The store will make life easier for residents.
   **D.** The store will stock common products such as soda, gum, candy, and potato chips.

Option C is correct. The writer says that the store will make life more convenient for residents. The answer option closest in meaning to this is Option C. Options A and B support the opinion of Neighbor 2. The products in Option D are not the ones Neighbor 1 is interested in, so Option D is incorrect.

9. Which of the following is something that Neighbors 1 and 2 could agree upon?

    **A.** Park Heights is an elitist community that does not respond to people's needs.

    **B.** Park Heights is a community that they care about.

    **C.** The store can provide after-school jobs for teens.

    **D.** The store will make life easier for residents.

Option B is correct. While the two neighbors disagree, it is clear that they both value their town and want it to improve. They only disagree about the specifics. For this reason, the other options (A, C, and D) are incorrect.

TIP: To answer a textual comparison item, first read all the passages. Then focus on each passage one at a time. Reread the first passage and answer all the items about it—in this case item 8. Then reread the second passage and answer all the items about it. Last, answer the items that are about both passages—in this case, item 9.

Textual comparison items will generally ask only for these kinds of information: (1) Similarities among the opinions; (2) Differences among the opinions; (3) Ways the people agree; and (4) Ways the people disagree.

# C. Social Studies Review

This section will help you refresh your understanding of reading and interpreting social studies information in the four main areas on the test: history, civics/government, economics, and geography.

## 1. History

**History** is the study of our past. History studies and examines past events in order to understand their causes and effects and their impact on subsequent events and the future. History items on the HiSET Social Studies section can address U.S. and world history and include items about government, politics, economics, culture, and society.

### a. The Boston Tea Party

*Items 1 and 2 are based on the information below.*

The **Boston Tea Party** is a key event that contributed to the increasing hostility between the American colonists and Britain that led to the American Revolution. One of the colonists' main complaints with the British was summed up in the phrase, "No taxation without representation." From Britain's point of view, the colonies were expensive to administer. After the French and Indian War, Britain had wanted the colonists to pay for a larger part of the expense of defending the colonies. The colonists believed that they should have a voice in the taxes they paid. In May 1773, Britain had passed the **Tea Act,** which imposed a tax on tea that colonists were required to pay. In several places, colonists had successfully protested against the tax and had not been required to buy the tea and pay the tax. But in Boston, the British governor insisted that the colonists pay the tax. To protest, late at night on December 16, 1773, a group of colonists disguised as Native Americans boarded a ship in the harbor waiting to unload a cargo of taxed tea and threw all the tea into the water. The British responded with a series of new laws, the **Coercive Acts,** which the colonists called "the Intolerable Acts." These laws deepened the conflict, and ultimately led to the calling of the **First Continental Congress** and the outbreak of war.

---

1. Why did Britain impose the tax on tea?

   A. To punish the colonists
   B. To raise money to pay for the colonies' defense
   C. To help them win the French and Indian War
   D. To decrease tea consumption

---

This is an example of an interpreting information item. Option B is correct. Defending the colonies had been costly, and Britain wanted the colonists to pay a bigger share of this expense. The tax on tea was one of these measures. This answer is stated directly in the passage. Option A is incorrect because the Coercive Acts, not the tax on tea, were intended to punish the colonists. Option C is incorrect because Britain had already won this war. The cost of the war, not winning it, was therefore Britain's concern. While taxes can be used to decrease consumption of certain items (such as alcohol or tobacco), this was not the intent of the tea tax, which was implemented to raise money.

---

2. Which of the following was a <u>direct</u> result of the Boston Tea Party?

   A. The French and Indian War
   B. The tea tax
   C. The Intolerable Acts
   D. The Revolutionary War

---

This is an example of an analyzing information item. Option C is correct. According to the information, Britain imposed the Intolerable Acts to punish the colonists for resisting the tax on tea. Therefore, Option B is incorrect. Option A is incorrect because the cost of the French and Indian War is one of the reasons Britain wanted to raise taxes. Option D is incorrect because the Revolutionary War was an indirect result of the Boston Tea Party, not the immediate result. Several other events, such as the formation of the First Continental Congress, led to the outbreak of war.

## b. The Dred Scott Case

*Items 3 and 4 are based on the information below.*

The **Dred Scott case** involved a dispute over the legal status of slaves in the United States. The existence of slavery in parts of the United States, but not others, created considerable tension among the states, especially in locations where people opposed slavery. While the idea that slavery could exist in one part of the country but not the rest was proposed as a compromise, it caused many problems and disputes. One dispute was whether a slave could be taken to a state where slavery was not legal. Dred Scott was a slave whose master lived in Missouri, a slave state. When the master took him to Illinois, where slavery was illegal, Dred Scott sued for his freedom in federal court. The case was finally decided by the Supreme Court, which ruled 7 to 2 that slaves could not sue in federal court because they could not hold citizenship in the United States. The court also ruled that the slave owner's property rights would be violated if Dred Scott successfully sued for his freedom. This appalling decision outraged public opinion in the north and led to increasing opposition to slavery.

---

3. What did the Supreme Court decide in the Dred Scott case?

   A.  Aspects of slavery could be practiced in places where slavery was not legal.
   B.  The court had no jurisdiction over cases about slavery.
   C.  Cases about slavery had to be decided in accordance with local law.
   D.  Slavery was legal in Illinois.

---

Option A is correct. While it was illegal to buy and sell slaves in Illinois, it appeared from the case that slave owners could take their slaves there or anywhere in the United States. Because the court issued a ruling, Option B is incorrect. The ruling showed that the court believed it had jurisdiction. Option C is contradicted by the passage. Local law did not count, according to the court. Even if slavery was illegal, slaves could be brought to that place. Option D is incorrect. The court said that slave owners could bring slaves to places where it was illegal. This, however, did not make slavery legal in those places.

---

4. Which of the following is the most logical inference that can be drawn from the Dred Scott case?

   A.  The compromise to contain slavery to parts of the United States was working.
   B.  Slavery could spread to all parts of the United States, even where it was illegal.
   C.  The slavery issue could be settled through the courts and law.
   D.  Most Americans were willing to accept slavery even if they did not agree with it.

---

Option B is correct because the court ruled that Scott's master could take him to states where slavery was illegal. Therefore, slavery could spread to those states. The remaining options are contradicted by the passage. The compromise was not working because slavery could not be stopped from spreading to free states, according to the decision (Option A). Public opinion was outrage and opposition to slavery grew because of the ruling, so Options C and D are incorrect.

## c. Genghis Khan

*Items 5 and 6 refer to the following information.*

**Genghis Khan** was the founder of the **Mongol Empire,** a far-reaching empire that is still the largest empire in world history. Genghis Khan was born to a poor, nomadic family in what is now known as Mongolia. He unified Mongolian tribes and created a fierce fighting machine that terrorized its victims. To terrorize and subjugate his enemies, Khan often killed the entire population of a city or town. By the end of Khan's life, large portions of present-day China and Central Asia had been conquered. Later conquests included all of China, Korea, and parts of Russia, Central Europe, and the Middle East. Khan introduced many reforms. For example, he gave the Mongolian language, which had not been written previously, a writing system. He also gave religious freedom to the people living under Mongolian rule.

5. Which of the following places was NOT conquered by the Mongolian Empire?

   A. China
   B. Vietnam
   C. Central Asia
   D. Parts of Russia

This is an interpreting information item. According to the information, all the places in the options except Vietnam were conquered by the Mongolian Empire, so Option B is correct.

6. How is Genghis Khan <u>most likely</u> regarded in Mongolia today?

   A. A hero and a symbol of Mongolia's greatness.
   B. An excellent general but a poor ruler.
   C. A divisive leader of the Mongolian people.
   D. A tolerant, forgiving ruler.

Option A is correct. His wide conquests and important reforms made him a hero among Mongolians. Option B is contradicted by the information, since he introduced so many reforms and was able to administer such an expansive empire. Option C is contradicted by the information. Genghis Khan, in fact, unified the Mongolian tribes. Option D is incorrect because though he was tolerant of people's religions, he ordered the slaughter of entire cities in order to further his conquests.

# 2. Civics/Government

**Civics and government** include the study of types of government, politics, power and authority, individual rights and responsibilities, justice, and the roles and practices of the informed citizen. HiSET civics/government items can focus on U.S. government and civics or on international and global contexts.

## a. The Branches of Government

*Items 1 and 2 are based on this diagram.*

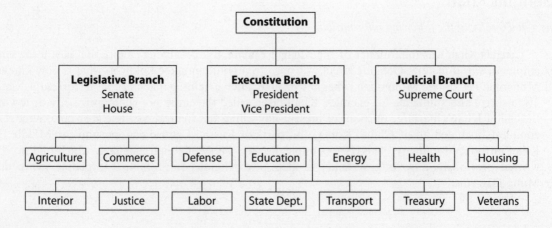

1. According to the diagram, which of the following is part of the legislative branch?

   A. The Supreme Court
   B. The Department of Justice
   C. The Senate
   D. The President

Of the four answer options, only the Senate (Option C) is part of the legislative branch. The Supreme Court (Option A) heads the judicial branch. The Department of Justice (Option B) and the President (Option D) are both parts of the executive branch.

2. According to the diagram, which of these is NOT a responsibility of the executive branch?

   A. Defending the country from attack
   B. Ensuring that the country has a good educational system
   C. Ensuring that the country has an adequate supply of gas, oil, coal, and electricity
   D. Passing new legislation

Option D is correct. Passing new legislation is a function of the legislative branch. The other options are incorrect because they are the roles of the departments that report to the president and are thus part of the executive branch: Option A is the role of the Defense Department, Option B is the role of the Department of Education, and Option C is the role of the Department of Energy.

# b. Motor Voter Laws

*Items 3 and 4 refer to the following information.*

   **Motor voter laws** permit citizens to register to vote when they obtain or renew their driver's licenses, apply for public assistance, or interact with the government in other ways. The purpose of the laws was to expand voting rights by making it easier for citizens to register to vote. In the past, registering to vote often necessitated a special trip to a government office, which was difficult or impractical for many people. The law made it easier for people to register to vote at driver's licenses offices, post offices, public aid offices, public libraries, and other government offices. However, not all political parties agreed. Many Republicans, who opposed the legislation, said that motor voter provisions would result in increased voting fraud. Democrats countered that Republicans were opposed because the voters who signed up tended to vote Democratic.

3. According to the information, what is the stated purpose of motor voter laws?

   A. To add more Democratic voters to the polls
   B. To reduce election fraud
   C. To increase citizen's civic participation
   D. To encourage people to use services such post offices and public libraries

Option C is correct. According to the information, the purpose of the laws was to increase participation by encouraging people to register and, therefore, be able to vote. Option A is the reason Democrats gave for why Republicans opposed the laws. Option B is not supported by the information and does not make sense.

Option D is incorrect because the laws' intention was to make registration easier by allowing people to register in places they already go, not to increase the use of those places.

---

4. Which of the following could be offered as proof that motor voter laws did not result in increased fraud?

   **A.** The number of registered voters increased.
   **B.** The percentage of citizens voting in presidential elections went up.
   **C.** Arrests for voter fraud declined after the laws went into effect.
   **D.** Police found that someone registered to vote in five different states.

---

Only Option C offers proof that the laws did not invite increased fraud. Options A and B are possible consequences of the laws, but are not signs that fraud did not increase. Option D is a sign that fraud went up, so it is incorrect.

# 3. Economics

**Economics** refers to the study of the production, distribution, and consumption of goods and services. It includes principles of supply and demand, differences between needs and wants, technology and the economy, and the long-term and short-term effects of government on the economy.

## a. Inflation

*Items 1 and 2 refer to the following information.*

> **Inflation** is the gradual increase of prices over time. **Deflation** is the decrease of prices over time. Inflation often occurs at times of economic growth, but too much inflation can cause the economy to slow down as prices increase too quickly and consumer spending falls. Deflation causes the real value of money to increase, since consumers can purchase more goods and services. However, deflation makes the cost of debt go up, so it's harder to earn money to repay the debt because of lower prices and incomes.

---

1. Who benefits from inflation?

   **A.** Debtors, because it's easier for them to repay the debts
   **B.** Consumers, because prices go down
   **C.** Savers, because the value of their savings goes up
   **D.** Employers, because wages go up

---

Option A is correct; it is indirectly implied in the passage. If deflation hurts debtors because it's harder for them to repay the debts, then it stands to reason that inflation will help debtors pay back their debts because over time their income will rise, but their debt will remain the same. Option B is incorrect because prices go up, not down, during inflation. Option C is incorrect because the value of savings will go down during inflation, since prices of goods and services increase during inflation. It is true that wages will go up during inflation, but this will benefit workers, not employers (Option D), since employers have to pay the higher wages.

2. Under which economic conditions would we <u>most likely</u> see deflation?

    **A.**    New technology makes production of goods and services faster and cheaper and raises quality.

    **B.**    An economic boom causes consumer spending to skyrocket.

    **C.**    A growing economy causes wages to rise rapidly.

    **D.**    Falling interest rates stimulate companies to invest in new factories and design innovative products.

Widespread availability of inexpensive, high-quality products would most likely cause prices to fall, so Option A is correct. The remaining options (B, C, and D) would most likely result in inflation, so they are incorrect.

# 4. Geography

**Geography** studies aspects of the land, its features, and how people use and interact with the land. It includes economic, political, and social factors. It also examines the environment and environmental conservation. Geography items include understanding and interpreting maps, documents, and case studies.

## a. Rainfall

*Items 1 and 2 refer to the following information and map.*

       Taipei and Yilan City are both located on the island of Taiwan. Taiwan is a subtropical island south of Japan and north of the Philippines. In the summer, strong south winds blow humid air toward Taiwan from the tropics. In the winter, the winds shift and blow from west to east across tall mountain ranges.

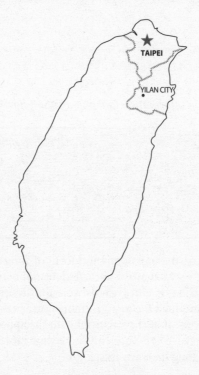

1. What would the weather <u>most likely</u> be like in Yilan City in the summer?

   A. Cold and rainy
   B. Cool and dry
   C. Warm and damp
   D. Hot and humid

Option D is correct. The summer heat from Taiwan's subtropical location, plus winds blowing humid air from the tropical regions south of Taiwan would make Yilan City hot and humid in the summer. Therefore, the other options (A, B, and C) are incorrect.

2. What would the weather <u>most likely</u> be like in Yilan City in the winter?

   A. Cold and rainy
   B. Cool and dry
   C. Warm and damp
   D. Hot and humid

Option A is correct. Cooler winter temperatures, coupled with air blowing from west to east, would cause rainfall to increase as the air from winds blowing from the west crosses the mountains, where it precipitates and falls as rain. Therefore, Yilan City would most likely be cold and rainy in the winter. The other options (B, C, and D) are incorrect.

> **TIP:** Geography items are the least frequently tested items on the HiSET. Therefore, if you are short on time preparing for the test, or when taking the test, leave the geography items for last.

# D. Practice

## 1. Items

*Items 1 through 3 refer to the following information and map of the Lincoln Highway.*

In the early twentieth century, the most common form of long-distance transportation was the railroad. The United States had a very extensive and efficient rail network that continued to grow. At this time, few people had cars. Outside of cities, roads were mostly unpaved, which made travel extremely difficult. While some cities maintained farm roads to bring crops to the town, roads were not extensively used for intercity travel. However, all of this changed with the appearance of Henry Ford's Model T car, the first mass-produced, inexpensive car. Suddenly, it became more important to have intercity roads so people could use their cars for long distance travel.

While most of us are familiar with the **interstate system,** a network of roads that was first developed in the 1950s, few people remember the **Lincoln Highway,** which was the nation's first coast to coast highway. The Lincoln Highway was the brainchild of an early automobile pioneer from Indiana, Carl G. Fisher. Fisher realized that for automobiles to be successful, better roads were needed, and began to push for the creation of the Lincoln Highway. The highway formally opened to traffic in 1913, and ran from New York's Time Square to Lincoln Park, San Francisco. The original route was 3,389 miles long and ran through 13 states: New York, New Jersey, Pennsylvania, Ohio, Indiana, Illinois, Iowa, Nebraska, Colorado, Wyoming, Utah, Nevada, and California. The road was unpaved gravel in most places, but was a major improvement over the mostly dirt roads that prevailed in America's countryside up until then. The highway inspired a number of similar highways, such as the Dixie Highway and the Yellowstone Highway.

1. Why was the Lincoln Highway an improvement over previous roads?

    A.  It was faster and more efficient than trains.
    B.  It was part of a network of interstate highways.
    C.  It was designed for intercity travel.
    D.  It was paved with cement.

2. If a driver started in Chicago, how many states would the driver pass through on the way to Los Angeles?

    A.  six
    B.  seven
    C.  eight
    D.  nine

3. In many places, the road was built by offering towns on the proposed route a special deal. If the town supplied the labor to build the road, the town would receive the construction materials for free. Why would the people agree to pay for the labor to build the highway through their town?

    A.  People would move away to larger cities because travel was easier.
    B.  Traffic and pollution would increase.
    C.  The highway would bring business to the town.
    D.  The people would be more motivated to buy cars.

*Items 4 through 6 refer to the following letter to the mayor.*

Dear Mayor Quinn,

I am very concerned about access to quality childcare in our town. I am the mother of three young boys, ages 7 years, 5 years, and 3 months. I was a stay-at-home mom after my first son was born, but after my second son was old enough to go to daycare, I returned to work in order to help my husband support our family. However, after my third son was born, I was unable to find affordable infant care and had to quit my job. All of the providers I found were either too expensive or not of sufficient quality. The only infant care program I could find was so expensive that the weekly charge cost more than my week's paycheck. I am lucky because my husband has a good job, so by cutting a few expenses, we will make it. But what would a single mother do?

I would like to request that Parkville Public Schools open a free or low-cost infant care program for moms who want or need to work in order to support their families. I would like to speak to you about this in person and also address the board of education.

Sincerely,

Tiffany Brooks

4. What problem is the letter writer concerned about?

   **A.** The town lacks good, affordable preschool programs.

   **B.** The public school system is closing the preschool program.

   **C.** The mayor has cut the school budget.

   **D.** Mothers of young babies cannot find caregivers.

5. Which of the following is the <u>most effective</u> action the letter writer could take to get the public schools to start the program?

   **A.** Complain to the governor of the state.

   **B.** Remove her other two sons from the childcare program as a protest.

   **C.** Start a website that gives referrals to mothers who cannot find appropriate care for young babies.

   **D.** Start a petition drive to show that the idea has widespread support.

6. The first amendment to the U.S. Constitution states:

> Congress shall make no law respecting an establishment of religion, or prohibiting the free exercise thereof; or abridging the freedom of speech, or of the press; or the right of the people peaceably to assemble, and to petition the government for a redress of grievances.

Which of the following first amendment rights is the letter writer using?

   **A.** Freedom of the press

   **B.** The right to ask the government to redress a grievance.

   **C.** The right to peaceably assemble

   **D.** Freedom of religion

*Items 7 and 8 refer to the following information.*

The **law of supply** says that when the price of a good or service goes up, the supply will go up. The **law of demand** says that when the price of a good goes up, the demand goes down. Supply and demand are at equilibrium when the supply and the demand are equal. That is, the amount of goods produced is equal to the amount of goods consumed. This is highly efficient because producers are selling as many goods as they produce, and consumers are buying as much of the goods as they want. This relationship can be summed up in a graph.

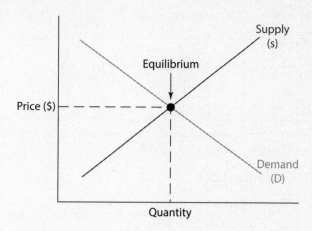

7. A certain brand of sunglasses suddenly becomes very popular. Which of the following is the <u>best</u> explanation of what will happen?

    A.   The price will go up.
    B.   The price will go down.
    C.   The price will stay the same.
    D.   The change in price cannot be predicted.

8. The supply and demand for baggy jeans were in equilibrium for many years until skinny jeans became popular. Then the price of baggy jeans went down. Which of the following is the best explanation of why the price of the baggy jeans went down?

    A.   The supply increased.
    B.   The supply decreased.
    C.   The demand increased.
    D.   The demand decreased.

*Item 9 refers to the following bar graph.*

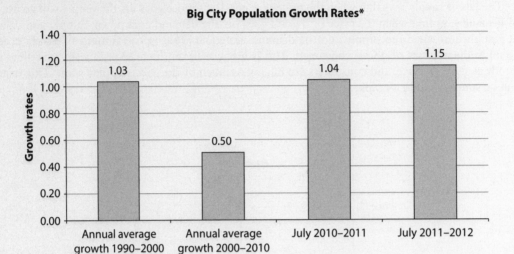

**Big City Population Growth Rates***

* Cities over one half million population

*Source: U.S Census Bureau*

9. What happened to the growth rate of the population of big cities in 2000–2012?

   A. Initially, growth rates dropped and then increased in subsequent years.
   B. Initially, growth rates increased and then dropped in subsequent years.
   C. Growth rates stayed more or less the same during the period.
   D. Growth rates steadily increased during the period.

10. Philosopher and historian George Santayana once famously wrote, "Those who cannot remember the past are condemned to repeat it." What was Santayana's view of history as expressed in this quotation?

    A. Studying history can help us see into the future.
    B. By examining our past, we can avoid the mistakes of the past.
    C. History inevitably repeats itself in a never-ending cycle.
    D. People cannot change the course of history.

# 2. Answer Explanations

1. **C. It was designed for intercity travel. (Interpreting Information/History)** Option C is correct because this information is stated directly in the passage. Option A is not possible because driving on a gravel road is slower and less efficient than taking a train. Option B is incorrect because the Lincoln Highway spurred the growth of other, later highways. Those highways did not exist at the time the Lincoln Highway was built. Option D is contradicted by the information; the highway was paved with gravel, not cement.

2. **C. eight (Interpreting Information/History)** The driver would pass through these eight states: Illinois, Iowa, Nebraska, Colorado, Wyoming, Utah, Nevada, and California. Therefore, the other options (A, B, and D) are incorrect.

3. **C. The highway would bring business to the town. (Analyzing Information/History)** Option C is correct because increased business is a logical result of building the highway through a town that would motivate the townspeople to pay for its construction. Option A is not a reason to support building the highway. While pollution was not a major concern at the time the Lincoln Highway was built, traffic and pollution are reasons to oppose the highway, not to build it (Option B). Option D is the reason the promoters of the highway wanted to build it, not the local citizens.

4. **D. Mothers of young babies cannot find caregivers. (Applying Information/Government and Civics)** Option D restates information given directly in the passage, so it is correct. Option A is incorrect because the town has good preschool programs, according to the letter. Options B and C are not supported by the information.

5. **D. Start a petition drive to show that the idea has widespread support. (Applying Information/ Government and Civics)** Option D is correct because starting a petition would show the mayor and the school board that many citizens support the idea. Option A is incorrect because the governor would most likely not be interested in such a local matter. Option B would not accomplish her goal, so is incorrect. Option C is incorrect because while people could use the website to find private infant care providers, it would not accomplish the goal of getting the school system to start a free or low-cost infant care program.

6. **B. The right to ask the government to redress a grievance. (Applying Information/Government and Civics)** Option B is correct because she is writing to the mayor to ask him to fix a problem, which means she is asking the government to redress a particular grievance. Option A is incorrect because she wrote a letter to the mayor; she didn't publish it in a newspaper or online. Option C is incorrect because she is not organizing a protest march or meeting. Option D is incorrect because religion is not involved in this matter.

7. **A. The price will go up. (Analyzing Information/Economics)** Option A is correct because the laws of supply and demand indicate that as demand increases, prices increase. Therefore, the other options are incorrect.

8. **D. The demand decreased. (Applying Information/Economics)** Option D is correct because demand for baggy jeans most likely went down when styles changed. Option A is incorrect because manufacturers would not increase production of a kind of jeans that is out of style. Options B and C would result in increasing, not decreasing, prices, so they are incorrect.

9. **A. Initially, growth rates dropped and then increased in subsequent years. (Interpreting Information/ Geography)** Option A is correct because population growth rates dropped in 2000–2010, and then increased between 2010 and 2012. For this reason, the other options (B, C, and D) are incorrect.

10. **B. By examining our past, we can avoid the mistakes of the past. (Analyzing Information/History)** Option B is correct because the word *condemned* in the sentence indicates that unless we study history, we will repeat the mistakes we made in the past. Option A is incorrect because it is impossible to see into the future. Option C is not supported by the information; Santayana believes that we will repeat our own mistakes, not that history operates in a cycle. Option D contradicts the quotation; we can change the course of history by paying attention to the lessons of the past.

# IX. Language Arts: Reading Full-Length Practice Test with Answer Explanations

**40 Items**
**Time: 65 Minutes**

**Directions:** This is a test of your skills in understanding various kinds of reading material. The reading texts come from a variety of published works. Some are literary and some are informational. A number of items follow each passage.

Each passage begins with an introduction that presents information that may help you while you read. After you read each passage, continue on to the items that follow it. For each item, choose the best answer. You may refer back to the passage as often as you wish.

---

*Items 1 through 8 refer to the passage below.*

**This excerpt from a short story, based on a true story, is about Jan Rodrigues, a sailor on a Dutch ship that is exploring the area that is now New York City in 1613. Of African descent and born in Santo Domingo, Rodrigues decides to stay on the island of Manhattan when the ship leaves.**

The canoe scudded to a stop at the steep, rocky shore. There was no slip, so he tossed the rope, which he had knotted to a crossbar and weighted with a pierced plumb square just larger than his thumb, forward into the foliage. Carefully he clambered toward the spray of greenery, the fingers of the thicket and its underbrush clasping the soles of his boots, his stockinged calves, his ample linen breeches. A thou-
(5)   sand birds proclaimed his ascent up the incline; the bushes shuddered with the alarm of creatures stirred from their lees; insects rose in a screen before his eyes, vanishing. When he had secured the boat and settled onto a sloping meadow, he sat, to wet his throat with water from his winesack, and orient him-self, and rest. Only then did he look back.

The ship, the *Jonge Tobias,* which had borne him and the others across more nautical miles than he
(10)  had thought to tally, was no longer visible, its brown hulk hidden by the river's curve and the outcrop-ping topped by fortresses of trees. The water, fluttering like a silk shroud, now white, now silver, now azure, ferried his eyes all the way over itself east—he knew from the captain's compass and his own canny sense of space, innate since he could first recall—to the banks of a vaster, still not fully charted island, its outlines an ocher shimmer in the morning light, etching themselves on his memory like augu-
(15)  ries. Closer, at the base of the hill, fish and eels drew quick seams along the river's nervous surface. From hideouts in the rushes toads serenaded....

Excerpt from "Mannahatta," by John Keene. *TriQuarterly,* Winter/Spring 2014.

1. What is the character doing in the excerpt?

   A.  Leading a group of sailors to a source of fresh water on the island

   B.  Landing a canoe on the shore of an island

   C.  Getting ready to return to his ship after exploring the area

   D.  Hiding on the island in order to avoid work on the ship

2. How can the setting best be described?

   A.  Full of hidden dangers

   B.  Lush with plant and animal life

   C.  Dry, rocky, and harsh

   D.  Urban with many skyscrapers

3. What is the *Jonge Tobias?*

   A.  The ship of Dutch explorers who find Jan Rodrigues living on Manhattan Island

   B.  The canoe that Jan Rodrigues rowed to the island

   C.  The sailing ship that brought Jan Rodrigues to North America

   D.  The boat that brought Jan Rodrigues from Santo Domingo to the Netherlands

4. What does the author mean when he says that the water "ferried [Jan Rodrigues's] eyes all the way over itself east" (lines 11–12)?

   A.  A ferryboat transported Jan Rodrigues to another island in the east.

   B.  Strong currents in the water pulled his boat to the east.

   C.  Jan Rodrigues paddled his canoe to the east.

   D.  The water drew Jan Rodrigues's attention to the east.

5. Which of the following details foreshadows Jan Rodrigues's impending separation from the ship?

   A.  "Carefully he clambered toward the spray of greenery, the fingers of the thicket and its underbrush clasping the soles of his boots" (lines 3–4)

   B.  "He sat, to wet his throat with water from his winesack" (line 7)

   C.  The *Jonge Tobias* "was no longer visible, its brown hulk hidden by the river's curve and the outcropping topped by fortresses of trees" (lines 9–11)

   D.  "Closer, at the base of the hill, fish and eels drew quick seams along the river's nervous surface" (line 15)

6. Which of the following individuals does Jan Rodrigues <u>most closely</u> resemble?

   A.  Pocahontas, the daughter of a Native American tribal leader in the Virginia area, who helped European settlers in the region

   B.  Leif Erikson, a Norse explorer thought by many to be the first European to land in North America

   C.  Jean-Baptiste Point Du Sable, of African descent, who was the first non-Native American inhabitant of what is now Chicago

   D.  Peter Minuit, an early Dutch settler of the New York area, who purchased Manhattan Island from Native Americans

7. All of the following details indicate that the excerpt is set in the past EXCEPT:

   A. "The canoe scudded to a stop at the steep, rocky shore." (line 1)

   B. "There was no slip, so he tossed the rope, which he had knotted to a crossbar and weighted with a pierced plumb square just larger than his thumb, forward into the foliage." (lines 1–3)

   C. "Carefully he clambered toward the spray of greenery, the fingers of the thicket and its underbrush clasping the soles of his boots, his stockinged calves, his ample linen breeches." (lines 3–4)

   D. "...the banks of a vaster, still not fully charted island, its outlines an ocher shimmer in the morning light..." (lines 13–14).

8. Several years later, Dutch settlers arrive on Manhattan Island and find Jan Rodrigues living there. Which of the following would <u>most likely</u> happen?

   A. Jan Rodrigues would welcome the new settlers and help them start their settlement.

   B. Jan Rodrigues would keep his distance from the new settlers.

   C. The new settlers would kill Rodrigues since he is probably allied with hostile Native Americans.

   D. The new settlers would move to another location because another settler is already present.

*Items 9 through 16 refer to the poem below.*

**Written in 1914, this poem depicts the ghost of Abraham Lincoln walking the streets of his hometown, Springfield, Illinois, contemplating World War I, which had just broken out in Europe.**

## Abraham Lincoln Walks at Midnight

It is portentous, and a thing of state
That here at midnight, in our little town
A mourning figure walks, and will not rest,
Near the old court-house pacing up and down.

(5) Or by his homestead, or in shadowed yards
He lingers where his children used to play,
Or through the market, on the well-worn stones
He stalks until the dawn-stars burn away.

A bronzed, lank man! His suit of ancient black,
(10) A famous high top-hat and plain worn shawl
Make him the quaint great figure that men love,
The prairie-lawyer, master of us all.

He cannot sleep upon his hillside now.
He is among us: – as in times before!
(15) And we who toss and lie awake for long
Breathe deep, and start, to see him pass the door.

His head is bowed. He thinks on men and kings.
Yea, when the sick world cries, how can he sleep?
Too many peasants fight, they know not why,
(20) Too many homesteads in black terror weep.

The sins of all the war-lords burn his heart.
He sees the dreadnaughts scouring every main.
He carries on his shawl-wrapped shoulders now
The bitterness, the folly and the pain.

(25) He cannot rest until a spirit-dawn
Shall come; – the shining hope of Europe free:
The league of sober folk, the Workers' Earth,
Bringing long peace to Cornwall, Alp and Sea.

It breaks his heart that kings must murder still,
(30) That all his hours of travail here for men
Seem yet in vain. And who will bring white peace
That he may sleep upon his hill again?

"Abraham Lincoln Walks at Midnight," by Vachel Lindsay.

9. Which of the following is a location NOT visited by Lincoln during his ghostly wanderings?

   A.  His former home
   B.  The market
   C.  The old courthouse
   D.  Europe

10. What is the speaker's attitude toward Lincoln?

   A.  He thinks that Lincoln represents important values.
   B.  He believes that Lincoln is an irrelevant figure from the past.
   C.  He thinks that Lincoln is a frightening, unwanted presence.
   D.  He thinks that Lincoln is too focused on trivial places from the past.

11. According to the speaker, why is Lincoln's ghost wandering the streets of Springfield in 1914?

   A.  He is horrified by the war in Europe.
   B.  He is haunted by the millions of deaths in the Civil War.
   C.  He misses familiar locations from his hometown.
   D.  He is lonely and wants to find his wife and children.

12. What does the speaker mean when he says, "He stalks until the dawn-stars burn away" (line 8)?

   A.  Lincoln's ghost will not rest until stars burn out in fiery supernovas.
   B.  Lincoln's ghost is going to attack someone or something.
   C.  Lincoln will return to his grave forever in the morning.
   D.  Lincoln's ghost wanders the streets nightly until sunrise.

13. All of the following details show that the ghost is of Abraham Lincoln EXCEPT

   A.  he is a "bronzed, lank man" (line 9).
   B.  he is wearing a "famous high top-hat" (line 10).
   C.  he is described as a "prairie-lawyer" (line 12).
   D.  "He thinks on men and kings" (line 17) fighting World War I.

14. According to the speaker, when will Lincoln's ghost be at peace again?

   A.  When dawn breaks and Lincoln returns to his tomb
   B.  When peace and justice rule the world
   C.  When Europe is democratic and at peace
   D.  When the United States enters the war against Germany

15. Which of the following statements would the speaker most likely agree with?

   A.  The Civil War was a noble war for a good cause, and World War I was an unjust war started by tyrants.
   B.  The Civil War haunts and tortures Lincoln's conscience.
   C.  World War I was started to promote democratic government in Europe.
   D.  The Civil War was the internal struggle of one country, and World War I was a global conflict.

16. Based on details in the poem, what would the speaker most likely say about recent wars in Afghanistan and Iraq?

   A.  He would say that they are needless and wrong, like all wars.
   B.  He would say that the U.S. should never preoccupy itself with foreign wars, such as World War I or these wars.
   C.  He would say that the wars would have to result in democratic governments in the countries to be just.
   D.  He would say that the United States is always justified in using war to achieve its aims.

*Items 17 through 24 refer to the passage below.*

**A television critic wrote the following article about how TV programming has changed over the years.**

Sometimes it seems like TV never changes. Game shows, sports shows, news, situation comedies, and police dramas all seem to be staples of American television and are some of America's longest running television programs. However, a quick comparison of television program listings from today and from 40 years ago would show some dramatic differences. Two types of TV programs that were extremely
(5)   popular 40 or 50 years ago—variety shows and westerns—are now gone almost completely. What happened to these types of shows and what does that tell us about how television has changed in recent years?

Westerns used to be among the most popular—and common—shows on television. In 1969, the peak of the genre's popularity, 26 different westerns were on prime-time television, and that was at a time
(10)  when there were only three major networks and no cable television. For many years, the longest running entertainment show on network television was *Gunsmoke,* which ran for 20 years.

What happened to the television western? First, audiences began to tire of the genre, which probably was overexposed with so many westerns on television. In addition, people's interests in rural-themed shows declined, and audiences became much more interested in urban-oriented programs that examined
(15)  the lives and problems of everyday Americans. Finally, there was considerable backlash against the violence in television westerns, which many people began to consider inappropriate for young audiences.

Variety shows, another staple of early television, also declined in popularity at about the same time, but for different reasons. Typically, these shows consisted of a host who introduced various musical and comedy acts. Variety shows such as *The Ed Sullivan Show* included acts of interest to every member of
(20)  the family, and families would often watch together. An episode might include a famous comedian for the whole family, a popular singer for the parents, a new rock and roll band for teenagers, an opera singer or pianist for classical music lovers, and a clown, puppet, or animal act for children. While these shows seemed stodgy at times, they drove pop culture. For example, *The Ed Sullivan Show* introduced the Beatles, the Rolling Stones, the Doors, and Elvis Presley to national audiences.

(25)  Variety shows declined in popularity for different reasons than westerns. Through the 1960s, few families had more than one television set. However, the rise of cheaper consumer electronics and increasing affluence allowed families to have as many television sets as family members, or sometimes even more. Thus, shows no longer had to appeal to the whole family. Each family member could watch the specific kind of show they wanted. Soon afterward, cable television led to highly specialized networks
(30)  that appealed to specific audiences, such as popular music, sports, or even game shows. Then came the VCR, followed by the DVD player and DVRs, which meant that people did not have to watch shows when they were on the air, but could watch any time. This freed families from having to watch TV together.

So what, if anything, has stayed the same in prime-time television? The situation comedy seems to be
(35)  the longest-running and most successful genre. This kind of program started with shows such as *I Love Lucy,* which went on the air in 1951, ran for 6 years, and has never gone off the air. Today, the longest running show on television, *The Simpsons,* is a situation comedy. This show began its 26th season in 2014.

17. Which of the following kinds of TV shows have largely disappeared from television?

    A. Police dramas
    B. Variety shows
    C. Situation comedies
    D. Sports shows

18. Which of the following is NOT a reason that accounts for the decline of television westerns?

    A. Excessive violence
    B. People tired of shows set in the country
    C. Audience's growing interest in urban themes
    D. The rise of cable television

19. Which of the following is an example of overexposure of westerns?

    A. Over 25 of them were on the air at their peak of popularity.
    B. *The Simpsons* started its 26th season in 2014.
    C. The Ed Sullivan show seemed stodgy at times.
    D. *I Love Lucy* went on the air in 1951.

20. Which of the following is NOT a reason that variety shows lost popularity?

    A. Teenagers could have their own televisions in their rooms.
    B. Cable television gave people a much wider choice of programs.
    C. Video recorders let people skip commercials.
    D. Technology lets people record and watch shows whenever they want.

21. Which of the following is a generalization that can be drawn from the information in the passage?

    A. Television programming is affected as much by technology as by viewers' tastes.
    B. Cable television killed the best shows on television.
    C. People will watch whatever is on television, whether they like it or not.
    D. Television is a vast wasteland of bad programming.

22. Which kind of television program was most affected by changes in television technology?

    A. Situation comedies
    B. Westerns
    C. Variety shows
    D. Sports shows

23. What is the author's main purpose in writing this article?

    A. To criticize television for excessive violence
    B. To analyze the success of *The Simpsons* and other situation comedies
    C. To show why people considered westerns stodgy
    D. To explain why the types of shows on television change over time

24. Based on the information in the article, which of these events would be most likely to occur?

    A. Prime-time game shows will become popular again.
    B. More specialized cable networks will continue to launch.
    C. Several new westerns will go on the air soon.
    D. Television networks will stop making new situation comedies.

*Items 25 through 32 refer to the excerpt from a play below.*

**This passage is from a play about a professor who studies the many accents of English, from upper-class to lower-class varieties. He studies the accents by recording them in writing and in audio recordings. One woman whose accent he studied is now asking for his assistance.**

MRS. PEARCE: *[hesitating, evidently perplexed]* A young woman wants to see you, sir.

HIGGINS: A young woman! What does she want?

MRS. PEARCE: Well, sir, she says you'll be glad to see her when you know what she's come about. She's quite a common girl, sir. Very common indeed. I should have sent her away, only I thought per-
(5)   haps you wanted her to talk into your machines. I hope I've not done wrong; but really you see such queer people sometimes— You'll excuse me, I'm sure, sir—

HIGGINS: Oh, that's all right, Mrs. Pearce. Has she an interesting accent?

MRS. PEARCE: Oh, something dreadful, sir, really. I don't know how you can take an interest in it.

HIGGINS *[to Pickering]* Let's have her up. Show her up, Mrs. Pearce *[he rushes across to his work-*
(10)   *ing table and picks out a cylinder to use on the phonograph].*

MRS. PEARCE: *[only half resigned to it]* Very well, sir. It's for you to say. *[She goes downstairs].*

HIGGINS. This is rather a bit of luck. I'll show you how I make records. We'll set her talking; and I'll take it down first in Bell's visible Speech; then in broad Romic; and then we'll get her on the phono-
graph so that you can turn her on as often as you like with the written transcript before you.

(15)   MRS. PEARCE: *[returning]* This is the young woman, sir.

*The flower girl enters in state. She has a hat with three ostrich feathers, orange, sky-blue, and red. She has a nearly clean apron, and the shoddy coat has been tidied a little.*

HIGGINS: *[brusquely, recognizing her with unconcealed disappointment, and at once, baby-like, making an intolerable grievance of it]* Why, this is the girl I jotted down last night. She's no use: I've got
(20)   all the records I want of the Lisson Grove lingo; and I'm not going to waste another cylinder on it. *[To the girl]* Be off with you: I don't want you.

THE FLOWER GIRL: Don't you be so saucy. You ain't heard what I come for yet. *[To Mrs. Pearce, who is waiting at the door for further instruction]* Did you tell him I come in a taxi?

MRS. PEARCE: Nonsense, girl! What do you think a gentleman like Mr. Higgins cares what you
(25)   came in?

THE FLOWER GIRL: Oh, we are proud! He ain't above giving lessons, not him: I heard him say so. Well, I ain't come here to ask for any compliment; and if my money's not good enough I can go elsewhere.

HIGGINS: Good enough for what?

(30)   THE FLOWER GIRL Good enough for ye—oo. Now you know, don't you? I'm come to have lessons, I am. And to pay for em too: make no mistake.

HIGGINS: *[stupent]* WELL!!! *[Recovering his breath with a gasp]* What do you expect me to say to
you?

THE FLOWER GIRL: Well, if you was a gentleman, you might ask me to sit down, I think. Don't I
(35)   tell you I'm bringing you business?

HIGGINS: Pickering: shall we ask this baggage to sit down or shall we throw her out of the window?

THE FLOWER GIRL: *[running away in terror to the piano, where she turns at bay]* Ah—ah—ah—
ow—ow—ow—oo! *[Wounded and whimpering]* I won't be called a baggage when I've offered to pay like
any lady.

(40)   *[Motionless, the two men stare at her from the other side of the room, amazed.]*

PICKERING: *[gently]* What is it you want, my girl?

THE FLOWER GIRL: I want to be a lady in a flower shop stead of selling at the corner of Tottenham Court Road. But they won't take me unless I can talk more genteel. He said he could teach me. Well, here I am ready to pay him—not asking any favor—and he treats me as if I was dirt.

(45)    MRS. PEARCE: How can you be such a foolish ignorant girl as to think you could afford to pay Mr. Higgins?

THE FLOWER GIRL: Why shouldn't I? I know what lessons cost as well as you do; and I'm ready to pay.

HIGGINS: How much?

Excerpt from *Pygmalion,* by George Bernard Shaw.

25. Why does Higgins invite the young woman up to his office initially?

A.   Mrs. Pearce recommended that he see her right away.

B.   He thinks it is a good opportunity to make money by giving lessons.

C.   It is a good opportunity for him to show his research methods to Pickering.

D.   He is interested in helping her become a lady.

26. What is Mrs. Pearce's attitude toward the Flower Girl?

A.   She believes that Higgins can help her solve her problems.

B.   She thinks that her accent is interesting and that Higgins should study it.

C.   She believes that the woman is lower class and lacks good manners.

D.   She thinks that Higgins should meet as many different kinds of people as possible.

27. Why does Higgins try to send the Flower Girl off at first?

A.   He does not want to associate with members of the lower class.

B.   He is not interested in studying her accent.

C.   He is not interested in buying flowers.

D.   He already has a good sample of her accent in his files.

28. What is indicated about the Flower Girl when she says, "I won't be called a baggage when I've offered to pay like any lady" (lines 38–39)?

A.   She is willing to stand up for herself.

B.   She will never be able to improve her situation.

C.   She has low self-esteem.

D.   She has plenty of money.

29. What is the meaning of the word "genteel" (line 43), as used in the passage?

A.   gently

B.   properly

C.   cleanly

D.   convincingly

30. Which of the following expresses a major difference between Higgins and the Flower Girl?

A.   Higgins behaves like a gentleman, while the Flower Girl does not act like a lady.

B.   Higgins is only interested in conducting his studies, while the Flower Girl is interested in using his research to improve herself.

C.   Higgins wants to record more of the Flower Girl's speech, but she does not want him to record her speech.

D.   Higgins is interested in the Flower Girl as an object of study, while the Flower Girl is interested in being friends with him.

31. Which of the following actions show that Higgins does not act like the upper-class gentleman he claims to be?

    A. He lives in a nice home and has a servant.
    B. He tells her to "Be off" (line 21).
    C. He studies people's accents.
    D. He is a professor.

32. Which of the following is <u>most likely</u> to happen next?

    A. Higgins will throw her out of the house.
    B. Higgins will record her speech.
    C. Higgins will agree to give her lessons.
    D. Higgins will ask Mrs. Pearce to help her.

*Items 33 through 40 refer to the passage below.*

**This passage discusses perceptions and realities of global warming.**

## How Can There Be Global Warming? It's Snowing Out!

While scientists continue to warn about the effects of global warming, some people wonder whether it really is the threat it is predicted to be. Chicago, for example, recently had one of the coldest winters on record, followed directly by a very mild and cool summer. These apparent disparities can be explained in two ways: the nature of global warming itself and the differences between climate and weather.

(5)  Global warming refers to a documented increase in Earth's average surface temperature. Since the early twentieth century, the average surface temperature has increased about 1.4°F. Most of this increase happened in the last 30 years. Scientists estimate that global temperatures will rise an additional 0.5° to 3.1°F in the twenty-first century.

Scientists now believe that the main cause of global warming is an increase in $CO_2$ emissions, primar-
(10) ily from burning fossil fuels, but also from cement production and deforestation. Cement production releases $CO_2$ not only from burning of fossil fuels used to make and transport cement, but also from the chemical processes that take place in the manufacture of cement. Deforestation raises $CO_2$ levels in at least two ways. First, carbon dioxide stored in wood is released when trees are burned or decay. In addition, as a consequence of deforestation, there are fewer trees to use carbon dioxide gas in photosynthesis.
(15) Scientists believe that all this carbon dioxide rises in the atmosphere and forms a layer that traps energy from the sun, which raises temperatures at the earth's surface.

Global warming affects different parts of the earth in different ways, which is why it sometimes seems like global warming is not really happening. The greatest temperature changes are in the polar regions, where rising temperatures will have the greatest impact, resulting in the continued melting of glaciers.
(20) This will, in turn, lead to rising sea levels. Scientists believe that the rising temperatures have disrupted all of Earth's weather patterns. They predict increased precipitation and more hurricanes, tornados, floods, and other kinds of extreme weather; however, they also believe that subtropical deserts will expand as well. They also note that even though people in locations such as Chicago may not think that they are experiencing global warming, average temperatures have increased in those places, too. This is
(25) the difference between climate and weather. That is, even though the weather may not seem warmer than usual, the climate itself has changed.

All of this points to the urgency of reducing $CO_2$ emissions as soon as possible. All countries, devel-
oping and developed, need to switch to renewable sources of energy, reduce fossil fuel use, switch to kinds of cement that produce less $CO_2$, and reduce deforestation. But, scientists caution, even a coordi-
(30) nated global effort to reduce the emission of $CO_2$ will only slow rising temperatures because of the large amount of carbon dioxide that has already accumulated in the atmosphere.

33. Why do some people believe that global warming is not a serious issue?

    A. They do not live in polar regions.
    B. Reducing $CO_2$ emissions will stop average temperatures from continuing to rise.
    C. Average temperatures have not risen significantly.
    D. They think that summer weather is cooler than usual.

34. Which of the following is NOT a cause of global warming?

    A. Deforestation
    B. Burning fossil fuel
    C. Cement manufacture
    D. Solar power

35. Which of the following statements best explains why global warming will cause both increased precipitation and the expansion of subtropical deserts?

    A. Weather is different from climate to climate.
    B. Global warming has disrupted all weather patterns but in different ways.
    C. Increased temperatures have caused glaciers to melt.
    D. Average global temperatures have risen 1.4°F.

36. Which of the following statements best describes the tone of the article?

    A. Rational and scientific
    B. Emotional and alarming
    C. Calm and reassuring
    D. Sarcastic and belittling

37. What is the meaning of the word "mild" (line 3), as used in the passage?

    A. Slight
    B. Hot
    C. Not extreme
    D. Not spicy

38. All of the following are facts mentioned in the passage EXCEPT

    A. cement production is the largest source of $CO_2$ emissions.
    B. deforestation releases carbon and carbon dioxide stored in wood.
    C. rising temperatures will have the biggest impact in arctic regions.
    D. melting glaciers will cause sea levels to rise.

39. What is the writer's main point?

    A. Global warming is not as serious a problem as people think.
    B. Global warming is a serious problem regardless of people's impressions.
    C. Deforestation is a major cause of global warming.
    D. We can stop global warming by making changes to cement production.

40. Which of the following will most likely occur if $CO_2$ emissions are reduced?

    A. Average global temperatures will drop about 1.4°F.
    B. Average global temperatures will increase 0.5° to 3.1°F.
    C. Average global temperatures will stop rising.
    D. The increase in average temperatures will slow down.

# Answer Key

| | | | | | | | | |
|---|---|---|---|---|---|---|---|---|
| 1. | B | 9. | D | 17. | B | 25. | C | 33. D |
| 2. | B | 10. | A | 18. | D | 26. | C | 34. D |
| 3. | C | 11. | A | 19. | A | 27. | D | 35. B |
| 4. | D | 12. | D | 20. | C | 28. | A | 36. A |
| 5. | C | 13. | D | 21. | A | 29. | B | 37. C |
| 6. | C | 14. | C | 22. | C | 30. | B | 38. A |
| 7. | A | 15. | A | 23. | D | 31. | B | 39. B |
| 8. | B | 16. | C | 24. | B | 32. | C | 40. D |

# Answer Explanations

1. **B. Landing a canoe on the shore of an island (Comprehension/Prose Fiction)** This answer can be determined from the first line of the excerpt, so Option B is correct. For this reason, the other options are incorrect. Additionally, the character is alone, so Option A is incorrect. He has just arrived on the island, so Option C is incorrect. Option D is not supported by details in the passage.

2. **B. Lush with plant and animal life (Comprehension/Prose Fiction)** The author's description of foliage (line 3), thicket and underbrush (lines 3–4), birds (line 5), bushes (line 5), insects (line 6), fish and eels (line 15), and toads (line 16) all indicate that this is an area with rich plant and animal life, so Option B is correct. For this reason, Option C is incorrect. Option A is not supported by details in the passage. Option D describes present-day Manhattan and is therefore incorrect.

3. **C. The sailing ship that brought Jan Rodrigues to North America (Comprehension/Prose Fiction)** This information is stated directly in the passage in the first sentence of paragraph 2 (lines 9–11), so Option C is correct. For this reason, the other options are incorrect.

4. **D. The water drew Jan Rodrigues's attention to the east. (Analysis/Prose Fiction)** This is an example of figurative language. *Ferry* means "to move over water." In this case, the water figuratively moved Jan Rodrigues's attention to the large island. Therefore, Option D is correct. Option A is incorrect because this story is set before the time that this area was settled and ferryboats transported people. Options B and C do not make sense because Jan Rodrigues is on the small island and not in the canoe when this action takes place.

5. **C. The *Jonge Tobias* "was no longer visible, its brown hulk hidden by the river's curve and the outcropping topped by fortresses of trees" (lines 9–11) (Inference/Prose Fiction)** Describing the ship as hidden from view in the distance behind him hints that soon the main character will become separated from the ship. The details in the remaining options do not imply that the character and the ship will soon become separated, so are incorrect.

6. **C. Jean-Baptiste Point Du Sable, of African descent, who was the first non-Native American inhabitant of what is now Chicago (Synthesis/Prose Fiction)** Both Du Sable and Rodrigues are early non-Native American settlers of future urban areas who are of African descent. For this reason, Option C is correct.

Option A is incorrect because Pocahontas is a Native American, not a settler. Option B is incorrect because Leif Erikson is of European, not African descent. Though Minuit is an early settler of a future large city, Option D is incorrect because Minuit is of European, not African descent.

7. **A. "The canoe scudded to a stop at the steep, rocky shore." (line 1) (Inference/Prose Fiction)** All the options except Option A include indications that the excerpt is set in the past, so Option A is the answer. The lack of a boat slip (Option B), the old fashioned stockinged calves and linen breeches (Option C), and the fact that Manhattan island is not charted, or mapped (Option D), are all details that show that the passage is set in the past.

8. **B. Jan Rodrigues would keep his distance from the new settlers. (Generalizing/Prose Fiction)** Option B is most likely correct because Rodrigues, of African descent, seems to be trying to get away from European people by settling in an uninhabited area. Therefore, it seems likely that he would keep his distance from the newcomers. For this reason, Option A is incorrect. Option C is not a logical action, since we do not know if Rodrigues allied himself with the Native Americans or whether they were hostile at that time. Option D is not supported by the details in the passage. For example, the passage indicates Rodrigues did not own the land, so there is no reason for the settlers to move elsewhere.

9. **D. Europe (Comprehension/Poetry)** The only place not mentioned in lines 4–8 as a location visited by Lincoln's wandering ghost is Europe. Worries about the war in Europe stirred Lincoln's ghost, according to the speaker, but the places that Lincoln visited are all in his hometown of Springfield, Illinois. Therefore, the answer is Option D, and the remaining options (A, B, and C) are incorrect.

10. **A. He thinks that Lincoln represents important values. (Interpretation/Poetry)** Option A is correct because the language and details in the poem, such as "portentous, and a thing of state" (line 1) and "quaint great figure that men love" (line 11), show that the speaker deeply respects Lincoln and his values. For this reason, Option A is correct. Option B is incorrect because the speaker seems to think that Lincoln and his values are relevant to the war being fought in Europe. Option C is not supported by the details in the passage. Option D is incorrect because Lincoln's ghost is wandering those places from his past because his soul is disturbed by current events in Europe.

11. **A. He is horrified by the war in Europe. (Interpretation/Poetry)** Option A is correct because details and language in the poem such as, "Too many peasants fight, they know not why,/Too many homesteads in black terror weep" (lines 19–20) and "The sins of all the war-lords burn his heart./He sees the dreadnaughts [warships] scouring every main [seacoast]" (lines 21–22), show that he feels that the war in Europe is horrifying. For this reason, Options C and D are incorrect. Option B is incorrect because the speaker does not mention the Civil War at all.

12. **D. Lincoln's ghost wanders the streets nightly until sunrise. (Analysis/Poetry)** This is an example of figurative language and refers to Lincoln's haunting the streets until the last stars that appear in the night sky disappear when the sun rises. Therefore, Option D is correct. Option A is a literal interpretation of the word *burn,* which refers to the rising sun, not the stars burning out, so it is incorrect. Option B is a literal interpretation of the word *stalks,* and refers to Lincoln's ghost wandering the streets, not to his looking for a victim. Option C is incorrect because the speaker says that the ghost wanders the streets every night because of the war in Europe: "He cannot rest until a spirit-dawn/Shall come; – the shining hope of Europe free" (lines 25–26).

13. **D. "He thinks on men and kings" (line 17) fighting World War I. (Comprehension/Poetry)** Option D is correct because World War I occurred after Lincoln's death. All of the details in Options A, B, and C are well-known features of Lincoln, so they are incorrect: He was a tall, lanky man, wore a top hat, and was a lawyer from Illinois, the prairie state.

14. **C. When Europe is democratic and at peace (Analysis/Poetry)** According to the details in the poem, Lincoln is appalled not by the horrors of the war, but its unjustness, since it was started by murderous kings (line 29) and not for a just cause, as in the case of the American Civil War. For this reason, Option A is incorrect. Option B is too general. The speaker is concerned about the war in Europe, not worldwide peace and democracy. Option D is incorrect because the speaker believes that Lincoln would think that the war itself is unjust, not that one country should be defeated.

15. **A. The Civil War was a noble war for a good cause, and World War I was an unjust war started by tyrants. (Synthesis/Poetry)** Option A is correct because the speaker seems to admire Lincoln, his values, and his leadership, and contrasts those with the events in Europe. Option B is incorrect because Lincoln's ghost was stirred by events in Europe. Option C is contradicted by details in the passage. The speaker seems to believe that the World War I was not fought for noble purposes. While Option D may be true, it is not the reason that the speaker abhors the war in Europe.

16. **C. He would say that the wars would have to result in democratic governments in the countries to be just. (Inference/Poetry)** The speaker's concern seems to be just causes, not pacifism; one way for the wars to be just would be for them to result in democratic governments in the region. For this reason, Options A and D are incorrect. Option B is incorrect because he believes that the war in Europe is problematic because it is unjust, not because it is a foreign war.

17. **B. Variety shows (Comprehension/Informational Texts)** This answer is stated directly in the passage in line 5, so Option B is correct. For this reason, the other options (A, C, and D) are incorrect.

18. **D. The rise of cable television (Comprehension/Informational Texts)** Option D is correct because the passage states in paragraph 5 (lines 29–30) that cable television led to the decline of variety shows, not westerns. The other options (A, B, and C) are factors mentioned in paragraph 3 (lines 12–16) as reasons for the decline of the television western, so they are incorrect.

19. **A. Over 25 of them were on the air at their peak of popularity. (Comprehension/Informational Texts)** This many programs in the limited prime-time hours of only three television networks would lead to overexposure, so Option A is correct. Options B and D are incorrect because these programs are situation comedies, not westerns. Option C is incorrect because this is an example of a variety show.

20. **C. Video recorders let people skip commercials. (Comprehension/Informational Texts)** Option C is correct because skipping commercials would affect all TV shows, not just variety shows. The other options (A, B, and D) are mentioned in the passage as reasons that variety shows lost popularity, so they are incorrect.

21. **A. Television programming is affected as much by technology as by viewers' tastes. (Generalization/Informational Text)** According to the information, westerns declined in popularity because of changes in taste, while changes in technology seemed to affect variety shows, so Option A is correct. The remaining options (B, C, and D) are not supported by information in the passage, so they are incorrect.

22. **C. Variety shows (Inferences/Informational Text)** Option C is correct because the passage discusses changes in television technology only in reference to variety shows. Therefore, the other options (A, B, and D) are incorrect.

23. **D. To explain why the types of shows on television change over time (Analysis/Informational Text)** This answer can be inferred from the details in the passage. In the first paragraph of the passage, the writer lists kinds of TV shows on the air, as well as two kinds of shows that are no longer popular, and then goes on to discuss the reasons for the change over time. The option that best expresses this main purpose is Option D. While the author mentions the excessive violence of westerns, it is only a detail, not the writer's main purpose in writing, so Option A is incorrect. The writer mentions *The Simpsons*

as an example of a kind of television show that has remained popular, which is unrelated to the main idea of the passage, so Option B is incorrect. Option C is not mentioned in the passage so is incorrect.

24. **B. More specialized cable networks will continue to launch. (Generalization/Informational Text)** According to the information in the passage, cable networks have been successful in capturing the attention of specific kinds of viewers, so they will most likely continue to launch. Option A is not supported by information in the passage. Option C is contradicted by information in the passage. Westerns seem unrelated to audiences' lives and interests, according to the passage. Option D is contradicted by the information in the passage. According to the passage, situation comedies have remained popular since the 1950s.

25. **C. It is a good opportunity for him to show his research methods to Pickering. (Comprehension/Drama)** Option C is correct because Higgins says, "This is rather a bit of luck. I'll show you how I make records" (lines 12–14) and then goes on to describe his methods of transcribing and recording speech. Mrs. Pearce is skeptical of the Flower Girl and is reluctant to show her in, so Option A is incorrect. Giving lessons does not come up until later in the excerpt, so Option B is incorrect. Option D is not supported by details in the excerpt, so it is incorrect.

26. **C. She believes that the woman is lower class and lacks good manners. (Interpretation/Drama)** Mrs. Pearce's skeptical attitude and her comment that the Flower Girl is "quite a common girl" (line 4) whose accent is "dreadful" (line 8) indicate that Option C is correct. Mrs. Pearce never brings up helping her, so Option A is incorrect. Mrs. Pearce also does not seem to understand Higgins's research and is reluctant to show her into the room, so Option B is incorrect. Option D is contradicted by the details in the passage. For example, she says that Higgins sees "such queer people sometimes" (lines 5–6).

27. **D. He already has a good sample of her accent in his files. (Comprehension/Drama)** Option D is correct because in lines 19–20, Higgins says, "Why, this is the girl I jotted down last night. She's no use: I've got all the records I want of the Lisson Grove lingo." He already associated with her, so Option A is incorrect. He already recorded her speech and others with the same sort of speech, so Option B is incorrect. She has not come to see Higgins to sell flowers, so Option C is incorrect.

28. **A. She is willing to stand up for herself. (Interpretation/Drama)** Option A is correct because her words show that she considers her offer as good as any lady's offer. Option B is not supported by the details in the passage. Option C is contradicted by her words. If she had low self-esteem, she would not stand up for herself in this way. Option D is contradicted by the details in the passage. She seems to be a poor, lower-class woman who sells flowers to passers-by to scrape together some money.

29. **B. properly (Comprehension/Drama)** Option B is correct because she says that she wants to learn to speak like a lady, or in proper English. Therefore, the other options (A, C, and D) are incorrect.

30. **B. Higgins is only interested in conducting his studies, while the Flower Girl is interested in using his research to improve herself. (Synthesis/Drama)** Option B is correct because the excerpt makes it clear that Higgins is only interested in gathering data for his research, while she wants to take lessons from him in order to get a better job. Higgins seems rude and dismissive, while the Flower Girl stands up for her dignity as a lady, so Option A is incorrect. Option C may have been true earlier in the play, but is not true now. When the Flower Girl enters the room, Higgins remarks that he already transcribed her speech the day before. Option D is contradicted by details in the passage. While Higgins is interested in her as an object of study, she is not interested in friendship but in language lessons.

31. **B. He tells her to "Be off" (line 21) (Interpretation)** Option B is correct because such a brusque response shows that he is not polite or considerate of her feelings—two of the marks of a gentleman. All the other options (A, C, and D) are consistent with being a gentleman.

32. **C. Higgins will agree to give her lessons. (Generalization/Drama)** Only the offer to pay for lessons seems to get Higgins's attention, suggesting that he will agree to do so. Therefore, Option C is correct. For this reason, Option A is not correct. There is no reason for Higgins to record her speech again (Option B) because he has already said he has enough samples of her particular accent. Option D is not supported by the details in the excerpt. Mrs. Pearce does not seem to like or approve of the Flower Girl much, so she would not be a logical person to ask to help her.

33. **D. They think that summer weather is cooler than usual. (Comprehension/Informational Texts)** Option D is correct because the passage states that local weather conditions in places such as Chicago lead some people to believe that global warming is not really happening. Option A is not supported by information in the passage. Option B is contradicted by the passage; per the passage, reducing $CO_2$ emissions will slow rising temperatures, but not stop temperatures from rising. An increase of 1.4°F is a significant increase, so Option C is incorrect.

34. **D. Solar power (Comprehension/Informational Texts)** Option D is correct. Solar power does not release $CO_2$, so it is not a cause of global warming. The remaining options (A, B, and C) are mentioned in the passage as causes of global warming, so they are incorrect.

35. **B. Global warming has disrupted all weather patterns but in different ways. (Synthesis/Informational Texts)** Option B is correct because only this option explains why precipitation can increase in some locations and decrease in others. Option A explains why cities like Chicago can experience mild summers and severe winters but still have average rising temperatures. Option C is a true statement, but it does not explain both increased precipitation and expansion of deserts. Option D is incorrect because the increase in average global temperatures does not explain why the effects of the increase are not the same everywhere.

36. **A. Rational and scientific (Interpretation/Informational Texts)** Option A is correct because the careful presentation of facts and scientific data and the logical argumentation make the tone rational and scientific. For this reason, Options B and D are incorrect. Option C is incorrect because while the article is calm, it is not reassuring; rather, it points out a problem that needs to be dealt with urgently.

37. **C. Not extreme (Comprehension/Informational Text)** Option C is correct because a cool summer is not extreme. For this reason, Option B is incorrect. Option A is related to another use of the word *mild,* such as a slight or mild cold. Option D is related to the meaning of the word *mild* when used to talk about food. Mild food is food that does not have a lot of spices in it.

38. **A. cement production is the largest source of $CO_2$ emissions. (Comprehension/Informational Texts)** Option A is contradicted by the information in the passage. According to the passage, the primary source of $CO_2$ emissions is the burning of fossil fuels (lines 9–10). All of the other options (B, C, and D) are mentioned in the passage as facts, so they are incorrect.

39. **B. Global warming is a serious problem regardless of people's impressions. (Analysis/Informational Texts)** The passage is about why global warming is a problem even though people do not perceive changes in their climate or weather. Option B expresses this idea most clearly. Option A is contradicted by the last paragraph, which states that immediate action is needed. Option C is only a detail in the passage, so it is incorrect. Option D is not supported by information in the passage.

40. **D. The increase in average temperatures will slow down. (Generalizing/Informational Texts)** This answer is stated directly in the last paragraph: "...even a coordinated global effort to reduce the emission of $CO_2$ will only slow rising temperatures because of the large amount of carbon dioxide that has already accumulated in the atmosphere" (lines 29–31). For this reason, Options A and C are incorrect. Option B is incorrect because this option shows the amount of future temperature increase anticipated under current conditions.

# X. Language Arts: Writing Full-Length Practice Test with Answer Explanations

## Part 1

**50 Items**

**Time: 75 Minutes**

**Directions:** This is a test of the skills involved in writing and revising written materials. There are two text selections similar to the kinds of documents high school students typically write. Each selection is presented twice: first in a box in a normal format, and then in a spread-out format with certain parts of the text underlined and numbered.

Skim the boxed text quickly to get an idea of the text's purpose, organization, and style. Then continue to the spread-out version.

Each numbered section of the text corresponds to an item in the right-hand column. Select the answer option that

- Makes the sentence grammatically correct
- Expresses the idea in the clearest or most appropriate way
- Is worded consistently with the style and purpose of the writing
- Organizes the ideas most effectively

If you believe that the underlined original version is best, choose Option A, "No change." For organization items, you may find it helpful to refer to the boxed text. For spelling items, indicate which of the three words is misspelled in the context of the passage, or choose Option A, "None."

*Items 1 through 19 are based on the following text selection.*

**A magazine writer prepared this draft of an article. Quickly skim the draft in the box below. Then go to the spread-out version and review the suggested revisions, choosing the best option for each item.**

Do you ever feel like you are drowning in email? Millions of people do. Experts agree that American workers are spending on email too much time. An average person sends or receives 100 to 200 emails per day at work. As well as a smaller number of personal emails. Some workers spend 2 to 3 hours per week just working on email. That's time that could be spend on other tasks. In addition, all this email increases stress, according to dr. Darla Day, a nationally recognized expert in workplace efficiency. Day "said, an inbox full of unanswered email, with more coming in every minute, is a reminder of unfinished tasks with new tasks coming in all the time." Several years ago, some experts even proposed a small tacks on email to cut down on excessive junk email. That was probably a bad idea, but there is still many things we can do to cut down on all this email. Experts propose a number of suggestions.

First, the reason that email distracts us is most likely because we pay so much attention to them. To cut down on time spent on email, reduce the number of times you check email each day. You might check email at the beginning of the day, mid-morning, before lunch, mid-afternoon, and just before quitting time. In addition, turn off email notifications so you are not interrupted each time you receive an email, or use the notifications wisely. For example, set your mail software so that high priority emails, such as messages from bosses or important customers, have a special notification sound, or message. Emails from less important sources can have a different notification, or no notification at all, based on their priority. This way, only email you really need to see right away can interrupt us.

Second, try to reduce the amount of email. One way to receive less email, is to send less email. So think of other ways to communicate, such as the telephone, text messaging, or social media. The telephone is particularly valuable in avoiding a chain of emails on the same subject. When a topic requires a lot of clarification and discussion the phone is probably better than email. Texting is a good way to send short messages. For example, instead of sending someone an email to tell them your location, simply send a text. Another way to reduce email is to get your name off mailing lists. Many of us simply delete unwanted emails each time we receive won. This is fine for random emails, but when we get daily ads and promotions, newsletters, and other subscriptions, a better solution is to opt out of the unwanted emails. To opt out, click on the special opt-out link in the email. Many people don't do this because it seems like extra work.

Finally, keep your email inbox organized. Delete unwanted emails, use folders to save other emails for later reference, and answer emails right away. Always use subject lines on email you send this way it's easier to find an email or the response you are looking for. If your email software offers you the possibility of organizing email by sender or topic, use it. This way, you can easily find all the emails from a particular sender or a certain topic.

## [1]

[1] Do you ever feel like you are drowning in email? [2] Millions of people do. [3] Experts agree <u>that American workers are spending on email too</u><sub>1</sub> <u>much time</u><sub>1</sub>. [4] An average person sends or receives 100 to 200 emails per day at <u>work. [5] As well as</u><sub>2</sub> a smaller number of personal emails. [6] Some workers spend 2 to 3 hours per week just working on email. [7] That's time that <u>could be spend</u><sub>3</sub> on other tasks. [8] In addition, all this email increases stress, according to <u>dr.</u><sub>4</sub> Darla Day, a <u>nationally</u><sub>4</sub> recognized <u>expert</u><sub>4</sub> in workplace efficiency. [9] <u>Day "said, an</u><sub>5</sub> <u>inbox full of unanswered email, with more coming</u><sub>5</sub> <u>in every minute, is a reminder of unfinished tasks</u><sub>5</sub> <u>with new tasks coming in all the time."</u><sub>5</sub> [10] Several

1. **A.** (No change)
   **B.** that American workers too much time are spending on email
   **C.** that American workers are spending too much time on email
   **D.** that on email American workers are spending too much time

2. **A.** (No change)
   **B.** work,
   **C.** work as well as
   **D.** work, as well as

3. **A.** (No change)
   **B.** could be spent
   **C.** could spend
   **D.** could spent

4. Which of the following words, if any, should be capitalized?
   **A.** (None)
   **B.** dr.
   **C.** nationally
   **D.** expert

5. **A.** (No change)
   **B.** Day "said, an inbox full of unanswered email, with more coming in every minute, is a reminder of unfinished tasks with new tasks coming in all the time".
   **C.** Day said, "An inbox full of unanswered email, with more coming in every minute, is a reminder of unfinished tasks with new tasks coming in all the time."
   **D.** Day said, "An inbox full of unanswered email, with more coming in every minute, is a reminder of unfinished tasks with new tasks coming in all the time".

years ago, some experts even <u>proposed</u> a small <u>tacks</u>
　　　　　　　　　　　　　　　6　　　　　　　　6

on email to cut down on excessive <u>junk</u> email. [11]
　　　　　　　　　　　　　　　　6

That was probably a bad idea, but there <u>is</u> still many
　　　　　　　　　　　　　　　　　　7

things we can do to cut down on all this email. [12]

<u>Experts propose a number of suggestions.</u>
　　　　　　　　　　　8

## [2]

First, the reason that email distracts us is <u>most</u>
　　　　　　　　　　　　　　　　　　　　　9

<u>likely</u> because we pay so much attention to <u>them</u>. To
9　　　　　　　　　　　　　　　　　　　　　10

cut down on time spent on email, reduce the number

of times you check email each day. You might check

email at the beginning of the day, mid-morning,

before lunch, mid-afternoon, and just before quit-

ting time. In addition, turn off email notifications so

you are not interrupted each time you receive an

email, or use the notifications wisely. For example,

set your mail software so that high priority emails,

such as messages from bosses or important custom-

ers, have a special notification <u>sound, or</u> message.
　　　　　　　　　　　　　　　　11

Emails from less important sources can have a dif-

ferent notification, or no notification at all, based

on their priority. This way, only email you really

need to see right away can interrupt <u>us</u>.
　　　　　　　　　　　　　　　12

6. Which of the following words, if any, is
   misspelled?
   A.　(None)
   B.　proposed
   C.　tacks
   D.　junk

7. A.　(No change)
   B.　be
   C.　are
   D.　were

8. Which of the following would be the best
   choice for Sentence 12?
   A.　(No change)
   B.　Move it before Sentence 10.
   C.　Make it the first sentence in Paragraph 2.
   D.　Remove the sentence completely.

9. A.　(No change)
   B.　mostly like
   C.　mostly likely
   D.　most like

10. A.　(No change)
    B.　theirs
    C.　it
    D.　itself

11. A.　(No change)
    B.　sound, or, message
    C.　sound or message
    D.　sound; or message

12. A.　(No change)
    B.　you
    C.　yourself
    D.　your

## [3]

Second, try to reduce the amount of email. One way to receive less <u>email, is</u> to send less email. So
<sub>13</sub> think of other ways to communicate, such as the telephone, text messaging, or social media. The telephone is particularly valuable in avoiding a chain of emails on the same subject. <u>When a topic requires a</u>
<sub>14</sub>
<u>lot of clarification and discussion the phone</u> is prob-
<sub>14</sub>
ably better than email. Texting is a good way to send short messages. <u>For example</u>, instead of sending
<sub>15</sub>
someone an email to tell them your location, simply send a text. Another way to reduce email is to get <u>your</u> name off mailing lists. Many of us simply
<sub>16</sub>
delete unwanted emails each time we <u>receive</u> <u>won</u>.
<sub>16</sub> <sub>16</sub>
This is fine for random emails, but when we get daily ads and promotions, newsletters, and other subscriptions, a better solution is to opt out of the unwanted emails. To opt out, click on the special opt-out link in the email. Many people don't do this because it seems like extra work. [17]

13. **A.** (No change)
    **B.** email, it is
    **C.** email; is
    **D.** email is

14. **A.** (No change)
    **B.** When a topic requires a lot of clarification and discussion, the phone
    **C.** When a topic requires a lot of clarification, and discussion the phone
    **D.** When a topic, requires a lot of clarification and discussion the phone

15. **A.** (No change)
    **B.** In contrast
    **C.** Nevertheless
    **D.** However

16. Which of the following words, if any, is misspelled?
    **A.** (No change)
    **B.** your
    **C.** receive
    **D.** won

17. The writer wants to add a sentence at the end of Paragraph 3. Which of the following would be the best choice?
    **A.** However, providing an opt-out link is required by federal law.
    **B.** However, opting out means you will miss valuable offers and information.
    **C.** However, many people like to receive these emails.
    **D.** However, opting out will reduce the amount of unwanted email.

**[4]**

Finally, keep your email inbox organized. Delete unwanted emails, use folders to save other emails for later reference, and answer emails right away. Always use subject lines on email you send this way it's easier
18
to find an email or the response you are looking for. If your email software offers you the possibility of organizing email by sender or topic, use it. This way, you can easily find all the emails from a particular
19
sender or a certain topic.
19

18. **A.** (No change)
    **B.** send this way its
    **C.** send, this way it's
    **D.** send. This way it's

19. **A.** (No change)
    **B.** from a particular sender, or a certain topic
    **C.** from a particular sender or on a certain topic
    **D.** from a particular sender or certain topic

*Items 20 through 38 are based on the following text selection.*

**Quickly skim the draft business letter in the box below from the West Park Community Center's executive director to the Parkton Chess Club president. Then go to the spread-out version and review the suggested revisions, choosing the best option for each item.**

---

Dear Mr. Luera:

We want to thank the Parkton Chess Club for its interest in using our facility for our meetings. We understand that the outdoor chess tables near Pine Avenue Beach is not useful to the club during the winter months. Therefore, we are happy to assign the club space in our Community Center for its games and meetings. During the colder months of the year. We have assigned the club the use of Meeting Room 23 for a three-month trial beginning October 1 of this year. The club may use this meeting room on a daily basis, as follows:

A.  Club members are welcome to meet and use the facility from 11 a.m. to 4 p.m. every day the community center is open to the public.

B.  Club members may use the storage closet in the room to store chess sets and other equipment used by the club. However, food and beverages may not be kept in the closet. We'll issue a closet key to the president, vice president, and secretary of the club. We reserve the rite to check the closet and its contents to ensure the safety, and security of the building.

C.  All members of the club should be residents of Parkton, 13 years old or older, and have a valid pass for the community center. Users's passes are available for children, adults, and seniors. Senior passes are free, and other passes have a small monthly fee.

D.  Club members may bring food or drinks to the room, they cannot cook or make coffee. Coffee machines are located on the lower level of the Community Center, and two coffee shops are located just outside the park entrance on Western Avenue.

E.  Club members are responsible for leaving the room clean, orderly, and it should be free of trash. All trash should be disposed of in the large bins at the end of the hall. The building is a green facility, so please cooperate by using the recycling bins for all recyclable material. The facility is open every day of the year except Thanksgiving Day, Christmas Day, and New Year's Day.

F.  This agreement is valid for a period of three months. You should file an application for renewal on or before Tuesday, January 3 2017 to continue using the facility.

As a registered community organization, our other facilities are also available to the club. You already asked about renting the center's large multifunction room for the club's annual Tournament of Chess Champions. Unfortunately, the room is not available the day you requested. Please call the center's facility manager, Cora Witherspoon, to find a date that works for the club. The rental fee for that room will go up 20 percent for all rentals booked after January 1, so we urge you to contact Ms. Witherspoon right away.

Thank you again for your interest in using the center for Parkton Chess Club activities. We hope the club members will enjoy using our facility for many years to come.

Sincerely,

Ned Barnes,
Executive Director

---

## [1]

We want to thank the <u>Parkton Chess Club</u> for its
[20]
interest in using our facility for <u>our</u> meetings. We under-
[21]
stand that the outdoor chess tables near Pine Avenue

Beach <u>is</u> not useful to the club during the winter months.
[22]
<u>Therefore</u>, we are happy to assign the club space in our
[23]
Community Center for its games and <u>meetings. During</u>
[24]
the colder months of the year. We have assigned the

club the use of Meeting Room 23 for a three-month

trial beginning October 1 of this year. The club may use

this meeting room on a daily basis, as follows:

20. **A.** (No change)
    **B.** Parkton chess Club
    **C.** Parkton chess club
    **D.** parkton chess club

21. **A.** (No change)
    **B.** your
    **C.** their
    **D.** its

22. **A.** (No change)
    **B.** have
    **C.** are
    **D.** has

23. **A.** (No change)
    **B.** Unfortunately
    **C.** In addition
    **D.** In contrast

24. **A.** (No change)
    **B.** meetings; during
    **C.** meetings during
    **D.** meetings, during

**[2]**

A. Club members are welcome to meet and use

the facility from 11 a.m. to 4 p.m. every day

the community center is open to the public.

**[3]**

B. Club members may use the storage closet in

the room to store chess sets and other equip-

ment used by the club. However, food and bev-

erages may not be <u>kept</u> in the closet. <u>We'll</u>
2525

issue a closet key to the president, vice presi-

dent, and secretary of the club. We reserve the

<u>rite</u> to check the closet and its contents to
25

ensure the <u>safety, and security of the building</u>.
26

**[4]**

C. All members of the club <u>should be residents of</u>
27

<u>Parkton, 13 years old or older, and have a</u>
27

<u>valid pass for the community center</u>. <u>Users's</u>
2728

<u>passes</u> are available for children, adults, and
28

seniors. Senior passes are free, and other

passes have a small <u>monthly</u> fee.
29

25. Which of the following words, if any, is
misspelled?
- A. (None)
- B. kept
- C. We'll
- D. rite

26.
- A. (No change)
- B. safety, and for the security of the building
- C. safety; and to protect the security of the building
- D. safety and security of the building

27.
- A. (No change)
- B. should have resided in Parkton, be 13 years old or older, and have a valid pass for the community center
- C. should reside in Parkton, be 13 years old or older, and have a valid pass for the community center
- D. should reside in Parkton, 13 years old or older, and have a valid pass for the community center

28.
- A. (No change)
- B. User passes
- C. User's passes
- D. User passes'

29.
- A. (No change)
- B. month
- C. every month
- D. month's

## [5]

**D.** [1] Club members may bring food or drinks to the <u>room, they cannot</u> cook or make coffee. [2]
<sub>30</sub>
Coffee machines are located on the lower level of the Community Center, and two coffee shops are located just outside the park entrance on Western Avenue. |31|

## [6]

**E.** [1] Club members are responsible for leaving the room <u>clean, orderly, and it should be free</u>
<sub>32</sub>
<u>of trash</u>. [2] All trash should be disposed of in
<sub>32</sub>
the large bins at the end of the hall. [3] The <u>building</u> is a <u>green</u> <u>facility</u>, so please cooperate
<sub>33</sub>     <sub>33</sub>   <sub>33</sub>
by using the recycling bins for all recyclable material. [4] The facility is open every day of the year except Thanksgiving Day, Christmas Day, and New Year's Day. |34|

## [7]

**F.** This agreement is valid for a period of three months. You should file an application for renewal on or before <u>Tuesday, January 3 2017</u>
<sub>35</sub>
to continue using the facility.

30. **A.** (No change)
    **B.** room, but, they cannot,
    **C.** room, but they cannot
    **D.** room but they cannot

31. The writer is considering whether or not to use the following sentence.

    > There are also several nice gift shops nearby.

    What would be the best choice for this sentence in Paragraph 5?
    **A.** Place it before Sentence 1
    **B.** Place it before Sentence 2
    **C.** Place it after Sentence 2
    **D.** (Do not use this sentence; Paragraph 5 is best as written.)

32. **A.** (No change)
    **B.** clean, and orderly, and free of trash
    **C.** clean, orderly, and be free of trash
    **D.** clean, orderly, and free of trash

33. Which of the following words, if any, should be capitalized?
    **A.** (None)
    **B.** building
    **C.** green
    **D.** facility

34. Which of the following would be the best choice for Sentence 4?
    **A.** (No change; the paragraph is best as written.)
    **B.** Move Sentence 4 before Sentence 2
    **C.** Move Sentence 4 before Sentence 3
    **D.** Remove Sentence 4.

35. **A.** (No change)
    **B.** Tuesday January, 3, 2017,
    **C.** Tuesday, January 3, 2017
    **D.** Tuesday, January 3, 2017,

## [8]

As a registered community organization, our
[36]
other facilities are also available to the club. You
[36]
already asked about renting the center's large multi-function room for the club's annual Tournament of Chess Champions. Unfortunately, the room is not
[37]
available the day you requested. Please call the center's facility manager, Cora Witherspoon, to find a date that works for the club. The rental fee for that room will go up 20 percent for all rentals booked after January 1, so we urge you to contact Ms. Witherspoon right away.

## [9]

[38] [1] Thank you again for your interest in using the center for Parkton Chess Club activities. [2] We hope the club members will enjoy using our facility for many years to come.

Sincerely,

Ned Barnes,
Executive Director

36. **A.** (No change)
    **B.** As a registered community organization, we will also let you use our other facilities.
    **C.** As a registered community organization, the club can also use our other facilities.
    **D.** As a registered community organization, we can also let the club use our other facilities.

37. **A.** (No change)
    **B.** Moreover
    **C.** Luckily
    **D.** In contrast

38. Which of the following would be the best choice for Paragraph 9?
    **A.** (No change; the letter is best as written.)
    **B.** Join Paragraph 9 to Paragraph 8.
    **C.** Join Sentence 1 of Paragraph 9 to Paragraph 8.
    **D.** Remove Paragraph 9 completely.

*Items 39 through 50 are based on the following text selection.*

**Quickly skim the draft newspaper article in the box below. Then go to the spread-out version and review the suggested revisions, choosing the best option for each item.**

Last Saturday, nearly 2,000 area residents joined in the citywide Day Of Service. Organized by the United City Charities and sponsored by over 250 local employers, the event was an opportunity for city residents to show pride and dedication to our town by volunteering for over 300 different charitable organizations. Area employers participated by encouraging employees to participate and donating food and supplies.

Volunteers worked on many projects around town. Many teams worked in area schools doing a variety of activities. For example, a team of accountants from Ahlbeck, Gadini, and Carson Accounting Service tutored area, middle, and high school, students in math. According to accountant Alfredo Gadini, "We met some great kids and had a good time helping them get ready for their final exams next week. We worked with both advanced math students and students who find math difficult." Another team built a new playground at Carpenter Elementary School. "All of our playground equipment was old and broken," observed Principal Pearl Goodman. "United City Charities provided us with funds for the new equipment, and the volunteers installed it in less than a day."

Several teams worked with the Eco-Maniacs, a community organization interested in protecting the environment. "We cleaned litter out of Rock Creek and Park Lake all day," said volunteer Mike McKasky, a customer service representative at Medill Communications. "We probably halled 1,000 pounds of refuse from our group's section of the creek." Dana Lewis, president of the Eco-Maniacs, said, "Were grateful for the aid that the United City Charities show us throughout the year, but we especially value the support of volunteers which are willing to work hard to make our community a better place."

Other volunteers worked at area hospitals and senior centers. A team of volunteers worked all day at Memorial Hospital. "Our team helped fix up an old storage area near the emergency room to build a new waiting room for families with children, said one volunteer. We washed and painted the walls and put in new flooring." According to the hospital, another team of volunteers will finish the job next week.

"This important event takes place yearly," said Latisha Harris, president of United City Charities. "While residents support our member charities through donations, todays' event is an opportunity for residents to become involved in the community in a personal way. It's a great opportunity to meet neighbors and make new friends while making our community better." This important community event takes place every year in October, but residents do not need to wait until next year to volunteer. Each year, we find that volunteers want to stay involved all year. "Our employees began participating in the Day of Service in 2011," said Thomas Ahlbeck, a partner at Ahlbeck, Gadini, and Carson Accounting. "Several of our employees volunteer in that school throughout the year weekly. It's great to know our work is helping children. Next year, we are going to offer after-school jobs to a few of the students during tax preparation season." According to Harris, "We refer volunteers to charities every day, and we have a matching program that helps volunteers find organizations that need their skills. Our 300 member charities are eager to have the support of our volunteers every day of the year."

**[1]**

Last Saturday, nearly 2,000 area residents joined
in the citywide <u>Day Of Service</u>. Organized by the
39   39    39
United City Charities and sponsored by over 250
local employers, the event was an opportunity for
city residents to show pride and dedication to our
town by volunteering for over 300 different charitable organizations. Area employers participated by
encouraging employees to participate and donating
food and supplies.

**[2]**

Volunteers worked on many projects around town.
Many teams worked in area schools doing a variety of
activities. For example, a team of accountants from
Ahlbeck, Gadini, and Carson Accounting Service
tutored <u>area, middle, and high school, students</u> in
40
math. According to accountant Alfredo Gadini,
"We met some great kids and had a good time helping them get ready for their final exams next week.
We worked with both advanced math students and
students who find math difficult." Another team
built a new playground at Carpenter Elementary
School. "All of our playground equipment was old
and broken," observed Principal Pearl Goodman.

39. Which of the following words, if any, should
NOT be capitalized?
**A.** (None)
**B.** Day
**C.** Of
**D.** Service

40. **A.** (No change)
**B.** area middle, and high school, students
**C.** area middle, and high school students
**D.** area middle and high school students

"United City Charities provided us with funds for the new equipment, and the volunteers installed <u>it</u> in
41
less than a day."

## [3]

Several teams worked with the Eco-Maniacs, a community organization interested in protecting the environment. "We cleaned litter out of Rock Creek and Park Lake all day," said volunteer Mike McKasky, a customer service representative at Medill Communications. "We probably <u>halled</u> 1,000 pounds of <u>refuse</u>
42 42
from our <u>group's</u> section of the creek." Dana Lewis,
42
president of the Eco-Maniacs, said, "<u>Were</u> <u>grateful</u> for
43 43
the <u>aid</u> that the United City Charities <u>show</u> us through-
43 44
out the year, but we especially value the support of volunteers <u>which</u> are willing to work hard to make
45
our community a better place."

## [4]

Other volunteers worked at area hospitals and senior centers. A team of volunteers worked all day at Memorial Hospital. "Our team helped fix up an old storage area near the emergency room to build a new waiting room for families with <u>children, said</u>
46
<u>one volunteer. We</u> washed and painted the walls and
46
put in new flooring." According to the hospital,

41. **A.** (No change)
    **B.** them
    **C.** themselves
    **D.** its

42. Which of the following words, if any, is misspelled?
    **A.** (None)
    **B.** halled
    **C.** refuse
    **D.** group's

43. Which of the following words, if any, is misspelled?
    **A.** (None)
    **B.** Were
    **C.** grateful
    **D.** aid

44. **A.** (No change)
    **B.** shows
    **C.** showing
    **D.** is showed

45. **A.** (No change)
    **B.** when
    **C.** where
    **D.** who

46. **A.** (No change)
    **B.** children, said one volunteer we
    **C.** children," said one volunteer. "We
    **D.** children", said one volunteer. "We

another team of volunteers will finish the job next week.

## [5]

[1] "This important event takes place yearly," said
<sub>47</sub>
Latisha Harris, president of United City Charities.

[2] "While residents support our member charities through donations, todays' event is an opportunity
<sub>48</sub>
for residents to become involved in the community in a personal way. [3] It's a great opportunity to meet neighbors and make new friends while making our community better." [4] This important community event takes place every year in October, but residents do not need to wait until next year to volunteer. [5] Each year, we find that volunteers want to stay involved all year. [6] "Our employees began participating in the Day of Service in 2011," said Thomas Ahlbeck, a partner at Ahlbeck, Gadini, and Carson Accounting. [7] "Several of our employees volunteer in that school throughout the year
<sub>49</sub>
weekly. [8] It's great to know our work is helping
<sub>49</sub>
children. [9] Next year, we are going to offer after-school jobs to a few of the students during tax preparation season." [10] According to Harris, "We refer volunteers to charities every day, and we have a

47. A. (No change)
    B. year,"
    C. each yearly,"
    D. each year"

48. A. (No change)
    B. todays
    C. today's
    D. todays's

49. A. (No change)
    B. volunteer in that school weekly throughout the year
    C. volunteer throughout the year in that school weekly
    D. throughout the year volunteer weekly in that school

matching program that helps volunteers find organizations that need their skills. [11] Our 300 member charities are eager to have the support of our volunteers every day of the year." 50

50. The writer is considering splitting Paragraph 5 into two paragraphs. The best place to begin a new paragraph would be with

A. Sentence 3.
B. Sentence 4.
C. Sentence 5.
D. Sentence 6.

**IF YOU FINISH BEFORE TIME IS CALLED, CHECK YOUR WORK ON THIS SECTION ONLY. DO NOT WORK ON ANY OTHER SECTION IN THE TEST.**

# Part 2

**1 Essay**

**Time: 45 Minutes**

**Directions:** This is a test of your writing skills. You have 45 minutes to prepare and write your response. Your essay will be scored based on the following criteria:

- Development and support of a main idea with examples and details
- Clear and effective organization of ideas, including an introduction, body, and conclusion; logical paragraphs; and effective transitions between and within paragraphs
- Appropriate language use, including varied vocabulary, varied sentence patterns, and appropriate voice
- Clarity and use of Standard Written English

---

A psychologist was recently interviewed on a local TV talk show about excessive violence in movies, television, and video games. He says that the violence people see is excessive and influences their behavior negatively.

---

Write an essay for the TV station's website to persuade readers to accept your opinion about whether violence in movies, television, and video games is excessive and affects people's behavior negatively. Think carefully about reasons that will help others understand your position as well as examples and details that you can use to support your position.

IF YOU FINISH BEFORE TIME IS CALLED, CHECK YOUR WORK ON THIS SECTION ONLY. DO NOT WORK ON ANY OTHER SECTION IN THE TEST.

# Answer Key

| | | | | |
|---|---|---|---|---|
| 1. C | 11. C | 21. D | 31. D | 41. A |
| 2. D | 12. B | 22. C | 32. D | 42. B |
| 3. B | 13. D | 23. A | 33. A | 43. B |
| 4. B | 14. B | 24. C | 34. D | 44. B |
| 5. C | 15. A | 25. D | 35. D | 45. D |
| 6. C | 16. D | 26. D | 36. C | 46. C |
| 7. C | 17. D | 27. C | 37. A | 47. A |
| 8. A | 18. D | 28. B | 38. A | 48. C |
| 9. A | 19. C | 29. A | 39. C | 49. B |
| 10. C | 20. A | 30. C | 40. D | 50. B |

# Answer Explanations

## Part 1

1. **C. that American workers are spending too much time on email (Misplaced Modifier/Language Facility)** Option C is correct. This prepositional phrase should go at the end of the clause because it modifies the entire predicate. For this reason, the other options (A, B, and D) are incorrect.

2. **D. work, as well as (Fragments/Writing Conventions)** Option D is correct. The original sentence is a fragment because it lacks a complete subject and verb. For this reason, Option A is incorrect. Option D corrects the error by joining the fragment to the previous sentence with a comma and the transitional phrase *as well as*. Option B is incorrect because it creates a kind of comma splice by omitting *as well as* and joining the phrase to the sentence. Option C is incorrect because it does not include the comma required to introduce a phrase with *as well as*.

3. **B. could be spent (Verb Tense/Language Facility)** Option B is correct. This verb phrase is in the passive voice, so the past participle *spent* is required. For this reason, Option A is incorrect. Options C and D omit a key part of the passive voice, a form of the verb *be*. Option C also needs the past participle *spent* instead of *spend*.

4. **B. dr. (Capitalization/Writing Conventions)** Option B is correct. The abbreviation *dr.* should be capitalized because it is part of a person's name. There is no need to capitalize the words in the other options (C and D) because they are not proper nouns.

5. **C. Day said, "An inbox full of unanswered email, with more coming in every minute, is a reminder of unfinished tasks with new tasks coming in all the time." (Punctuation/Writing Conventions)** Option C is correct because a quotation introduced with *said* needs a comma after *said,* opening quotation marks, and a capital letter. For this reason, Options A and B are incorrect. In addition, Option B incorrectly places the period outside of the closing quotation marks. For this reason, Option D is also incorrect.

315

6. **C. tacks (Spelling/Writing Conventions)** Option C is correct. The writer confused the homonym *tax* with *tacks.* The other words in the other options (B and D) are spelled correctly.

7. **C. are (Subject-Verb Agreement/Writing Conventions)** Option C is correct because the subject of this verb, *things,* is plural, so a plural verb is required. For this reason, Option A is incorrect. Option B is incorrect because *be* is not a complete verb, which makes the sentence a fragment. Option D is incorrect because there is no reason to use the past tense in this sentence.

8. **A. (No change) (Paragraph Structure/Organization)** Option A is correct. Sentence 12 acts as the thesis statement for the whole article, so it should be the last sentence in the introductory paragraph. For this reason, all the other options (B, C, and D) are incorrect.

9. **A. (No change) (Adjectives and Adverbs/Writing Conventions)** Option A is correct because *likely* is an adjective that is correctly modified by the adverb *most* (which means "to the greatest degree"). Options B and C are incorrect because *mostly* is an adjective that means "usually true or correct." Options B and D are also incorrect because the adjective *likely* is required here.

10. **C. it (Pronoun Reference/Writing Conventions)** Option C is correct because the antecedent of this pronoun is *email,* which is singular, so the singular pronoun *it* is required here. Therefore, Option A, which has a plural pronoun (*them*), is incorrect. A singular object pronoun, not a plural possessive pronoun (Option B) or a reflexive pronoun (Option D) is required here, so those options are incorrect.

11. **C. sound or message (Punctuation/Writing Conventions)** Option C is correct because when two nouns are joined by *and,* no punctuation is needed. Therefore, the remaining options (A, B, and D) are incorrect.

12. **B. you (Pronoun Reference/Writing Conventions)** Option B is correct because the sentence is referring to *you,* the object of the verb *interrupt,* so the object pronoun *you* is required. Therefore, Option A is incorrect. Option C is incorrect because there is no reason to use the reflexive pronoun *yourself* here because the subject of the sentence is *email,* not *you.* Option D is incorrect because there is no reason to use the possessive adjective *your* here in place of an object pronoun.

13. **D. email is (Punctuation/Writing Conventions)** Option D is correct because there is no reason to use a comma between the subject and the verb of the sentence. For this reason, Option A is incorrect. Option B is incorrect because adding *it* makes the sentence a comma splice. Option C is incorrect because a semicolon is used to join two independent clauses.

14. **B. When a topic requires a lot of clarification and discussion, the phone (Subordination/Language Facility)** Option B is correct because when a dependent clause comes before an independent clause, the two clauses are separated by a comma. For this reason, Option A is incorrect. Options C and D are incorrect because they lack the necessary comma after *discussion* and because there is no reason to include a comma between two nouns joined by *and* (Option C) or to separate the subject and the verb (Option D).

15. **A. (No change) (Transitional Words and Phrases/Organization)** Option A is correct. The transitional phrase *For example* correctly signals that the information in the sentence is an illustration of the idea presented in the previous sentence. The other options (B, C, and D) present transitional phrases that do not make sense.

16. **D. won (Spelling/Writing Conventions)** Option D is correct because the writer confused the homonym *won* with the word *one.* The words in the other options (B and C) are spelled correctly.

17. **D. However, opting out will reduce the amount of unwanted email. (Paragraph Structure/Relevance)** Option D is correct because it introduces information directly relevant to the topic of the paragraph: reducing unwanted email. Option A may be true, but is less relevant to the topic of the paragraph than Option D. Options B and C are incorrect because the main idea of the paragraph is reducing unwanted email, not the value of it.

18. **D. send. This way it's (Run-On Sentence/Language Facility)** Option D is correct because this sentence is a run-on. Dividing the sentence in two with a period and a capital letter creates two complete sentences. Therefore, Option A is incorrect. Option B does not correct the run-on and introduces a new error: There is no reason to change the subject and verb of the sentence to the possessive word *its*. Option C is incorrect because it creates a comma splice.

19. **C. from a particular sender or on a certain topic (Parallel Structure/Language Facility)** Option C is correct. This part of the sentence lacks parallel structure because *or* joins a prepositional phrase and a noun phrase. Option C corrects the problem by adding the preposition *on,* so that *or* joins two prepositional phrases. Option B is incorrect because adding a comma does not correct the faulty parallel structure. Option D is incorrect because deleting *a* does not fix the faulty parallel structure.

20. **A. (No change) (Capitalization/Writing Conventions)** Option A is correct because this is the complete name of the club, which is a proper noun. Therefore, all the words in the name should be capitalized. For this reason, Options B, C, and D are incorrect.

21. **D. its (Pronoun Reference/Writing Conventions)** Earlier in the sentence, the club is referred to as *its,* so *its* is the correct form of the pronoun to use here. The other options (A, B, and C) introduce unnecessary shifts in pronoun reference.

22. **C. are (Subject-Verb Agreement/Writing Conventions)** Option C is correct because the subject of this sentence is the plural noun *tables,* so a plural verb is necessary. For this reason, Option A is incorrect. There is no reason to change the verb to *have* or a form of *have,* so Options B and D are incorrect.

23. **A. (No change) (Transitional Words and Phrases/Organization)** Option A is correct because the transitional word *Therefore* indicates the correct relationship among ideas: cause-and-effect. The transitional words and phrases in the other options do not indicate the correct relationship among the ideas. *Unfortunately* (Option B) and *In contrast* (Option D) indicate contrast, and *In addition* (Option B) indicates addition of another supporting idea.

24. **C. meetings during (Sentence Fragments/Language Facility)** Option C is correct because the phrase *During the colder months of the year* cannot stand alone as a sentence. Option C corrects this error by joining it to the preceding sentence as an adverbial phrase that says when the action in the sentence took place. For this reason, Option A is incorrect. Option B is incorrect because there is no reason to use a semicolon to join this phrase to the preceding sentence. Semicolons are used to join two independent clauses. Option D is incorrect because there is no reason to use a comma to separate this adverbial phrase from the rest of the sentence.

25. **D. rite (Spelling/Writing Conventions)** Option D is correct because the writer confused the homonym *rite* ("ceremony") with *right* ("having legal authority to act in a certain way"). The words in the other options (A, B, and C) are spelled correctly.

26. **D. safety and security of the building (Punctuation/Writing Conventions)** Option D is correct because two nouns joined by *and* do not need a comma. Therefore, Option A is incorrect. Option B retains the unnecessary comma and introduces a parallel structure error. Option C introduces a parallel structure error and incorrectly uses a semicolon to join the two phrases.

27. **C. should reside in Parkton, be 13 years old or older, and have a valid pass for the community center (Parallel Structure/Writing Conventions)** Option C is correct because it corrects the faulty parallel structure by putting three verb phrases in parallel structure. For this reason, Option A is incorrect. Option B attempts to fix the parallel structure error, but introduces a verb tense error; there is no reason to use *should have resided*. Option D does not correct the parallel structure error; the second phrase is an adjective phrase and should be a verb phrase to match the other phrases in the sentence.

28. **B. User passes (Spelling/Writing Conventions)** Option B is correct. *User passes* is needed here to parallel *Senior passes* in the next sentence. For this reason, Option A is incorrect. There is no such word as *users's*. Option C incorrectly changes to possessive (*User's passes*). There is no reason to use an apostrophe after *passes* (Option D).

29. **A. (No change) (Adjectives and Adverbs/Writing Conventions)** Option B is correct because the adjective *monthly* is used correctly to modify *fee*. Therefore, the other options (B, C, and D) are incorrect.

30. **C. room, but they cannot (Run-On Sentence/Language Facility)** Option C is correct because this option corrects the comma splice in the sentence by adding *but*. Therefore, Option A is incorrect. There is no reason to add commas after *but* and *cannot,* so Option B is incorrect. Option D correctly inserts but; however, it neglects to precede *but* with a comma.

31. **D. (Do not use this sentence; the article is best as written.) (Relevance/Organization)** Option D is correct because this detail is not relevant to the article, so it should not be included. For this reason, the other options (A, B, and C) are incorrect.

32. **D. clean, orderly, and free of trash (Parallel Structure/Language Facility)** Option D is correct. The original sentence has faulty parallel structure, and Option D fixes this problem by making the third item in the list an adjective phrase. For this reason, Option A is incorrect. Option B is incorrect because commas are not needed when items in a list are each joined together with *and*. Option C is incorrect because the phrase *be free of trash* is not parallel with the other two words in the list, which are adjectives.

33. **A. (None) (Capitalization/Writing Conventions)** Option A is correct. None of the words are proper nouns or adjectives, so none of them need to be capitalized. For this reason, the other options (B, C, and D) are incorrect.

34. **D. Remove Sentence 4. (Relevance/Organization)** Option D is correct. Sentence 4 is not relevant to the main idea of the letter, which is the agreement between the community center and the club. For this reason, the remaining options (A, B, and C) are incorrect.

35. **D. Tuesday, January 3, 2017, (Punctuation/Writing Conventions)** Option D is correct because when writing the date, the day of the week, the date, and the year should all followed by commas. Only Option D has commas in all these places. The remaining options are incorrect: Option A omits the commas after *3* and *2017;* Option B omits the comma after *Tuesday* and adds an unneeded comma after *January;* and Option C omits the comma after *2017*.

36. **C. As a registered community organization, the club can also use our other facilities (Dangling Modifiers/Language Facility)** Option C is correct. The original sentence contains a dangling modifier; the main clause lacks a subject for the introductory phrase to refer to. Only Option C provides such a subject, *the club.* For this reason, Option A is incorrect. Options B and D both contain dangling modifiers because in each sentence, the initial phrase lacks a clear subject to refer to in the independent clause, so are incorrect.

37. **A. (No change) (Transitional Words and Phrases/Organization)** Option A is correct because *Unfortunately* indicates the correct relationship between the sentences: *Unfortunately* indicates that contrasting or contradictory information about the previous sentence is coming. The remaining options (B, C, and D) do not indicate this relationship between the sentences, so they are incorrect.

38. **A. (No change; the letter is best as written.) (Paragraph Structure/Organization)** Option A is correct. Paragraph 9 is the concluding paragraph of the letter, so it should stand alone. For this reason, the other options (B, C, and D) are incorrect.

39. **C. Of (Capitalization/Writing Conventions)** Option C is correct. *Of* is not a very important word in this proper noun, the name of an organization, so it should not be capitalized. The words in the remaining options (B and D) are important words that should be capitalized in a proper noun.

40. **D. area middle and high school students (Punctuation/Writing Conventions)** Option D is correct. There are only two items in the series, so commas are not needed to separate them. For this reason, Options A, B, and C, which use commas to separate the two items in the series, are incorrect. Option A has additional, unneeded commas after *area* and *school*. Option B has an additional unneeded comma after *school*.

41. **A. (No change) (Pronoun Reference/Writing Conventions)** Option A is correct because *it* is an object pronoun that agrees with the singular antecedent *equipment*. Option B is incorrect because *them* is a plural object pronoun. Option C does not make sense because the volunteers installed the *equipment*, not *themselves*. Option D is incorrect because an object pronoun is required, and *its* is a possessive adjective.

42. **B. halled (Spelling/Writing Conventions)** Option B is the answer because the writer confused the homonym *hall* ("a long, narrow passage in a building") with *haul* ("move something large and heavy with effort"). *Hall* is a noun; there is no such word as *halled*. The words in the other options (C and D) are spelled correctly.

43. **B. Were (Spelling/Writing Conventions)** Option B is correct. The writer confused the homonym *were* (a past tense form of the verb *be*) with the contraction *we're (we are)*. The words in the other options (C and D) are spelled correctly.

44. **B. shows (Subject-Verb Agreement/Writing Conventions)** Option B is correct because even though *United City Charities* ends in a final *-s*, this organization name is singular, so it needs a singular verb. For this reason, Option A, which has a plural verb, is incorrect. Option C is incorrect because *showing* is not a complete verb, which makes the sentence into a fragment. Option D does not make sense.

45. **D. who (Relative Clauses/Language Facility)** Option D is correct because the antecedent of this essential relative pronoun is human, so the only relative pronoun in the options that makes sense is *who*. The relative pronoun *which* (Option A) is used only in nonessential relative clauses and is not used to refer to people. The relative pronoun *when* (Option B) is used to refer to a time. The relative pronoun *where* (Option C) is used to refer to a location.

46. **C. children," said one volunteer. "We (Punctuation/Writing Conventions)** Option C is correct because it uses commas and quotation marks correctly: A comma is required after *children* and before the closing quotation marks, and opening quotation marks and a capital letter are required for *We*. Option B does not have the required quotation marks and capital letter; in addition, removing the period results in a run-on sentence. Option D is incorrect because after *children*, the comma should come before the closing quotation marks.

47. **A. (No change) (Adjective and Adverb Errors/Writing Conventions)** Option A is correct because the adverb *yearly* is used correctly in this sentence. It tells the frequency with which the action in the sentence takes place. Option B is incorrect because an adverb, not a noun, is needed to modify this sentence. Option C does not make sense. *Each year* (Option D) is a construction that can be used in place of *yearly,* but this option deletes the comma required before the closing quotation marks.

48. **C. today's (Spelling/Writing Conventions)** Option C is correct. *Today* is a singular noun, so an apostrophe and an *s* are needed to make it possessive. For this reason, Option A is incorrect. Option B omits the required apostrophe. Option D is an incorrect spelling of a possessive.

49. **B. volunteer in that school weekly throughout the year (Misplaced Modifiers/Language Facility)** Option B is correct because it places the modifier *weekly* closer to the verb it modifies. For this reason, Option A is incorrect. Options C and D contain different misplaced modifiers.

50. **B. Sentence 4 (Paragraph Structure/Organization)** Option B is correct because as written, Paragraph 5 has two main ideas: advantages of participating in the event and ways that people can participate throughout the year. The second topic begins with Sentence 4, so that is the best place to begin a new paragraph. For this reason, Option A is incorrect. Options C and D are incorrect because these options divide the information about participation throughout the year into separate paragraphs.

# Part 2

Use the Learner-Friendly HiSET Essay Scoring Rubric on pages 149–150 and these sample essays with score explanations to evaluate and score your essay. If possible, ask a teacher or a friend who is good at writing to evaluate and score your writing for you. Whether or not another person can review your essay, you should always use the rubric and sample essays to evaluate and score your essay yourself. Set aside your essay for a day or two so you can view it with fresh eyes. Then compare your essay to the sample essays. Find the sample essay that most closely resembles your essay. Then read the descriptions in the rubric for that score as well as the scores above and below it. Select the description that best matches your essay. That should give you a good idea of your final score. If you were able to have another person score your essay, compare the two results. Use the information you learn to figure out ways you can improve your writing.

## Sample Response, Score = 1

Bam! Zap! Kaboom! That's what happens when Batman punches or kicks or hits a bad guy. I love Batman, crime shows, and action movies with lots of car chases, explosions, guns, nives, and fighting. Kung fu movies are really fun my favorite kung fu movies star Jackie Chan, he is my very favorite actor, but I like Arnold Schwartzenegger movies, too.

**Explanation:** The information in the essay is not relevant to the topic. The essay does not have an introduction or conclusion, and it does not organize ideas into paragraphs or use transitions. It has little variety in vocabulary, a long and drawn out run-on sentence, and many errors in grammar and usage that impede understanding.

## Sample Response, Score = 2

I am writing to state my disagreement with the point of view expressed by a psychologist about excessive violence. I do not believe that there is excessive violence in TV, movies, and games. These games are not really, only fiction. The movies are just for entertainment, and so it is not a problem that they contane violent. Everyone who watches these shows and games knows that they are not real, only fake, and so will not be affected by them. The movies are fun, too. I like to watch car chases and explosions. These movies are good to see in 3D. Therefore, I do not believe that violence is excessive. I hope that everybody disagrees with these psychologists.

**Explanation:** The essay has one relevant idea, but the essay is repetitious. There is an attempt to write an introduction and conclusion, but ideas are not organized into paragraphs. The vocabulary is limited and awkward, and there are many errors in grammar and spelling that interfere with understanding.

## Sample Response, Score = 3

I heard that on a recent TV talk show, a psichologist complained that there is too much violints on TV and in games, but I disagree. I love to play a lot of different games, such as Car Chase and SWAT. These games have a lot of car chases, eplosions, and deaths, but I am not a violint person because of them. I am jus a normal guy who likes to play video games after work.

In addition, I like the games because they are interactive and fun. Sometimes my friends come over to play, or we play online together from our homes. When we see each other we can talk and laugh about our mos recent online adventures. We are not violint at all. In fact, I would say that the games are healthy because after I play, I don't feel stressed at all. I think that the games are a good way to relax and unwind. I feel the same way after watching an action movie. I really like action movies where the hero accomplishes an important goal, such as preventing a war or stopping a terrorist.

In conclusion, I think that this psichologist has the wrong idea about violints. The games and movies he complains about do not make me a violint person. They are ways to have fun with my friends and are good ways to unwind and relax. I think that this psichologist should lighten up and learn to have more fun.

**Explanation:** The essay includes relevant ideas, but they are not explained fully. The essay has an introduction and conclusion, but the introduction is very short. The essay has the beginning of a paragraph structure, but combines the introduction and first body paragraph. The tone is also too informal at times. The essay does not use transitions, but ideas are in a logical order. The essay has many errors in vocabulary, spelling, grammar, and sentence structure.

## Sample Response, Score = 4

A psychologist on a TV talk show recently said that movies, TV shows, and video games have too much violence. As a mother of three young boys, I am concerned about all of this violence. I think that seeing so much violence is bad for children, is a bad influence on adults, and prevents us from watching better options.

My three sons are fascinated by violent movies and TV shows. However, I have noticed that after they see a violent program or play a violent game, there behavior is different. They tend to disagree and fight more. One of the friends of my oldest son recently got into a fight in school after he and my son had gone to see a violent movie over the weekend. According to his mom, he was acting out the story he saw in the movie. And my youngest son always has terrible nightmares if he watch a violent TV show with his brothers.

I think that all of this violence is a bad influence on adults, too. Adults need to learn that they need to solve their problems with words, not guns. There is too much violence happening in our streets today. I think that people have become used to violence, and they are not upset or disturbed when it happens in real life, especially if it is not them. My old neighborhood had problems with drive-by shootings and gun fights with gang members and police. It was so bad we moved away. But, many people were not outraged by this violence, but just accepted it.

Third, all of these violent movies, TV shows, and games keep us from more valuable programs. There are many good programs on TV such as comedies and documentaries, but people are too busy watching crime and action shows. And there are a lot of fun video games, too, that are no violent.

In conclusion, people need to realize that all of this violence is very bad to children, has a bad effect on adults, and keeps us from more valuable programs and games. I hope that the government will do something about all this violence before it gets completely out of control.

**Explanation:** This essay has three main supporting ideas, each of which is somewhat developed, though there is still not enough information and detail. The essay has fairly well-developed introductory and concluding paragraphs, and groups related ideas into three supporting paragraphs. The essay uses mostly simple transitions between paragraphs. The essay has some problems with sentence structure and variety, as well as some errors in spelling and grammar, but these do not interfere with understanding.

## Sample Response, Score = 5

On a recent TV show, a psychologist brought up a very important issue in our society, violence in media. According to the psychologist, all of the violence in movies, TV shows, and games are having a negative effect on society. I do not agree with this psychologist. I believe that his point of view is exaggerated. Not all movies, films, and games are violent, people can distinguish fiction from reality, and many of the programs he complains about are interesting and fun.

First of all, the psychologist is focusing on only certain movies, TV shows, and games. There are many more shows, movies and games than the ones he is talking about, and people see a variety of different kinds of media each day. I like action movies, for example, but these are not the only movies I watch. Sometimes I like to watch a nice love story with my wife, or see a comedy or adventure. I also watch the news, read books and magazines online, and go to concerts. So while there are many movies that have a lot of violence, these are not the only kinds of media available to us.

In addition, I think that this psychologist is really underestimating people. He seems to think that people cannot tell fiction from reality. People know that these movies are not true and that the world does not really work this way, just as they know that things in a science fiction movie are not really true. For example, we all know that there are not violent explosions or big car chases with hundreds of police cars every day, though we enjoy seeing those things in movies. While I understand his concern that people will be influenced by this violence, I think that he needs to realize that people are not as foolish and gullible as he thinks.

Third, many of the movies and TV shows that he is complaining about take on important subjects or provide valuable entertainment. For example, I recently watched the film *True Lies* on cable. This is a really interesting action movie. It examines a lot of important issues such as honesty in our relationships. I think that this movie is really about patriotism and sacrifices people make to help our country. Other films, such as the Indiana Jones movies, have a lot of violence, but these movies are fun and enjoyable adventures that the whole family can watch.

In conclusion, though I share his concern that there is too much violence in the world, I do not think that these movies, shows, and games are the cause. I think that there are plenty of movies, TV shows, and games that are not violent, that people can tell fiction from fact, and that these movies take on important subjects and provide entertainment. I think that this psychologist has a very negative and narrow view about people and their abilities, and I hope that I can continue to watch and enjoy all the different kinds of entertainment that are available.

**Explanation:** This essay has three sophisticated main supporting ideas, and each one has well-developed supporting reasons, examples, or details. It also brings up and addresses a counterargument from the psychologist. The essay has an introduction and conclusion and organizes ideas into supporting paragraphs. The essay uses transitions in many places and has some variety in sentence patterns. It has a few errors, but these do not interfere with understanding.

## Sample Response, Score = 6

Are you concerned about violence and crime in our community? Last weekend, there were 7 deaths of young people in my city from violent shootings. In one case, a young girl was struck by a stray bullet fired in a drive-by shooting outside her house. According to a psychologist on a recent talk show, violence in the TV shows, movies, and games that people watch and play may have some role in this rising violence. I agree that all of this violence is excessive, that it influences people's behavior, and that people need to have better entertainment options.

According to a recent study I read in a magazine, people are exposed to a huge amount of violence in the media. According to the article, people on average see thousands of gunfights, car chases, explosions, fires, and deaths in a year. That is a huge amount of violence. In addition, people see the effects of war and terrorism on TV every day. After 9–11, people saw film of planes crashing into the World Trade Center again and again for days. And in a single video game, a player can kill hundreds of people, or even be killed himself. That is way too much violence.

Second, this violence seems to have an effect on people. The rate of crime and violence seems to go up every year. As I mentioned before, this summer has been especially violent in my city. The 7 deaths I just mentioned are just the beginning. It's only late August, and the number of murders is already greater than last year. I believe that seeing all of this violence is making people less sensitive to violence in their daily lives. This year, there has not been a single protest about the number of murders until the young girl was shot by accident. That upset people, but what about all the young men who were shot because of arguments that got out of control, drug dealing, or other crimes? No one seems to care, and the violence seems to keep on increasing.

Finally, there really are not many entertainment options that do not contain violence of one sort or another. We need more variety in TV, movies, and games. Very few television shows do not include violence of one sort or another. I am not completely opposed to violence, however. Violence is a part of life, so it should be part of movies and TV, when relevant, but the amount of it should be appropriate. We need more options, such as concert shows, comedies, documentaries, sports shows, and nature programs. All of these are valuable options that people could appreciate and enjoy without all of the violence. People also need to get away from the media and participate in real life. People should be playing sports, going to concerts, and eating in restaurants with family and friends.

In conclusion, while some violence is OK, there are too many violent programs, the programs have desensitized people to violence, and people need to find better options and find other things to do in addition to watching TV and movies. I hope that the number of violent programs will go down so that people will not be so violent in real life.

**Explanation:** This essay has three main supporting ideas, and each one has well-developed supporting reasons, examples, or details. It has an introduction that gets the reader's attention by asking a provocative question. It also brings up and addresses a counterargument in a key place by mentioning that some violence is acceptable, since it is a part of life. The essay organizes ideas into effective supporting paragraphs and uses transitions between and within paragraphs. It has few errors and variety in sentence patterns; grammar, vocabulary, and usage are sophisticated.

# XI. Mathematics Full-Length Practice Test with Answer Explanations

**50 Items**

**Time: 90 Minutes**

**Directions:** This is a test of your skills in applying mathematical concepts and solving mathematical problems. Read each item carefully and decide which of the five alternatives best answers the item.

There are relatively easy problems scattered throughout the test. Thus, do not waste time on problems that are too difficult; go on, and return to them if you have time.

---

1. What is the value of $6(4w - 5v^2)$ when $w = 3$ and $v = -2$?

   A. $-1,440$
   B. $-528$
   C. $-48$
   D. $192$
   E. $672$

2. A cleaning solution calls for $\frac{1}{2}$ cup of ammonia to be mixed with 2 cups of water. Which expression gives the correct amount of ammonia, $A$, that should be mixed with $\frac{1}{2}$ cup of water?

   A. $A = \frac{1}{2} \times \frac{1}{2}$

   B. $\dfrac{A}{2} = \dfrac{\frac{1}{2}}{\frac{1}{2}}$

   C. $\dfrac{A}{\frac{1}{2}} = \dfrac{\frac{1}{2}}{2}$

   D. $\dfrac{A}{\frac{1}{2}} = \dfrac{2}{\frac{1}{2}}$

   E. $A = \frac{1}{2} \times 2$

3. If $x + 4 = 9$, what is the value of $x^2 + 8x + 16$?

   A. $5$
   B. $25$
   C. $66$
   D. $81$
   E. $169$

4. A telephone number in the United States contains 10 digits (a 3-digit area code, a 3-digit prefix, and a 4-digit line number). The first digit in the area code and the prefix cannot be a 0 (that is to call an operator) or a 1. If there are no restrictions for the other digits, which expression correctly represents the number of possible telephone numbers in the United States?

   A. $10^{10}$
   B. $8 \times 10^{10}$
   C. $8 \times 10^{9}$
   D. $8^2 \times 10^{9}$
   E. $8^2 \times 10^{8}$

5. Marcus pays $95 for a plumber to visit his house and $35 per hour for the work done. Which equation represents the total amount, $A$, Marcus must pay if the plumber works for $t$ hours?

   A. $A = 95t + 35$
   B. $A = 35t + 95$
   C. $t = 95A + 35$
   D. $t = 35A + 95$
   E. $A = 120t$

6. A bull's-eye consists of three concentric circles. The innermost circle has a radius of 1, the middle circle has a radius of 3, and the outermost circle has a radius of 5. Which expression shows the area of the shaded part of the diagram below?

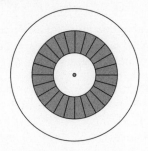

   A. $\pi$
   B. $8\pi$
   C. $9\pi$
   D. $16\pi$
   E. $25\pi$

7. A mole is a unit of measurement used in chemistry. The mass of one mole of water is 18.02 grams. The number of molecules in one mole of water is $6.22 \times 10^{23}$.

   Which expression correctly identifies how to find the mass of one molecule of water?

   A. $\dfrac{18.02}{6.22 \times 10^{23}}$

   B. $\dfrac{6.22 \times 10^{23}}{18.02}$

   C. $18.02 \times 6.22 \times 10^{23}$

   D. $18.02 + 6.22 \times 10^{23}$

   E. $6.22 \times 10^{23} - 18.02$

8. Nivine is evaluating the cost of the goods produced at her company. The cost of producing $n$ units of the company's best-selling product is $C = -20n^2 + 750n$. What is the cost of producing 30 units of the product?

   A. 4,500
   B. 17,250
   C. 18,000
   D. 21,300
   E. 21,900

9. Frank is checking some electrical circuits. The number of amps of electric current, $I$, that flow through a circuit with $V$ volts and resistance $R$ ohms is given by the formula $I = \sqrt{\dfrac{V}{R}}$. How many amps, rounded to the nearest tenth, are in a circuit with 120 volts and 20 ohms?

   A. 0.4
   B. 2.4
   C. 10.0
   D. 11.8
   E. 49.0

*Use the following summary and diagram to answer items 10 through 12.*

A summary of a survey completed by people attending a farmer's market indicating the methods by which they get local, state, and national news is shown.

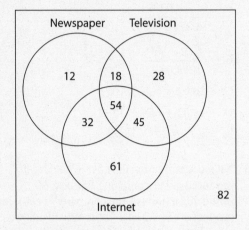

10. How many responders say that they get their news from sources <u>other than</u> a newspaper?

    A.  28
    B.  45
    C.  61
    D.  134
    E.  216

11. How many responders claim that they get their news from all three sources?

    A.  136
    B.  95
    C.  86
    D.  72
    E.  54

12. If a responder from this survey is selected at random, what is the probability that the responder gets news from the Internet but not from television?

    A.  $\dfrac{61}{332}$

    B.  $\dfrac{93}{332}$

    C.  $\dfrac{32}{332}$

    D.  $\dfrac{61}{105}$

    E.  $\dfrac{93}{105}$

13. The formula for converting degrees Celsius, $C$, from degrees Fahrenheit, $F$, is $C = \dfrac{5}{9}(F - 32)$.

    A typical temperature for a refrigerator is 40°F. What is the approximate corresponding temperature in degrees Celsius?

    A.  −14.4
    B.  −4.4
    C.  4.4
    D.  14.4
    E.  40

14. In the accompanying diagram of the Delta Corporation's logo, triangles $ABC$ and $DAC$, $BC = BA$ and $DC = DA$. The measure of $\angle DAC = 26°$, and the measure of $\angle B = 58°$. Which expression shows the measure of $\angle BAD$?

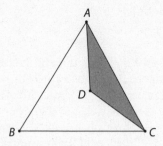

A. 30.5
B. 35
C. 61
D. 122
E. 128

15. The state legislature consists of $M$ members. Of these, $D$ members are Democrats. Which expression represents the ratio of the Democrats in the state legislature to those who are not Democrats?

A. $\dfrac{D}{M}$

B. $\dfrac{M}{D}$

C. $\dfrac{M-D}{D}$

D. $\dfrac{D}{M-D}$

E. $\dfrac{D}{M+D}$

16. A scale on a road map shows that 2.5 inches on the map corresponds to 90 miles on the road. The road map is put on a copier machine and a section of the map is enlarged with a 150% zoom feature. Two different points on this enlarged section of the map now appear to be 2.5 inches apart. What is the <u>actual</u> distance, in miles, between the two points?

A. 30
B. 60
C. 90
D. 135
E. 270

17. The weight of 1 mole of iron sulfate is 151.91 grams. If 1 mole of iron sulfate contains $6.022 \times 10^{23}$ molecules, which expression shows the weight of one molecule of iron sulfate?

A. $\dfrac{6.022 \times 10^{23}}{151.91}$

B. $\dfrac{151.91}{6.022 \times 10^{23}}$

C. $151.91 \times 6.022 \times 10^{23}$

D. $151.91 + 6.022 \times 10^{23}$

E. $6.022 \times 10^{23} - 151.91$

18. Which expression represents the number of hours in $w$ weeks, $d$ days, and $m$ minutes?

A. $w + d + m$

B. $168w + 24d + 60m$

C. $168w + \dfrac{d}{24} + \dfrac{m}{60}$

D. $168w + 24d + \dfrac{m}{60}$

E. $\dfrac{w}{168} + \dfrac{d}{24} + \dfrac{m}{60}$

19. Carly is planning a company meeting at the Flagship Hotel. The cost of renting a meeting room at the hotel is $650. The budget for the meeting is $2,100. The expectation is that 45 people will attend the meeting. If $C$ represents the amount spent per person for food and refreshments for the meeting, which of the following inequalities expresses the amount of money that can be spent per person on food and refreshments?

    A. $C + 650 \le 2{,}100$
    B. $45C \le 2{,}100$
    C. $45C + 650 \le 2{,}100$
    D. $C \le 45$
    E. $45C \le 2{,}100 + 650$

*The vertices of triangle ABC shown below have coordinates A(2, 4), B(9, 3), and C(2, 10). Use this information to answer items 20 and 21.*

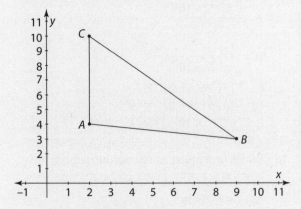

20. Which expression shows the area of triangle $ABC$? The formula for area of a triangle is $\frac{1}{2}$ base $\times$ height.

    A. $\sqrt{85}$
    B. 21
    C. 42
    D. $13 + \sqrt{85}$
    E. $13 + \sqrt{98}$

21. A line, $m$, through the point $(-3, 4)$ is drawn parallel to $\overline{BC}$. What is the value of the slope for $m$?

    A. $-7$
    B. $-1$
    C. $0$
    D. $1$
    E. $7$

22. A surveyor finds that three of the angles forming the corners of a parcel of land have measurements 70°, 125°, and 70°. The fourth corner of the parcel, $\angle C$, is in a pond and cannot be physically measured. Determine the number of degrees in the measure of this last angle.

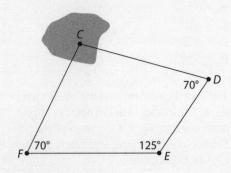

    A. 55
    B. 90
    C. 95
    D. 110
    E. 125

*The accompanying graph shows the relationship between the number of minutes past noon and the total number of meals sold by that time on a given weekday at the Rolling Gourmet Food Truck. Use this information to answer items 23 and 24.*

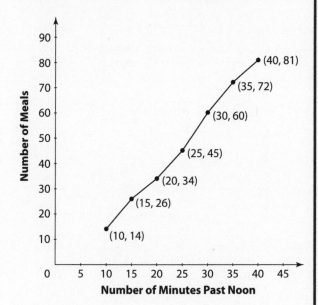

**Number of Minutes Past Noon**

23. During which time interval was the rate at which the meals were being sold the greatest?

   A. 10 to 15
   B. 15 to 20
   C. 20 to 25
   D. 25 to 30
   E. 30 to 35

24. What is average number of meals (rounded to the nearest one-hundredth) sold per minute during the 30-minute interval between $t = 10$ and $t = 40$?

   A. 1.80
   B. 2.03
   C. 2.23
   D. 2.60
   E. 11.57

25. To pay for the end-of-the-season cookout for his T-ball team, the coach needs to collect $2 for each player and $4 for each adult who will attend. If the coach receives a total of $66 for the adults and $t$ players, which expression represents the number of adults who paid to attend the cookout?

   A. $66 - 2t$
   B. $2t - 66$
   C. $4(66 - 2t)$
   D. $\dfrac{66}{4} - 2t$
   E. $\dfrac{66 - 2t}{4}$

26. One of the walls in Mr. and Mrs. Eslinger's living room is shaped as shown below. They decide that they will paint the upper region of the wall (designated *ABHCDEFG* in the diagram) a different color from the rest of the wall. What is the area, in square feet, of the upper region of this wall?

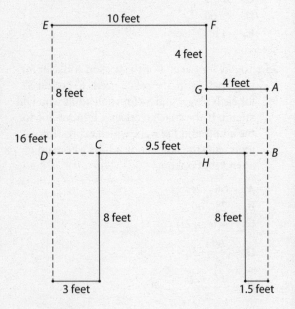

A. 56
B. 80
C. 96
D. 112
E. 224

27. The diagram below shows a Norman window, a rectangle with a semicircular section above it. What is the best estimate of perimeter of the frame of this window, to the nearest foot?

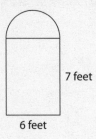

7 feet

6 feet

A. 13
B. 22
C. 26
D. 29
E. 39

*Use the data in the following table to answer items 28 and 29.*

A local radio station is determining if it should change the type of music it plays. The station surveyed listeners of different age groups about the kinds of music they want to hear. The summary is given below.

| Age Group | Classic Rock | Rap | Techno | Country | Totals |
|---|---|---|---|---|---|
| 13–19 | 47 | 174 | 191 | 121 | 533 |
| 20–29 | 127 | 79 | 34 | 219 | 459 |
| 30–39 | 219 | 45 | 12 | 178 | 454 |
| 40 or older | 321 | 12 | 0 | 156 | 489 |
| Totals | 714 | 310 | 237 | 674 | 1,935 |

28. What is the probability that a randomly selected listener who likes classic rock will be 40 years old or older?

   A.  $\dfrac{321}{489}$

   B.  $\dfrac{489}{1,935}$

   C.  $\dfrac{714}{1,935}$

   D.  $\dfrac{321}{714}$

   E.  $\dfrac{489}{714}$

29. What is the probability that a listener selected at random is between the ages of 30 and 39 or prefers country music?

   A.  $\dfrac{454}{1,935}$

   B.  $\dfrac{674}{1,935}$

   C.  $\dfrac{950}{1,935}$

   D.  $\dfrac{178}{454}$

   E.  $\dfrac{178}{674}$

30. If 40 bandages cost $3.50 and 60 bandages cost $5.10 and there is a linear relation between the number of bandages, $n$, in a package and its cost, $C$, which equation relates the number of bandages in a package and the cost per bandage?

   A.  $C = \$0.085n$
   B.  $C = \$0.0875n$
   C.  $C = \$0.08n$
   D.  $C = \$0.08n + \$0.30$
   E.  $C = \$0.30n + 0.08$

31. Allie spends $\frac{1}{3}$ of her monthly income on housing, $\frac{1}{4}$ on food, and $\frac{1}{8}$ on utilities. She deposits $\frac{1}{5}$ of her remaining income into her savings account. What part of her monthly income goes into her savings account?

    A. $\frac{7}{120}$

    B. $\frac{11}{120}$

    C. $\frac{17}{120}$

    D. $\frac{7}{24}$

    E. $\frac{17}{24}$

32. Stephan shoveled the snow that fell on the trapezoid-shaped sidewalk in front of the entrance to the building where he works. What is the total area, in square yards, of the sidewalk he shoveled? The formula for the area of a trapezoid is $\frac{1}{2}h(b_1 + b_2)$. The Pythagorean theorem is $a^2 + b^2 = c^2$.

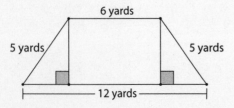

    A. 28
    B. 36
    C. 48
    D. 60
    E. 72

33. The diagram below shows a square floor tile with a circle in the center. Find the area of the shaded region. (Answer to the nearest tenth of a square inch.)

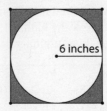

    A. 31.0
    B. 106.3
    C. 113.0
    D. 181.7
    E. 257.0

34. Due to a drop in the economy, Acme Inc. laid off 20% of its workforce in April. When the economy continued to stall, the company laid off 10% of the summer workforce in September. What percent of the original workforce was still employed after the September layoffs?

    A. 22
    B. 30
    C. 70
    D. 72
    E. 78

35. People between the ages of 1 and 70 should consume at least 600 units of vitamin D daily. Alice gets her vitamin D by drinking fat-free milk (which contains 150 units per 8 ounce serving) and from eggs (1 egg contains 25 units). Which expression represents the number of cups of milk, $m$, and the number of eggs, $e$, that Alice should consume each day to meet her vitamin D requirement? (*Note:* 1 cup = 8 ounces.)

    A. $150m + 25e \geq 600$
    B. $150m + 25e \leq 600$
    C. $150m + 250e = 600$
    D. $m + e > 600$
    E. $m + e < 600$

36. Alexis pays a total of $143.18, including sales tax, for a coat that was on sale with a 20% discount. The sales tax was 4% of the final price of the coat. Which expression will compute the original price of the coat, pre-sale and pre-tax?

   A. $143.18 × 0.80 × 0.04
   B. $143.18 × 0.80 × 1.04
   C. $\dfrac{\$143.18 \times 0.04}{0.80}$
   D. $\dfrac{\$143.18 \times 1.04}{0.80}$
   E. $\dfrac{\$143.18}{0.80 \times 1.04}$

37. Mr. and Mrs. Germain are landscaping part of their backyard. The landscaped portion of their backyard is a square measuring 16 feet per side. A circular garden will be included in the middle of the square with the circle touching each side of the square. The regions between the square and circle will be covered in stone. What is the number of square feet (rounded to the nearest whole number) that will be covered by the stone?

16 feet

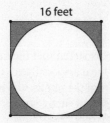

   A. 256
   B. 137
   C. 55
   D. 16
   E. 14

38. Arlene has $10 bills, $5 bills, and $1 bills in her wallet. The number of $1 bills is three times the number of $5 bills, and the number of $10 bills is two more than the number of $1 bills. The total value of the money in her wallet is $134. If $f$ represents the number of $5 bills in her wallet, which equation can be used to determine the number of $5 bills in her wallet?

   A. $10(f + 2) + 5f + 1(3f) = 134$
   B. $10(3f + 2) + 5f + 1(3f) = 134$
   C. $10(3f) + 5f + 1(3f + 2) = 134$
   D. $10f + 5(3f) + 1(3f + 2) = 134$
   E. $10f + 5(3f + 2) + 1(3f) = 134$

39. An experiment consists of spinning the spinner shown (all regions are the same size) and then rolling a six-sided die numbered 1 through 6. The phrase "the die shows" refers to the number at the top of the die. In the accompanying diagram, the die is showing a 2.

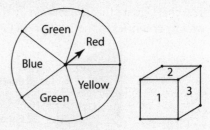

   What is the probability that the spinner lands in a region marked green and the die shows a 3?

   A. $\dfrac{1}{15}$
   B. $\dfrac{2}{15}$
   C. $\dfrac{17}{30}$
   D. $\dfrac{11}{15}$
   E. $\dfrac{5}{6}$

40. A teacher is checking 8 children's reading fluency. She had the children read a short passage aloud, and she recorded the number of seconds each one needed to read the passage. The recorded times were: 23, 12, 30, 19, 18, 43, 30, and 38. Which set of measures of central tendency is correct for the data?

A. Mean = 18.5, Median = 26.5, Mode = 30

B. Mean = 18.5, Median = 30, Mode = 26.5

C. Mean = 26.625, Median = 26.5, Mode = 30

D. Mean = 26.625, Median = 30, Mode = 26.5

E. Mean = 26.5, Median = 26.625, Mode = 30

*Use the data in the following graph to answer items 41 and 42.*

The chart shows the distribution of the medals won by countries in the 2014 Sochi Olympics.

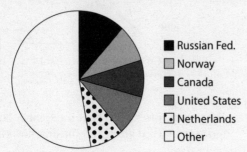

- ■ Russian Fed.
- □ Norway
- ■ Canada
- ▦ United States
- ⊡ Netherlands
- □ Other

41. If the measure of the angle of the sector representing Norway is 32°, about what percent of the medals awarded at Sochi were won by Norway?

A. 8
B. 9
C. 10
D. 32
E. 115

42. The host country, Russia, won 33 medals. If this represents approximately 11.4% of all the medals awarded in Sochi, how many total medals were awarded?

A. 256
B. 264
C. 289
D. 297
E. 376

43. A square that is made out of some flimsy material is bent to resemble a diamond. If the diagonals of the diamond are perpendicular to each other and bisect each other and the lengths of the diagonals are 12 and 16, what is the perimeter of the diamond?

 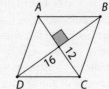

A. 10
B. 28
C. 20
D. 40
E. 112

44. A news report stated that the number of houses sold in the local area last year, 648, was down one-third from the number of houses sold the year before. How many houses were sold the year before?

A. 216
B. 324
C. 864
D. 972
E. 1,944

*Use the data in the following table to answer items 45 and 46.*

Team salaries for the 30 Major League Baseball (MLB) teams in 2014 are displayed.

| Salary (to the nearest $10 million) | Frequency |
|---|---|
| 240 | 1 |
| 210 | 1 |
| 180 | 1 |
| 160 | 2 |
| 150 | 1 |
| 130 | 4 |
| 110 | 5 |
| 100 | 1 |
| 90 | 6 |
| 80 | 5 |
| 70 | 1 |
| 50 | 2 |

*(Source: ESPN.com)*

45. What is the median salary (in millions of dollars) for the 30 teams?

   A. 52.3
   B. 105
   C. 110
   D. 120
   E. 130.8

46. If one of the major league baseball teams is selected at random, what is the probability that the team salary will be at least $110 million?

   A. $\dfrac{1}{5}$

   B. $\dfrac{7}{30}$

   C. $\dfrac{1}{3}$

   D. $\dfrac{1}{2}$

   E. $\dfrac{2}{3}$

47. Edwin wants to know the area of a rectangular fish pond in his backyard. If one of the sides of the pond is 8 feet, and the perimeter of the fish pond is 30 feet, then what is the total area of the fish pond, in square feet?

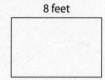

8 feet

   A. 22
   B. 38
   C. 56
   D. 176
   E. 240

48. A brick is in the form of a rectangular solid with a central hole that is also in the shape of a rectangular solid. The volume of the brick is equal to $L_1 \times W_1 \times H_1 - L_2 \times W_2 \times H_2$. Determine the number of cubic inches in the volume of the brick if $L_1 = 8$ inches, $W_1 = 3$ inches, $H_1 = 6$ inches, $L_2$ is half of $L_1$, $W_2$ is half of $W_1$, and $H_2$ is a third of $H_1$.

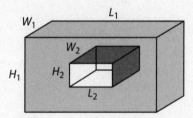

   A. 126
   B. 132
   C. 162
   D. 156
   E. 1,728

49. A business is said to "break even" when the costs and revenue are the same, or even. The revenue and cost functions for a company are shown in the accompanying graph. Which of the labeled points on the graph represent the point at which the company breaks even?

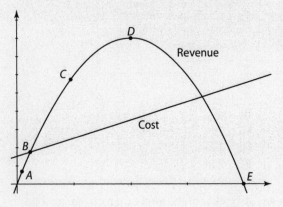

    A.  A
    B.  B
    C.  C
    D.  D
    E.  E

50. The results of a survey taken of the 298 employees of a certain corporation are displayed in the accompanying Venn diagram. According to this information, what is the probability that a manager selected at random will be a woman?

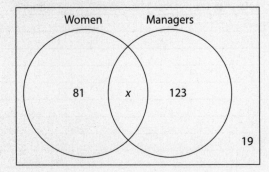

    A.  $\dfrac{75}{123}$

    B.  $\dfrac{75}{198}$

    C.  $\dfrac{75}{81}$

    D.  $\dfrac{75}{156}$

    E.  $\dfrac{75}{298}$

# Answer Key

| | | | | |
|---|---|---|---|---|
| 1. C | 11. E | 21. B | 31. A | 41. B |
| 2. C | 12. B | 22. C | 32. B | 42. C |
| 3. D | 13. C | 23. D | 33. A | 43. D |
| 4. E | 14. B | 24. C | 34. D | 44. D |
| 5. B | 15. D | 25. E | 35. A | 45. B |
| 6. B | 16. B | 26. C | 36. E | 46. D |
| 7. A | 17. B | 27. D | 37. C | 47. C |
| 8. A | 18. D | 28. D | 38. B | 48. B |
| 9. B | 19. C | 29. C | 39. A | 49. B |
| 10. E | 20. B | 30. D | 40. C | 50. B |

# Answer Explanations

1. **C. –48 (Numbers and Operations on Numbers: Order of Operations)** Option C is correct. When 3 and –2 are substituted, the expression becomes $6(4 \times 3 - 5(-2)^2) = 6(12 - 20) = 6(-8) = -48$. Option A is incorrect because 12 and –20 are multiplied to get –240; this result is then multiplied by 6. Option B is incorrect because $-5v^2$ is computed to be –100 by incorrectly multiplying 5 and –2 before squaring. Option D is incorrect because it wrongly computes $5v^2$ to be 20 and adds this to 12 rather than subtracting it from 12. Option E is incorrect because $5v^2$ is computed to be 100, and this is added to 12.

2. **C. $\dfrac{A}{\frac{1}{2}} = \dfrac{\frac{1}{2}}{2}$ ( Numbers and Operations on Numbers: Proportions)** Option C is correct because the proportion is written with the amount of ammonia written in the numerator and the amount of water in the denominator, with the right side of the equation representing the original mixture. Option A does not account for the original amount of water in the mixture. Options B and D are the same proportion with the numbers in the lower-left to upper-right diagonal interchanged. Option E does not have an appropriate meaning for this problem.

3. **D. 81 (Algebraic Concepts: Solving Linear Equations)** Option D is correct. If $x + 4 = 9$, then $x = 5$. Therefore, $x^2 + 8x + 16 = 5^2 + 8(5) + 16 = 25 + 40 + 16 = 81$. Option A represents the value of $x$, not of the expression $x^2 + 8x + 16$. Option B is the result of replacing $x$ with 1 in the expression $x^2 + 8x + 16$. Option C is the result of computing $5^2$ to be 10, not 25. Option E is the result of replacing $x$ with 9 in the expression $x^2 + 8x + 16$.

4. **E. $8^2 \times 10^8$ (Data Analysis: Probability and Statistics: Counting Principle)** Option E is correct because 2 of the slots in a 10-digit phone have 8 choices, while the remaining 8 slots have 10 choices. Option A ignores the restrictions stated for 0 and 1. Option B uses the 8 once and also contains 11 digits (using the 10 choices 10 times). Option C accounts for a 10-digit number but only one use of the restrictions on the first digit. Option D shows the number of possibilities for an 11-digit telephone number.

5. **B. $A = 35t + 95$ (Algebraic Concepts: Number Properties)** Option B is correct. Marcus pays $35 for each hour the plumber works on the job, so 35 and $t$ are multiplied together and 95 is added to the result: $A = 35t + 95$. Option A reverses these two values, indicating that the plumber is paid $95 per hour. Options C and D reverse the roles of the total amount $A$ and the number of hours $t$. Option E adds the hourly rate with the amount for the house call and makes this number the new hourly rate.

6. **B. $8\pi$ (Measurement and Geometry: Area and Perimeter)** Option B is correct because the correct area is the difference of the areas of the middle circle and the innermost circle. The area of the innermost circle is $\pi$ (Option A), and the area of the middle circle is $9\pi$ (Option C). Option D is the difference between the area of the outermost circle ($25\pi$) and the middle circle ($9\pi$). Option E is incorrect because it is the area of the outermost circle.

7. **A. $\dfrac{18.02}{6.22 \times 10^{23}}$ (Algebraic Concepts: Number Properties)** Option A is correct because it takes the mass of all the molecules and divides it by the number of molecules to compute mass per molecule: $\dfrac{18.02}{6.22 \times 10^{23}}$. Option B computes molecules per mass. Option C computes mass-molecules, a unit that is not appropriate, while options D and E have no meaning.

8. **A. 4,500 (Algebraic Concepts: Number Properties)** Option A is correct: $-20(30)^2 + 750(30) = -20(900) + 22{,}500 = -18{,}000 + 22{,}500 = 4{,}500$. Option B is the result of computing $20(30)^2 - 750$, Option C is $20(30)^2$, Option D is $-40(30) + 750(30)$, and Option E is $-20(30) + 750(30)$.

9. **B. 2.4 (Algebraic Concepts: Number Properties)** Option B is correct: $\sqrt{\dfrac{120}{20}} = \sqrt{6} \approx 2.4$. Option A reverses the 120 and 20 in the formula. Option C incorrectly subtracts the values 120 and 20, while Option D incorrectly adds them. Option E multiplies 120 and 20 and then takes the square root.

10. **E. 216 (Data Analysis: Probability and Statistics: Venn Diagrams)** Option E is correct because it adds up the number of responses outside the circle labeled newspaper: $61 + 45 + 28 + 82 = 216$. Option A represents people who get their news from television only. Option B represents those who get their news from both television and the Internet but not from other sources. Option C represents people who get their news from the Internet only. Option D represents people who get their news from only television and/or the Internet: $61 + 45 + 28 = 134$.

11. **E. 54 (Data Analysis: Probability and Statistics: Venn Diagrams)** Option E is correct because 54 responders, the intersection of the three circles, get their news from all three sources. Options A through D are incorrect because they include responders who do not get their news from all three sources. Option A wrongly adds to 54 the 82 people who get news from sources other than the newspaper, television, or the Internet: $82 + 54 = 136$. Option B represents responders who get their news from any two of the three sources ($18 + 32 + 45 = 95$) and omits the 54 who get their news from all three sources. Option C incorrectly adds to 54 the 32 responders who get their news from the Internet and the newspaper. Option D incorrectly adds to 54 the 18 who get their news from the newspaper and television.

12. **B. $\dfrac{93}{332}$ (Data Analysis: Probability and Statistics: Venn Diagrams, Probability)** Option B is correct because there are $61 + 32 = 93$ people who get their news from the Internet and the newspaper but not from television, and there are 332 total responders to the survey: $\dfrac{93}{332}$. Option A represents the

probability of those who get their news only from the Internet. Option C represents the probability of those who get their news from both the Internet and the newspaper, but not other sources. Options D and E have the wrong denominator: 105 represents the number of people who get their news from the Internet and/or the newspaper. Option D shows the probability that a person selected at random from 105 responders only get their news from the Internet. Option E represents the probability that a responder selected at random from 105 responders gets news from the Internet or from the Internet and the newspaper (32 + 61).

13. **C. 4.4 (Algebraic Concepts: Number Properties** Option C is correct because $\frac{5}{9}(40-32)=\frac{5}{9}(8)=\frac{40}{9}\approx 4.4$. Option A computes $\frac{9}{5}(32-40)$, while Option B incorrectly computes $\frac{5}{9}(32-40)$. Option D incorrectly computes $\frac{9}{5}(40-32)$, and Option E incorrectly computes $\frac{5}{9}(40+32)$.

14. **B. 35 (Measurement and Geometry: Angle Relationships)** Option B is correct. The measure of $\angle BAC = 61 : \left(\frac{180-58}{2}\right)$. The measure of $\angle DAC = 26$. Therefore, the measure of $\angle BAD = 61 - 26 = 35$. Option A is incorrect because there is no indication that segment $DA$ bisects $\angle BAC$. Option C is the measure of $\angle BAC$, and Option D is the sum of the measures of $\angle BAC$ and $\angle BCA$. Option E is the measure of $\angle ADC$.

15. **D. $\dfrac{D}{M-D}$ (Numbers and Operations on Numbers: Ratios)** Option D is correct. If $D$ members of the legislature are Democrats, then $M - D$ are not: $\dfrac{D}{M-D}$. Option A is incorrect because it shows the ratio of the number of Democrats to the number of members of the legislature. Option B is incorrect because it shows the ratio of the number of members of the legislature to the number of Democrats. Option C is incorrect because it is the reciprocal of the correct answer: the ratio of the number of non-Democrats to the number of Democrats. Option E is the ratio of the number of Democrats to the total of the number of members in the legislature and the number of Democrats.

16. **B. 60 (Numbers and Operations on Numbers: Ratios, Percent)** Option B is correct. Applying the magnification factor to the original map, two points on the map that were 2.5 inches apart are now $1.5 \times 2.5 = 3.75$ inches apart. The real life distance between these two points is still 90 miles. The scale for the enlarged map is now 3.75 inches = 90 miles. Write a proportion to find the distance corresponding to 2.5 inches on the new map:

$$\frac{3.75}{90} = \frac{2.5}{x}$$
$$3.75x = 2.5 \cdot 90$$
$$3.75x = 225$$
$$x = \frac{225}{3.75}$$
$$x = 60$$

Option A is incorrect because it changes the scale to $33\frac{1}{3}\%$. Option C is incorrect because it assumes no change in scale. Option D is incorrect because it increases the scale by 150%. and Option E is incorrect because it changes the scale to 300%.

17. **B.** $\dfrac{151.91}{6.022 \times 10^{23}}$ **(Numbers and Operations on Numbers: Order of Operations)** Option B is the answer because it divides the weight per mole by the number of molecules per mole to get the unit weight per molecule: $\dfrac{\text{grams}}{\text{mole}} \div \dfrac{\text{molecules}}{\text{mole}} = \dfrac{\text{grams}}{\text{molecule}}$ becomes $\dfrac{151.91}{6.022 \times 10^{23}}$.

18. **D. $168w + 24d + \dfrac{m}{60}$ (Numbers and Operations on Numbers: Order of Operations)** Option D is the correct answer. There are 24 hours in a day and 168 hours in a week ($24 \times 7 = 168$), so the number of hours in $w$ weeks and $d$ days is $168w + 24d$. Add to this that there are $\dfrac{m}{60}$ hours in $m$ minutes, and you have: $168w + 24d + \dfrac{m}{60}$. Option A adds the number of weeks, days, and minutes without converting them into hours, while Option B multiplies the number of minutes by 60 in an attempt to convert the answer into hours. Option C divides the number of days by 24 rather than multiplying, and Option E mistakenly divides the number of weeks and the number of days in an attempt to get hours.

19. **C. $45C + 650 \leq 2{,}100$ (Algebraic Concepts: Solving Inequalities)** Option C is the correct answer. The budget for the meeting is $2,100, so that is the most that can be spent. The costs for the meeting are the room rental ($650) and food and refreshments (45 times the cost per person $C$ for a total of $45C$). Option A adds the cost per person with the rent of the room. Option B only takes into account the cost of food and refreshments for the 45 people and does not include the room rental. Option D attempts to compare the price per person for food and refreshments to the number of people expected to attend the meeting. Option E adds the rental cost of the room to the amount of the budget (rather than adding the rental cost to the food cost).

20. **B. 21 (Measurement and Geometry: Area and Perimeter)** Option B is correct. The vertical segment $AC$ is the base and has length 6, while the horizontal segment from $A$ to $B$ forms the height and has length 7. The area of the triangle is $\dfrac{1}{2}(6)(7) = 21$. Option C is twice this number. Option A is an incorrect attempt to find the length of the segment $\overline{BC}$ using the lengths 6 and 7, while Option D uses this number to determine the perimeter of the triangle. Option E uses the correct length of $\overline{BC}$ in attempt to find the perimeter of the triangle.

21. **B. –1 (Algebraic Concepts: Slopes and Lines)** Option B is the correct answer. The slope of the line through points $B$ and $C$ is $-1$, so the slope of line $m$ must also be $-1$. To calculate the slope for $\overline{BC}$, substitute the coordinates for points $B$ (9, 3) and $C$ (2, 10) into the slope formula: $m = \dfrac{y_2 - y_1}{x_2 - x_1} = \dfrac{10 - 3}{2 - 9} = \dfrac{7}{-7} =$. Parallel lines have the same slope, so the slope of the new line $m$ is also $-1$. Option A is the change in the $y$-coordinate for the line through $B$ and $C$. Option C adds the changes in the vertical and horizontal values ($-7$ and 7) rather than dividing them. Option D has a sign error in computing the slope, and Option E is absolute value of the change in the $y$-coordinates for the line through $B$ and $C$.

22. **C. 95 (Measurement and Geometry: Polygons)** Option C is correct. The sum of the measures of the three angles in the quadrilateral is 265°. The sum of the interior angles of a quadrilateral is always 360°, so subtract 265 from 360 to find the measure of the remaining angle: $360 - 265 = 95$. Option A represents the supplement of angle $E$. Option B is incorrect; it is the result of a visual estimation that the angle is a right angle. Option D represents the supplement of either angle $D$ or angle $F$. Option E shows the same measure as angle $E$, the result of faulty reasoning to think that both pairs of opposite angles must have the same measure.

23. **D. 25 to 30 (Data Analysis: Probability and Statistics: Statistics)** Option D is correct because while each of the intervals in the answers is 5 minutes long, it is during the interval from 25 to 30 that the most meals, $60 - 45 = 15$, were sold.

24. **C. 2.23 (Data Analysis: Probability and Statistics: Statistics)** Option C is correct because during the 30-minute interval from time $t = 10$ to time $t = 40$, 67 meals were served ($81 - 14 = 67$), giving the rate of meals per minute to be $67 \div 30 = 2.23$. Option A is the rate from $t = 35$ to $t = 40$. Option B is the average number of meals sold per minute the entire time the truck was open: $81 \div 40 = 2.025 \approx 2.03$. Option C is the rate from $t = 20$ to $t = 30$. Option E is the average of the data representing the number of meals sold.

25. **E. $\dfrac{66 - 2t}{4}$ (Algebraic Concepts: Number Properties)** Option E is correct. It computes the amount of money collected for the adults by subtracting the money collected for the players, $2t$, from the total of 66 and then dividing the difference by 4 because that is the cost for each adult: $\dfrac{66 - 2t}{4}$. Option A is the amount of money paid for the adults. Option B is a negative number. Option C incorrectly multiplies the money paid by the adults by \$4. Option D incorrectly divides the total amount paid by all by the \$4 per adult cost and then subtracts the amount paid by the players.

26. **C. 96 (Measurement and Geometry: Area and Perimeter)** Option C is correct. The area of the upper region can be computed in two different ways.

**Method 1:**

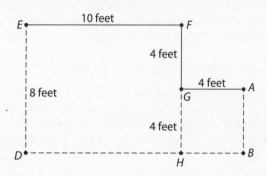

Find the areas for *DEFGH* ($8 \times 10 = 80$) and *GABH* ($4 \times 4 = 16$) and add them together to get 96 square feet.

**Method 2:**

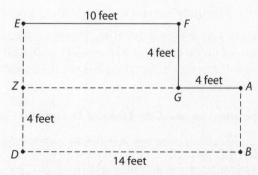

Find the areas of *ZEFG* ($4 \times 10 = 40$) and *ZGABD* ($4 \times 14 = 56$) and add them together to get 96 square feet.

Option A is incorrect because it is just the area of *ZGABD*. Option B is incorrect because it is just the area of *DEFGH*. Option D is incorrect because it is the area of the upper region with the cut-out in the upper-right corner included. Option E is incorrect because it is the area of the largest rectangle that can be made in the picture (with the cut-outs in the upper right and lower center included).

27. **D. 29 (Measurement and Geometry: Area and Perimeter)** Option D is correct. The dimensions of the window, in feet, are 6 by 7. The diameter of the semicircular section of the window is 6. The perimeter of the arc of the semicircle is half of the circumference of the circle: $\frac{1}{2} \times 6 \times \pi \approx 9.4$. Because the top of the rectangle is not part of the perimeter of the window, the perimeter is calculated by adding the length of the bottom and two sides of the rectangle (7 + 7 + 6 = 20) and half the circumference of the circle (20 + 9.4 = 29.4). The answer closest to this result is Option C, 29. Option A is half the perimeter of all four sides of the rectangle: $\frac{1}{2}(6+6+7+7)$, while Option C is the perimeter of all four sides of the rectangle. Option B is the sum of half of the perimeter of all four sides of the rectangle and the perimeter of the semicircle. Option E is the perimeter of the bottom and two sides of the rectangle and the circumference of the full circle.

28. **D. $\frac{321}{714}$ (Data Analysis: Probability and Statistics: Probability)** Option D is correct because of the 714 listeners who prefer to listen to classic rock, 321 are 40 years of age or older. Option A is incorrect because it represents the proportion of the responders who prefer classic rock that are age 40 or older. Option B represents the proportion of all the responders who are 40 or older. Option C represents the proportion of all the responders who prefer classic rock. Option E is a ratio of the number of responders 40 or older to the number of responders who prefer classic rock.

29. **C. $\frac{950}{1,935}$ (Data Analysis: Probability and Statistics: Probability)** Option C is correct because the number of people in the age 30–39 range is 454, the number of people who prefer country music is 674, and there are 178 people who are in both categories. Therefore, of the 1,935 listeners who responded to the survey, 950 fit one category or the other: 454 + 674 – 178 = 950. Option A is incorrect because this is the probability the person selected was age 30–39. Option B is incorrect because this is the probability the person prefers country music. Option D is the probability of a country music preference given the age is 30–39, while Option E is the probability of being age 30–39 given the preference of country music.

30. **D. $C = \$0.08n + \$0.30$ (Algebraic Concepts: Slope)** Option D is correct because the slope of the linear relation is $\frac{5.10-3.50}{60-40} = 0.08$. Substitute 3.50 for $C$ and 40 for $n$ into $C = 0.08n + b$ to determine that $b = 0.30$: 3.50 = 0.08(40) + $b$; 3.50 = 3.2 + $b$; $b$ = 0.30. Therefore, the correct equation is $C = \$0.08n + \$0.30$. Option A takes the cost for 60 bandages and divides by 60, while Option B does the same for the cost of 40 bandages. Option C has the correct slope but not the correct value for $b$, while Option E interchanges the values for slope and $b$.

31. **A. $\frac{7}{120}$ (Numbers and Operations on Numbers: Order of Operations)** Option A is the correct answer. Allie spends $\frac{1}{3}+\frac{1}{4}+\frac{1}{8}=\frac{8}{24}+\frac{6}{24}+\frac{3}{24}=\frac{17}{24}$ of her monthly income on the items described, leaving her $\frac{7}{24}$ of her monthly income. One-fifth of this amount, or $\frac{7}{24}\times\frac{1}{5}=\frac{7}{120}$, goes into her savings account.

Option B subtracts $\frac{7}{24}$ and $\frac{1}{5}$. Option C is $\frac{1}{5}$ of $\frac{17}{24}$. Option D is the part of her income she has left after paying for housing, food, and utilities. Option E is the part of her salary used to pay for housing, food, and utilities.

32. **B. 36 (Measurement and Geometry: Areas and Perimeter)** Option B is the correct answer. You first have to compute the height of the trapezoid by using the symmetry of the trapezoid and the Pythagorean theorem.

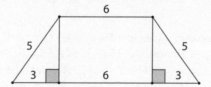

The height of the trapezoid is 4: $3^2 + h^2 = 5^2$; $9 + h^2 = 25$; $h^2 = 16$; $h = 4$. You can then use the formula for the area of the trapezoid, $\frac{1}{2}h(b_1 + b_2)$, substituting $h = 4$, $b_1 = 6$, and $b_2 = 12$: $\frac{1}{2}(4)(6+12) = (2)(18) = 36$. You can also add the area of the rectangle ($4 \times 6$) and the area of the two triangles to get the correct answer: $2 \times \frac{1}{2}(3 \times 4) + 24 = 12 + 24 = 36$. Option A is the perimeter of the trapezoid. Option C is the product of the height and the lower base. Option D is the product of the length of a leg and the lower base. Option E fails to use the $\frac{1}{2}$ in the area of the trapezoid formula.

33. **A. 31.0 (Measurement and Geometry: Areas and Perimeter)** Option A is the correct answer. Find the area of the shaded region by first calculating the area of the square and the area of the circle. The radius of the circle is equal to half the side of a square, so a side is 12, making the area of the square $12^2 = 144$. The area of the circle is $\pi r^2$: $\pi(6)^2 = 36\pi \approx 113$. Then subtract: $144 - 113 = 31$. Option B is the difference between the area of the square and $12\pi$. Option C is the area of the circle only. Option D is the sum of the area of the square and $12\pi$. Option E is the sum of the area of the square and the circle.

34. **D. 72 (Numbers and Operations on Numbers: Percent)** Option D is the answer. After the April layoffs, Acme had 80% of its workforce still employed. With 10% of these people, or 8% of the original workforce, laid off in September, this leaves 72% of the original workforce. Option A is 20% + 10% of 20%, which does not make sense in this problem. Option B is the sum of the layoff rates. Option C is the difference between 100% and the sum of the layoff rates. Option E subtracts 10% of 20% from the 80% who are still working.

35. **A. $150m + 25e \geq 600$ (Algebraic Concepts: Solving Inequalities)** Option A is correct because the sum of the vitamin D obtained from drinking milk and eating eggs must be greater than or equal to the 600 units needed: $150m + 25e \geq 600$. Option B has the wrong inequality sign, while Option C is an equation and does not account for the possibility of exceeding the 600 units. Options D and E do not measure the amount of vitamin D consumed, just the number of glasses of milk and eggs consumed.

36. **E.** $\dfrac{\$143.18}{0.80\times1.04}$ **(Numbers and Operations on Numbers: Order of Operations)** Option E is correct because you need to divide the final price by 1.04 to find the sale price of the coat before tax and then divide the sale price by 0.80 to find the original price of the coat: $\dfrac{\$143.18}{0.80\times1.04}$. Option A is not correct because even though it uses the percentages of the problem, it uses 0.04 instead of 1.04 and multiplies when it should be dividing. Option B is not correct because it multiplies by 1.04 when it should be dividing. Option D is incorrect because it multiplies the final sale price by the tax impact, essentially meaning that the coat is taxed twice.

37. **C. 55 (Measurement and Geometry: Area and Perimeter)** Option C is correct. The diameter of the circle is the same length as the side of the square, 16 feet, so the radius of the circle is 8 feet. The area of the shaded region is the area of the square ($16 \times 16 = 256$) minus the area of the circle ($\pi 8^2 = 64\pi = 200.96$, which rounds to 201): $256 - 201 = 55$. Option A is incorrect because that is the area of the square. Option B is incorrect because it is the difference between the area of the circle and the perimeter of the square. Option D is the area of one fourth of the square, not of the shaded areas. Option E is the difference between the perimeter of the square and the circumference of the circle.

38. **B. $10(3f + 2) + 5f + 1(3f) = 134$ (Algebraic Concepts: Number Properties)** Option B is the correct answer. If $f$ represents the number of $5 bills, then $3f$ represents the number of $1 bills. Because there are two more $10 bills than there are $1 bills, the number of $10 bills is represented by $3f + 2$. The total value of the $10 bills is $10(3f + 2)$, the total value of the $5 bills is $5f$, and the total value of the $1 bills is $1(3f)$. Add these together to get the total value of $134: $10(3f + 2) + 5f + 1(3f) = 134$. Option A represents the situation where the number of $10 bills is two more than the number of $5 bills. Option C has the number of $1 bills being two more than the number of $10 bills. Options D and E are based on the basic variable being the number of $10 bills.

39. **A. $\dfrac{1}{15}$ (Data Analysis: Statistics and Probability: Probability)** Option A is correct because it is the product of the probability of getting a green on the spinner, $\dfrac{2}{5}$, and getting a 3 on the die, $\dfrac{1}{6}$: $\dfrac{2}{5} \times \dfrac{1}{6} = \dfrac{2}{30} = \dfrac{1}{15}$. Option B is incorrect because it computes with the probability of getting a 3 as $\dfrac{1}{3}$. Option C is incorrect because it adds the correct probabilities from Option A. Option D is incorrect because it adds with the incorrect probability from Option B. Option E is incorrect because it divides the correct probability of getting a 3 by the correct probability of spinning a green.

40. **C. Mean = 26.625, Median = 26.5, Mode = 30 (Data Analysis: Probability and Statistics: Central Tendency)** Option C is correct. The mean is found by computing the sum of the data values and dividing by the number of data points: $\dfrac{23+12+30+19+18+30+43+38}{8} = \dfrac{213}{8} = 26.625$. The median is found after arranging the data in increasing order: 12, 18, 19, 23, 30, 30, 38, 43. The median is midway between 23 and 30: $\dfrac{23+30}{2} = 26.5$. The mode is the data value that is used most often: 30. Options A and B are not correct because the mean is not found by determining the number midway between the two middle points in the unsorted data. Option D is incorrect because the median and mode are interchanged, while Option E is incorrect because the values stated are not matched with the correct measure of central tendency.

41. **B. 9 (Measurement and Geometry: Circles)** Option B is correct because 32° is approximately 9% of 360°: $32 \div 360 = 0.088$, or 8.8%. Option B, 9, is the closest to this answer. Option A is incorrect because it improperly rounds 8.8% to 8%. Option C is incorrect because it approximates 32° as being one-tenth of the circle's 360°. Option D is incorrect because the number of degrees in the central angle is not the same as the percent of the circle it occupies. Option E is incorrect because it multiplies 360 by .32, or 32%; 32 is the measure of degrees of the angle, not the percentage of the circle.

42. **C. 289 (Measurement and Geometry: Circles)** Option C is correct. Since 33 is 11.4% of all the medals distributed, divide 33 by 0.114 to get 289 (rounded to the nearest whole number). Option A is the 289 total medals minus the number won by the Russians. Option B is the result of subtracting the medals earned by Russia from 33 times 9. Option D is the result of multiplying 33 by 9. Option E is the product of 33 and 11.4, rounded to the nearest whole number.

43. **D. 40 (Measurement and Geometry: Perimeter)** Option D is correct. Each half of the diagonals form right triangles, and the lengths of the legs of the right triangles are 6 and 8. Use the Pythagorean theorem to determine that the length of a side of *ABCD* is 10: $6^2 + 8^2 = c^2$; $36 + 64 = c^2$; $100 = c^2$; $c = 10$. Therefore, the perimeter of *ABCD* is 40: $10 + 10 + 10 + 10 = 40$. Option A is incorrect because it is the length of only one side. Option B is the sum of the lengths of the diagonals. Option C is the sum of the lengths of two sides. Option E is four times the sum of the lengths of the diagonals.

44. **D. 972 (Numbers and Operations on Numbers: Order of Operations)** Option D is correct. If the market is down one-third, then 648 represents two-thirds of the houses sold the previous year. Set up and solve the proportion $\frac{2}{3} = \frac{648}{x}$. Multiplying the cross-products yields $2x = 1{,}944$ or $x = 972$. Option A is the result of taking one-third of 648. Option B is half of 648. Option C is the result of taking 216 and adding it to 648. Option E is the result of multiplying 648 by 3 (or the result of solving the proportion $\frac{1}{3} = \frac{648}{x}$).

45. **B. 105 (Data Analysis: Probability and Statistics: Central Tendency)** Option B is correct because it is the median salary for the 30 teams. To find the median, list all salaries in order and determine the average of the two middle values (in bold): 50, 50, 70, 80, 80, 80, 80, 80, 90, 90, 90, 90, 90, 90, **100, 110,** 110, 110, 110, 110, 130, 130, 130, 130, 150, 160, 160, 180, 210, 240. The middle values are 100 and 110: $100 + 110 = 210$; $210 \div 2 = 105$.

Option A is incorrect because it is the sum of the salary groups divided by 30. Option C is incorrect because it is the mean salary for the 30 teams. Option D is the median of the twelve stated salary groups. Option E is the mean of the twelve stated salary groups.

46. **D. $\frac{1}{2}$ (Data Analysis: Probability and Statistics: Probability)** Option D is correct. When you add the frequencies for the number of teams with salaries of $110 million or more, you get a total of 15 teams: $5 + 4 + 1 + 2 + 1 + 1 + 1 = 15$. This means 15 out of the 30 teams, or $\frac{1}{2}$, have salaries of at least $110 million. Option A is incorrect because it represents the salary levels in excess of $110 million without including the number of teams at each level. Option B is incorrect because it represents the salary levels of at least $110 million without including the number of teams at each level. Option C is incorrect because it represents the salary levels in excess of $110 million. Option E is incorrect because it represents the salary levels of at most $110 million.

47. **C. 56 (Measurement and Geometry: Area and Perimeter)** Option C is the correct answer. If the perimeter is 30 then the length of the remaining sides is $\frac{30-2(8)}{2} = \frac{30-16}{2} = \frac{14}{2} = 7$, making the area of the rectangle 56: $8 \times 7 = 56$. Option A is incorrect; it is the difference between 30 and 8 and represents only three sides of the perimeter. Option B is the sum of the perimeter of all four sides and the given side $(30 + 8)$. Option D is the product of the given side and the other three sides of the perimeter $(8 \times 22)$, and Option E is the product of the given length and the perimeter $(8 \times 30)$.

48. **B. 132 (Measurement and Geometry: Volume of a Cube or Rectangular Solid)** Option B is correct. $L_2 = 4$ inches, $W_2 = 1.5$ inches, and $H_2 = 2$ inches. The value of $L_1 \times W_1 \times H_1 - L_2 \times W_2 \times H_2 = (8 \times 3 \times 6) - (4 \times 1.5 \times 2) = 144 - 12 = 132$. Option A is incorrect because it uses $H_2 = 3$ inches (one-half of $H_1$ rather than one-third of $H_1$). Options C and D add the dimensions of the central hole from Options A and B, respectively, rather than subtracting them. Option E incorrectly multiplies the six dimensions together.

49. **B. $B$ (Algebraic Concepts: Coordinate Plane)** Option B is the correct answer because point $B$ is the point at which Revenue is equal to Cost so Profit = Revenue – Cost = 0. Point $A$ shows a point where Cost > Revenue. Point $C$ shows the point where Revenue > Cost so Profit > 0. Point $D$ shows a point where Revenue is greatest, and point $E$ shows a point where Revenue = 0.

50. **B. $\frac{75}{198}$ (Data Analysis: Probability and Statistics: Venn Diagrams)** Option B is correct. The number of people in the intersection of the two circles is 75: $298 - 81 - 123 - 19 = 75$. The number of managers is $123 + 75 = 198$, 75 of whom are women. Because 123 are not contained in the circle categorizing the women, 123 must be men. Therefore, the probability that a manager is a woman is $\frac{75}{198}$. Option A is the ratio of women managers to men managers. Option C is the ratio of women managers to women who are not managers. Option D is the probability that a woman selected at random is a manager. Option E is the probability that an employee selected at random is a woman manager.

# XII. Science Full-Length Practice Test with Answer Explanations

**50 Items**

**Time: 80 Minutes**

**Directions:** This is a test of your skills in analyzing information in the area of science. Read each item and decide which of the four answer options is the best answer.

Sometimes, several items are based on the same information or graphic. You should read this material carefully and use it to answer the items.

---

*Items 1 through 7 refer to the following information.*

Very tall skyscrapers, such as Taiwan's Taipei 101, need to be strong enough to withstand the forces of high winds while also bending or swaying slightly so they do not break apart. However, the swaying can cause discomfort to people on high floors of the building. If the swaying is excessive, it can cause damage to the building. To counteract the swaying, engineers designed a large damper, a kind of pendulum with a very heavy ball at the bottom. The damper extends from the 92nd to 87th floors of the 101-story skyscraper and is intended to stabilize the building.

**91st Floor** [390.60 m]
(Outdoor Observation Deck)

**89th Floor** [382.20 m]
(Indoor Observation Deck)

**88th Floor**

**87th Floor**

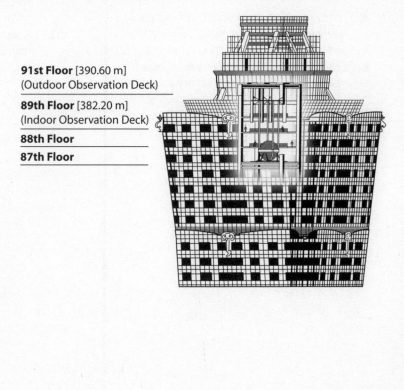

1. What is the relationship between the damper and the swaying of the building from wind striking it?

   A. Swaying of the damper transfers energy from the swaying to the foundations of the building many feet below the surface.

   B. Energy from the swaying is transferred from the building to the damper, so the damper sways instead of the building.

   C. Some wind strikes the damper instead of the building, which reduces the stress of the wind on the building.

   D. The damper is not effective in reducing swaying of the building because the swaying of the damper causes the building to sway more.

2. On March 31, 2002, during the construction of Taipei 101, a massive earthquake struck Taipei. What is the most likely effect of an earthquake on the damper?

   A. Movement of the damper will increase as energy from the moving building is transferred to the damper.

   B. Movement of the damper will increase because the damper will absorb vibrations from the lower floors of the building.

   C. Movement of the damper will decrease so that it can absorb the earthquake's vibrations.

   D. Movement of the damper will decrease as vibration from the earthquake counteracts its movement.

3. The damper in Taipei 101 would protect it from which of the following events?

   A. An earthquake cracks the foundation of the building.

   B. A windstorm causes winds in excess of 90 km/h.

   C. A subway train derails several blocks from the building.

   D. A compact car goes out of control late at night and crashes into the base of the building.

4. Which of the following does the damper in Taipei 101 most resemble?

   A. The cushion on a chair, which makes the chair more comfortable to sit on.

   B. A roll bar on a jeep, which protects occupants from harm if the vehicle turns over.

   C. A shock absorber on a car, which absorbs vibrations from bumps in the road.

   D. A valve or plate in a chimney that regulates the flow of air out of the chimney.

5. In which of the following places would a damper help prevent unwanted vibrations?

   A. A huge aircraft carrier has a damper to counteract the motion of the ocean.

   B. A large ocean liner uses dampers to prevent vibrations from the ship's engines from disturbing passengers.

   C. A cargo ship captain places the heaviest cargo in the bottom of the ship to keep it from capsizing.

   D. A human-powered paddle boat uses a damper to prevent vibrations from the paddles from stirring up the water of a small lake.

6. Based on the information, which of the following, in addition to earthquakes, is a risk typical of Taiwan that most logically encouraged architects to add a damper to the design of Taipei 101?

   A. Typhoons
   B. Volcanos
   C. Floods
   D. Blizzards

7. A stress crack is a harmless crack that appears in the interior walls of a tall building because of the motion of the building. What should engineers do when stress cracks appear in Taipei 101?

   A. Make plans to repair the damper because it is not working as expected.

   B. Keep a detailed log of the cracks because they can indicate that a major failure of the building is coming.

   C. Repair the cracks because they are not a major hazard to the building or its occupants.

   D. Evacuate the building because the cracks show that the building is on the verge of collapse.

*Items 8 through 16 refer to the following information.*

Fish are the most numerous groups of vertebrate animals, with over 32,000 known species. One of the main characteristics of fish is that they take in oxygen and release carbon dioxide through gills. Gills are specialized breathing organs that allow fish to obtain oxygen that is dissolved in water. Gills typically appear inside of flaps on the sides of the fish's head or body. Inside the gills are thin layers of tissue that allow water to pass by. Most fish are able to take in water through their mouths and push it out through their gills. As the oxygenated water passes along the gill tissue, oxygen is absorbed and carbon dioxide is excreted. Some fish, such as most shark species, cannot pass water from their mouths to their gills. These fish have gill flaps that take in and release water. Most shark species can pump water through these flaps, but a few species, such the great white shark, do not have this ability. Instead, water passes through these sharks' gills as they swim. If these sharks stop swimming, they will suffocate. This is one of the reasons some shark species look so sinister—they never stop swimming.

However, not all fish use gills, or do not use them exclusively to exchange gases. These fish obtain oxygen from the air. Some of these fish, such as the mudskipper, are amphibious, but others live exclusively in the water and surface to get oxygenated air. Often these fish live in environments with oxygen-poor water, such as very shallow or muddy water.

| Air-Breathing Fish | |
|---|---|
| **Fish** | **How They Breathe** |
| Mudskipper, anguillid eels | Air is absorbed from the atmosphere through the skin. |
| Electric eels | Air is absorbed from the atmosphere into the mouth cavity. |
| Catfish | Air is absorbed in the digestive tract. |
| Lungfish | Air enters the lungs from the mouth and exits through the gills. |
| Gar and bowfin | Air enters a special swim bladder from the mouth and exits through the gills. (The swim bladder is an organ that fish can fill with air in order to control their buoyancy in water.) |

8. Why do <u>most</u> air-breathing fish need this ability?

    **A.** They lack well-developed gills and only have gill flaps.

    **B.** They cannot release carbon dioxide into the water.

    **C.** Rising ocean temperatures are causing fish to look for oxygen in the air.

    **D.** The water they live in lacks dissolved oxygen.

9. Which species of fish obtains oxygen in a way <u>most</u> similar to humans?

    **A.** Electric eels

    **B.** Lungfish

    **C.** Gar

    **D.** Catfish

10. What is the main difference between gills and gill flaps?

    **A.** Sharks use their gill flaps to look sinister to scare their prey.

    **B.** Gill flaps are much less efficient in obtaining oxygen than gills.

    **C.** Fish can pump water from their mouths through gills but not through gill flaps.

    **D.** Gills and gill flaps are located on different parts of a fish's body.

11. Which of the following is most likely an additional risk for air-breathing fish?

   A. They cannot swim at deep levels.
   B. They are at risk of meeting predators when they rise to the surface to obtain air.
   C. They lack a way to obtain oxygen if they cannot obtain it from the water.
   D. They cannot obtain food while they are breathing air.

12. Water contains a much lower percentage of oxygen than air does. Which of the following statements can most logically be inferred from this sentence and the information in the passage?

   A. It's easier for air-breathing fish to get oxygen from the air than from the water.
   B. Air-breathing fish obtain more of their oxygen from the atmosphere than from water.
   C. Fish that breathe through gills consume less oxygen than air-breathing fish.
   D. Gills are much more efficient in absorbing oxygen than are lungs.

13. The amount of dissolved gases in water decreases as the temperature of the water rises. Scientists believe that ocean temperatures are rising because of global warming. What effect will rising ocean temperatures have on fish that obtain oxygen only through gills?

   A. The fish will begin to suffocate from lack of oxygen.
   B. The fish will develop other ways to breathe similar to air-breathing fish.
   C. The fish will have to swim faster to get enough water to pass through their gill flaps.
   D. The fish will have to move to deep ocean depths to find colder, oxygen-rich water.

14. An electric eel is swimming in oxygen-poor water and needs to breathe from the air. What will the electric eel do?

   A. Inhale air into its lungs through its mouth and expel it through its gills.
   B. Rise to the surface and float with the top part of its body out of the water.
   C. Rise to the surface and swallow some air.
   D. Rise to the surface and open its mouth.

15. A frog can obtain oxygen through its skin, tongue, and lungs. What is the most logical reason frogs need to breathe in all these ways?

   A. Frogs' lungs are not strong enough to obtain enough oxygen for the frog to live outside of water.
   B. Frogs cannot use their lungs when out of water, so they need to absorb oxygen through their bodies.
   C. Frogs are amphibious, so they need to breathe on land and in water.
   D. Like air-breathing fish, frogs live in oxygen-poor water.

16. Which of these fish does a frog's breathing most resemble?

   A. Electric eels
   B. Gar
   C. Lungfish
   D. Catfish

*Items 17 through 19 refer to the following information.*

Environmental scientists often express concern about invasive species. Typically, an invasive species is considered to be a species that is not indigenous to a certain habitat and is causing environmental harm. These species may have been brought to the new environment purposefully or may have arrived by accident.

One example of a species considered to be invasive is the so-called Asian carp. The Asian carp actually refers to approximately nine species of carp that were introduced to many places around the world, including North America, from Asia. Long used as food in Asia, the fish are not considered harmful there. Of the varieties considered most harmful in North America, black carp are known to overconsume and deplete supplies of certain shellfish, some of which are already endangered themselves; grass carp are known to overconsume aquatic plants, which causes harm to complex food webs, and silver carp are known to overconsume plankton, which also disrupts food webs. At present, scientists are concerned that if Asian carp enter Lake Michigan, they will spread through the entire Great Lakes and cause harm to this extensive system of freshwater lakes.

One characteristic of the Asian carp that may help it spread is its ability to jump. When startled, an Asian carp can jump 5 feet or more. There have been cases of fishers and recreational boaters being hit, cut, or even knocked out of their boats by a jumping Asian carp. Some scientists believe that this ability to jump will make it especially hard to keep this species out of the Great Lakes.

The term *invasive species* has been called imprecise by many scientists. They believe that the term has been applied inconsistently and actually has three different definitions that are used interchangeably:

| | |
|---|---|
| Definition 1 | A widespread non-indigenous species that causes harm to its new habitat. Examples: Asian carp, kudzu vines, and starlings |
| Definition 2 | A native species that has become a dominant or overpopulated in its environment because of a lack of natural predators, such as deer in an urban forest preserve, where natural predators of deer have all been killed off. |
| Definition 3 | A widespread non-indigenous species, whether harmful to the new habitat or not, such as ornamental carp, which were imported from Asia and kept in decorative ponds because of their beauty. Sweet clover, another example, was introduced from Europe and has been domesticated for use as animal food. These species are often called introduced species. |

Because of the confusion caused by these terms, some scientists claim that the term *invasive species* is too broad and imprecise and should be replaced with more precise terms and definitions.

17. Why is the Asian carp widely considered an invasive species?

   A. It is living outside its natural habitat and causing damage to its new habitat.
   B. Some varieties were deliberately brought to the United States to control weeds in freshwater systems.
   C. It is trying to invade the Great Lakes.
   D. It was introduced from Asia.

18. Which of the three definitions of invasive species does the Asian carp most closely resemble?

   A. Definition 1, because its ability to jump can injure people
   B. Definition 1, because it harms indigenous species
   C. Definition 2, because it lacks natural predators
   D. Definition 3, because Asian carp have long been grown in China for use as food

19. The natural predator of elk is the wolf. After wolves were hunted to extinction in Yellowstone Park, the elk population exploded. A controversial plan to reintroduce wolves to Yellowstone Park resulted in the population of elk being reduced to a more manageable level. Populations of other animals were affected, too. In this example, which of the animals are an invasive species?

   A. Wolves, because they were reintroduced to the environment
   B. Wolves, because they are overconsuming elk
   C. Elk, because their population grew out of control and negatively affected their habitat
   D. Elk, because they were not native to Yellowstone Park

*Item 20 through 23 are based on the following passage.*

Stephan has a window box garden on the balcony of his apartment on the 23rd floor of a high-rise building in Chicago. He has a tomato plant, a pepper plant, and a squash vine growing. One day, he notices that a small insect is harming his pepper plant. He looks up information on the insect and finds that it is a pepper weevil. This species originated in Mexico, the original habitat of the pepper plant. In the United States, this pest is found in southern states. Apparently, this pest cannot survive the harsh winters of the north.

The pepper weevil reproduces by laying eggs inside the bud or pepper pod. When the eggs hatch, the larvae feed on the bud or pod until they become pupa. When the adult weevils emerge, they are soon able to reproduce. A single pair of pepper weevils can produce 5 to 20 generations of offspring during a single growing season and are particularly harmful on farms where large amounts of peppers are grown. Once established, pepper weevils are hard to eradicate. Insecticides only work on adults, and by the time damage to the plant is noticed, the infestation may have already damaged the crop.

Stephan didn't notice the pepper weevils when he bought the plant at a local garden store, but a week later he saw them. A label on the plant said that it was grown at a plant nursery in Texas. He is worried that they may get on some of his other plants.

20. Which invasive species does the pepper weevil most resemble?

   A.  Deer
   B.  Asian carp
   C.  An ornamental goldfish
   D.  Sweet clover

21. Which of the following is the most likely way the pepper weevil got on Stephan's pepper plants?

   A.  The eggs were already on the plant when it left the plant nursery in Texas.
   B.  Pepper weevils moved from Stephan's tomato plant to his pepper plant.
   C.  A bird deposited eggs on the plant when it foraged for food on the balcony.
   D.  An adult pepper weevil flew to Stephan's garden and laid eggs on the pepper plant.

22. What is the best way for Stephan to ensure that his pepper plants do not get pepper weevils in next year's garden?

   A.  Grow next year's pepper plants from seeds.
   B.  Spray next year's pepper plants with weed killer.
   C.  Buy his pepper plants from a different garden store.
   D.  Pull out this year's pepper plant and throw it away.

23. Which is the correct order of the stages of the life of a pepper weevil?

   A.  larva, egg, pupa, adult
   B.  pupa, egg, larva, adult
   C.  egg, larva, pupa, adult
   D.  egg, adult, pupa, larva

24. Erosion is process by which rock or soil is moved to another location by air or water. Which of these is an example of erosion?

    A. Constant exposure to crashing waves makes rocks on a beach round and smooth.
    B. Cracks in a cliff gradually grow wider as roots from trees grow into the cracks and make them wider.
    C. Strong winds blow away topsoil from the farms in a local area.
    D. Topsoil is depleted because farmers grow corn on their land year after year.

25. A customer leaves a shopping cart in a supermarket parking lot on a windy day. A strong gust of wind pushes the shopping cart, which makes it start to roll across the parking lot. Which of the following events would most likely cause the shopping cart to stop rolling?

    A. Friction inside the wheels causes the cart to slow down and then stop.
    B. The cart gradually rolls to a stop because it runs out of energy.
    C. Gravity pulls the shopping cart downhill.
    D. Another gust of wind causes the cart to change direction.

26. Which of the following parts of Newton's laws best accounts for the shopping cart coming to a stop?

    A. An object in motion tends to stay in motion.
    B. An object will change speed or direction if another force acts on it.
    C. An object at rest tends to stay at rest.
    D. For each action, there is an equal and opposite reaction.

*Items 27 and 28 refer to the following definitions.*

| Force | Something that makes an object move |
|---|---|
| Speed | Rapidity of the movement of an object |
| Velocity | Speed of an object in a direction |
| Acceleration | A change in speed or direction |

27. The gust of wind that puts the cart in motion is an example of which of the following?

    A. Force
    B. Speed
    C. Velocity
    D. Acceleration

28. Which of the following is an example of velocity?

    A. A spaceship is moving toward the moon at 500 kilometers per hour.
    B. A spaceship is sitting on the launch pad waiting to take off.
    C. A spaceship used rockets to turn to avoid colliding with space debris.
    D. The spaceship's powerful engines blasted it into outer space.

*Items 29 through 36 refer to the following information.*

Ultraviolet light is a kind of electromagnetic radiation. The wavelength of ultraviolet light is shorter than that of visible light and longer than the wavelength of X-rays. It is called ultraviolet light because the frequency of UV waves is higher than that of violet light, which is normally the highest frequency of light visible to humans. Ultraviolet light can pass through many substances, but is blocked by others, including ozone.

Ozone is a special form of oxygen composed of three oxygen atoms. A thin, blue gas with a slightly unpleasant odor, ozone is considered a pollutant close to Earth. It is abundant in a layer of the atmosphere high above Earth. This layer blocks some, but not all ultraviolet light. Ozone molecules are less stable than $O_2$ molecules, and easily break down into $O_2$ molecules, especially when in contact with certain human-made gases. Many scientists believe that these gases are responsible for a large hole, or opening, in the ozone layer over the South Pole.

Ultraviolet light can cause radiation burns on human skin in large enough doses, which results in sunburn. People with light skin are particularly susceptible to sunburn. Continued doses of UV light over many years can lead to various forms of skin cancer. Since certain kinds of UV light cause our skin to produce vitamin D, increased exposure to UV light can increase our body's production of vitamin D. Scientists believe that it is possible that increased exposure to UV light could raise people's vitamin D levels to unsafe amounts.

The amount of UV light to reach Earth in various locations varies, depending on factors such as the thickness of the ozone layer in that location, the elevation above sea level, and the season. The amount of ultraviolet light that reaches a particular location on Earth varies each day, depending on the amount of cloud cover and the time of day. More UV light can pass through the atmosphere when the sun is high in the sky than when it is nearer the horizon. More UV light can reach Earth in summer than winter because of the tilt of the Earth, which affects the concentration of UV rays.

The UV index is a scale used to measure the amount of UV light reaching Earth each day. It is calculated every day for every U.S. ZIP Code using weather and satellite data.

| UV Index | |
|---|---|
| 2 or less | Low |
| 3–5 | Moderate |
| 6–8 | High |
| 9–10 | Very high |
| 11+ | Extreme |

29. Why is UV light called ultraviolet?

   A.  It gives objects exposed to it a glowing violet fluorescent appearance.
   B.  Its waves have a higher frequency than those of violet light.
   C.  It is stronger and brighter than violet light.
   D.  It looks violet to the human eye.

30. If the UV index in Chicago is 3, what is the UV level?

   A.  Low
   B.  Moderate
   C.  High
   D.  Very high

31. Which of the following is true of the hazards of UV light?

   A.  UV light is a cause of global warming.
   B.  Vitamin D production is a benefit of increased exposure to UV light.
   C.  Overexposure to UV light can have serious health consequences.
   D.  UV light is causing ozone levels to decline.

32. Tim's new car has a sunroof. He can open the sunroof in two ways. Inside the car, a kind of opaque covering can be slid back. The opening is still closed by a glass cover, but light can enter the car through the glass. When a button on the dashboard is pressed, the glass sunroof cover slides back so air can enter the car.

Tim always drives to work at 12 p.m. On Tuesday, he drove the car with the opaque slide open and the glass cover closed. On Wednesday, he opened the glass cover and the opaque slide. Tim got a bad sunburn on Wednesday, but not on Tuesday. Both days were equally sunny and the UV index was the same. What explains the difference?

   A.  Ultraviolet light, which causes sunburns, cannot travel through glass easily.
   B.  The sun produced more ultraviolet light on Wednesday than on Tuesday.
   C.  The glass was not tinted darkly enough to block the ultraviolet light on Wednesday.
   D.  Tim didn't get sunburned on Tuesday because he went to work later in the day, when sunlight is not as direct.

33. Which of these places would most likely have a very high UV index?

    A. Denver, Colorado, which has a high elevation, on a sunny summer day

    B. San Francisco, California, on foggy winter day

    C. Chicago, Illinois, on a sunny winter day

    D. Buenos Aires, Argentina, on a cloudy July morning

34. Which of the following is NOT a possible long-term risk associated with increased UV exposure from ozone depletion?

    A. Incidence of skin cancer will increase.

    B. Rising vitamin D levels will produce toxic reactions.

    C. Fossil fuels will be depleted.

    D. Food crops will be damaged by excessive radiation.

35. What is the relationship between tilt of the Earth in summer and UV light reaching Earth's surface?

    A. In summer, UV rays are stronger than in winter.

    B. Cloudy weather blocks more sunlight in winter than in summer.

    C. The sun produces more UV light in summer than in winter.

    D. Earth's tilt toward the sun in summer means that the UV rays reach Earth more directly.

36. Which of the following is the most logical way to preserve the ozone layer?

    A. Reduce the use of fossil fuels, which cause global warming.

    B. Eliminate the discharge of gases that cause ozone molecules to break down to $O_2$.

    C. Use special machines to create a new ozone layer at Earth's surface.

    D. Use more sunscreen and sunblock to stop the effects of increased UV exposure.

*Items 37 through 40 refer to the following information.*

The guinea pig is a small rodent native to South America. In guinea pigs, black fur is a dominant trait (B) and white fur a recessive trait (b). When guinea pigs reproduce, they will receive a copy of one gene for fur color from each parent. If an offspring receives two dominant genes (BB) or a dominant and a recessive gene (Bb), the offspring will have black fur. The only way for the offspring to have white fur is if it receives two copies of the recessive gene (bb). The Punnett square below shows the possible combinations of genes for a guinea pig with one dominant and one recessive gene (Bb) crossed with another guinea pig with two copies of the recessive gene (bb).

|   | B | b |
|---|----|----|
| b | Bb | bb |
| b | Bb | bb |

37. A guinea pig has white fur. Which genes did it inherit from its parents?

   A.  BB
   B.  Bb
   C.  bB
   D.  bb

38. What are the odds that an individual offspring of the two guinea pigs will have white fur?

   A.  0
   B.  1:8
   C.  1:4
   D.  1:2

39. Another guinea pig with two copies of the gene for black fur (BB) is crossed with a white guinea pig. What are the odds that an individual offspring will be white?

   A.  0
   B.  1:8
   C.  1:4
   D.  1:2

40. Two guinea pigs with one copy of the dominant gene and one copy of the recessive gene are crossed. What are the odds that an individual offspring will have the combination Bb?

   A.  0
   B.  1:8
   C.  1:4
   D.  1:2

*Items 41 and 42 are based on the following information.*

Sublimation happens when a material changes from a solid to a gas without becoming a liquid. The opposite of sublimation is deposition—when a material changes from a gas to a solid without passing through the liquid phase.

41. Which of the following is an example of sublimation?

   A.  When mixed, vinegar and baking soda foam up and gas is released.

   B.  In a freezer, ice cubes gradually become smaller and thinner.

   C.  On a very hot day, rain falling on a sidewalk quickly turns to vapor.

   D.  A scientist uses hydrogen and oxygen to synthesize water.

42. Which of the following is an example of deposition?

   A.  Frost forms on the windows of a car overnight.

   B.  Snow on a road hardens into ice as cars drive over it.

   C.  When salt is spread on ice, it melts.

   D.  Dry ice disappears into a cloud of gas.

*Items 43 through 45 refer to the following information.*

The solar system consists of the sun and everything in its orbit: 8 major planets, approximately 173 moons in orbit around those planets (including 66 in orbit around Jupiter), 8 dwarf planets, and many other objects, such as comets. As technology has advanced, the number of known objects in the solar system has increased. For example, the number of known moons in the solar system doubled between 2003 and today. The number of planets, however, decreased by one. In 2006, members of the International Astronomical Union (IAU) voted to redefine Pluto as a dwarf planet. The reason for this was simple: Shortly before, astronomers had found another potential planet, Eris, further in distance from the sun than Pluto. Measurements seemed to indicate that it was larger than Pluto. The discoverers were certain that soon it would be named a new planet. However, if scientists accepted Eris as a planet, they would have to accept two more orbiting bodies as planets, too. Instead, the scientists voted to change the definition of planet, and count Eris as a dwarf planet. The IAU decided that objects like Pluto and Eris, part of a band of large and small space debris called the Kuiper Belt, were simply larger members of this group, and reclassified them as dwarf planets. This way, they avoided having a large number of objects in the Kuiper Belt being named as major planets.

43. Approximately how many moons are in orbit around major planets?

   A.  1
   B.  8
   C.  66
   D.  173

44. Why has the number of known bodies in the solar system increased?

   A.  Astronomers voted to change the definitions of objects in the solar system.
   B.  Debris from space travel has formed new bodies in the solar system.
   C.  New planets and other bodies continue to form in the solar system.
   D.  Improved telescopes permit astronomers to see into space better than in the past.

45. Which of the following is the <u>most logical</u> reason astronomers voted to narrow the definition of planet to include only 8 planets?

   A.  Pluto is too distant from the sun to be considered a planet.
   B.  Objects in the Kuiper Belt are not in orbit around the sun.
   C.  Objects in the Kuiper Belt are different from the 8 major planets.
   D.  Pluto was not really in orbit around the sun.

*Items 46 through 50 refer to the following information.*

In anatomy, an organ is defined as a collection of tissues that forms a structural unit and has a defined function. While many people do not consider it an organ, the skin is our body's largest organ. An average adult has about 20 square meters of skin. On humans, skin has several vital functions. First, skin protects us from microbes. Skin forms a barrier that prevents dirt, microbes, and other unwanted materials from getting inside our bodies and making us sick. Skin also helps us regulate body temperature. If our temperature rises or falls, our body can adjust sweat production. The evaporation of sweat absorbs heat from our bodies and cools us, for example. Third, skin contains nerve cell endings for the sense of touch. Through our skin we can feel such sensations as hot and cold. Finally, vitamin D is synthesized in the skin when skin is exposed to certain forms of ultraviolet light.

46. Which of the following is NOT a reason skin is considered an organ?

   A.   It has a defined function.
   B.   Adults have 20 square meters of skin on average.
   C.   It is a structural unit.
   D.   It is a collection of tissues.

47. What will happen if your skin receives a small cut?

   A.   You will feel pain.
   B.   Your temperature will rise.
   C.   You will feel cold.
   D.   You will begin to sweat.

48. When sweat evaporates from our bodies, our bodies are cooled. Which of these statements best explains why sweating cools us?

   A.   It is an exothermic reaction.
   B.   It is an endothermic change.
   C.   It removes water from our bodies.
   D.   It removes salt from our bodies.

49. Which of the following is a way skin regulates body temperature when you feel cold?

   A.   The small blood vessels in the skin narrow so that blood flow is reduced and heat is conserved.
   B.   You begin to shiver, which generates heat.
   C.   You sweat more, which warms your body.
   D.   Goose bumps raise the small hairs on your body, which provide insulation.

50. Which of the following is NOT a function of the skin?

   A.   Production of an essential nutrient
   B.   Detecting important sensations
   C.   Regulating our core body temperature
   D.   Warning us of far-off danger

# Answer Key

| | | | | |
|---|---|---|---|---|
| 1. B | 11. B | 21. A | 31. C | 41. B |
| 2. A | 12. D | 22. A | 32. A | 42. A |
| 3. B | 13. A | 23. C | 33. A | 43. D |
| 4. C | 14. D | 24. C | 34. C | 44. D |
| 5. B | 15. C | 25. A | 35. D | 45. C |
| 6. A | 16. C | 26. B | 36. B | 46. B |
| 7. C | 17. A | 27. A | 37. D | 47. A |
| 8. D | 18. B | 28. A | 38. D | 48. B |
| 9. B | 19. C | 29. B | 39. A | 49. A |
| 10. C | 20. B | 30. B | 40. D | 50. D |

# Answer Explanations

1. **B. Energy from the swaying is transferred from the building to the damper, so the damper sways instead of the building. (Interpreting Information/Physical Science)** Option B is correct because by swinging, the damper absorbs and counteracts the building's swaying motion. Option A is not correct because the damper is connected to the upper floors of the building, not the foundation. Option C is not correct because the damper is inside the building, so it cannot be struck by the wind. Option D is incorrect because the damper will absorb energy.

2. **A. Movement of the damper will increase as energy from the moving building is transferred to the damper. (Applying Information/Physical Science)** Option A is correct because as vibrations transfer to the damper, the damper will move more and the building will move less. For this reason, Options C and D are incorrect. Option B is incorrect because the damper is designed to absorb movement from the top floors of the building, not from the lower floors. Vibrations from the earthquake will travel through the building to the upper floors, where the damper will absorb them.

3. **B. A windstorm causes winds in excess of 90 km/h. (Applying Information/Physical Science)** Option B is correct because only this event would cause the building to sway. The damper would protect the building from swaying caused by the earthquake, but it would not prevent the foundation from cracking, so Option A is incorrect. Options C and D are events that would most likely not create vibrations strong enough to affect the building.

4. **C. A shock absorber on a car, which absorbs vibrations from bumps in the road. (Applying Information/ Physical Science)** Option C is correct because both a shock absorber and the damper are designed to absorb vibrations. Option A is incorrect because a cushion is designed to soften the effect of gravity pulling down on us. Option B is not correct because a roll bar is not made to absorb energy; it is made to prevent injury in case of a roll-over accident. Option D is incorrect because the damper inside a chimney is designed to close off the chimney, not absorb energy.

5. **B. A large ocean liner uses dampers to prevent vibrations from the ship's engines from disturbing passengers. (Applying Information/Physical Science)** Option B is correct because a damper would absorb the engine vibrations. Option A is incorrect because a damper would not absorb this type of motion. Option C is incorrect because this is an example of ballast, which lowers the center of gravity of a boat, so it will remain upright. Option D is incorrect because a damper cannot prevent the boat's paddles from disturbing the water.

6. **A. Typhoons (Application/Physical Science)** Option A is correct because a typhoon would produce swaying from high winds, which the damper can absorb. The risks in the other options (B, C, and D) are not ones that would cause swaying of the building, so they are incorrect.

7. **C. Repair the cracks because they are not a major hazard to the building or its occupants. (Applying Information/Physical Science)** Option C is correct because the information makes it clear that stress cracks are not a major problem, but simply something that is expected from the swaying of the building. Therefore Options A, B, and D are incorrect.

8. **D. The water they live in lacks dissolved oxygen. (Interpreting Information/Life Science)** Option D is stated directly in the passage, so it is correct. Option A is true of many fish that do not breathe from the air, so it is incorrect. Options B and C are not supported by the information.

9. **B. Lungfish (Applying Information/Life Science)** Option B is correct because lungfish have lungs similar to human lungs. Option A is incorrect because electric eels can absorb oxygen through their mouths. Option C is incorrect because gar can get oxygen through their swim bladders. Option D is incorrect because catfish absorb oxygen in their digestive tracts.

10. **C. Fish can pump water from their mouths through gills but not through gill flaps. (Analyzing Information/Life Science)** Option C can be inferred from information in the passage, so it is correct. Options A, B, and D are not supported by information in the passage.

11. **B. They are at risk of meeting predators when they rise to the surface to obtain air. (Analyzing Information/Life Science)** Option B is correct because rising to the surface exposes the fish to predators that do not live in water, such as birds. Option A is not a risk, so it is incorrect. Option C is contradicted by the information. Option D does not make sense. The animals can continue to look for and consume food while taking in oxygen from the air.

12. **D. Gills are much more efficient in absorbing oxygen than are lungs. (Analyzing Information/Life Science)** Option D is a correct inference because the information says that water contains a much lower percentage of oxygen than air. Therefore, gills must be more efficient in obtaining oxygen from the water in order for the fish to survive. Options A, B, and C cannot be inferred from the information.

13. **A. The fish will begin to suffocate from lack of oxygen. (Applying Information/Life Science)** Option A is correct because reduced oxygen will cause the fish to suffocate. Option B is not supported by the information in the passage. Option C does not make sense because as the fish swim faster, they will require more oxygen, so they would suffocate anyway. Option D is not supported by the information. Oxygen levels vary by depth. The most oxygen-rich water is near the surface, and oxygen levels generally decrease with depth, but at very deep levels, begin to increase again. However, fish may not be able to survive in such cold, dark, depths.

14. **D. Rise to the surface and open its mouth. (Analyzing Information/Life Science)** Option D is correct because electric eels absorb oxygen into their mouths, so they would need to open their mouths. Option A describes how a lungfish obtains oxygen from the atmosphere. Option B describes how mudskipper and anguillid eels obtain oxygen from the air. Option C describes how catfish obtain oxygen from the air.

15. **C. Frogs are amphibious, so they need to breathe on land and in water. (Applying Information/Life Science)** Option C is correct because amphibious animals live on both land and water. Therefore, a frog would have ways to obtain oxygen both on land and in water. Options A, B, and D are not supported by the information.

16. **C. Lungfish (Analyzing Information/Life Science)** Option C is correct because both frogs and lungfish use lungs for breathing at least part of the time. For this reason, the other options (A, B, and D) are incorrect.

17. **A. It is living outside its natural habitat and causing damage to its new habitat. (Interpreting Information/ Life Science)** Option A is correct because it matches the definition of invasive species in the information. Option B may be correct, but does not explain why the animal is harming its new habitat. Options C and D are incorrect because they do not explain how the fish are harmful.

18. **B. Definition 1, because it harms indigenous species (Interpreting Information/Life Science)** Option B is correct because harming indigenous species is one of the main characteristics of an invasive species. Option A is incorrect because, while true, it does not establish that the fish harm their new habitat. Option C is incorrect because this definition applies only to native species. Option D is incorrect because Asian carp are grown as food in Asia, not North America, where they are considered invasive.

19. **C. Elk, because their population grew out of control and negatively affected their habitat (Applying Information/Life Science)** Option C is correct because it matches one definition of invasive species in the information. Option A is incorrect because wolves were the natural predator of elk until they were killed off. Option B is not supported by the information. Option D is incorrect because elk are a native species.

20. **B. Asian carp (Analyzing Information/Life Science)** Option B is correct because this is the only option that is an invasive species. Therefore, the other options (A, C, and D) are incorrect.

21. **A. The eggs were already on the plant when it left the plant nursery in Texas. (Analyzing Information/Life Science)** Pepper weevils only live on pepper plants in the southern U.S., so the eggs had to be on the plant before it was shipped to Chicago. Option B is incorrect because pepper weevils do not grow on tomato plants. Option C is not supported by the information in the passage. Option D is incorrect because pepper weevils do not exist naturally in the Chicago area.

22. **A. Grow next year's pepper plants from seeds. (Applying Information/Life Science)** If Stephan grows next year's pepper plants from seeds, he will be able to avoid getting weevils from plants shipped from southern states where the weevils live. Option B would kill plants, not insect pests. Stephan's pepper plants could still get pepper weevils if the new garden store gets its pepper plants from nurseries in southern states, so Option C is incorrect. Option D will not make any difference on next year's garden because the pepper weevil cannot live through the Chicago winter. Therefore, his plants could get the weevils again next year unless he takes other precautions.

23. **C. egg, larva, pupa, adult (Analyzing Information/Life Science)** Option C matches the order given in the information. Therefore, the other options (A, B, and D) are incorrect.

24. **C. Strong winds blow away topsoil from the farms in a local area. (Applying Information/Earth Science)** Option C is correct because this is the only option that involves a natural force moving rock or soil to another location. Options A and B are examples of weathering. Option D is an example of soil depletion from inappropriate farming methods.

25. **A. Friction inside the wheels causes the cart to slow down and then stop. (Interpreting Information/ Physical Science)** Option A is correct because Newton's First Law says that an object in motion tends to stay in motion unless acted upon by another force. Friction is a force that slows the cart. Therefore, Option B is incorrect. Options C and D are incorrect because these additional forces would result in acceleration—a change in direction or velocity. In Option C, the velocity would increase. In Option D, the direction would change, and the speed would possibly increase.

26. **B. An object will change speed or direction if another force acts on it. (Generalizing/Physical Science)** Option B is correct because another force, friction, acted on the cart, which caused it to stop. Option A is incorrect because the cart did not stay in motion. Option C is incorrect because the cart was not at rest. Option D is incorrect because this example is not about action and reaction forces.

27. **A. Force (Generalizing/Physical Science)** Option A is correct because the gust of wind made the cart move. The other options (B, C, and D) are incorrect because they deal with the movement of the object.

28. **A. A spaceship is moving toward the moon at 500 kilometers per hour. (Application/Physical Science)** Option A is correct because this option is about both speed and direction. Option B is not about speed or direction because the spaceship is not in motion. Option C is incorrect because this example is about acceleration—a change in speed or direction. Option D is incorrect because it is about a force.

29. **B. Its waves have a higher frequency than those of violet light. (Interpreting Information/Physical Science)** This information is stated directly in Paragraph 1. Option A is incorrect; although UV light can make objects fluoresce, materials will fluoresce in several colors. Option C is not supported by information in the passage. Option D is incorrect because UV light is not visible light.

30. **B. Moderate (Interpreting Information/Physical Science)** Option B is stated directly in the table. Therefore, the other options (A, C, and D) are incorrect.

31. **C. Overexposure to UV light can have serious health consequences. (Generalizing/Physical Science)** Option C is correct because too much UV light can result in skin cancer and overproduction of vitamin D. Option A is not supported by the information in the passage. Option B is contradicted by the information; our bodies do not have the capacity to regulate vitamin D production, which can cause a health hazard if too much accumulates in our bodies. Option D does not make sense; decreasing ozone levels are causing the amount of UV light reaching Earth to increase.

32. **A. Ultraviolet light, which causes sunburns, cannot travel through glass easily. (Interpreting Information/ Physical Science)** Option A is correct because glass filters much, but not all, of the ultraviolet light in sunlight. Option B is incorrect because while sunlight can vary depending on events on the sun such as solar flares, the changes are not sufficient to cause an increased potential for sunburn. In addition, the UV index was the same both days. Option C is incorrect because the glass itself, not the tinting, is enough to filter out most UV light. Option D is contradicted by the information, which states that Tim went to work at the same time both days.

33. **A. Denver, Colorado, which has a high elevation, on a sunny summer day (Application/Earth Science)** Option A is correct because this location has several factors that would contribute to a high UV index: sunny weather, high altitude, and daytime hours during the summertime. Option B is incorrect because on a foggy winter day, not much UV light could get through. Option C is incorrect because UV light would not be high in winter. Argentina is in the southern hemisphere, so it is not likely to have high UV index in July, which is a winter month in South America.

34. **C. Fossil fuels will be depleted. (Analyzing Information/Earth Science)** Option C is a consequence of overreliance on fossil fuels, not of UV exposure. The problems in the other options (A, B, and D) are more likely the consequences of increased exposure to UV light, so they are possible long-term risks.

35. **D. Earth's tilt toward the sun in summer means that the UV rays reach Earth more directly. (Analyzing Information/Earth Science)** Energy from the sun passes through Earth's atmosphere more directly when Earth is tilted toward the sun than when it is tilted away. There is no support in the information for Option A. Cloudy weather (Option B) blocks an equal amount of UV radiation whether in summer or in winter. Option C is incorrect because although the amount of UV light produced by the sun may vary, the production of UV light by the sun is not a result of seasons on Earth.

36. **B. Eliminate the discharge of gases that cause ozone molecules to break down to $O_2$. (Applying Information/Earth Science)** Option B is the only option that would reduce ozone depletion in the upper atmosphere. Option A would reduce greenhouse gases, not gases that cause ozone depletion. Ozone at Earth's surface is a source of pollution, so Option C is incorrect. Option D may ward off some effects of increased UV exposure, but it will not help preserve the ozone layer.

37. **D. bb (Interpreting Information/Life Science)** Option D is correct because a guinea pig will have white fur only if it receives two copies of the recessive gene (bb). Therefore, the other options (A, B, and C) are incorrect.

38. **D. 1:2 (Analyzing Information/Life Science)** Option D is correct because of the four possible combinations of genes in the Punnett square, only two result in white fur. Therefore, the odds are 1:2. The other options (A, B, and C) are incorrect.

39. **A. 0 (Analyzing Information/Life Science)** The offspring of a guinea pig with two dominant genes will always be black because the offspring will always receive a copy of the dominant gene from this parent. The other options (B, C, and D) are incorrect.

40. **D. 1:2 (Applying Information/Life Science)** Option D is correct because the Punnett square produced will have these combinations of the genes: BB, Bb, Bb, bb. Therefore the odds are 2:4 or, simplified, 1:2. The other options (A, B, and C) are incorrect.

41. **B. In a freezer, ice cubes gradually become smaller and thinner. (Applying Information/Physical Science)** Option B is correct because the solid ice became water vapor without passing through a liquid state. Options A and D are examples of chemical reactions, not changes in state. Option C is an example of evaporation, not sublimation.

42. **A. Frost forms on the windows of a car overnight. (Applying Information/Physical Science)** When frost appears, water vapor in the air crystalizes in a thin layer on the glass without passing through a liquid state. Option B is a physical change to snow as it becomes compacted into ice. Option C is an example of melting. Option D is an example of sublimation.

43. **D. 173 (Interpreting Information/Earth Science)** The number 173 is stated directly in the passage, so Option D is correct. The other options (A, B, and C) are incorrect.

44. **D. Improved telescopes permit astronomers to see into space better than in the past. (Interpreting Information/Earth Science)** This information is stated directly in the passage, so Option D is correct. Option A only accounts for the classification of objects, not their total number, which would remain the same regardless of their classification. Only objects from natural sources are considered heavenly bodies, so Option B is incorrect. Option C is not supported by the information.

45. **C. Objects in the Kuiper Belt are different from the 8 major planets. (Interpreting Information/Earth Science)** Option C is correct because the scientists believed that Pluto and Eris shared more characteristics with the Kuiper Belt than with the 8 major planets. Options A and D are not supported by the information. Option B is contradicted by the information.

46. **B. Adults have 20 square meters of skin on average. (Interpreting Information/Earth Science)** Option B is the answer because, while it is stated directly in the passage, it is the only option that is not part of the definition of an organ as described in the first sentence of the passage. The remaining options (A, C, and D) are stated directly in the passage, so they are incorrect.

47. **A. You will feel pain. (Applying Information/Life Science)** Option A is correct because pain is one of the sensations our skin can detect. It is part of the sense of touch. The remaining options (B, C, and D) do not happen when we receive a cut.

48. **B. It is an endothermic change. (Applying Information/Life Science)** Option B is correct because evaporation causes an endothermic change—heat is required for the water to evaporate. Since water absorbs heat from the body in order to evaporate, the body is cooled. Option A is not correct for two reasons: Evaporation is a physical change, not a chemical reaction, and is endothermic. Options C and D are true of sweating, but they are not reasons sweating cools our bodies.

49. **A. The small blood vessels in the skin narrow so that blood flow is reduced and heat is conserved. (Analyzing Information/Life Science)** Option A is correct because heat from blood passing near the skin can leave the body. By reducing blood flow, less heat is lost. Option B is incorrect because shivering is caused by skeletal muscles, not the skin. Option C is contradicted by the information; we sweat to cool our bodies. Option D is incorrect because the thin, light hair on our bodies is not sufficient to warm us.

50. **D. Warning us of far-off danger (Interpreting Information/Life Science)** Option D is correct because hearing and vision warn us of far off danger. Option A is incorrect because skin produces vitamin D, an essential nutrient. Option B is incorrect because the sense of touch helps us detect sensations such as pain. Option C is incorrect because our skin regulates body temperature through sweat, blood level contraction, and the sense of touch.

# XIII. Social Studies Full-Length Practice Test with Answer Explanations

**50 Items**

**Time: 70 Minutes**

**Directions:** This is a test of your skills in analyzing information in the area of social studies. Read each item and decide which of the four answer options is the best answer.

Sometimes, several items are based on the same information. You should read this material carefully and use it to answer the items.

*Items 1 through 7 refer to the following information and timeline.*

**The U.S. Constitution has been amended several times to expand voting rights. Look at the timeline.**

| Amendments to the U.S. Constitution: Voting Rights | |
|---|---|
| 1870 | The Fifteenth Amendment gave all male citizens the right to vote regardless of race. |
| 1920 | The Nineteenth Amendment gave female citizens the right to vote in all elections. |
| 1961 | The Twenty-third Amendment gave District of Columbia residents the right to vote for President. |
| 1964 | The Twenty-fourth Amendment abolished the poll tax. |
| 1971 | The Twenty-sixth Amendment lowered the voting age to 18 for all (from 21 for males and 18 for females in some states). |

1. In what year did women gain the right to vote in all elections?

   A. 1870
   B. 1920
   C. 1961
   D. 1964

2. Which amendment to the Constitution granted the right to vote to males between the ages of 18 and 21?

   A. Nineteenth
   B. Twenty-third
   C. Twenty-fourth
   D. Twenty-sixth

3. Which of the following is <u>most likely</u> a reason the voting age for males was lowered to 18 in 1971?

   A. Because studies showed that males lacked the maturity of females at age 18
   B. So males could consume alcoholic beverages at a younger age
   C. Because before 1971 male citizens could be drafted into the military during the Vietnam War at age 18 but could not vote
   D. Because women lacked equal rights at the time

4. What was year of the first presidential election in which Washington, D.C., voters were eligible to vote?

   A. 1960
   B. 1964
   C. 1968
   D. 1972

5. Which of the following values and beliefs are most responsible for these amendments?

    A. Honesty and integrity
    B. Freedom of religion
    C. Equality and fairness
    D. Gender equality

6. In what year did African American men gain the right to vote?

    A. 1870
    B. 1920
    C. 1961
    D. 1964

7. What is the most likely effect of the amendments on voting?

    A. Many unqualified people will start to vote.
    B. More people will cast votes in elections.
    C. More people are eligible to vote.
    D. Fewer people will register to vote.

*Items 8 through 11 refer to the following map and information.*

A highly connected Internet user is defined as an individual who can connect to the Internet in multiple locations from multiple devices. For example, an individual with a connected smartphone that can be used on the go, a connected desktop computer at work, and a connected laptop computer at home would be considered highly connected. Recently, the number of highly connected individuals was estimated to be 27% of the U.S. population. This represents a plurality of the population of the United States, which means that a large portion of the U.S. population are frequent Internet users. Unfortunately, the second largest group is people with no Internet access at all. Approximately 15.9% of the U.S. population falls into this group. This map shows which states have highly connected Internet users above, at, and below the national average of 27%.

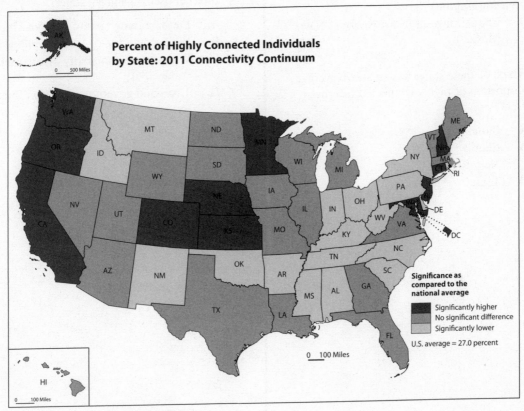

**Percent of Highly Connected Individuals by State: 2011 Connectivity Continuum**

Significance as compared to the national average

Significantly higher
No significant difference
Significantly lower

U.S. average = 27.0 percent

*Source: www.census.gov/prod/2013pubs/p20-569.pdf*

8. Which of these regions of the U.S. has the greatest proportion of highly connected Internet users?

   A. New England (Maine, Massachusetts, New Hampshire, Vermont, Rhode Island, Connecticut)
   B. The South (Virginia, North Carolina, South Carolina, Alabama, Georgia, Arkansas, Louisiana, Mississippi, Kentucky, Tennessee)
   C. The west coast (California, Oregon, Washington)
   D. The southwest (Texas, Arizona, New Mexico)

9. Which of these states has an above-average proportion of highly connected Internet users?

   A. Indiana
   B. Illinois
   C. Nebraska
   D. Texas

10. How many states have a lower percentage of highly connected Internet users than the national average?

    A. 15
    B. 16
    C. 17
    D. 18

11. Which of the following factors would most increase the percentage of highly connected Internet users in a given state?

    A. Laws banning texting while driving
    B. Widespread use of landline phones
    C. Widespread availability of Internet connectivity
    D. Taxes and government fees on Internet services

*Items 12 through 15 refer to the following information.*

An economist recently compared the average prices of Big Mac sandwiches in countries around the world. The results are summed up in the table.

| Big Mac Prices in Selected Countries | |
|---|---|
| Country | Average Price in U.S. Dollars (before all taxes) |
| Norway | $7.76 |
| Switzerland | $6.83 |
| Brazil | $5.86 |
| Canada | $5.25 |
| Euro Zone | $4.95 |
| Britain | $4.93 |
| Australia | $4.81 |
| United States | $4.80 |
| Turkey | $4.42 |
| Japan | $3.64 |
| China | $2.73 |
| Russia | $2.55 |
| Indonesia | $2.43 |
| South Africa | $2.33 |
| India (Chicken Mac) | $1.75 |
| Ukraine | $1.63 |

12. In which of the countries in the table is a Big Mac sandwich the least expensive?

    A. Russia
    B. Indonesia
    C. India
    D. Ukraine

13. Based on the information, which of the following countries most likely has the highest cost of living?

    A. Brazil
    B. South Africa
    C. Canada
    D. United States

14. Which of the following factors makes prices in different countries most difficult to compare?

    A. Tax rates are higher in some countries than others.
    B. The countries have different forms of government.
    C. Big Macs are not made from beef in all countries.
    D. Not all the countries use the metric system.

15. Which of the following would provide a more reliable estimate of the cost of living in various countries?

    A. Compare another, more common product, such as the price of milk.
    B. Compare an assortment of products and services people commonly use.
    C. Compare the exchange rates of the various countries' currencies to the U.S. dollar.
    D. Compare average salaries in the various countries.

*Items 16 and 17 refer to the following information.*

According to the U.S. Department of Energy, 2014 was the first year that more energy was produced from wind power, solar power, and biomass than from hydropower. Of all these renewable energy sources, hydropower was long the mainstay. However, declining costs for producing wind and solar power, along with federal and state laws mandating that power companies increase their use of renewable sources, resulted in significant increases in the use of the three non-hydro sources. In addition, drought conditions in several parts of the country reduced the availability of hydropower and forced utility companies to look to other renewable sources to comply with the state and federal mandates.

16. Which of the following is a reason that wind power, solar power, and biomass surpassed hydropower?

   A.  The non-hydro sources have become much cheaper to produce recently.
   B.  Less coal is available for use in power plants.
   C.  Utility companies are unable to produce hydropower because of a bad drought.
   D.  Governments banned further use of hydropower, so utility companies had to look for alternatives.

17. Which of the following can most logically be concluded from the information?

   A.  Non-hydro sources will continue to surpass hydropower.
   B.  Solar power is considered a reliable source of electricity.
   C.  More electricity is now generated from solar power than from hydropower.
   D.  Solar power is cheaper than hydropower.

*Items 18 through 23 refer to the following information.*

The Confederacy formed when states where slavery was legal seceded from the Union after the election of Abraham Lincoln to the presidency. Eventually, eleven states seceded: Virginia, North Carolina, South Carolina, Georgia, Florida, Tennessee, Alabama, Mississippi, Louisiana, Arkansas, and Texas. Four slaveholding states (Missouri, Kentucky, Delaware, and Maryland) remained in the Union, but did not give up slavery. (West Virginia broke away from Virginia in 1863 to join the Union.) President Lincoln vowed that he would not attack the Confederacy unless they attacked first because he continued to consider them U.S. states and the people American citizens.

On the outbreak of actual fighting at Fort Sumter, the Union capital, Washington, D.C., was vulnerable to Confederate attack from nearby Virginia, just across the Potomac River, or from Maryland, which, though remaining within the Union, had strong sympathy for the Confederacy. An extensive network of forts and other military installations, including rifle pits, bunkers, cannon emplacements, and stockades at bridgeheads, were built in a circle 37 miles in circumference surrounding Washington, D.C., to protect it from invasion. By the conclusion of the war, 68 different forts ringed the capital.

Only one Civil War battle took place within the boundaries of Washington, D.C., the battle of Fort Stevens. Located in northwest Washington, D.C., not far from the border with Maryland, Fort Stevens was attacked by troops commanded by Confederate General Jubal Early on July 11–12, 1864. Early's troops entered Maryland and then attacked from the north. The fort's strong fortifications plus the prompt arrival of reinforcements from Washington, D.C., caused Early to withdraw his troops after only two days of fighting.

The Battle of Fort Stevens holds two distinctions: It is the only Civil War battle fought within the limits of Washington, D.C., and the battle marks the only time that a sitting U.S. President was fired on in a war. Lincoln, his wife, Mary Todd Lincoln, and several others rode to the fort to view the fighting. According to one account, Lincoln was standing on one of the parapets of the fort to observe more closely when enemy shots were fired, killing another member of the presidential party. Supposedly, one of the Union soldiers shouted out to Lincoln, "Get down, you fool!"

18. Why was Washington, D.C., vulnerable to attack at the start of the war?

    A.  Lincoln refused to attack the Confederacy first.

    B.  It was one of the most fortified cities in the world.

    C.  Many of its residents were confederate sympathizers.

    D.  A Confederate state was located just across the Potomac River.

19. According to the passage, Washington D.C.,'s fortifications were built in a large circle around the entire city. What does this information indicate about the fortifications and the city's vulnerability to attack?

    A.  Fortifications along the Maryland border were unnecessary because Maryland was a Union state.

    B.  The city could be attacked from all sides because the Confederacy was so near.

    C.  Lincoln needed to surround the city in case of a popular uprising of Washington, D.C., citizens against the Union.

    D.  Lincoln was afraid the Union army was not strong enough, so he built more forts than necessary.

20. Which of the following is a conclusion that can be drawn from the information?

    A. Lincoln should have moved the capital to a safer place before the war.

    B. The Confederacy would have captured Washington, D.C., if Fort Stevens had fallen.

    C. Lincoln was a brilliant military strategist.

    D. The network of forts and other defensive structures were important in safeguarding Washington, D.C.

21. Which of the following statements shows that the Battle of Fort Stevens is unique in U.S. history?

    A. It is the first time Washington, D.C., needed fortification.

    B. It is the only time Washington, D.C., was attacked during a war.

    C. It is the only time that a U.S. President was fired upon in war.

    D. It is the only time that a U.S. President has visited a war zone.

22. According to the information, Lincoln's wife, Mary Todd Lincoln, accompanied him to the battle along with others. Which of the following can be inferred from this statement?

    A. Mary Todd Lincoln's desire to go to the battle was a sign of her growing mental illness.

    B. People's attitude toward war was more casual than today.

    C. Lincoln thought that everyone should experience the war to see how terrible it was.

    D. Lincoln did not like his wife, so he did not object to her accompanying him to such a dangerous place.

23. Why did the soldier call Lincoln a fool?

    A. Many people doubted Lincoln's leadership during the war.

    B. The heat of the moment made the soldier speak carelessly.

    C. The soldier was a Confederate sympathizer.

    D. The soldier didn't know that the person was the President.

24. Songs have long been an important part of U.S. Presidential election campaigns. One of the most notable is the sunny, "Happy Days Are Here Again," which was the theme song of Franklin Delano Roosevelt's campaign for President. This bouncy song was an ideal way to frame Roosevelt's positive message about how he could end the Depression with his promise of a "New Deal" for the American people. The song's upbeat melody and catchy lyrics also formed a perfect counterpoint to the dour, conservative image of President Herbert Hoover, who many Americans blamed for not acting decisively to prevent the Depression.

    Why was "Happy Days Are Here Again" an effective song for Roosevelt's campaign for President?

    A. It reminded people of Herbert Hoover's patriotism.

    B. It announced to people that Roosevelt had promised to end Prohibition.

    C. It made people feel optimistic that Roosevelt could solve their problems.

    D. It made people feel worse because it contrasted so greatly with the Depression.

*Items 25 and 26 refer to the following information and graph.*

**A fast-food chain recently analyzed service speed in its drive-throughs in order to improve customer service. This table summarizes the results.**

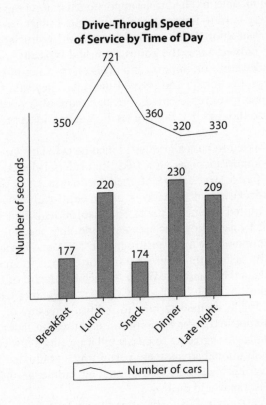

**Drive-Through Speed of Service by Time of Day**

25. What is the busiest time of day for the chain?

    **A.** Breakfast
    **B.** Lunch
    **C.** Snack
    **D.** Dinner

26. According to the chart, dinner has the slowest service speed and the fewest number of cars. Which of the following statements is the <u>most logical</u> explanation of this information?

    **A.** The chain has more workers on duty at dinner time than at lunch time.
    **B.** Customers don't like to eat fast food for dinner.
    **C.** Orders are much larger at lunch time than at dinner time.
    **D.** Customers order more complicated menu items at dinner time than at other times.

*Items 27 through 35 refer to the following information.*

Because taxation was a major issue in the American Revolution, the writers of the Constitution made it particularly hard for the government to impose taxes. In particular, the Constitution said that any direct tax (such as an income tax) had to be apportioned among the states according to population. This provision made it very hard to impose a tax on income. In fact, several court decisions stated that an income tax was unconstitutional. Yet, many citizens and politicians believed that an income tax would be fairer than the indirect taxes the government had typically used to raise funds up until that time. Indirect taxes included taxes on imports and taxes on the sales of certain products. They believed that these taxes were disproportionate and favored the rich. They said these taxes hit the poor harder than the rich because these taxes represented a greater share of a poor person's total income than a wealthy person's. They also thought that these taxes did not provide a predictable revenue stream for the government.

Many tax reformers wanted to pass a graduated income tax. This kind of tax imposed progressively higher tax rates as individuals' incomes increased. Reformers believed that this was fairer, since the wealthy could afford to pay a larger share of their income in taxes than ordinary, working people. However, court rulings declaring income taxes unconstitutional stated that an amendment to the Constitution would be required for such a tax to be constitutional. This ruling convinced the reformers that an amendment to the Constitution was necessary, and they began to push for one in Congress.

The amendment was opposed by a powerful senator, Nelson Aldrich, of Rhode Island. Aldrich, a Republican, was a wealthy eastern financier, and supported their interests in Congress. They believed that an income tax would tax them unfairly. When Aldrich first heard of the idea of a graduated income tax, he called it "Communistic." Aldrich, chair of the Senate Finance Committee, blocked the tax bills as long as he could, but finally seemed to bow to political pressure of supporters of an income tax. Aldrich engineered what appeared to be a compromise but was in fact a plan to derail the income tax proposal forever. In exchange for agreeing to pass a bill imposing a low corporate income tax, which he wanted, he allowed a constitutional amendment permitting a graduated income tax to be sent to states for ratification. He was certain that the constitutional amendment would fail to win ratification, and that the calls for an income tax would die down.

Aldrich's plan, however, backfired. Shortly after the amendment was sent to the states for ratification, a reformist movement swept the country, and Democratic majorities were elected to both the House of Representatives and the Senate, as well as to many state legislatures. As part of the reformist victory, the proposed constitutional amendment was ratified by enough states to become part of the Constitution.

27. Which of the following is NOT a reason that reformers supported a graduated income tax instead of indirect taxes?

    A. They believed in Communism.
    B. They believed that indirect taxes affected the poor unfairly.
    C. They believed that an income tax would provide a better revenue stream for the government.
    D. They believed that the rich could afford to pay more than the poor.

28. Why was an income tax difficult to impose?

    A. It was opposed by influential Democrats in Congress.
    B. The courts said that an income tax was unconstitutional.
    C. It was hard to get people to pay their taxes.
    D. An income tax was unfair to the poor.

29. What is the meaning of the word *disproportionate* as used in paragraph 1?

    A. Smaller than necessary
    B. Larger than necessary
    C. Larger than appropriate
    D. Smaller than appropriate

30. Why did Aldrich suddenly allow the proposal for a constitutional amendment to go forward?

    A. He decided that a graduated income tax was not Communistic after all.
    B. He agreed with the reformers that indirect taxes were unfair to the poor.
    C. He allowed it to go forward, thinking that it would not be ratified by the states.
    D. He realized that the amendment was going to pass despite his opposition, so he stopped opposing it.

31. Why did Aldrich's plan backfire?

    A. The Supreme Court ruled that a graduated income tax was constitutional.
    B. Popular support for the amendment gained momentum, and the amendment was ratified by the states.
    C. Congress raised the tax rates on corporations.
    D. A Republican majority was elected to both the House and the Senate.

32. What is the most likely reason that Aldrich opposed a graduated income tax?

    A. He wanted to tax the poor more heavily than the rich.
    B. He thought that an income tax would harm the economy.
    C. He represented the interests of the wealthy, whom the tax bill singled out for higher taxes.
    D. He felt that taxes were too high in general, and should be lowered or abolished.

33. Which of the following is NOT a measure that the reformers would have supported and Aldrich would have opposed?

    A. A proposal to increase federal regulation of interstate railroads
    B. A plan to allow for the people to call for referendums
    C. A plan to support corporate monopolies that dominated the economy
    D. A proposal to regulate food and drug companies

34. Which of the following is an opinion about the graduated income tax?

    A. It hit the rich harder than the poor.
    B. It was declared unconstitutional.
    C. A reformist movement supported it.
    D. It is Communistic.

35. Based on the information in the passage, which of the following is a theme of U.S. history at this time?

    A. Disagreement among different sections of the country
    B. Conflict with foreign countries
    C. Disagreement between reformers and the wealthy
    D. Conflict over civil rights

*Items 36 through 39 refer to the following political cartoon captioned "Killed in Committee."*

Killed in Committee

Source: www.senate.gov/artandhistory/art/artifact/Ga_Cartoon/Ga_cartoon_38_00597.htm

36. What is the main idea of the cartoon?

   A. Aldrich used his power to stop needed reforms.

   B. Aldrich is a fierce defender of the Constitution.

   C. Aldrich is a good leader because he blocked bad legislation.

   D. Senate committees serve a vital function in government.

37. In the cartoon, what do the flies represent?

   A. Problems that Aldrich and his committee solved.

   B. Needed legislation that Aldrich blocked in his committee.

   C. Reformist politicians who Aldrich opposed.

   D. Other senators on Aldrich's committee.

38. Which of the following is an opinion expressed by the cartoonist?

   A. The country has able leaders who can solve its problems.

   B. Senate committees operate in open, democratic ways.

   C. Business interests have bribed Aldrich.

   D. Companies such as Standard Oil have too much power and influence.

39. How would the cartoonist represent progressive income tax in the cartoon?

   A. As another dead fly caught in the web of Aldrich's committee

   B. As a can of insecticide that is about to spray and kill Aldrich

   C. As a fly that is alive and flying, with a label that says "State ratification."

   D. As another special interest holding up another part of the web.

*Items 40 through 42 refer to the following information.*

The law of demand says that price and demand are interrelated: As price goes up, demand will go down. However, the law of demand affects different products in different ways. If a product is considered a necessity, such as milk or bread, demand will not be affected very much by price because consumers will continue to buy the product. This is called inelastic demand.

On the other hand, demand may be elastic. When demand is elastic, even a small change in price will affect demand. Demand for items that consumers feel are unnecessary or luxuries are elastic. For example, if the price of a certain brand of jeans goes up, consumers may switch to another brand, or not buy the jeans at all. The following graphs show how inelastic and elastic demand work.

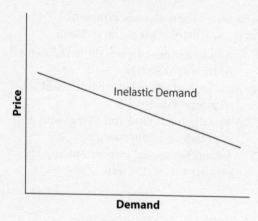

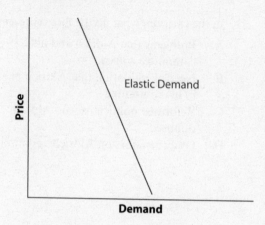

40. Which of the following illustrates the relationship between price and demand?

   A. When the demand goes up, supply goes up.

   B. When demand goes down, the price goes up.

   C. When the price goes up, demand goes down.

   D. When the price goes up, the demand goes up.

41. What is inelastic demand?

   A. Price increases will cause an immediate drop in demand.

   B. Price increases will cause consumers to think the product is better and buy it.

   C. Price increases will not affect demand very much.

   D. Changes in supply will not affect the price.

42. Which of the following is an example of inelastic demand?

   A. Freezing cold weather causes iceberg lettuce prices to skyrocket, and lettuce sales decline.

   B. The price of gold more than doubles, so sales of gold jewelry drops off.

   C. A bumper strawberry harvest causes prices to drop so far that many farmers plow their crops under.

   D. The price of broccoli drops by 75% but people don't buy much more.

*Items 43 through 47 refer to the following information.*

In many ways, the 1950s were the golden age of the automobile. World War II had ended in 1945, and the victorious United States transitioned to a peacetime economy. During the war, few automobiles were produced for consumer use, so in 1945, most cars on the road were old and dilapidated. By the 1950s, car production soared. By some estimates, there were 25 million cars registered in 1950. Approximately 6 million new cars were manufactured in 1950 alone, and nearly 58 million cars were manufactured during the decade. By 1958, the number of registered cars in the United States had more than doubled to 67 million. This had a tremendous impact on life in the United States.

In cities, public transportation and living patterns changed enormously. Streetcars and light rail were replaced with buses, and both walking and public transportation use declined as people increasingly drove their cars. Because people could drive to work, they no longer needed to live near their jobs or have access to public transportation. This facilitated another major change: the rise of the suburb.

In the past, suburbs were near large cities and connected to them by rail lines. In the 1950s, the wide availability of the car, with the addition of the new highway system, permitted a large exodus of city residents to new suburbs, many of which had little or no public transportation. As a result, suburbs grew at a high rate.

The automobile also introduced new kinds of businesses and pastimes, such as drive-in restaurants and drive-in movies. Though these had existed before, the widespread availability of cars caused these kinds of businesses to boom.

43. How many cars were on U.S. roads by the end of the 1950s?

    A.  6 million
    B.  25 million
    C.  58 million
    D.  67 million

44. Which of the following is the <u>most logical</u> explanation of why car sales boomed in the 1950s?

    A.  The Korean War caused steel production to be directed to military uses.
    B.  After winning World War II, people felt optimistic about the future.
    C.  People who had lived through the Depression felt worried about spending money.
    D.  The Cold War made people feel anxious about the future.

45. How did the widespread use of cars affect living patterns in the United States?

    A.  People with automobiles no longer needed to live in central cities, so they could move to the suburbs.
    B.  Streetcars were replaced with buses.
    C.  Prosperous Americans could afford to live in attractive suburbs.
    D.  Developers used mass-production techniques pioneered in the auto industry to build attractive, affordable housing in the suburbs.

46. What is the meaning of the word *dilapidated* in paragraph 1?

    A.  Out of order
    B.  In poor condition
    C.  Ruined
    D.  Rusty

47. Consider the two statements below.

> I. Large central cities are now growing at a faster rate than suburbs.
>
> II. Nowadays, Americans use drive-through banks, pharmacies, restaurants, coffee shops, and wedding chapels.

Which of the statements, if either, shows that the automobile culture of the 1950s had a lasting impact on American society?

- **A.** I only
- **B.** II only
- **C.** I and II
- **D.** Neither I nor II

*Items 48 through 50 refer to the following information and ad.*

Bruce Ritter and Pete Quimby are both running for mayor of Parkton. Recently, Quimby's supporters put these billboards up around town.

> Bruce Ritter is a billionaire who doesn't pay his taxes!
>
> Last year, Ritter made nearly 20 million dollars from his businesses and investments, but paid a lower percentage of his income in taxes than most people in town. Plus he used loopholes to avoid paying Social Security taxes for 2 years.
>
> Workers in his hazardous factories make minimum wage while Ritter rakes in millions—at your expense! Do you want a mayor who pays his fair share? Don't vote for Ritter!

48. What is the main purpose of this ad?

- **A.** To help win support for Quimby's proposal to lower everyone's taxes.
- **B.** To get Ritter to pay his fair share of taxes.
- **C.** To put doubt in people's minds about Ritter.
- **D.** To encourage people to like Quimby.

49. What is the <u>most likely</u> reason the ad includes the detail that Ritter is a billionaire?

- **A.** The ad writers hope people will believe he got his money in dishonest ways.
- **B.** The ad writers think people admire large employers.
- **C.** The ad writers think ordinary people don't like extremely wealthy people.
- **D.** The ad writers want people to think Ritter does not have good ideas.

50. Quimby supporters are responsible for the billboards. Why didn't they include Quimby's name in the billboard ad?

- **A.** Quimby is a modest person.
- **B.** Quimby wants to present a positive image to voters.
- **C.** Quimby does not believe the ad's claims, so he didn't want his name in it.
- **D.** Quimby did not pay his taxes either, so he is afraid of being attacked.

# Answer Key

| | | | | |
|---|---|---|---|---|
| 1. B | 11. C | 21. C | 31. B | 41. C |
| 2. D | 12. D | 22. B | 32. C | 42. D |
| 3. C | 13. A | 23. B | 33. C | 43. D |
| 4. B | 14. A | 24. C | 34. D | 44. B |
| 5. C | 15. B | 25. B | 35. C | 45. A |
| 6. A | 16. A | 26. D | 36. A | 46. B |
| 7. C | 17. B | 27. A | 37. B | 47. B |
| 8. C | 18. D | 28. B | 38. D | 48. C |
| 9. C | 19. B | 29. C | 39. C | 49. C |
| 10. C | 20. D | 30. C | 40. C | 50. B |

# Answer Explanations

1. **B. 1920 (Interpreting Information/Civics and Government)** Option B is correct. The year 1920 is stated directly in the timeline.

2. **D. Twenty-sixth (Interpreting Information/Civics and Government)** Option D is correct. This information is stated directly in the timeline.

3. **C. Because before 1971 male citizens could be drafted into the military during the Vietnam War at age 18 but could not vote (Applying Information/Civics and Government)** Option C is correct. It was unfair to deny men the right to vote but compel them to serve in the military. Option A would be a reason to keep the voting age higher for men than women. Option B does not make sense. Option D may be true, but it is not a reason to keep the voting age higher for men than for women.

4. **B. 1964 (Interpreting Information/Civics and Government)** Option B is correct. According to the information, District of Columbia residents were granted the right to vote in 1961. Therefore, the first presidential election in which they could vote was in 1964 (presidential elections occur on a 4-year cycle). For this reason, the other options (A, C, and D) are incorrect.

5. **C. Equality and fairness (Evaluating Information/Civics and Government)** Option B is correct because all of these amendments made voting rights fairer and more equal. For this reason, the other options (A, B, and D) are incorrect.

6. **A. 1870 (Interpreting Information/Civics and Government)** Option A is correct. This information is stated directly in the timeline; therefore, the other options (B, C, and D) are incorrect.

7. **C. More people are eligible to vote. (Analyzing Information/Civics and Government)** Option C is correct because each one of the amendments granted the right to vote to more individuals. Option A is not supported by the information. Though more people are eligible to vote, that does not mean that more people will actually vote, so Option B is incorrect. Option D cannot be inferred from the information.

8. **C. The west coast (California, Oregon, Washington) (Analyzing Information/Geography)** Option C is correct because all the states in this region have above-average rates. Option A is incorrect because only two of the states in this region have rates above the national average: New Hampshire and Connecticut. Options B and D are incorrect because none of the states in these regions have rates above the national average.

9. **C. Nebraska (Interpreting Information/Geography)** Option C is correct. Of the four states in the options, only Nebraska has an above-average proportion of Internet users. Therefore, the other options (A, B, and D) are incorrect.

10. **C. 17 (Analyzing Information/Geography)** Option C is correct because the map shows that these 17 states have below-average rates: Idaho, Montana, New Mexico, Oklahoma, Arkansas, Mississippi, Alabama, South Carolina, North Carolina, Tennessee, Kentucky, West Virginia, Indiana, Ohio, Pennsylvania, New York, and Delaware. Therefore, the other options (A, B, and D) are incorrect.

11. **C. Widespread availability of Internet connectivity (Applying Information/Geography)** Option C is correct. Of the four factors in the options, only widespread connectivity would increase the percentage of highly connected users. Option A would most likely not have any effect since users can still text at other times. Option B would have no positive effect since highly connected users can still use multiple devices to connect in multiple locations. Option D would tend to decrease the number of highly connected users.

12. **D. Ukraine (Interpreting Information/Economics)** Option D is correct. According to the table, a Big Mac costs $1.63 in Ukraine. This price is lower than in every other country in the list. Therefore, the remaining options (A, B, and C) are incorrect.

13. **A. Brazil (Analyzing Information/Economics)** Option A is correct. Of the four countries in the options, the price of the sandwiches is the most expensive in Brazil. Therefore, it's likely that Brazil has the highest cost of living of the four countries, judging only from the information.

14. **A. Tax rates are higher in some countries than others. (Analyzing Information/Economics)** Option A is correct because while taxes are not included in the information, they are part of the total cost of the sandwich. Since tax rates can vary widely from country to country, it's difficult to compare the prices. Options B and D would not make the information more difficult to compare. Only one country, India, makes this sandwich with chicken instead of beef (Option C), and this is a very minor difference that affects only one country in the list.

15. **B. Compare an assortment of products and services people commonly use. (Analyzing Information/Economics)** Option B is correct because only this option will give a bigger picture of the cost of living in the various countries. Examining the cost of another individual item, milk (Option A), would most likely not give a more reliable estimate because it has the same limitation as the information on sandwiches—the comparison is based on only one item. Comparing exchange rates (Option C) or average salaries (Option D) would not provide data on the cost of living in the various countries.

16. **A. The non-hydro sources have become much cheaper to produce recently. (Interpreting Information/Geography)** Option A is correct. This information is state directly in the passage. Option B is not supported by the information. Option C is too broad: The drought has reduced, not eliminated, the ability to produce hydropower. Option D is not supported by the information.

17. **B. Solar power is considered a reliable source of electricity. (Analyzing Information/Geography)** Option B is correct because the government and the companies would not be using solar power unless they thought it was reliable. Option A cannot be concluded from the information. Many factors can affect which power sources are used in the future. Option C is not supported by the information.

The information says that the amount of electricity generated from biomass, wind power, and solar power together has surpassed hydropower. Therefore, the amount of electricity produced only from solar power is likely less than the amount of electricity produced from hydropower. Option D is incorrect because the information says that the cost of solar power has declined. It does not say whether it has become less expensive than hydropower.

18. **D. A Confederate state was located just across the Potomac River. (Interpreting Information/History)** Option D is correct. This information is stated directly in the passage. The proximity of a Confederate state (Virginia) and the lack of fortifications at the start of the war made Washington, D.C., vulnerable, not Lincoln's desire to avoid initiating the war (Option A). Option B does not make sense. The capital was not fortified in 1860, and fortifications made it less, not more, vulnerable to attack. Option C is not supported by the information. According to the information, many Maryland residents, not D.C. residents, were confederate sympathizers.

19. **B. The city could be attacked from all sides because the Confederacy was so near. (Evaluating Information/History)** Option B is correct because Virginia was nearby, and troops could get to Washington, D.C., by crossing the Potomac River or by passing through Maryland, just as General Early's troops did. Option A is contradicted by the information. Maryland had many Confederate sympathizers living in it, which made it a convenient route for the Confederacy to invade Washington, D.C. Options C and D are not supported by the information and do not make sense.

20. **D. The network of forts and other defensive structures were important in safeguarding Washington, D.C. (Generalizing/History)** Option D is correct because the Battle of Fort Stevens shows that the network of fortifications was important in defending the capital against attack. Option A is not supported by the information. Option B cannot be concluded from the information. The Confederate troops would have had to attack other fortifications and defeat many other soldiers guarding the capital to take control of the city. While Option C may be true, it cannot be inferred from the information in the passage.

21. **C. It is the only time that a U.S. President was fired upon in war. (Generalizing/History)** Option C is correct. This information is stated directly in the passage and makes the battle unique. Options A and B are not supported by the information. Washington, D.C., needed fortification during the War of 1812 and was, in fact, attacked and burned by the British. Option D is not supported by the information and is, in fact, untrue. For example, President Barak Obama visited Afghanistan several times as President.

22. **B. People's attitude toward war was more casual than today. (Evaluating Information/History)** Option B is correct because Lincoln's visit to the front with a large party including his wife shows that people took battle less seriously than they do today. The remaining options (A, C, and D) are not supported by the information and do not make sense.

23. **B. The heat of the moment made the soldier speak carelessly. (Analyzing Information/History)** Option B is correct because the President was in danger, and the soldier shouted out without thinking. Option A is incorrect because while it is true that many people had doubts about Lincoln's leadership during the war, that was no reason for the soldier to call him a fool at that moment. Option C is not supported by the information. If the soldier were really a Confederate sympathizer, he would not have told Lincoln to get out of the line of fire. Option D is not likely. Lincoln's presence at the battle was not a secret to the Union soldiers and his unusual height made him recognizable.

24. **C. It made people feel optimistic that Roosevelt could solve their problems. (Interpreting Information/ Civics and Government)** Option C is correct because the information makes it clear that the optimistic lyrics and bouncy melody made people believe that Roosevelt had the answers to the nation's problems. Therefore, Option D is incorrect. Option A is incorrect because the song contrasted with Hoover's

our, conservative image. Option B is incorrect; though the song was later associated with ending prohibition, this was not Roosevelt's intent when the song was selected.

**3. Lunch (Interpreting Information/Economics)** The time of day with the highest point on the line graph is Lunch, with 721 cars. Breakfast (Option A) has only 350 cars. Snack (Option C) has only 360 cars. Dinner (Option D) has only 320 cars.

**D. Customers order more complicated menu items at dinner time than at other times. (Analysis/Economics)** Option D is correct because preparing complicated menu items takes extra time, which would account for the slower service speeds. Option A would result in faster service at dinner time, so it is incorrect. Option B accounts for fewer cars at dinner time than lunch time, but does not explain the slower service time at dinner, so it is incorrect. Option C would result in slower service times at lunch, so it is incorrect.

27. **A. They believed in Communism. (Interpreting Information/History)** Option A is correct because this was Aldrich's accusation, and does not reflect the reformers' actual beliefs. The other options (B, C, and D) are given as reasons the supporters wanted a graduated income tax, so they are incorrect.

28. **B. The courts said that an income tax was unconstitutional. (Interpreting Information/History)** Option B is stated directly in the passage, so it is correct. Option A is incorrect because influential Republicans, such as Aldrich, opposed the income tax. Option C is not supported by the information. Option D is contradicted by the information. Reformers said that an income tax was fairer to the poor.

29. **C. Larger than appropriate (Interpreting Information/History)** Option C is correct because the information makes clear that indirect taxes represented a larger portion of the incomes of poor people than rich people. The phrase closest in meaning to this is *larger than appropriate*. Therefore, the other options (A, B, and D) are incorrect.

30. **C. He allowed it to go forward, thinking that it would not be ratified by the states. (Interpreting Information/History)** Option C is directly stated in the passage, so it is correct. The remaining options (A, B, and D) are contradicted by the information. Aldrich continued to oppose the idea of an income tax, but he thought that it would not pass.

31. **B. Popular support for the amendment gained momentum, and the amendment was ratified by the states. (Interpreting Information/History)** Option B paraphrases information stated directly in the passage, so it is correct. Options A and C are not supported by the information. Option D is contradicted by the information. A reform-minded Democratic majority was elected to both the House and the Senate.

32. **C. He represented the interests of the wealthy, whom the tax bill singled out for higher taxes. (Analyzing Information/History)** Option C is correct because it is implied in the passage. Aldrich was a wealthy financier, and the bill singled out the wealthy for higher taxes, so that is the most logical reason Aldrich would oppose it. The remaining options (A, B, and D) are incorrect because they are not supported by the information.

33. **C. A plan to support corporate monopolies that dominated the economy (Applying Information/History)** Option C is correct because Aldrich, a wealthy financier, would have supported any proposal that supported business interests, such as corporate monopolies, but reformers would have opposed such a plan. The reformers would have supported and Aldrich would have opposed increased regulation (Option A), since it would harm corporate interests. The reformers would have supported and Aldrich would have opposed a plan for people to call referendums because this would have given more voice to common people. The reformers would have supported and Aldrich would have opposed regulation of food and drug companies (Option D) because that would harm corporate interests.

34. **D. It is Communistic. (Evaluating Information/History)** Option D is correct. This statement represents Aldrich's opinion about the graduated income tax. The other options (A, B, and C) are stated as facts in the information.

35. **C. Disagreement between reformers and the wealthy (Generalizing/History)** Option C is correct because the reformers and the wealthy disagreed about an income tax, and a reform movement gained control of many state legislatures, the U.S. Senate, and House of Representatives, and ratified the amendment. This indicates that disagreement between the wealthy and reformers was a major theme of the period. The remaining options (A, B, and D) are not supported by the information.

36. **A. Aldrich used his power to stop needed reforms. (Interpreting Information/History)** The cartoon represents vital issues of the day caught and killed in the web of Aldrich's committee, so Option A is correct. For this reason, Options C and D are incorrect. Option B is not supported by the cartoon.

37. **B. Needed legislation that Aldrich blocked in his committee. (Interpreting Information/History)** Option B is correct because two of the flies are labeled "house bill" and another is labeled "needed legislation," so the flies represent bills that Aldrich stopped. Therefore, Option A is incorrect. Option C is incorrect because the flies represent laws and reforms, not reformers. Option D is not supported by the cartoon.

38. **D. Companies such as Standard Oil have too much power and influence. (Analyzing Information/History)** Standard Oil is represented as a tower holding up one side of the web. This shows that a web of interests in government and business was stopping needed reforms. Therefore, Option D is correct. Options A and B are contradicted by the cartoon. Option C is not supported by the cartoon. While Aldrich favored business interests, there is no indication that the business interests bribed him.

39. **C. As a fly that is alive and flying, with a label that says "State ratification." (Applying Information/History)** The progressive income tax amendment ultimately escaped the web of Aldrich's committee through state ratification, so Option C is correct. Option A is incorrect because Aldrich was not able to stop this proposal. There is no indication that the progressive income tax ended Aldrich's career or reduced his power, so Option B is incorrect. Option D is incorrect because the progressive income tax was something Aldrich opposed, so would not be represented as something that supported Aldrich's web.

40. **C. When the price goes up, demand goes down. (Interpreting Information/Economics)** Option C is directly stated in the information, so it is correct. This makes the other options incorrect. Option A is a result of the interaction of the laws of supply and demand. Option B misstates the law and makes no sense; when demand drops, prices are likely to drop, too. Option D also misstates the law and makes no sense; increased prices will make people less likely to buy a product.

41. **C. Price increases will not affect demand very much. (Interpreting Information/Economics)** Option C is correct. The answer is stated directly in the information. Option A is a description of elastic demand. Option B is not supported by the information. Option D is about supply, not demand, and misstates the law of supply. The law of supply says that an increase in price will cause an increase in supply.

42. **D. The price of broccoli drops by 75% but people don't buy much more. (Applying Information/Economics)** Option D is correct because a change in price did not affect demand very much. This is an example of inelastic demand, in which changes in price have a relatively small impact on demand. Option A is an example of elastic demand. Demand for lettuce was strongly affected by the increase in price. Option B is also an example of elastic demand. Option C is an example of the interaction of the laws of supply and demand. If the supply of a product is too great, producers will adjust their output. In this case, the farmers are destroying their crops because it costs more to produce and ship the berries than they will earn. A possible consequence of their action is that the reduced supply will cause prices to go back up again.

43. **D. 67 million (Interpreting Information/History)** Option D is correct because this information is stated directly in the passage. Option A (6 million) is the number of cars produced in 1950. Option B (25 million) is the number of registered vehicles in 1950. Option C (58 million) is the number of vehicles produced in the 1950s.

44. **B. After winning World War II, people felt optimistic about the future. (Analyzing Information/History)** Option B is correct because people who feel happy and optimistic are more likely to spend money on expensive purchases, such as new cars, than people who are worried and fearful. Option A is a reason for car sales to decline, so it is incorrect. Options C and D are reasons for people to avoid expensive purchases, so they are incorrect.

45. **A. People with automobiles no longer needed to live in central cities, so they could move to the suburbs. (Analyzing Information/History)** Option A is correct. According to the information in the passage, people with cars no longer needed to live near their jobs or public transportation, which facilitated migration to the suburbs. Option B is not a reason that living patterns changed, so it is incorrect. Option C is not related to automobiles, so it is incorrect. Option D is another reason that suburbs grew dramatically, but it does not mention automobile ownership, which was necessary for people to move to the suburbs.

46. **B. In poor condition (Interpreting Information/History)** The cars were still on the road but were old and worn. The option closest in meaning to this is Option B. Options A and C are incorrect because the cars were still on the road, so they could not be out of order or ruined. While a dilapidated car may be rusty, this is not the only condition that makes a car dilapidated, so Option D is incorrect.

47. **B. II only (Evaluating Information/History)** Option B is correct because only Statement II shows the continued effects of the automobile culture that started in the 1950s. Statement II shows that the kinds of automobile-oriented businesses that boomed in the 1950s have expanded today. Statement I is incorrect because increased growth rates of large, central cities in recent years is a change from high growth rates of suburbs that resulted from the automobile culture.

48. **C. To put doubt in people's minds about Ritter. (Analyzing Information/Civics and Government)** Option C is correct because this ad is intended to make people question whether Ritter's actions make him fit to hold public office. Option A is not correct because the ad is not about Quimby's proposal. Option B is incorrect because Quimby's goal is to win the election, not to get Ritter to pay his taxes. Option D is incorrect because the ad is not about Quimby because his name is not mentioned.

49. **C. The ad writers think ordinary people don't like extremely wealthy people. (Evaluating Information/Civics and Government)** Option C is the most likely reason among the options for including this detail. Option A is not supported by the ad because it does not say he made his money dishonestly. Option B is not a reason to include a detail in an attack ad. Option D is incorrect because the ad is focused on Ritter's image, not his ideas.

50. **B. Quimby wants to present a positive image to voters. (Analyzing Information/Civics and Government)** Option B is correct because Quimby wants to remain distant from the ad in order to maintain a positive image with voters. Option A does not make sense. If Quimby were really modest, he would not be running for public office. Option C is not correct because his motivation in leaving off his name is to avoid association with attack ads. If Quimby did not believe the ad's claims, he would have either stopped his supporters from producing the ads or publicly stated his opposition to them. Option D is not supported by the information. In addition, if Quimby really had a tax problem, he would most likely not bring up the issue of taxes at all.